FUNDAMENTALS OF ADULT EDUCATION

ISSUES AND PRACTICES FOR LIFELONG LEARNING

Edited by

DEO H. POONWASSIE
Senior Scholar, University of Manitoba

ANNE POONWASSIE
Continuing Education and Development

THOMPSON EDUCATIONAL PUBLISHING, INC.

Toronto

Information on how to obtain copies of this book may be obtained from:
Web site: www.thompsonbooks.com
E-mail: publisher@thompsonbooks.com
Telephone: (416) 766-2763
Fax: (416) 766-0398

National Library of Canada cataloguing in publication data

Main entry under title:

Fundamentals of adult education : issues and practices for lifelong learning

1st ed.

Includes bibliographical references and index.
ISBN 1-55077-125-6

1. Adult education – Canada. I. Poonwassie, Deo H. II. Poonwassie, Anne.

LC5254.F86 2001   374'.971   C00-933245-6

Copy Editing: Elizabeth Phinney
Cover Design: Elan Designs
Cover Image: Andrew Valko, RCA

Every reasonable effort has been made to acquire permission for copyright materials used in this book and to acknowledge such permissions accurately. Any errors or omissions called to the publisher's attention will be corrected in future printings.

We acknowledge the support of the Government of Canada through the Book Publishing Industry Development Program for our publishing activities.

Printed in Canada.
 2 3 4 5   06 05 04 03

Table of Contents

Acknowledgements

We wish to thank Dr. Romulo Magsino, dean of the Faculty of Education, and Dr. John Young, head of the Department of Educational Administration, Foundations and Psychology, both at the University of Manitoba, for their support and encouragement in completing this book. We also know that contributors to this volume worked diligently to meet deadlines, and to each of these writers we say thank you.

We are grateful to Andrew Valko, RCA, for producing an attractive cover design for this book. We also thank Keith Thompson at Thompson Educational Publishing for his patience and professional assistance in completing this project.

Permission was received to reproduce the following material:

- James A. Draper, "The Metamorphoses of Andragogy," *The Canadian Journal for the Study of Adult Education* 12, no. 1 (1998).

- Gordon Selman, "Stages in the Development of Canadian Adult Education," *Canadian Journal of University Continuing Education* X, no. 1 (January 1984).

- Mark Selman, "Philosophical Considerations," Chapter 10 in *The Foundations of Adult Education in Canada* by Gordon Selman, Michael Cooke, Mark Selman, and Paul Dampier (Toronto: Thompson Educational Publishing, 1998).

- Council of Ministers of Education, Canada, Summary of *The Survey of Trends in Adult Education and Training in Canada (1985-1995)*.

Preface

The practice of adult education today takes many forms: skills training, professional development, personal development, leisure activities and programs for ethnic groups, the elderly and specially targeted populations. And there are many organizations involved in providing these services, such as volunteer organizations, universities, colleges, business, public school boards and governments.

In Canada, the main professional organizations supporting these diverse activities are the Canadian Association for Adult Education (CAAE), established in 1935, and the Institut Canadien d'Education des Adultes (ICEA), established in 1952 as the French-language adult education institute. There are several provincial adult education associations that provide services to adults in urban and rural areas. Examples of other organizations are: the YMCA and YWCA, the Women's Institutes and church groups.

In North America, growth in adult education as an area of academic study grew exponentially in the 1960s and thereafter (Jarvis 1991, 1). In Canada, as early as 1889, Queen's University began offering courses through their extension services (Selman and Dampier 1991, 68). Since the 1950s, several universities across Canada have developed graduate programs in adult education at both the masters and doctoral levels. Today, the Canadian Association for the Study of Adult Education (CASAE) promotes research and study in adult education. Its membership includes scholars, researchers and educational institutions in post-secondary education. The Canadian Association for University Continuing Education (CAUCE), which is comprised mainly of activists in the field of continuing education, attempts to bridge the gap between theory and practice.

Adult education and lifelong learning are also world-wide activities supported by international organizations such as the International Council for Adult Education (ICAE), which was founded in 1973 by J. Roby Kidd, together with adult educators from other countries. Its membership consists mainly of national organizations involved in the promotion of adult education. UNESCO, a major arm of the United Nations, has also assumed some responsibility for these activities and has developed programs to support the initiatives of member countries in reaching their goals.

The Purpose of This Book

This book is intended to contribute to the study and practice of adult education in Canada. While it has been prepared mainly for beginning students at universities and colleges, more experienced practitioners and students will find the selections helpful and stimulating. Instructors and community workers will also find this book useful, since it covers many areas that are basic to the practice of adult education. The contributors include researchers and practitioners from universities, colleges, high schools, governments and international organizations. In addition, both males and females of different ethnic backgrounds are represented. They provide the reader with current research, stimulating thoughts and insightful commentary.

The volume is divided into three sections, though readers may choose not to follow them sequentially. Section I, "Foundations of Adult Education," contains five chapters carefully selected to provide the reader with a basic understanding of the field in terms of definition, history, philosophy, theory building and learning theory. If one is to comprehend the practice and study of adult education, primary information that provides the raison d'être of the field is essential. This section presents information so that the reader can begin to formulate a conceptual framework for analysis of theory and practice in adult education.

Section II, "The Practice of Adult Education," includes seven chapters chosen to present the reader with some of the skills and information required of practitioners of adult education. While the reader may not become an expert practitioner after reading this section, there will be sufficient information to expose him or her to the types of skills that are required in the preparation for practice. The reader will be introduced to needs assessment, program planning, facilitating adult learning and prior learning assessment. Information will be provided as to the places where adult education programming occurs, such as university continuing education units and community colleges.

Section III, "Issues in Adult Education," introduces several current topics that are of concern to adult education practitioners and researchers. This section contains eight chapters, each dealing with a different topic, including UNESCO, access in adult education, labour education, technical-vocational education, the professionalization of adult educators in Quebec, women and adult education, distance education, First Nations adult education and the purpose of education in a civil society. No attempt was made to prioritize these topics, except to place the article by Alan Thomas at the end as a sort of final word from a leading figure in Canadian adult education. This section is clearly not exhaustive and the references at the end of each chapter provide ample direction for further reading.

Taken as a whole, we think that these selections will give the reader a good overview of the current state of adult education.

Emerging Issues in Adult Education

To conclude this preface, we would like to suggest some emerging areas of interest that readers may wish to pursue.

Information technology. Looming large in the arena of adult education is the presence of information technology. This revolution in the means for dissemination of knowledge (and propaganda) has increased communication, especially among those who can afford the new technology. The implications of increased use of this technology for adult education activities are enormous and revolutionary; if used properly, communicative competence will be enhanced and large numbers of people will benefit through a heightened consciousness of their realities.

Globalization. Alongside this new technology is the advent of increased globalization. The international inequities forged by the activities of multinational corporations and industrial nations divide the world into two main groups—those who enjoy the highest standard of living and are literate, consumer driven, knowledgeable, healthy and wealthy, and those whose lives are controlled by the first group and who are illiterate, subsistence driven, uninformed, disease prone and poor. Clearly there are several nations that rest somewhere between these extremes, but the overall devastation in the lives of the poor is real and unheralded. As Sumner (1999) states: "Corporate globalization is an overwhelmingly successful example of the system's ability to colonize the lifeworld" (p.74).

Elitism. Along with the corporate mentality comes the built-in elitism that is displayed in adult education activities. As governments trim funds for education, the ability to pay for adult education courses plays a significant role in who benefits from these programs. As pointed out in two national surveys—*From the Adult's Point of View* (1982) and *The Adult Education and Training Survey* (1992)—those with more schooling seek more, and those with less tend to participate less in adult education and training. Is there a role for adult educators in promoting social equality in our society?

Counselling. Adult learners sometimes need counselling in career choices, academic possibilities and personal affairs. This is not unusual because of the many responsibilities that can become a burden when trying to pursue further education and training. Helping adults to make the correct choices is complicated and requires a professional with considerable skills. When adults seek assistance, it is usually because they have exhausted other possibilities and have come to the stark realization that their own resourcefulness is inadequate. This makes them vulnerable, and a skilful and ethical counsellor will recognize this and act accordingly.

Multiculturalism. As a multicultural nation, Canada can boast of the presence of virtually all peoples of the world. They make major contributions to the well-being of adults in the areas of sport and recreation, language education, business training, cultural enrichment, providing and receiving employment, academics and research. The contribution of all ethic groups to the social fabric of this country needs to be celebrated and much work remains to be done in this area.

Internationalism. It is important to expose the reader to the role of adult education in other countries. The UNESCO report on Education for All Status and Trends (1997) entitled *Adult Education in a Polarizing World* states that "the society that mankind will inhabit in the 21st century is being shaped by new and powerful forces that include the globalization of economic activity, the growing importance of knowledge as a prerequisite for participation in fundamental human activities and the increasing democratization of political systems" (p.7). Basic adult education is still being challenged as a human right in many parts of the world. In order for readers to get a realistic picture of adult education, they must become aware of what is happening in other parts of the world.

Further readings on each of these topics can be obtained from current journals, books and pamphlets on adult education and other respective subject areas. Many of these issues are discussed in this volume.

Deo H. Poonwassie and Anne Poonwassie
January 2001

References

Canadian Association for Adult Education. 1982. *From the adult's point of view.* Toronto: Canadian Association for Adult Education.

Human Resources Development Canada. 1995. *The 1992 adult education training and survey.* Ottawa: Statistics Canada. Government of Canada.

Jarvis, P. 1991. Growth and challenges in the study of adult education. In *Adult education evolution and achievements in a developing field of study,* edited by J.M. Peters et al. (pp.1-13). San Francisco: Jossey-Bass.

Selman, G., and P. Dampier. 1991. *The foundations of adult education in Canada.* Toronto: Thompson Educational Publishing.

Sumner, J. 1999. Global vision or corporate nightmare? The privatization of adult education in the new millennium. *The Canadian Journal for the Study of Adult Education* 13 (2): 73-85.

UNESCO. 1997. *Adult education in a polarizing world. Education for all status and trends/1997.* Paris: UNESCO.

Contributors

- **Walter Archer** is currently at the Faculty of Extension, University of Alberta, where he is Associate Dean, Research, and Acting Director of the Master of Arts in Communications and Technology. His main research interests are distance education and the formation and operation of consortia in adult and higher education.

- **Nancy Buchanan,** M.Ed., is a research co-ordinator and policy analyst in the area of women's health. She is also an instructor in the Women's Studies Program at the University of Manitoba.

- **Élisabeth Barot** has a doctorate in Spanish and Latin American Studies from the University of Pau, France. Her master's degree in Political Science was obtained from the University of Ottawa. Dr. Barot has been a program officer with the Canadian Commission for UNESCO since 1992. Her special responsibilities have been in the areas of human rights, social and human sciences, women and youth. From 1987 until 1992, she was an officer with the Association of Universities and Colleges of Canada. She has authored numerous papers and publications, in addition to organizing a variety of national and international meetings in her area of expertise.

- **Anthony Bos**, Ph.D., is the President of Keewatin Community College in Manitoba. He has over twenty years of history in education administration in the community college system, with special emphasis on adult education and community partnerships.

- **Paul Bouchard** is Associate Professor and Graduate Program Director in Adult Education at Concordia University in Montreal. His research interests include workplace learning, self-directed learning strategies and distant learning environments. Dr. Bouchard is currently serving as President of the Canadian Association for the Study of Adult Education (CASAE).

- **Marshall Wm. Conley**, Ph.D., is the author of more than 120 publications and professional papers. Prior to taking early retirement in June 2000, he was Professor of Political Science, teaching International Organization and Human Rights at Acadia University. Currently, he is Senior Consultant at Knowledge House Inc., an education and ICT firm located in Halifax, Nova Scotia. Dr. Conley has been a member of Canadian delegations to the UNESCO (Paris) General Conference in 1995, 1997 and 1999, as well as some twelve others in New York, Geneva, Vienna and Paris. He is Vice-President, Canadian Commission for UNESCO.

- **Dianne L. Conrad** has been an adult education practitioner in Alberta for twenty years. The Assistant Director of an on-line master's program at the University of Alberta, she is currently completing her doctoral research in on-line learners' patterns of participation.

- **James A. Draper** was a Professor in the Department of Adult Education, Ontario Institute for Studies in Education, University of Toronto, from 1967 to 1995, teaching international/cultural/comparative studies, community development, issues relating to adult illiteracy and foundation studies. He was a founding member and later President of the Canadian Association for the Study of Adult Education. In 2000, he was the recipient of the Diamond Jubilee Award by the Indian Adult Education Association for his outstanding contribution to adult education in India, the first non-Indian to receive a national award in adult education.

- **Karen Magro** completed her doctorate degree in Adult Education at the Ontario Institute for Studies in Education, University of Toronto. She teaches at the Winnipeg Adult Education Centre and the University of Manitoba.

- **Margot Morrish**, M.Ed., completed studies at the University of Manitoba, focusing on intercultural aspects of family violence prevention. Margot works in the field of immigrant/refugee settlement in program development, community education and service accessibility.

- **Anne Percival** is Professor and Dean of the Continuing Education Division at the University of Manitoba. She has a doctorate in Adult Education from Columbia University and an MBA from the University of Manitoba. Anne has worked as a program planner in management development and as an instructional designer in distance education. Her teaching and research interests are in program planning and professional practice in adult education. She is the author of *Practising Theory: A Guide to Becoming an Effective Adult Education Programmer.*

- **Donovan Plumb** has worked as an adult education consultant, trainer and university educator for more than fifteen years. His interests include adult learning theory, effective communications, distance education and adult education and cultural change. He teaches adult education at Mount Saint Vincent University, Halifax, Nova Scotia.

- **Anne Poonwassie**, M.Ed., is an adult education consultant and facilitator in the area of adult professional development. She teaches facilitating adult education in the Continuing Division at the University of Manitoba and has shared her expertise in numerous publications.

- **Deo H. Poonwassie**, Ph.D., is Senior Scholar in the Department of Educational Administration, Foundations and Psychology at the University of Manitoba. He has practised and published in the fields of adult education, teacher training and international education.

- **Gordon Selman** is Professor Emeritus at the University of British Columbia. His field of research and publication is the history and development of adult education in Canada and British Columbia. He is a former president of the Canadian Association for Adult Education and the Canadian Association for University Continuing Education and he chaired the organizing committee for the Canadian Association for the Study of Adult Education. He is a co-author of *The Foundations of Adult Education in Canada*, 2d ed. (Thompson Educational, 1998) and author of *Adult Education in Canada: Historical Essays* (Thompson Educational, 1995), among other works.

- **Mark Selman** is Executive Director of the Learning Strategies Group, Faculty of Business, Simon Fraser University. His professional career has been focused on university involvement in community and mid-career education. He has a Ph.D. in Philosophy of Education from the University of British Columbia and has written primarily about issues in philosophy and adult education, including co-authoring *The Foundations of Adult Education in Canada*, 2d ed. Dr. Selman has held several board and executive positions in professional organizations including President of the Canadian Association for the Study of Adult Education.

- **Atlanta Sloane-Seale** is an Assistant Professor and Program Director at the University of Manitoba, Continuing Education Division. Her areas of interest include program planning, accessibility and equity.

- **Bruce Spencer** is a Professor in the Centre for Work and Community Studies at Athabasca University, Alberta. He is the author and editor of several books and monographs on adult and workers' education, including *The Purposes of Adult Education: A Guide for Students*, and (with Sue Scott and Alan Thomas) *Learning for Life: Canadian Readings in Adult Education*, both published by Thompson Educational Publishing.

- **Thomas J. Sork** is Professor of Adult Education in the Department of Educational Studies, University of British Columbia. His current research interests are in the human dynamics of educational planning and professional ethics in adult education.

- **Alan M. Thomas** is Professor of Adult Education at the Ontario Institute for Studies in Education, University of Toronto. He is the author of *Beyond Education: A New Perspective on Society's Management of Learning* (Jossey-Bass, 1991).

- **Michael R. Welton** is Professor of Adult Education at Mount St. Vincent. His research interests include adult education history, work and learning and active citizenship. His recent books are *In Defense of the Lifeworld* (1995) and, with Jim Lotz, *Father Jimmy: The Life and Times of Jimmy Tompkins* (1997). He is currently editing an adult education theory reader with Donovan Plumb, *Knowledge Shift: Lifelong Learning in the Networked World* (to be published by Thompson Educational).

- **David N. Wilson**, Professor of Adult, Comparative and Higher Education at the Ontario Institute for Studies in Education, University of Toronto, served with UNESCO, ILO and Asian Development Bank on leaves of absence. He has worked in TVET in Africa, Asia, Canada, Caribbean, Eastern Europe and Latin America for over thirty years. He is President of the International Society for Educational Planning, World Council of Comparative Education Societies and former President of the Comparative and International Education Society of Canada and the Comparative and International Education Society (USA).

- **Angelina (Angie) T. Wong**, Ph.D., is Professor of Extension at the University of Saskatchewan. After more than a decade in distance education, she re-directed her research and project development towards prior learning assessment. Since 1996, she has spearheaded prior learning assessment (PLA) investigations for the province's two universities.

DEDICATION

**This book is dedicated to our son, Alex Raja,
who is a lifelong learner**

I
THE FOUNDATIONS OF
ADULT EDUCATION

1

The Metamorphoses of Andragogy

James A. Draper

Evolution of the concept *andragogy* is integral to understanding the development of adult education as a field of practice. In this chapter, the term *adult education* might have been used in place of *andragogy*, as historically and presently the terms are frequently used synonymously. Andragogy has been selected for the title of this article because it illustrates the classical root of the development of adult education, and also provides a link between North America and Western Europe. In Canada, the graduate program in adult education at the University of Montreal has traditionally used the term *androgogie*.

Another reason for using the term andragogy stems from an underlying assumption within graduate programs in adult education in Canada: that graduates should have a basic appreciation and understanding of the development of ideas, theory, programs and concepts relating to their chosen field of study and practice. For example, graduates should be familiar with such organizations as the Mechanics' Institutes, the Women's Institutes, the Workers' Educational Association, the Antigonish Movement, the National Farm Radio Forum, as well as with such concepts as the social gospel, mathetics, lifelong learning and community development. Being familiar with the evolution of andragogy is the foundation for professionalism in adult education.

This article uses andragogy as a vehicle to illustrate the issues that adult educators perceived and grappled with over the years in defining their specialized field of practice and theory, which gives meaning to contemporary practice. The concepts we use are important to our professional history—for example, the use of andragogy by adult educators to distinguish their practice from pedagogy (the traditional education of children). Much of the struggle to develop an appropriate vocabulary and to understand the intentional learning of adults has been a philosophical as well as a methodological one and therefore has generated debate among practitioners.

Historical Reflections

The history of non-formal education, for children and adults, is as old as the history of human beings. Learning and education are synonymous with living, and people have always organized their learning in order to survive, to understand and to create. *Education* as used here refers to organized or intentional learning.

I. Origin of the Concept and Terminology

In the 1700s and into the 1800s, a number of forces and factors influenced the way in which learning was organized and also the content and location for that learning. These factors included the Industrial Revolution and the mobility of people from rural to urban areas to work in factories and other non-traditional occupations; the increasing technological sophistication of navigation, war and commerce; the number of private societies that were established to educate the masses of society, many of whom were illiterate (such as the Society for Promoting Christian Knowledge, the Society for Encouraging the Industrious Poor and the Society for the Diffusion of Useful Knowledge). Various organizations were being established during this time, all of which had an educational component, such as the Mechanics' Institutes (1825 in England), cooperatives, trade unions, correspondence societies and the development of university extension programs.

All of these and other activities helped to extend the educational opportunities for the working masses of society (including the opportunities to become literate, at least to the point of being able to read the scriptures). The rapid increase in educational programs for adults meant that more planners of these programs were in a position to observe the characteristics of adults as learners, as well as the factors that motivated adults to learn, the values placed on knowledge and the ways adults used knowledge. Nevertheless, in the early beginnings, the teaching done in the majority of these adult programs paralleled the way in which children were generally taught, often using an authoritarian and lecture approach.

One of the first detailed descriptions of these new adult schools, and probably the first history of English adult education, was given in the book by Thomas Pole, a medical doctor who was, among other things, a member of the Bristol, England, society for teaching the adult poor to read the Holy Scriptures. His book, published in 1814, was called *A History of the Origin and Progress of Adult Schools*; it provided "an account of some of the beneficial effects already produced on the moral character of the labouring poor; and considerations on the important advantages they are likely to be productive of to society at large." The book included an appendix containing rules for the governance of adult school societies, and the organization of the schools. Pole laments that

> benevolent individuals, or preceding generations, have exerted themselves for the education of youth; but that these exertions have been inefficient or too limited, is proven by the great proportion of the labouring poor, arrived to years of maturity, who have suffered, and are still suffering inexpressible loss in respect to their mental concern, from the lamentable ignorance which still prevails amongst them (p.i).

Pole was among the first persons to note the phenomenon of adult education and its role in society and coined the term *adult education* to identify the phenomenon.

During Pole's time elementary education was regarded as an act of charity, and during this time and with varying motives there was a vigorous initiation of charity schools and the provision of inexpensive devotional literature for adults and for children. These and other programs later became the foundation upon which theories of popular education for adults were eventually based.

In 1833 the term *andragogy* was coined by Alexander Kapp, a German grammar school teacher. The term was intended to describe the educational theory of the Greek philosopher Plato. Selecting the Greek root of the term andragogy was intended to make a distinction between the teaching of adults, as opposed to pedagogy, the teaching of children. The term reflected the various programs for adults being established during this period, although it appears that *andragogy* and *adult education* were used synonymously.

Perhaps the most innovative and far-reaching institution created during these times was the Folk High Schools, founded by Bishop N.F.S. Grundtvig (1783-1872) of Denmark. Warren (1989) points out that Grundtvig conceived these schools for adults as a reaction against the system of education of children and the irrelevance of education to living a productive life. Warren comments:

> The "black schools" of Denmark ... resembled the German model which forced people up or out of the system in accordance with their success in emotionless logic and endless memorization channelled all too often through foreign Latinity. This tyrannical combination, Grundtvig asseverated, would stifle rather than enlighten the human development of any soul (p.216).

Warren continues:

> Since the kind of schools envisioned by Grundtvig did not exist, they would need to be created. In these folk high schools, students would be encouraged to bloom rather than be educated to conform (p.216).... Lectures mostly must be discarded because students were there not only to be taught by teachers but to teach their instructors in turn (p.217).

Warren goes on to compare the andragogical assumptions of American adult educators and those of N.F.S. Grundtvig, and notes the major effect that Grundtvig's thinking had on E.C. Lindeman, referred to as the father of adult education in the U.S.A.

Davies (1931) points out that, "Grundtvig had a rooted aversion to teaching methods which consisted in criticizing and theorizing without reference to concrete experience" (p.89). He further elaborates on Grundtvig's thoughts on education:

> With the period of youth, from eighteen onwards, there comes, according to Grundtvig, the moment of "spiritual creation" which gives the educator his [or her] richest opportunity. Hence the process of education would be incomplete, and would fail to a great extent of its effect, unless the claims of this period were taken into account, and schools established to give young people, not a technical or vocational education, but an "education for life", and one which would fit them to go on educating themselves after they left the school (p.87).

The folk high schools, intended primarily to provide peasants with education, spread initially to other Scandinavian countries and then elsewhere. They have greatly influenced the development of a philosophy relating to the education of adults.

II. Influence of Humanistic Social Philosophy

A number of simultaneous forces that were taking place in the 1800s profoundly influenced the thinking about adult education in the next century. The tendency to compare the education, needs and experiences of children and adults; a reaction against authoritarian, void-of-life, rote memory; and the lecture approach (characteristic of the pedagogy of the times) encouraged a number of people to think of education for adults as different from the education of children. The development of thinking about adult education as essentially non-formal was, in part, a reaction against perceptions of formal education.

Other, sociological forces were in evidence as well. A humanist philosophy was increasingly being expounded during these times, and this philosophy influenced those who were involved in conceptualizing the practice of adult education. This philosophy helped to provide an alternative to the traditions of pedagogy, which an increasing number of adult educators were looking for. The Enlightenment of the eighteenth century was a protest against forces threatening humanity, such as industrialization, which represented the mechanization of mankind, as well as political forces that threatened cultural identity. These were the early years of the social sciences as we know them today. The growth of these social sciences, including adult education, paralleled the continued growth of the humanities.

The humanistic philosophy focused on the dignity and autonomy of human beings. It expressed itself as a revolt against authority and developed a holistic view of people. In educational practice, it became learner/student-centred; it encouraged learners to be self-directing, to seek their potential; and it believed that individuals should be, and should want to be, responsible for their own learning. The humanist assumption was that people have a natural tendency to learn and that learning will flourish if nourishing, encouraging environments are provided. The process or journey of the educational experience itself was being valued, and the role of "teacher" and "student" were being re-examined and described, such that the teacher frequently came to be seen as a facilitator and also as a recipient learner. These humanistic ideas developed over time, but they paralleled the development of educational thoughts about adults as learners.

Griffin (1987) observes that by the end of the nineteenth century, "ideas and concepts of adult education could be thought of primarily as an exercise in applied adult learning theory in a social context" (p.159). Griffin explains:

> The origins of adult leaning discourse can be traced to nineteenth century social and political thought, notably to varieties of sociological functionalism, political liberalism, and theories of progress and change. These ideas, unlike those of other, school-oriented education theory, had not been transformed by ideological conflicts in the public sphere. As a result, there was scope for a much more systematic analysis of adult education in relation to alternative social policy models, thereby bringing it into line somewhat with our approach to other social policies of welfare or redistribution, with which adult education is often, in practice, linked (p.159).

This concept of learning within a humanizing social context provided the impetus for expansion in usage of both the concepts and the terminology of andragogy during the early to mid-twentieth century.

Andragogy in the Twentieth Century

Eugen Rosenstock, a German social scientist and a teacher in the Academy of Labour in Frankfort, is credited with re-introducing the term *andragogy* in 1924. He urged that a separate method and philosophy be used for adult education and claimed that it was insufficient to translate pedagogical concepts into an adult situation. Knowles (1984) explains that Rosenstock advocated that "the teachers should be professionals who could cooperate with the pupils; only such a teacher can be, in contrast to a 'pedagogue,' an 'andragogue'" (p.80).

As with the development of new thought, a number of events increasingly focused on adult education as a field of practice as well as a field of study, meaning that adult education was developing its own body of knowledge and research. One can note for instance the 1929 World Conference on Adult Education held in England, sponsored by the World Association of Adult Education. The conference was intended to encourage international co-operation in adult education.

I. International Expansion of Adult Education and Usage of the Term Andragogy

In 1947, a division of adult education within UNESCO was established, followed over the years with world conferences on adult education in 1949, 1960, 1972, 1985 and 1997. The 1960 event took place in Montreal, reflecting Canada's visibility and leadership in the international field. In 1964 UNESCO launched the Experimental World Literacy Program. In 1965, the UNESCO international committee for the advancement of adult education accepted Paul Legrand's report recommending the endorsement of the principles of lifelong education. The establishment of the International Council for Adult Education in 1973 and the various events it has organized since then, and the development of graduate departments of adult education or andragogy in most regions of Canada, contributed to the specialization of adult education. Kidd and Timus (cited in Husen and Postlethwaite 1985) point out in the *International Encyclopedia of Education* that

> in some countries, indeed, particularly in Europe, the term "andragogy" has been coined.... Its use has been strongly resisted in some parts of the world, but in most countries where adult education is established as a field of practice, the area covered by andragogy is nevertheless recognized as a distinctive field of study (p.100).

Similarly, speaking about socialist states, Livecka (cited in Husen and Postlethwaite 1985) says,

> the need to develop principles and practices appropriate to adult education led to the formulation of the concept of andragogy. Research and study in Yugoslavia, Hungary, and Poland has concentrated on the development of its theory and application. In other socialist states, although andragogy may not be an accepted term, theoretical research has concerned itself with the same problems, notably the place of adult education in a system of lifelong education and the place of adult education in socialist thought and life (p.175).

Also writing in the *International Encyclopedia of Education* and cited by Husen and Postlethwaite, A. Krajnc of Yugoslavia (now Slovenia) points out that andragogy

> has only achieved general acceptance in a few European countries–Poland, the Federal Republic of Germany, the German Democratic Republic, the Netherlands, Czechoslovakia, and Yugoslavia. It also appears sometimes in other professional literature, for example in UNESCO documents. In English-speaking countries the adoption of the term has on the whole been resisted. Such penetration as it has achieved in the United States has been greatly assisted by Malcolm Knowles' advocacy (p.267).

W. Rokicka, documentalist with the UNESCO International Bureau of Education (in her personal communication with Shirley Wigmore at the Ontario Institute for Studies in Education) writes that although the term andragogy is found in some UNESCO documents, UNESCO does not recommend the usage of the term andragogy and seldom uses it in its publications.

In spite of resistance in some quarters, the term andragogy has a relatively widespread usage in some quarters, as illustrated in a study undertaken by Claude Touchette (1982), a professor of andragogy at the University of Montreal. He elaborates on the diversity of the term, pointing out that "the term *andragogy* is synonymous with the term *adult education*." Touchette points out that whereas the French-language publication of UNESCO's Fourth Conference on Adult Education, held in Paris in 1985, uses the term *andragogy* in the broader sense, the English version uses the term *continuing education* (p.26). Touchette goes on to report that

> according to directory data, 17 universities out of 95 (that is 18%) teach andragogy. These universities are located in Italy, Sweden, Poland, Yugoslavia, Quebec, The Dominican Republic, Tanzania and India. No mention is made of universities in Venezuela, Peru, Costa Rica, Germany and the Netherlands, which also have andragogy programs. For most of these universities, as for Quebec, the meaning of the term *andragogy* encompasses all dimensions of the phenomenon of adult education and cannot be reduced to a single methodology or approach, as certain English-language publications suggest. This wide definition is derived from the German and Yugoslavian conceptualizations of andragogy (p.27).

II. Drawing a Sense of Commonalities among Differences in Terminologies

Perhaps one of the most extensive theoretical discussions on andragogy written in Europe is the article by Ger Van Enckevort (1971), who was with the Dutch Centre for Adult Education. In his article "Andragology: A New Science" he cites the characteristics of andragogy specified by professor Ten Have, and claims that *andragology* "is a social phenomenon of a specific kind (p.44) ... cannot be considered as merely an application of the behavioural sciences and/or of sociology (p.45-46) ... [and] is an effort to break down the separations between the different forms of andragogical action and theory" (p.46).

When speaking of approaches to theory building and research in adult education in East Europe, a Canadian, Jindra Kulich (1984), points out that adult education in the East European countries is viewed very broadly so as to include formal, non-formal and cultural educational programs. He also points out, "A spirited debate has been going on in Central and Eastern Europe since the late 1950s as to the place of the study of adult education in the system of the social sciences" (p.128). Kulich also points out that Polish authors vary considerably in their position on the use and relationship of andragogy and pedagogy. Some argue that "andragogy is an independent science, drawing on many social sciences and it has close ties with pedagogy" (p.129). But Kulich says that the terms adult pedagogy and andragogy are used "interchangeably to denote the study of education, self-education and training of working youth and adults" (p.128). In these writings one can note that there is some agreement on andragogy being a science, sometimes viewed within the social sciences. Kulich concludes by saying:

> The term adult pedagogy is quite common in East European writing and, although illogical in terms of the definition of pedagogy as the education of children and youth, prevalent elsewhere, is consistent with a Central and East European view of pedagogy as the all-embracing science of education (p.135).

There is a great deal of literature that relates to the discussions about the meaning and place of andragogy but only a few more examples will be given. The Andragogy Group (1981) at the University of Nottingham in England speaks of pedagogy with adults versus andragogy and goes on to elaborate on the assumptions on which they base their continuum, the poles of which are traditional and progressive education. Within the African context, Kabuga (1977) voices the opinion that, "education in any society ... which employs the techniques of pedagogy is oppressive, silencing and domesticating ... and is premised on the authority of the teacher as well as on a static culture" (p.1). However, he says, andragogy is "premised on a dynamic culture" (p.2), and the application of andragogy is relevant and meaningful in education at all levels.

Finally, Savicevic (1968) concludes that andragogy is "a relatively independent scientific discipline within the general science of education. This means that andragogy is not a 'branch' of pedagogy, although it is an integral part of the general science of education. However, a sharp line cannot be drawn between pedagogy and andragogy, because they both study the education process in various fields" (p.52). The next section carries this debate to North America.

The Andragogy Debate in North America

In 1926 Lindeman published "Andragogik: The Method of Teaching Adults" in the *Worker's Education Journal* and also published his book *The Meaning of Adult Education*. The following year, Anderson and Lindeman published *Education through Experience*. Although these publications introduced the term andragogy to North America, it was not popularized until over four decades later.

In *The Meaning of Adult Education*, Lindeman (1926, 1961) proclaimed his belief in the humanizing aspect of education:

> The resource of highest value in adult education is the learner's experience. If education is life, then life is also education (p.6).... The best teaching method is one which

emerges from situation-experiences (p.115).... The first step toward liberation is taken when an individual begins to understand what inhibits, frustrates, subjugates him [or her]. We learn to be free when we know what we desire freedom for and what stands in the way of our desire (p.46).

He also expressed his perception of education for adults as distinctly purposeful:

> My conception of adult education points toward a continuing process of evaluating experiences, a method of awareness through which we learn to become alert in the discovery of meanings (p.85).... Orthodox education may be a preparation for life but adult education is an agitating instrumentality for changing life (p.104).... Teachers of youth assume that their function is to condition students for a preconceived kind of conduct; teachers of adults, on the other hand, will need to be alert in learning how the practical experiences of life can enliven subjects. The purpose of adult education is to give meaning to the categories of experiences, not to classifications of knowledge (p.123).

Although Lindeman wrote about *Andragogik*, reflecting a European influence, in his major writings he uses the term *adult education*, implying that he perceives the terms to be synonymous. In his writings he also reacts against orthodox pedagogic education and searches for an in-depth alternative and idealistic method of educating adults.

I. The Progressive Philosophy Underlying the Introduction of Andragogy in North America

Particularly during the early twentieth century, in Canada and the United States, a progressive philosophy was developing, which paralleled the introduction of the concept of andragogy (in Europe) and the humanistic philosophy which it implied. This progressive philosophy promoted the attainment of freedom through understanding and the relationship of education to one's daily life. Educators saw progressivism as a way of democratizing knowledge; they valued a problem-solving and learner-centred approach to education, valued the experience of learners and placed a great deal of emphasis on the experiential and also the experimental contribution it made to education. Education was seen as an instrument of social change and the teacher was perceived as being a facilitator of change and growth. As with the humanistic philosophy discussed earlier, progressive and other forces worked together to break the traditional monopoly on knowledge.

The social, geographical, political and economic context within Canada, at any given time, determined not only *what* adults learned, but *why* and *how*. New paradigms of practice were being created through such activities as the Antigonish Movement, the Mechanics' Institutes, the Workers' Educational Association, the Women's Institutes, the Banff School of Fine Arts, Frontier College and the expansion of university extension programs. All of these programs (Draper 1998) and many more were intended to extend the opportunities for adult learning; to introduce innovative ways of organizing and delivering educational programs, dealing with the economic and other realities of daily living; and to humanize society. The writings of Fitzpatrick, Corbett and Kidd illustrate these changes, as does Coady's (1939) book *Masters of Their Own Destiny*.

In the United States, through his 1970 publication *The Modern Practice of Adult Education: Andragogy Versus Pedagogy*, Malcolm Knowles drew serious attention to andragogy in the North American context. In it he presented his initial perception of pedagogy and andragogy as separate and opposing educational ideologies, saying that pedagogy is based on a now obsolete premise—that is, the idea that the purpose of education is to transmit culture. The title of Chapter 3 of his book poses his thoughts at that time: "Andragogy: An Emerging Technology for Adult Learning—Farewell to Pedagogy." Knowles' 1970 theorizing states that andragogy differs from the assumptions about child learning, on which traditional predagogy is based, in four distinct ways:

> An adult's self-concept moves from one of being a dependent personality toward one of being a self-directing human being; he [*sic*] accumulates a growing reservoir of experience that becomes an increasing resource of learning; his readiness to learn becomes oriented increasingly to the developmental tasks of his social roles; his time perspective changes from one of postponed application of knowledge to immediacy of application, and accordingly his orientation toward learning shifts from one of subject centeredness to one of problem centeredness (p.39).

A critical examination of these and other points made by Knowles shows that all of the above assumptions can be applied to children and youth.

By the middle of the decade, Knowles had modified his thoughts from those expressed in 1970. In the second edition of his book, published in 1980, Knowles writes that "Andragogy is simply another model of assumptions about learners to be used alongside the pedagocial model of assumptions" (p.43). He now refers to *pedagogy* as the body of theory and practice on which teacher-directed learning is based and *andragogy* as that which is based on self-directed learning. The pedagogical orientation is characterized by dependent concepts of the learner, subject-centredness, a formal authority-oriented climate, planning primarily done by the teacher as the authority figure and evaluation being primarily done by the teacher. The andragogical orientation would be the opposite of these as poles on a spectrum.

Following Knowles' 1970 publication, in 1972 came *A Trainers Guide to Andragogy*, a United States Department of Health, Education and Welfare publication. The andragogical process is referred to and described:

> The development, organization, and administration of programs in applied andragogy involves continuous circular application of the following seven steps, namely, setting a climate for learning, establishing a structure for mutual planning, assessing interests, needs and values, formulating objectives, designing learning activities, implementing teaming activities, and evaluating results (reassessing needs, interests and values) (pp.10-11).

Later in this publication, when discussing "andragogy—a balance of freedom and control," it is stated that "the educational model of andragogy is based on the psychology of William James and the educational theory of John Dewey both of which envision man [*sic*] as capable of directing his own destiny" (p.91). This statement is interesting, since much of Dewey's writings were about progressive education for children.

II. Stimulation of Critical Discussion and Research

Knowles' original and subsequent writing sparked considerable discussion from his colleagues in Canada and the United States. Houle (1972) was one of the first persons to give a critical response to Knowles, taking the position that learning and education are essentially the same for children and adults:

> If pedagogy and andragogy are distinguishable, it is not because they are essentially different from one another but because they represent the working out of the same fundamental processes at different stages of life (p.222).

Similarly, Brundage and MacKeracher (1980) say, "To the extent that adults and children are different, learn in different ways, and need to be helped to learn in different ways, it is appropriate to discuss andragogy and pedagogy as separate issues. To the extent that adults and children are similar, the dichotomy is inappropriate" (p.6).

More recently, there followed in the Journal of Adult Education a series of articles expressing the opinions of various adult educators. Yonge (1985) comments:

> A Pedagogy-Andragogy difference cannot be justified by focusing on teaching and learning. When the Pedagogic and the Andragogic are viewed as two modes of human accompaniment, the critical differences between them become clear. The Pedagogic involves an adult accompanying a child so the latter may eventually become an adult. The Andragogic involves an adult accompanying another adult to a more refined, enriched adulthood. Thus, there is a difference in the participants and in the aims. Both agogic events involve a relationship of authority, but Pedagogic authority rests on a different base and is of a different character than Andragogic authority. These differences qualify the meaning of everything that occurs in these contexts: e.g. the "same" teaching strategy will have a different meaning in these two types of situations (p.166).

Yonge does conclude however that andragogy should not be used as a synonym or substitute for adult education, which he says is much broader than the use of andragogy in his paper (p.13).

Also in the *Journal of Adult Education*, Elias (1979) argued that there is no important difference between teaching children and teaching adults, which he illustrated by critiquing Knowles' original five assumptions about andragogy. McKenzie (1979) responded to Elias' thoughts and presented a philosophical position that assumes an existential difference between adults and children. Davenport and Davenport (1985a) published "A chronology and analysis of the andragogy debate" and conclude "it is time for the andragogy debate to move to a higher level" (p.158). That same year (1985b) they published "Andragogical-Pedagogical Orientations of Adult Learners: Research Results and Practice Recommendations." Carlson (1989) points out that "Knowles appropriates the term for his own purposes ... he cast aside the humanistic European definition of andragogy ... and redefined andragogy as 'an emerging technology for adult learning'" (p.225).

In "A Critical Theory of Adult Learning and Education," Jack Mezirow (1981) outlines a charter for andragogy. He says that "andragogy, as a professional perspective of adult educators, must be defined as an organized and sustained effort to assist adults to learn in a way that enhances their capability to function as self-directed learners" (p.137). Mezirow goes on to present a twelve-point charter of andragogy, of which the first three points are cited here. A theory of adult learning and education is intended to:

1. progressively decrease the learner's dependency on the educator;
2. help the learrier understand how to use learning resources—especially the experience of others, including the educator, and how to engage others in reciprocal learning relationships;
3. assist the learner to define his/her learning needs—both in terms of immediate awareness and of understanding the cultural and psychological assumptions influencing his/her perceptions of needs (p.137).

III. Viability of Andragogy as a Theory

In recent years in North America, questions have been raised about the viability of andragogy as a theory. Merriam (1988), for instance, discusses the term under the heading of theories of adult learning and goes on to say: "The best known 'theory' of adult learning is andragogy. It is based upon four assumptions, all of which are characteristics of adult learners.... This theory ... has given adult education 'a badge of identity' which distinguishes the field from other areas of education" (p.189). However, Merriam comments: "It has also caused more controversy, philosophical debate, and critical analysis than any other concept/theory/model proposed thus far ... [s]ince he [Knowles] no longer claims andragogy to be unique to adults." In her writings about adults as learners, Cross (1981) comments:

> Whether andragogy can serve as the foundation for a unifying theory of adult education remains to be seen. At the very least, it identifies some characteristics of adult learners that deserve attention. It has been far more successful than most theory in gaining the attention of practitioners, and it has been moderately successful in sparking debate; it has not been especially successful, however, in stimulating research to test the assumptions. Most important, perhaps, the visibility of andragogy has heightened awareness of the need for answers to three major questions: (1) Is it useful to distinguish the learning needs of adults from those of children? If so, are we talking about dichotomous differences or continuous differences? Or both? (2) What are we really seeking: Theories of learning? Theories of teaching? Both? (3) Do we have, or can we develop, an initial framework on which successive generations of scholars can build? Does andragogy lead to researchable questions that will advance knowledge in adult education? (pp.227-228).

In theorizing about andragogy as a relational construct, Pratt (1988) develops an interesting model of dependency-competence and states some andragogical presuppositions, arguing that

> andragogy and pedagogy can better be compared and understood if we consider the variations in learner dependency with respect to specific situations and attempt to analyze the type of teacher-learner relationships best suited to those variations. Thus, both andragogy and pedagogy may partly be defined via the nature of relationships that develop out of situational variations and the characteristics of learner dependency (p.164).

Similarly, Joblin (1988) helps to deal with the empirical questions that are raised in comparing the andragogical and pedagogical approaches, pointing out that "arguments, then, can be presented that both defend and refute the notion that adults are more self-directed than children and youth" (p.122).

In examining the North American literature on andragogy, one can only conclude that the metamorphoses of the concept continues. It has been referred to as a theory of learning, as a philosophical position, as a political reality and as a set of hypotheses. In the extensive listing in the database of the U.S. Education Resources Information Center (ERIC) clearinghouse on adult, career and vocational education, the term andragogy has also been referred to as a learning system, a technique, a process, a set of principles, a method, a new technology, a model and "a process oriented toward problem solving" (Brown 1985). In fact andragogy was only adopted as an ERIC descriptor in 1984, but not without debate on the appropriateness of the root of the term and its gender bias. A flavour of this debate is illustrated by Mohring (1989) in a paper called "Andragogy and Pedagogy: A Comment on Their Erroneous Usage." Mohring comments:

> Using andragogy to stand for educating adults and pedagogy for educating children is etymologically inaccurate. Although pedagogy derives from "pais", meaning child, from antiquity pedagogy also stands for education without reference to learners' ages. Andragogy derives from "aner", meaning adult male, not adult of either sex. Given the efforts to eliminate "sexist" words, why introduce a new one? We would be served better by using English than by using etymologically inaccurate Greek. If Greek is desired, "teleios", not "aner", is the Greek word for the English "adult". Andragogy should yield to teleiagogy, thereby including adults of both sexes (p.i).

Feelings continue to be mixed about the term andragogy, and the debate continues. Not all of the debate is as critical as Hartree (1984):

> Whilst in a sense he [Knowles] has done an important service in popularizing the idea of andragogy, it is unfortunate that he has done so in a form which, because it is intellectually dubious, is likely to lead to reflection by the very people it is most important to convince. The debate surrounding andagogy may have served to bring it to the public eye, but it is also likely to damage its credibility (p.209).

Tennant (1986) expresses similar feelings as those expressed by Hartree:

> Moreover, it is important to abandon some of the myths about adult learning which have general currency ... the myth that our need for self-direction is rooted in our constitutional makeup; the myth that self-development is a process of change towards higher levels of existence; and the myth that adult learning is fundamentally (and necessarily) different from child learning (p.121).

Podeschi (1987) comments that there is confusion about andragogy in the American adult education field and that this is partly explained because "theoreticians who debate andragogy are caught often in an unconscious complexity about the kind of issue in which they are involved: empirical proof or philosophical premise" (p.14).

In his article "Andragogy after Twenty-Five Years," Pratt (1993) sets out to answer one central question: What contribution has andragogy made to educators' understanding of adult learning? He comments:

> For some, andragogy has been a prescriptive set of guidelines for the education of adults. For others, it represents a philosophical position vis-a-vis the existential nature of adults. For still others, it is an ideology based on beliefs regarding individual freedom, the relationship between individual and society, and the aims of adult education.... Andragogy has been adopted by legions of adult educators around the world and has influenced the practice of adult education across an impressive range of settings. Very likely, it will continue to be the window through which adult educators take their first look into the world of adult education (p.15).

Pratt concludes, "While andragogy may have contributed to our understanding of adults as learners, it has done little to expand or clarify our understanding of the process of learning. We cannot say, with any confidence, that andragogy has been tested and found to be, as so many have hoped, either the basis for a theory of adult learning or a unifying concept for adult education" (p.21).

The next and last section summarizes and presents some reflections on what has been presented in this chapter.

Summary and Reflections

I. The Early Years

Pole was the first to write extensively about the phenomenon of adult learning; he coined the term adult education in 1814. His writings emphasized that there was a need to extend the opportunities for adult learning (initially focusing on moral education and reading the Christian scriptures). It was not enough, he said, for society to focus only on the education of children. Kapp coined the term androgogy, meaning the education of adults, as compared to pedagogy. Grundtvig continued the criticism of the authoritarianism of pedagogy and the irrelevance of what was generally taught in the schools, especially to young adults. He spoke of the need for a philosophical shift in educational thought, such that experience was valued, and that there was a need to develop innovative methods in educating adults. He expressed the idea of "education for life." Out of his efforts came the Danish Folk High Schools (primarily providing non-formal education for young adults who needed an education at a higher level than elementary school).

A humanist philosophy was being expounded during these times, as a revolt against authority. This philosophy focused on the dignity and autonomy of human beings and continued to search for and develop alternative methods of teaching adults. By the end of the nineteenth century, a discourse on adult learning had begun.

II. The European Perspective

In the twentieth century, andragogy was reintroduced. Rosenstock urged a separate method and philosophy for adult education. The *International Encyclopedia* noted the similarities of meaning of adult education and andragogy, as fields of practice. Adult education was also seen as a distinctive field of study, reflected in the various university graduate programs that were being established. Krajnc held that adult education and andragogy were synonymous terms. Touchette's international study supported this view and concluded the andragogy encompasses all dimensions of the

phenomenon of adult education and cannot be reduced to a single methodology. Van Enckevort argued that adult education was not merely an application of the behavioural sciences but was a separate field. In his
international writings, especially on Eastern Europe, Kulich places the
study of adult education as a theory or science within the social sciences. He
reported that adult education was to be viewed broadly, to include formal,
non-formal and cultural educational programs. Savicevic also saw adult education in broad terms and as a separate discipline. However, a negative
stereotype of pedagogy prevailed as part of the struggle to legitimize adult
education as a distinct field of practice and study.

III. The North American Perspective

Grundvig greatly influenced Lindeman as did humanist and progressive
thought. Lindeman (and others) theorized about adult learning in terms of
the role of experience, the factors that inhibited learning and the application of knowledge and self-evaluation as ways of distinguishing—at least ideally—between the education of adults (andragogy) and the education of
children (pedagogy).

Knowles was introduced to andragogy by a colleague from Europe and
perpetuated the dichotomy between andragogy (adult education) and pedagogy. In contrast, Houle viewed pedagogy and andragogy as representing
the same fundamental processes, albeit at different stages of life. Yonge saw
the two concepts as representing different modes of human development.
Tennant even argued that andragogy promoted some myths about adult
learning. Pratt's view was that what adult and child education hold in common is situational variations and characteristics of learner dependency.

IV. Reflections

A discussion on andragogy is not irrelevant to the metamorphoses of
adult education in Canada. Beginning in the 1700s in Western Europe, attempts were made to describe the practice of adult education and to distinguish it, at least theoretically, from pedagogy, the traditional education of
children. Adult educators began to observe that using these formal traditional approaches to education (pedagogy in schools and universities) did
not necessarily work, especially in non-formal educational settings for
adults. They began to ask "Why?" and "What should be?" As a way of communicating what was perceived to be different about the education of adults
(and since part of the distinction was to contrast the education of adults with
the education of children), it seemed natural that early adult educators
would look for a word that was grounded in the classical Greek language, as
with the origins of pedagogy. Hence the term andragogy was coined.

The early uses of andragogy were intended to contrast (often more ideally than in practice) a philosophical difference between the methods used
to teach adults and the methods used to teach children. The perceived voluntary act of learning was an important influencing factor that led adult educators to explore alternative approaches to organizing learning. Such
educators also acknowledged the importance of the learning process, apart

from the content to be learned. Humanistic and humanitarian forces greatly influenced the initial meaning given to andragogy. Adult educators also began to recognize and articulate the importance that experience had when adults engaged in education, the things that motivated adults to learn and the ways adults retained their learning through application and practice.

The evolution of andragogy was carried into the North American scene by Lindeman, although he generally used the term adult education. In his early writings, Knowles perpetuated the differences between pedagogy and andragogy (preferring this term rather than adult education) and to a great extent defined andragogy by what it was not, compared to pedagogy. That is, pedagogy was seen to represent formal schooling, it was authoritarian, other-directed learning and subject-matter oriented. Andragogy, on the other hand, represented a less authoritarian, out of school education, an inner or self-directed form of learning that was problem or project oriented, a learner-centred approach to learning and was essentially non-formal. Andragogy had a goal of changing the status quo and therefore was linked to social change and liberalization.

In today's context, these distinctions between andragogy and pedagogy are essentially theoretical and present a false dichotomy. In retrospect, the debate seems naïve and ignores the attempts by pedagogues to seek alternative methods for teaching children. All one has to do is to examine the reality of practice in educational programs for children and those for adults to see that each represents all variations for organizing learning. All of the philosophical traditions, be they liberal, behaviourist, progressive, humanistic or radical (see Elias and Merriam 1984) are witnessed in educational (formal and non-formal) programs for adults and children. Some settings in which adults (and children) learn are authoritarian, others, humanistic; some are directed by outside forces, others are self-directed by individual learners; some programs do not allow for individual interpretation or value the experience that the learner brings to an educational setting, others do allow for these things and so on. The method used in an educational setting is relative and contextual.

Although the debate in Europe shifted away from defining andragogy (adult education) by what it was not (compared to pedagogy), the popularizing of andragogy in North America by Knowles focused on the differences between these two terms, emphasizing the humanistic characteristics of andragogy and ignoring the humanistic character of pedagogy. If andragogy is defined as being humanistic and progressive, then how is adult education defined if the two terms are not synonymous?

Much of the debate on andragogy and pedagogy seems to imply that there is a simplistic consistency in human development—for example, it is not experience alone that sets adults apart from children nor is it even accumulated experience (as this also applies to children) but the kind of experience that one has. In some situations, children have far more experiences and knowledge than adults. The debate, as presented here, also ignores the immense amount of non-formal education engaged in by children, or the extent to which adults commit themselves to formal education. Both approaches span the lifetime of individuals. Mezirow's charter of andragogy, one might argue, applies just as well to children as to adults.

Is andragogy a theory, as argued by some? If so, what is the theory? From the data presented in this article, there is strong evidence that andragogy/adult education are not theories of learning. However, from the field of study of adult education (for example, university graduate programs) come theories, principles and assumptions that help to explain and understand (adult) learning.

It is intentional learning that is the essence of adult education/andragogy. Therefore, one can argue that the generic definition of adult education/andragogy is not determined by the content, skills, attitudes or values being learned (such as literacy education or professional continuing education); by any particular age group of adults; by the sponsoring agency or location of the educational program; or by the methods of teaching and learning being used. These are only variables for describing specific educational programs. The key to which philosophical orientation is most appropriate at a given point in time is determined by the intent of the adult learner and the time and resources available.

Over the years, adult education has come to be viewed as a process of facilitating and managing the intentional (formal and non-formal) learning of adults (always accompanied by incidental or informal learning). A criticism might be made that the above view of adult education is too broad and all encompassing (although internationally and historically the tendency has been to use a broader rather than a narrower definition). The same comment could be said of other fields of study, all of which use "all-encompassing" definitions to define their fields (for example, political science, sociology, economics, geology, anthropology and psychology).

In conclusion, tracing the metamorphoses of andragogy/adult education is important to the field's search for identity. In searching for meaning (historically and contemporarily) adult educators have had to engage in debate to create and refine the terms that they use, as well as to strengthen the theoretical base of their field of practice and study (through research) within the social sciences. The search for meaning has also been an attempt to humanize and understand the educational process.

References

Anderson, M.L., and E.C. Lindeman. 1927. *Education through experience.* New York: Workers Education Bureau.

Andragogy Group. 1981. *Towards a developmental theory of andragogy.* Nottingham, England: Nottingham University, Department of Adult Education.

Best, F. 1988. The metamorphoses of the term 'pedagogy.' *Prospects* 18 (2): 157-196.

Brown, H.W. 1985. Lateral thinking and andragogy: Improving problem solving in adulthood. *Lifelong Learning* 8 (7).

Brundage, D.H., and D. MacKeracher. 1980. *Adult learning principles and their application to program planning.* Toronto: Ontario Ministry of Education.

Carlson, R. 1989. Malcolm Knowles: Apostle of andragogy. *Vitae Scolasticae* 8 (1): 217-233.

Coady, M. 1939. *Masters of their own destiny.* New York: Harper and Brothers.

Corbett, E.A. 1957. *We have with us tonight.* Toronto: Ryerson.

Cross, P.K. 1981. *Adults as learners.* San Francisco: Jossey-Bass.

Davenport, J., and J. Davenport. 1985a. A chronology and analysis of the andragogy debate. *Adult Education* 35 (3): 152-159.

——. 1985b. Andragogical-pedagogical orientations of adult learners: Research results and practice recommendations. *Lifelong Learning* 9 (1): 6-8.

Davies, N. 1931. *Education for Life (A Danish pioneer).* London: Williams and Norgate.

Draper, J.A. 1998. Introduction to the Canadian chronology. *The Canadian Journal for the Study of Adult Eduction* 12 (2): 33.

Draper. J.A., and J. Carere. 1998. Selected chronology of adult education in Canada. *The Canadian Journal for the Study of Adult Education* 12 (2): 44.

Elias, J.L. 1979. *Andragogy revisited.* Adult Education 29 (4): 252-256.

——., and S. Merriam. 1984. *Philosophical foundations of adult education.* Malabar, Fla.: Robert E. Krieger.

Fitzpatrick, A. 1920. *The university in overalls.* Toronto: Frontier College Press.

Griffin, C. 1987. The professional organisation of adult education knowledge. In *Adult education as social policy*, edited by P. Jarvis. London: Croom Heim.

Hartree, A. 1984. Malcolm Knowles' theory of andragogy: A critique. *International Journal of Lifelong Education* 3 (3): 203-210.

Houle, C.0. 1972. *The design of education.* San Francisco: Jossey-Bass.

Husen, T., and T.N. Postlethwaite, eds. 1985. *The international encyclopedia of education: Research and studies.* Vol. 1. Oxford, England: Pergamon.

Joblin, D. 1988. Self-direction in adult education: An analysis, defense, refutation and assessment of the notion that adults are more self-directed than children and youth. *Lifelong Education* 2 (2): 115-125.

Kabuga, C. 1977. Why Andragogy? *Adult Education and Development* 9 (September): 1-3. Reprinted as Appendix L: Andragogy in developing countries in *The adult learner: A neglected species* by M.S. Knowles (pp.233-239). 4th ed. Houston, Tex.: Gulf Publishing (1990),

Kidd, J.R. 1950. *Adult education in Canada.* Toronto: Canadian Association for Adult Education.

Knowles, M.S. [1970] 1980. *The modern practice of adult education: Andragogy versus pedagogy.* Rev. ed. Chicago, Ill.: Follett.

——. 1984. *The adult learner: A neglected species.* 3rd ed. Houston, Tex: Gulf Publishing.

Kulich, J. 1984. Approaches to theory building and research in adult education in East Europe. *International Journal of Lifelong Education* 3 (2): 127-136.

Lindeman, E.C. 1926. Andragogik: The method of teaching adults. *Worker's Education Journal.*

——. [1926] 1961. *The meaning of adult education.* Montreal: Harvest House.

McKenzie, L. 1979. A response to Elias. *Adult Education* 29 (4): 256-260.

Merriam, S.B. 1988. Finding your way through the maze: A guide to the literature on adult learning. *Lifelong Learning* 1 (6): 187-198.

Mezirow, J. 1981. A critical theory of adult learning and education. *Adult Education* 32 (1): 123-139.

Mohring, P.M. 1989. Andragogy and pedagogy: A comment on their erroneous usage (Project No. 29). St. Paul, Minn.: University of Minnesota, Department of Vocational and Technical Education.

Podeschi, R.L. 1987. Andragogy: Proofs or premises. *Lifelong Learning* 14: 16.

Pole, T. [1814] 1968. A history of the origin and progress of adult schools. London: The Woburn Press.

Pratt, D.D. 1988. Andragogoy as a relational construct. *Adult Education* 38 (3): 160-181.

——. 1993. Andragogy after twenty-five years. In *An update on adult learning theory,* edited by S.B. Merriam. San Francisco: Jossey-Bass.

Savicevic, D.M. 1968. *The system of adult education in Yugoslavia.* Syracuse, N.Y.: Syracuse University, Publications Program in Continuing Education.

Tennant, M. (1986). An evaluation of Knowles' theory of adult learning. *International Journal of Lifelong Education, 5*(2), 113-122.

Touchette, C. 198). *The field of adult educationlandragogy in 96 universities.* Paris: UNESCO.

UNESCO. 1973. Summary of the Faure Report: International Commission on the Development of Education (Occasional paper No. 9). Ottawa, Ont.: Canadian Commission for UNESCO.

United States Department of Health, Education, and Welfare. 1972. *A trainers guide to andragogy (its concepts, experience and application).* Washington, D.C.: Author.

Van Enckevort, G. 1971. *Andragology: A new science.* Aontas [Irish National Adult Education Association] (1): 37-52.

Yonge, G.D. 1985. Andragogy and pedagogy: Two ways of accompaniment. *Adult Education* 35 (2): 13-166.

2

Stages in the Development of Canadian Adult Education

Gordon Selman

W e do not have a comprehensive account of the development of adult education in Canada. There is not even such a description for any province or region. The varied nature of the field is reflected in three volumes that come as close as anything to providing a general picture of adult education in this country, two edited by J.R. Kidd, *Adult Education in Canada* (1950) and *Learnng and Society* (1963) and the third edited by Kidd and G.R. Selman, *Coming of Age* (1978). Each of these is comprised of articles dealing with various aspects of adult education occurring over the last several decades and, taken together, they represent something of the panorama of programs, institutions and people which have constituted Canadian adult education.

Adult education in Canada has gained a considerable reputation internationally for imagination and excellence. National Farm Radio Forum and Citizens'20 Forum, the extension work of St. Francis Xavier University, Frontier College, the Joint Planning Commission, the Banff School and the Women's Institute movement are some of the well-known Canadian projects that have gained recognition abroad and in some cases have been borrowed and adapted for use elsewhere. It is all the more surprising, therefore, that we have not managed as yet to produce a general history of Canadian adult education.

Canada has created many programs and institutions, such as those mentioned above, which are original and unique responses to our experience as a people in this northern half of the North American continent. We have also borrowed institutional forms from other sources, mostly from Britain (Mechanics' Institutes, the YMCA, the Workers' Educational Association and newer forms of distance education) and the United States (correspondence education, types of agricultural extension, school board and college programs and the newer form of university extension).

There have been compelling reasons prompting Canadians to learn. We have been an immigrant society and we have had to adjust to new conditions. We have jointly undertaken the enterprise of nation building, with all its challenges at both the personal and community level. In addition to these ongoing factors, we have experienced a series of major shocks and crises that have required a response on a massive scale, based largely on our capacity to learn. These have included such events as the two World Wars and the Depression, the technological revolution of recent decades and the periodic stresses and strains within Canadian confederation.

In recent years, three efforts have been made by Canadian scholars to sum up the history of adult education in Canada within certain time frames. The earliest of these was in a paper by J.R. Kidd (1979). He took as his starting point the creation of Canada and extended that first period to the outbreak of World War I. Subsequent periods extended to 1945, and thence to the present time. In those periods, he saw progressive stages of development, down to the present "Coming of Age." In a second recent interpretation, Selman and Kulich (1980) have set their focus on more recent decades, focusing on the field's growing professionalism. Their milestone years were 1935, 1960 and 1979. In the most recent such analysis, Alan Thomas (1981) deals with what he terms the "modern period." Thomas organizes his study into three periods: the 1930s to 1955, the late 1950s to mid-1960s and the years since 1966, during which he sees an increased recognition of non-formal education and a readiness to focus less on adult education and more on adult learning.

In what follows, an effort is made to establish periods of development that go back to the earliest days of European settlement in Canada and that, it is suggested, provide a satisfactory framework within which to seek coherence and some measure of consistency in the development of the field. Such time frames are, of course, artificial creations, but they are sometimes helpful in identifying significant trends and notable milestones in the advancement of the field of activity.

Before 1867

This was largely a period of scattered, informal beginnings under private and voluntary auspices. It was a time of book clubs, literary and scientific societies, music, handicraft and art associations. It has been pointed out that the well-known "l'ordre de bon temps" group formed at Port Royal in 1605, in which members took turns in entertaining and edifying fellow group members, may be seen as the earliest peer learning group in what later became Canada.

An important development of this period was the creation of large numbers of Mechanics' Institutes in several of the colonies, the earliest appearing in Nova Scotia, Quebec and Ontario in the early 1830s (approximately a decade after their origins in Britain). The first YMCAs appeared in Montreal, Toronto and elsewhere in the 1850s and night classes under their sponsorship were organized beginning about the time of Confederation. Libraries, under public and private auspices, had their beginnings at this time. Several of what were to become long-lived cultural associations, such as L'institut Canadien of Montreal (1844) and the Royal Canadian Institute of Toronto (1849), were formed in this period.

Aside from public libraries, little is known about the origins of public support for adult education in this period. In 1851, the Government of Upper Canada began to subsidize the classes offered by the Mechanics' Institutes, and the Toronto School Board offered night school classes for a few years beginning in 1855.

1867-1914

In this period, adult education was still predominantly under private auspices, but some important steps were taken by government and other public authorities and institutions that laid the groundwork for the expansion of the public sector.

As the population increased and settlement pushed west and north, there was a continuation of the phenomenon of study groups, institutes and associations devoted to educational and cultural matters. Mechanics' Institutes, YMCAs and after 1868, YWCAs were formed in increasing numbers. In 1895 there were 311 Mechanics' Institutes in Ontario alone. Representative of the wide range of other voluntary organizations that were active in the field are the National Council of Women (founded in 1893) and the forerunner of the home and school movement founded in Beddeck, Nova Scotia, two years later.

Agricultural extension, under private and public auspices, came into its own in this period. The Grange (the first in 1872), Farmers' Institutes (the first in 1894) and other agricultural societies flourished. The C.P.R. and the federal government operated experimental farms beginning in the mid-1880s. After the turn of the century, the federal and some provincial departments of agriculture became engaged on a large scale in educational activities by means of information services, demonstration schools and through the appointment of district agriculturalists. Co-operative education was under way early in the new century. In 1913, the federal Parliament passed the *Agricultural Instruction Act*, which made federal funds available for use by the provinces for agricultural extension work, an important step in itself, but also significant in that it pioneered the means subsequently to be used by Ottawa to fund other types of vocational education as well. Other departments of government, for instance Marine and Fisheries and the Geological Survey, began to offer educational services in this period.

Public educational institutions began in greater numbers to get into the field. The Toronto School Board re-instituted its night classes in 1880 on a permanent basis. Night classes in technical subjects were greatly expanded at the turn of the century. Queen's University became the first university in Canada to begin extension work on a permanent basis in 1889, and the University of Toronto and McGill soon followed suit. After the turn of the century, with the creation of provincial universities in Saskatchewan and Alberta, these two adopted the more broadly based approach to university extension that had been pioneered at the University of Wisconsin.

Three other important organizations had their origins in this period. The first Women's Institute was founded in Stoney Creek, Ontario, in 1897. An organization devoted to the education of rural women and improving the quality of rural life, the Women's Institute movement subsequently spread quickly and became world-wide. The Canadian Reading Camp Association began in 1899 and has continued its work in frontier camps and communities ever since, changing its name in 1919 to Frontier College. The origins of co-operative education in Canada are obscure, but the founding of the Caisse Populaire in 1900 should be noted in that connection.

1915-1939

A traumatic period in the life of the country, these twenty-five years also witnessed the beginning of a conscious adult education movement in Canada and the creation of a number of noteworthy projects. The best known program during World War I was Khaki College, which made available a wide range of educational services to Canadian armed forces personnel in Britain and Europe. In World War II, such services were organized by the Canadian Legion Educational Services, which was formed in 1939 and served both overseas and Canadian-based armed forces personnel.

A number of important adult education institutions were created in Canada during this period. University extension was begun at many universities, the best-known project being the co-operative education program of St. Francis Xavier University in Nova Scotia, often referred to as the Antigonish Movement. Begun in 1928, the work addressed itself to the impoverished fishermen, farmers and industrial workers of northern Nova Scotia and proved so successful, under the leadership of the Rev. Moses Coady, that it gained international fame and has over the decades been studied and adapted for use in many countries in the Third World. The Workers' Educational Association was established in several centres in Canada in 1918, and although it had a short history in most places, it has continued its activity ever since in Ontario. Sir George Williams University, long an evening college and an important source of part-time degree study, was founded in Montreal in 1926. The Banff Centre, originally the Banff School of Fine Arts, was founded under University of Alberta auspices in 1933 and began its remarkable success story in the depth of the Depression. The first of the famous institutes on public affairs was held at Lake Couchiching in 1932. And in the late 1930s, two of our most important national institutions were created, the Canadian Broadcasting Corporation (CBC) and the National Film Board.

In 1935, following an organizational meeting the previous year and the carrying out of the first national survey of adult education in Canada (Sandiford 1935), the Canadian Association for Adult Education (CAAE) was established. Founded largely by university and government people, the CAAE was originally intended to be a clearing house and information centre for adult education in Canada, but under the dynamic leadership of E.A. Corbett, it was soon, partly because of the crisis presented by the World War, transformed into a direct programming agency, largely in the field of citizenship education.

Certain government services developed extensively during this period. In 1919, with the passage of the *Technical Training Assistance Act*, the federal government provided funds for use by the provinces in vocational training, a device that was used to circumvent the constitutional barrier to Ottawa's direct involvement in education. This device was used consistently up until the 1960s, making it possible to channel federal funds into "training" programs. Further important legislation in 1937 made possible much significant educational provision for unemployed adults in the later years of the Depression, including vocational training in many fields and the well-known "Youth Training Schools." At the provincial level, the pace of development varied from one province to another. Taking British Columbia as an example, where the Minister of Education and his government (elected in late 1933) were very much of the interventionist, New Deal tradition, many progressive steps were taken in order, in the words of the day, to "improve the morale of the people." The measures adopted included free evening classes in vocational subjects for the unemployed, the imaginative extension of correspondence education, life-skills and social education (in partnership with voluntary associations) for women from families on relief, a progressive *Apprenticeship Act*, implementation of regional library services, an innovative recreation and leadership training project ("Pro-Rec") and the organization of hundreds of drama and play reading groups.

The crisis of the Depression and the deep concern about the future of Canadian society produced many efforts during the 1930s to study and re-think the basic elements of man's relationship to his fellow man, and the nature and role of government. A great deal of this effort was directly related to politics and produced several political movements, most notably the Co-operative Commonwealth Federation Party in 1932. But much of such study group activity was carried out under other sponsorship, for instance the groups under United Church auspices that prepared and issued a major proposal, "Christianity and the Social Order" and other policy statements. The Social Gospel movement was very lively in these desperate days, as were many forms of radical political advocacy.

1940-1959

This was a vibrant time in the life of Canada, in war and peace, and also in the field of adult education. Many of the best-known accomplishments in Canadian adult education were created or gained prominence during these years and there was considerable expansion of provision by public authorities for this work.

The war-time period mobilized Canadians to unaccustomed tasks on an unprecedented scale. Whether in the armed forces, war industries or the vast network of civilian and voluntary support services, Canadian men and women responded, and learned, as never before. Canada emerged from the war with an expanded economy and a new sense of identity as a nation. The educational efforts of the Wartime Information Board and many other organizations during the war years contributed to these changes.

The CAAE, under the leadership of Corbett and his successor, J.R. Kidd, made remarkable contributions in these two decades. Foremost among these were the two projects in the field of citizenship education undertaken in co-operation with the Canadian Broadcasting Corporation, National Farm Radio Forum and Citizens' Forum. Listening groups were organized at the local level across Canada and each week were provided with background information and stimulation by means of a pamphlet (produced by the CAAE) and a broadcast (produced by the CBC) on the week's topic. The local groups, having read the pamphlet and heard the broadcast, then discussed the subject, afterwards reporting their opinions on certain questions listed in the pamphlet. By such feedback, the opinions of the groups were obtained, as were suggestions for future topics. These programs attracted a great deal of international attention and were adopted for use in many other countries. The CAAE also organized the Joint Planning Commission in this period, a remarkably successful and flexible instrument for consultation and joint planning at the national level for public and private agencies in the fields of adult education, cultural and social development. The CAAE also provided significant leadership in two other areas of adult education that emerged in these years, human relations training and study-discussion groups in the liberal arts.

The post-war period was one of continuing large-scale immigration to Canada and both government, through the newly formed Citizenship Branch, and the voluntary sector, with the effective leadership of the Canadian Citizenship Council, provided services to many "New Canadians."

Cold War tensions and Canada's active role as a leading middle power on the world scene at this time encouraged the activities of several important organizations concerned with education about international affairs, including the United Nations Association, the Canadian Institute on Public Affairs and the Canadian Institute on International Affairs. Canadian adult educators, most notably J.R. Kidd, also began to play an important role at UNESCO and elsewhere in the international dimensions of the adult education movement.

Local and provincial governments in parts of Canada became involved more actively in the field. The community centre movement swept the country, creating new means of making educational and recreational services accessible at the neighbourhood level. School board adult education programs began to expand rapidly in some areas, most notably in British Columbia. Whereas in 1945, only one province in Canada had a formally constituted adult education section within its Department of Education, by 1957 seven provinces had taken that step. In Saskatchewan, the landmark Royal Commission on Agriculture and Rural Life demonstrated how the research and public hearings of such a body could be used as an educational instrument among the citizens. In Manitoba, the provincial government launched an important community development project among the Métis people. The federal government also greatly expanded its educational work with the native people, Indian and Inuit.

The National Film Board gained world recognition in this period for the excellence of its productions. In order to carry out its mission of interpreting Canada to Canadians, it devised an outstandingly successful domestic distribution system. Through its field staff, and in co-operation with other agencies in each province, it created a far-flung series of local film councils and film distribution circuits through which its excellent documentaries and other non-commercial productions were seen by a remarkable number of Canadians on a regular basis.

This was a period, especially in the 1950s, in which a sense of professionalism was emerging in adult education. Organizations of adult educators began to appear in some provinces and the CAAE inaugurated a series of regional conferences in both the west and the Maritimes. Several universities offered individual credit courses on the subject of adult education for the first time in the 1950s (many of them taught by J.R. Kidd) and in 1957, the University of British Columbia introduced the first full-degree (masters) program in Canada in this field.

1960-1982

The most recent period has seen enormous strides made in the field of adult education and this account can at best mention only some highlights. In very broad terms, the 1960s may be seen as a period of important federal initiatives and the subsequent years as ones of more active provincial leadership, perhaps reflecting the state of Canadian Confederation in general. Canada's stature in the field of adult education was demonstrated in 1960, when UNESCO's Second World Conference on Adult Education was held in Montreal and J.R. Kidd was elected as its president. The conference is generally seen to have articulated for the field that adult education had passed the stage of being seen largely as a remedial activity, something one engaged in to make up for something that was missed earlier, and instead should be seen as part of a normal pattern of lifelong learning in which all persons would expect to take part as a customary dimension of adult life.

The federal government has made enormous contributions to adult education in these years. The character of technical and vocational education in Canada has been transformed as a result of three major pieces of federal legislation: the *Technical and Vocational Training Assistance Act* (1960), which made unprecedented amounts of money available for vocational training facilities and programs and made possible the creation of many of our colleges, vocational schools and technical institutes; the *Occupational Training Act* (1967), which continued this development and also brought the federal authorities into a more direct role in purchasing training and selecting and supporting students; and the *National Training Act* (1982), which appears to be placing greater emphasis on training on-site in industry and on high-skill vocations. Related to the vast expansion of vocational education has been the federal role in the development of adult basic education (ABE) and English-as-a-second-language instruction. In both these areas, federal efforts have accelerated educational provision (the role of the NewStart Corporations in six provinces was an important dimension of ABE) and has resulted in pressure on the provinces to increase their efforts as well. Another important area of federal contributions flowed from the War on Poverty approach that originated in the mid-1960s and that spawned a great range of community development, local initiative and social development agencies and policies. The bilingualism drive in Canada, within the civil service and outside it, has spurred much educational activity. Finally, in this necessarily selective review of federal initiatives, mention should be made of the large federal grants to the labour movement in recent years to help strengthen its educational activities.

Developments at the provincial level are perhaps even more diverse and impressive and only some examples can be mentioned. That important new policy approaches were under consideration was signified by the reports of the Parent, Wright and Worth Commissions in Quebec, Ontario and Alberta. Policies to match these progressive recommendations were not always forthcoming, but in the last decade significant steps have been taken in such areas as the creation of community colleges, the expansion of school board adult education programs and fresh approaches to distance education offerings. Examples of more specific measures include the community college policy in Saskatchewan, policies on further education and community schools in Alberta, and the use of community development and ABE in Quebec and elsewhere.

Distance education and educational broadcasting have made great advances in recent years. Many long-established institutions have greatly expanded their distance education offerings (the University of Waterloo being a leading example) and new, special purpose institutions such as Athabasca University in Alberta and the Open Learning Institute in British Columbia have been created. Educational broadcasting has made great progress, especially in Quebec, Ontario, Saskatchewan and British Columbia.

Community colleges have been mentioned in passing. The vast expansion of the college system (and similar institutions such as post-secondary institutes) has enormously increased the opportunities for adult education in some parts of the country. Colleges from the outset have been designed with the educational needs of adults and part-time students in mind and they have altered the face of educational provision for adults in Canada.

Several program areas of adult education have greatly expanded in recent years. The professions have seen clearly the urgency of continuing professional education for their members and have mounted substantial programs. Major businesses have in some cases developed very large training enterprises within their organizations. The Women's Movement, which has emerged in the last twenty years, has placed great emphasis on appropriate counselling and educational provision for women, in their various roles and circumstances. Access to university degree study on a part-time basis has increased greatly, with institutions such as York University and the University of Toronto creating new colleges to serve the needs of part-time students. Community development programs proliferated impressively in the 1960s and early 1970s, with the National Film Board, Indian Affairs, the ARDA program, the Centre for Community Studies (Saskatchewan), several institutions in Quebec and Memorial University of Newfoundland being among the leading agencies in this work. Related to community development has been the growth of a broadly based community education movement.

With the increased acceptance of adult or lifelong education as a normal expectation for increasing numbers of Canadians has come an increasing professionalization of the field. Professional training programs, largely at the graduate level, are available in most provinces. Many organizations of adult educators have been formed, provincially and nationally, some relating to the field as a whole (such as the CAAE) and some being concerned with particular areas of practice (ABE, English as a second language, university extension, training in industry and so on). A national organization concerned with research about the field, the Canadian Association for the Study of Adult Education, was founded in 1981.

The most recent attempt to estimate the participation rate of Canadian adults in adult education activities was completed in 1980 by Brundage and Clark (1980) and indicated that approximately 23 percent of adults were participating each year. Clearly adult education has become an accepted part of life for a great, and growing, section of our population.

At the time of writing [1983], the depressed economy and resulting austerity budgets are causing havoc in adult education. Programs are being cut back and cancelled, many adult educators are losing their jobs or having them reduced in scope. Programs that are least able to pay their way out of fees are particularly vulnerable and many of the people who are most in need of adult education opportunities are facing long waiting lists or the elimination of services entirely. The situation is not entirely dark, of course, and adult educators, who as a breed are all too accustomed to functioning on slender resources, are accomplishing much. It is hoped that as times improve, opportunities for adults in Canada to continue their growth and development through learning will be provided on an ever-increasing scale, and with a degree of imagination and vigour that is consistent with our historical tradition.

1983 to 1999 (*by Deo H. Poonwassie*)

The robust spirit of adult educators chronicled above by Professor Selman was the very foundation of adult education as a social movement. However, the economic and social changes in the 1980s and 1990s forced formal adult education into a mode of training to provide skills for a competitive work force, and a much greater entrepreneurial ethic replaced the genre of adult education as a social movement. Although much has been accomplished in strengthening vocational and technical training, the *National Training Act* of 1982 endorsed the centralization and privatization of training through the establishment of Labour Force Development Boards, and subsequently the federal government ceased its practice of funding guaranteed places for training at community colleges.

Fiscal restraint and bringing down the deficit was the call for public economic discipline, and economic constraints affected adult education in public educational institutions; hence the concerted effort for economic self-sufficiency and profit making by many organizations. The shift from the provision of adult education services by the public sector to the private sector has been remarkable (Selman et al. 1998).

Technological development is having a profound effect on adult education and continuing professional education. The distance mode of delivery is seen as the great equalizer in accessibility to training and education. Unfortunately, these modes cater to those who have already achieved a certain level of formal education and who have developed a propensity for self-directed learning. Those with some education get more, and others with less are often ignored. Computer-assisted learning, teleconferencing, interactive videoconferencing and print correspondence courses are quite expensive to deliver; in a self-supporting or a profit-making milieu, the costs are passed on directly to the consumer (students) or private sponsoring agent. Again, those who cannot afford the tuition and accompanying costs (day care, books and so on) do not have access to such innovations. Indeed, the same applies to the Internet and various forms of computer-assisted instruction.

The traditional methods of adult education, such as small-group discussion and learning, are gradually being replaced with the new technologies. The principles of economic efficiency and competition are changing the modes of delivery in adult education and further eroding the major foundations of social interaction in adult education. Conversely this juggernaut of technological change is the current and future wave of innovation that is having indelible influences in society. Adult education must embrace these changes and use them to further enhance lifelong learning for all. The work has merely begun.

In 1992 Statistics Canada published its *Adult Education and Training Survey*; this research was undertaken to determine the importance of adult education and training in Canada, the motivation of learners, the obstacles they encounter and to discover the nature and relevance of the training they received (p.6). The findings of this survey revealed that, in 1991, one in four adults participated in adult education or training activities; learners' activities were directed mainly at career-related skills; employers supported 47 percent of the study programs; the school system was the most important provider of training activities to adult learners, followed by commercial suppliers and employers; and about 6 million programs and courses were taken for job-related reasons. It can be reasonably concluded that adult education activities are central to our learning society.

The two recessions in 1981 and 1991 resulted in high unemployment from downsizing and from both public- and private-sector reorganization. The shift from a resource-based economy to service activities forced a new direction in adult training. Adults were now vigorously involved in learning about new technologies, as careers or jobs required different competencies and skills. The still-nagging reality of literacy needs of adults and a doubled immigrant and/or refugee population between 1981 and 1991 significantly increased the demand for adult education and training.

The *Adult Education and Training Survey* (1992) report contributed significant information on adult education and training, emphasizing the expanding need for job re-training and the gradual but steady shift from the public sector to the private domain as primary providers of adult learning needs (p.16). The *Survey of Trends in Adult Education and Training in Canada* (1985-1995) undertaken by the Council of Ministers of Education, Canada (CMEC), is the Canadian report prepared for the Fifth International Conference on Adult Education (CONFINTEA) sponsored by UNESCO (1997). The summary of this report is illuminating:

> During these ten years, Canadian adult education experienced major changes in organizational structure, responded to shifting economic pressures, and addressed new

needs among learners. Approaching the end of the century, it is dealing with major challenges around citizenship, equity, and the use of new information technologies.

Participation in adult education increased throughout this period, following previously documented patterns whereby those with the most previous education and the highest incomes were most likely to become involved. With the devolution of much federal funding and responsibility falling to the provinces, issues of equity will increasingly be debated. While policies on equity have been put in place, funding cutbacks have made them increasingly difficult to implement.

Increasing and persistent unemployment has provoked much debate about the value of skills training. Public investment in this area rose in the late 1980s, but was declining by the end of this period. Partnerships involving employers, labour and equity-seeking groups grew and then shrank with the availability of public funds, with the exception of some joint Sectoral Councils. With reductions in overall social spending, training funds were focused on the unemployed.

Literacy work gained visibility and importance, along with a strengthened organizational infrastructure, although it remains a vulnerable part of the field. Changes in labour force and social security policy have re-shaped the opportunities available to adults who complete the programs.

Within these broad structural changes, many innovative smaller initiatives have occurred. Aboriginal groups have developed the capacity for economic development; community groups have shaped special programs for women and immigrants and governments have provided incentives to prior learning and assessment recognition (PLAR). Experiments in distance education have been undertaken in schools, libraries, businesses and homes across the country, and the needs of refugees, laid-off workers and people with AIDS have posed new challenges to the traditional content and methods of adult education.

Financial support for both providers and participants remains a key issue in public policy debate and organizational politics. It also directs the research support and professional development available to adult educators, as well as the public recognition given to lifelong learning.

Particular areas of attention now include opportunities for women, the environment, health, citizenship, community development and new information technologies. In each, the pressures of change in the economic and social structure work in tension with the aspirations of individuals and groups to shape the particularly Canadian approach to adult education for the next century (pp.3-4).

CONFINTEA was held in Hamburg, Germany. *The Hamburg Declaration* was discussed under ten themes: (1) adult learning and democracy: the challenges of the twenty-first century; (2) improving the conditions and quality of adult learning; (3) ensuring the universal right to literacy and basic education; (4) adult learning, gender equality and equity and the empowerment of women; (5) adult education and the changing world of work; (6) adult education in relation to the environment, health and population; (7) adult learning, culture, media and new information technologies; (8) adult learning for all: the rights and aspirations of different groups; (9) the economics of adult learning; and (10) enhancing international co-operation and solidarity (UNESCO n.d., 11).

Each of these themes has been part of the history of adult education in Canada and will continue to engage adult educators in this century. While there are formal programs for studying and promoting adult education, the informal learning of adults must be recognized as extensive and pervasive throughout the adult population (Livingstone 1999). With the ageing Canadian population, this trend will take on larger proportions and importance.

During the last decade, activities by the Canadian Association for Adult Education (CAAE) and some provincial organizations, for example, the Manitoba Association for Adult and Continuing Education (MAACE), became mortally constricted. The demise of several adult education organizations could be explained, in part, by their inability to change their mission and practice in light of a fast-changing society. The types of services provided by these organizations were being supplied more efficiently by other organizations in the private sector and by the Internet services using new technologies. The leadership and members of these organizations were unable to redefine their roles in a society propelled by economic constraints, globalization, new information technologies and rapid development of the knowledge industry. We must also remember that most people in these organizations were volunteers who had the responsibility of full-time employment.

The key publications cited above provide us with information that indicates two decades (1980-2000) of changing directions in Canadian adult education. The major shifts in the use of technology, the exponential growth of adults learning (formal and informal),the rise in big business domination (sometimes known as globalization), the increase of adult education services by the private sector and the dormancy of public-service adult voluntary organizations all underscore the need for a rejuvenation of services for adult learning. The voluntary sector is especially crucial for the practice of adult education and must be used as a rich source for enhancing the quality of life in our society.

References

Brundage, D., and R. Clark. 1980. Canada. In *Adult learning opportunities in nine industrialized countries*, by Peterson et al. Princeton: Educational Testing Service.

Council of Ministers of Education, Canada. 1996. *Survey of trends in adult education and training in Canada (198 -1995)*. A report to the Canadian Commission for UNESCO. Toronto: CMEC.

Human Resources Development Canada. 1995. *The 1992 adult education and training survey*. Ottawa: Statistics Canada.

Kidd, J.R. 1979. *Some preliminary notes concerning the heritage of Canadian adult education*. Vancouver: University of B.C. Centre for Continuing Education.

———., ed. 1950. *Adult education in Canada*. Toronto: Canadian Association for Adult Education.

———., ed. 1963. *Learning and society*. Toronto: Canadian Association for Adult Education.

———., and G. Selman, eds. 1978. *Coming of age*. Toronto: Canadian Association for Adult Education.

Livingstone, D.W. 1999. Exploring the icebergs of adult learning: Findings of the first Canadian survey of informal learning practices. *The Canadian Journal for the Study of Adult Education* 13 (2): 49-72.

Sandiford, P., ed. 1935. *Adult education in Canada: A survey*. Toronto: University of Toronto (typescript multilith).

Selman, G., and J. Kulich. 1980. Between social movement and profession: A historical perspective on Canadian adult education. *Studies in Adult Education* 12 (2): 109-16.

Selman, G., M. Cooke, M. Selman, and P. Dampier. 1998. *The foundations of adult education in Canada*. 2d ed. Toronto: Thompson Educational Publishing.

Thomas, A.M. 1981. Education: Reform and renewal in the 80s. In *Canadian education in the 1980's*, edited by J.D. Wilson. Calgary: Detsefig. Originally published in *Canadian Journal of University Continuing Education* 10 (1) (1984): 7-16. Reprinted with the permission of the CJUCE.

UNESCO. n.d. CONFINTEA. *Adult education: The Hamburg declaration. The agenda for the future.* Hamburg: UNESCO-Institute for Education.

3

Philosophical Considerations

Mark Selman

Adult educators do not usually think of their day-to-day decision making as proceeding from philosophical premises. Commonly, like people working in other fields, they act in ways that seem appropriate or natural, and in many cases, according to standards of accepted practice within their place of employment. But if we think about it, we realize that when educators do make decisions about how to act, their decisions are based on their values and their fundamental beliefs about the way things are. By examining philosophical issues that lie behind some of these decisions, we become more aware of the implications and consequences of particular ways of thinking and acting.

After a few introductory remarks to explain the purposes of discussing philosophical issues in this context, this chapter begins by describing how philosophers distinguish the kinds of claims or statements made about issues that might be raised in an ordinary classroom situation. The distinctions they have developed are based on the sorts of evidence or support needed to establish the acceptability of those statements. Next, some of the assumptions held by adult educators and theorists are examined, including fundamentally different views about the nature of society, the role of adult education within society and the basis of our knowledge of the world. In each case, a connection is made between these general positions and the views of adult educators. Some of these ideas are applied to an examination of the concept of autonomy and other matters involved in what Malcolm Knowles calls *andragogy*, or "the science and art of helping adults learn."[1] The chapter concludes by recognizing some of the ways in which philosophy is changing and how these changes might relate to changes in disciplines and fields of practice such as adult education.

As Robert Blakely succinctly puts it, "We can—and usually do—refrain from asking philosophical questions, but we cannot avoid acting according to philosophical assumptions."[2] Given that our assumptions may be a result of all sorts of accidents of upbringing and experience, and that they may well be based on little evidence or ill-founded inference or may even be in contradiction with one another, some questioning of them is in order. In fact, it might be argued that relatively self-conscious reflection on one's fundamental beliefs and values is part of what makes an individual more than a simple product of environmental pressures, part of what accounts for a person's ability to be autonomous or self-determining.

In addition to this general reason for examining one's assumptions, educators have particular reasons to reflect on their views. Insofar as learning implies change, educators are involved in the activity of changing people, or at least of helping people change themselves. This carries with it certain responsibilities–among them a responsibility to have examined the beliefs and values that may be conveyed through their words and actions. Further, educators are constantly faced with the task of trying to understand how other people make sense of whatever is being studied. This task is obstructed if educators are not aware of their own basic assumptions, which make certain conclusions seem obvious to them, but which may not be shared by others.

Without suggesting that such reflection should in any way be restricted to the early, formative stages of a professional career, it is worth noting that reflection on fundamental assumptions may inform or help shape one's outlook and aspirations. It could influence, for example, one's choice of education or employment. Also, it may well become more difficult to find the time, or sufficient detachment from day-to-day pressures, to think through philosophical issues as one becomes involved in a career. So there are good reasons for reflecting on these issues at a relatively early stage of professional practice, as well as during one's subsequent career as a practitioner.

It may be helpful to distinguish between at least two of the many ways in which the word *philosophy* is used. Sometimes it is used to refer to a discipline or field of study. Most frequently, at least in Canada, philosophy in this sense is taken to refer to the Western tradition of philosophy, beginning with the Greek philosophers, including Plato and Aristotle, and also emphasizing modern European philosophical thought, from Descartes (writing in the 1600s) to the present. As such, the term *philosophical* refers to a certain set of issues in epistemology (the study of knowledge), metaphysics (questions that exceed in some way the scope of science), ethics (the study of good or right human conduct), and aesthetics (the study of art and beauty), as well as logic, language and thought. But *philosophy* is also used to refer more generally to people's most fundamental beliefs and values. The phrase "philosophy of life," for example, usually expresses this latter sense.

For the most part, this chapter is devoted to exploring philosophical considerations in the former sense, that is, issues that commonly arise for adult educators about which philosophers have had something important to say. As can be seen, such examinations can have starting points from the direct experiences of adult educators, from examinations of the ideas of those who theorize about adult education or from the works of philosophers that bear on issues involved in adult education. The sections that follow include all of these.

Philosophical Distinctions

To examine our fundamental beliefs and values, and those of theorists and practitioners in adult education, it will be helpful to have some conceptual tools. A few distinctions will therefore be introduced and explained. In order to establish the relevance of these distinctions, they will be discussed in the context of an adult educator who is trying to make practical decisions about how best to conduct her class.

Imagine, for this purpose, that an educator is teaching a class for nurses who are interested in learning how to orient and instruct new and inexperienced nurses being hired in a particular jurisdiction. One of the issues raised by a member of her class is that the experienced nurses feel that something should be done to help the new nurses think more critically about situations, rather than following instructions rigidly and being at a loss when even relatively minor obstacles interfere with standard procedures. The instructor (let's call her Sharon) has looked at a couple of articles about critical thinking but feels ill-equipped to address some of the issues raised by her class. They want to learn how to teach critical thinking but, through class discussion, Sharon realizes that none of them, herself included, has a very clear idea about what critical thinking really is, or how they could promote critical thinking in this context. Some of the issues raised in the discussion include: What does critical thinking mean, or what does it mean to be a critical thinker? Do you have to be an expert to teach critical thinking or can any teacher learn to do it? Are general courses of instruction in critical thinking worthwhile or should they develop a specialized program of their own?

Each of these questions raises different kinds of issues, calling for different sorts of answers that require different types of supporting arguments. Philosophers categorize different kinds of issues or claims according to the grounds that serve to support or undermine them. *Conceptual claims*, for instance, are claims that are true or false depending exclusively on the meaning of words. That is, the truth of a conceptual claim is evident to anyone who has a relatively complete understanding of what the words in it mean. While this might seem to indicate that conceptual claims are relatively straightforward, many of the central concepts in adult education are sometimes used in confusing and contradictory ways. The language used both to think about the world and to communicate with others affects what we can see and what we can say, and so conceptual issues have fundamental importance to the enterprise of education. In fact, many of the enduring issues in philosophy and education turn out to be conceptual ones.

The first question raised by Sharon and her class, about what critical thinking means, is a conceptual issue. Sometimes people speak and write as if it is quite clear what even complex terms mean, as if the meaning should be clear to any competent person with a dictionary. This is certainly not the case for terms such as *critical thinking*, which are used by different people for different purposes. Often such words are used as theoretic terms, in which case they may take on a special meaning. *Learning* is another example of such a term. If it is used by a behaviourist psychologist to mean "a change in behaviour," we must be careful not to extend any conclusions drawn using this particular definition of learning to the more general and varied uses of the term. It may be very relevant to learning to duck when passing under a low doorway but have little application to learning in the sense that one learns to care about one's workmates. Different senses, uses or ways of understanding a concept are called *conceptions*.

Philosophers have developed various strategies to clarify the meaning of terms. Although there isn't space here for any serious examination of these strategies, one thing to note is that conceptual questions cannot be settled by more research, at least not research in the traditional sense of conducting experiments and observing the results. If Sharon and her class want to find out what critical thinking means, there will be no point in looking to see what research has "proven" or in conducting their own experiments. It isn't a question of facts that can be established so much as a question of meaning. Instead, the class might look closely at what people who are teaching or writing about critical thinking are trying to achieve, or they might examine the philosophical debate over the nature of critical thinking.

A second type of issue is called *empirical.* Empirical issues are those that are determined on the basis of evidence supplied by our senses, either directly or indirectly. Claims about observable states of affairs in the world are the most obvious examples of empirical claims, but other claims for which only supporting evidence is available are also included. Examples of this latter category include claims about past events, claims about unobservable events such as subatomic collisions, or conditional claims, that is, claims about what would happen if such and such were the case.

For Sharon's class to answer their second question, about whether special expertise is required or whether they could themselves teach their students to think more critically on the job, they would be considering an empirical issue of this latter type. This is the sort of issue for which they might be able to find an answer in the research, although it would require care in evaluating whether or not the cases of published research that they found provided examples close enough to their own situation to be relevant. They would also want to be sure that the indicators of success or failure used in the research studies were a reasonable match for the conception of critical thinking that was relevant to their interests—in this case, defined as more independent and constructive thought on the part of their students while on the job.

In order to establish the soundness of an empirical claim, we do not usually employ reflection or philosophical methods of inquiry, but are more likely to rely on the standards and practices developed in the sciences or in the study of history. In education, however, it has often proven extremely difficult to sort out whether one method works better than another for accomplishing a given objective. This does not seem solely a matter of complexity, but also arises from the fact that education involves human intentions and feelings. Thus, in certain areas of human endeavour, empirical issues are inextricably connected to other sorts of issues.

Value judgements form a third category. While many value judgements are not generally referred to as being either true or false, reasons can be offered for or against accepting them, and some judgements are more justifiable than others. If, for instance, a particular taxation policy can be shown to be producing undesirable social consequences, such as drastically increasing unemployment, or if it could be shown to be in conflict with some fundamental principle of human justice, we would have reasons for accepting the value judgement that it is a bad taxation policy.

Thus, while value-related issues are often thought of as contentious and irresolvable, it is not the case, as some have thought, that value judgements are simply expressions of opinion that lack a rational or cognitive basis. On the contrary, trying to establish a relatively stable, consistent and coherent set of values is no less a rational enterprise than is the project of establishing a stable, consistent and coherent system of beliefs. Indeed, it seems to be the case that the two are closely related and are jointly involved in our coming to be a mature person. As the issue of what constitutes maturity is of central importance to defining the field of adult education, it is one to which we will return.

When Sharon and her class were considering their third question, whether general instruction is "worthwhile" or whether they "should" consider developing a more specialized program for their own purposes, they were considering value issues. Value judgements are often identifiable because they employ value terms such as worthwhile or good, or because they express judgements about what should or ought to be done. It is of particular importance in a practical field such as education to realize that practical judgements, such as those employing should and ought, are value judgements. As such, their acceptability is not determined by empirical research alone. Whether they are acceptable is also a matter of meeting other sets of standards. Which standards are relevant will depend on the sort of judgements being expressed.

Two broad categories of standards that are relevant for present purposes are those judgements that express *epistemological* and *ethical claims.* The first of these express judgements according to the adequacy of the methods and validations used in claims to knowledge. Such standards of adequacy are of obvious significance to the educational enterprise. Whether one is preparing a lecture, evaluating a textbook, reacting to a comment made in discussion or judging an assignment, an important issue will be to judge the adequacy of statements as assertions of knowledge. This will involve assessing whether they are true, whether there is evidence in support of claims that are made and whether the claims are significant or relevant to the points under discussion. If Sharon's class wanted to know whether improved results on a certain kind of standard test were good evidence for the quality of a critical-thinking program, they would be raising an epistemological issue.

Ethical judgements are those made about the adequacy of a person's (or a group's) conduct, especially as it relates to the interests of others. Two types of ethical issues that commonly arise in educational settings are issues involving the distribution of educational resources and those involving the treatment of individual students with (or without) respect. If, for instance, one of Sharon's students pointed out that the reason they ought to assist the new nurses to think independently was because that was the only approach consistent with treating them as mature persons, he or she would be making an ethical argument.

One fact worth noting about ethical disputes in particular is that there is often agreement at an abstract level about the value to be realized in a given situation (for example, respect for persons, fairness, solidarity) but disagreement at the level of practice about what counts in a particular context as acting according to these values, or about how to balance conflicting values. This can be seen from the example of Sharon's student who raised the issue of encouraging independent thought. It is comparatively easy to get people to agree that adult students ought to be treated as mature persons, but rather more difficult to reach agreement about what that means in terms of teaching methods.

Some Fundamental Assumptions in Adult Education

Having now a shared understanding of these distinctions, we will turn our attention to some of the ways in which adult educators differ over fundamental assumptions. It is important to recognize that no simple set of categories can do justice to the range of differences that exist between educators on such matters. As we will see, thinkers who share many assumptions can disagree sharply over others.

I. Functionalism and Conflict Theory

One important area in which educators disagree about fundamental issues is in their views of society and its relation to individuals. Only some aspects of this disagreement are, strictly speaking, philosophical, but it bears examination here because the different viewpoints have significant consequences for how the role of the educator is conceptualized. While this section may seem rather far removed from the familiar and practical situation of a class initiating new nurses into the workplace, which helped to ground our discussion of certain philosophical issues and claims, the wider perspective it offers can create a background for more familiar educational issues. For instance, thinking about critical thought from the perspective of Paulo Freire, as discussed below, can only be done within a political context we might not otherwise consider.

The disagreement between educators can perhaps be captured most succinctly by means of two contrasting metaphors: one portraying society as an organism and the other as a scene of conflict or struggle. The former is derived from a theory called *functionalism*, and is commonly associated with liberal thought; the latter, called *conflict theory*, is more common among Marxist and other more radical critics of existing Western social structures. It should be stressed, before exploring what is at stake in the acceptance of these metaphors, that theorists may vary greatly in how they make use of them–that while the metaphors may be used to point out general areas of disagreement, some liberals may have more in common with some more radical thinkers than they do with some other liberals, and vice versa.

According to those who see society as an organism, the various parts of society contribute to its overall efficient functioning in the same way that each organ of a body fulfils a necessary role. Schools, labour unions, the courts, businesses and other segments of society each function as required for the operation of society as a whole. Under changing circumstances, the system adapts by making adjustments in the relations between the various segments of society or in the roles of its institutions.

Usually associated with this view is the belief that society rewards most highly those roles that are most important. Thus, the ablest individuals are attracted to those positions that are critical to the welfare of the society as a whole. For educators who hold these sorts of beliefs about the way society works, the role of adult education is likely to be seen as facilitating the adjustment or improvement of society, particularly by increasing the number of qualified people for positions that are in social demand. Individual students will, it is thought, be able to improve their position by equipping themselves to take on more important functions, ones that are more highly valued and rewarded. In addition, society as a whole will benefit by having more capable people in important positions.

Conflict theorists have a very different view of the way society works. They see it as being composed of groups with fundamentally different and often incompatible interests. Relations between different groups are not based on mutual adaptation for the overall smooth functioning of society, but rather on constant struggle, with some groups trying to maintain positions of entrenched wealth and power over those without. For those who take this view, the belief that individuals succeed by equipping themselves better to fulfil roles important to society is seen as a myth, moreover as a myth that is useful for those in power as it tends to promote satisfaction with the status quo.

Educators who subscribe to this second view tend to see their role in one of three ways. The first suggests that most educational efforts are merely window dressing, that real change in societal relations can proceed only on the basis of a different economic structure. Educational reform, in this view, is likely to be seen as a distraction from the real problems, which are economic and political, or at best as treating the symptoms rather than the root causes of social inequality.

Other conflict theorists, however, have seen a more positive role for educators, believing that education can at least help to create the conditions necessary for the amelioration of political and economic inequities. In the field of adult education, Paulo Freire is one important writer who has taken this position. Based primarily on the experience of literacy work in Brazilian villages, Freire and his colleagues developed what he called a "pedagogy of the oppressed." In his book by that title, Freire argues that education is by its nature a political activity in that it either promotes the assumptions of the existing political and economic structures or it brings people to question them. In either case, it serves a political function.[3] In the context of the very poor villages in which Freire worked, the very fact of increased literacy among the villagers did indeed have significant political consequences. By becoming literate, they gained access to information about a range of possibilities unknown in the circumscribed world of their villages. They were no longer completely dependent on their employers, the landowners, as they found out about alternative social arrangements.

They could begin to question the apparent inevitability of existing states of affairs and social relations.

Freire describes this as a first step in the process of "conscientization," the process of becoming aware of contradictions in one's situation and becoming capable of acting to resolve them. Notice that, for Freire, meaningful or authentic education is not simply the passing on of facts, or even a deeper initiation into the cultural traditions of a society, but necessarily involves the fostering of critical thought regarding the sociopolitical context in which the learners are situated. Quite naturally, Freire's ideas have had the most influence in situations that resemble those in which his ideas were developed. In Canada, this has tended to be in working with groups facing the most severe obstacles to economic well-being and political autonomy, such as Native Indians, immigrant labourers, illiterate adults and prisoners.

The third conception of the role of educators is illustrated by the Italian Marxist Antonio Gramsci. In contrast to Freire, Gramsci offers a rather traditional, even conservative, account of school age education. His primary concern was that children of lower-class families were prevented from obtaining the best education available, and not that the education they obtained was ideologically biased.[4] It is only in adulthood, when people have started to work, that education should be focussed on specifically political objectives, primarily under the auspices of worker-controlled organizations such as labour unions and community-based groups.

II. Subject-Centred and Learner-Centred Approaches

The general distinction between the views of Freire and Gramsci are roughly paralleled by differences among liberal educators. On the one hand, educators who adopt a progressivist approach, usually derived in some way from the thought of John Dewey, tend to emphasize the active role of the learner in creating and defining the value of what is learned. Often this results in what is referred to as a "learner-centred" curriculum. On the other hand are those who, often drawing on the work of R.S. Peters, emphasize the importance of initiation into our cultural traditions and the intrinsic value of what is commonly called a liberal education. This approach tends to result in what is called a "subject-centred" curriculum.

Peters has associated this view with the idea that education is to be valued for its own sake, not primarily or essentially because of its utility or its value as a means towards achieving other goals. This is in contrast, of course, to those who see education's value as residing in its contribution towards individual advancement or social reform.

Many of these positions have entered into debates in adult education. The notion that educational planning should be driven by the interests of the participants is evident in a common saying from thirty years ago–that "adult education has no curriculum." In 1966, the Canadian Association for Adult Education issued *A White Paper*, in which it was stated, "Whatever a citizen chooses to learn is important simply because he chooses to learn it."[5] On the other hand, Colin Griffin has argued that "the primary conceptual framework for adult education ... has been constructed in terms of needs, access and provision rather than in terms of knowledge, culture and power." We need, he says, "a curriculum theory of adult education; one which is primarily concerned with the social and political definition, distribution and evaluation of knowledge."[6]

The view that education is to be valued for its own sake is evident in the 1936 statement of H.F. Munro, president of the Canadian Association for Adult Education, who wrote of "the enterprise of turning an individual into a genuinely competent and wise adult" and of "the love of learning for its own sake, with the consequent enlargement of our philosophical frontiers and the wisdom that knowledge, rightly pursued, brings in its train."[7] George Grant, the well-known Canadian political philosopher who once worked for the same association, wrote in the association's journal in 1953 that adult education stands for "no limited social ends, but for the highest end, the self-liberation of the human soul by the systematic examination of its own activities."[8] Northrop Frye, the eminent literary critic and educator, went so far as to say, in his book *On Education*, that attempts to be "relevant" are inimical to the realization of the most important values of education.[9]

On the other hand, Canada in particular has a long tradition of adult education projects undertaken with specific political, economic and social ends in mind. One of the most famous of these is the Antigonish Movement in the Maritimes, which used adult education as a focus for the organization of co-operative ventures among exploited fishermen and their families. The leading figure in the Antigonish Movement, the Rev. Moses Coady, believed, according to his biographer, that "the adult educator worth his salt was an aggressive agent of change and adult education a mass movement of reform."[10] In 1941, E.A. Corbett, in his Director's Report to the Canadian Association for Adult Education, said, "That's our job, to show people what a living, shining thing democracy can be."[11] It is interesting to consider our more everyday classroom concerns under the umbrella of the various ideals expressed above.

Three Philosophical Orientations

To gain an appreciation of the issues that lie behind these different positions, one must understand something of the place of epistemological concerns in the development of Western philosophical thought. Perhaps the most central project of Western philosophy has been to identify the grounds on which our knowledge is based; that is, on what basis we can identify the differences between those of our beliefs that are true and justified and those that are false or merely speculative. Philosophers such as Descartes have believed that it is possible to derive a foundation for our knowledge of reality from reason alone. This is referred to as *rationalism*. In contrast, British philosophers John Locke, Bishop Berkeley and David Hume believed that our knowledge of reality is based entirely on impressions of the world received through our sensory organs. Because, as mentioned above, claims that are based on information that can be verified through our senses are called empirical, this position is referred to as *empiricist*.

Since the end of the eighteenth century, this argument has been modified somewhat, largely because of internal contradictions in each of the major positions. Rather than searching for a foundation on which all knowledge could be grounded, philosophers have turned more to the problem of identifying those areas of knowledge or kinds of claims that can be said to be held on the basis of good reasons. One of the most celebrated moves in this direction was Kant's argument that human knowledge and understanding is restricted to the world as it appears to us, that we have no access to any ultimate or unconditioned reality. One of the implications of this argument is that many of the positions taken by earlier philosophers in attempting to determine the true nature of reality, which were quite apart from how the world appears to human beings, are meaningless as they are based on a confusion about how language can properly be used.

In this century, several major streams of philosophy have emerged as responses to these historical positions. In the English-speaking world, three have been particularly influential and each of these has had significant influence on educational theorizing. These three strains are positivism, pragmatism and analytic philosophy.

I. Positivism

The project of *positivists* generally has been to develop a scientific language that is more precise than our ordinary way of speaking, one that includes only claims that are logically true (analytic) and those that can be verified unambiguously by reference to observable states of affairs (empirical). While this has been an extremely influential philosophical doctrine, attempts to apply these notions in understanding human behaviour and social interactions have been quite contentious. One of the most dramatic of these attempts has been the psychological theory of *behaviourism*. Behaviourism is worth considering in detail, both because of its historical influence on educational practice and as an example of a practical theory based on this philosophical doctrine.

Behaviourists have argued that a scientific understanding of human action is desirable and is possible only if the concepts by means of which we understand how people act and react are operationalized in terms of their observable behaviours. In practical terms, this has been interpreted to mean that educators ought to state their aims in terms of the behaviours that they wish their students to exhibit. Thus, educators can develop clear, unambiguous criteria for the achievement of an educational objective, and can eventually establish what means of education are effective in bringing about different objectives.

As simple as this program sounds when described in a few sentences, it is fraught with conceptual difficulties. Chief among these has been that many of the concepts by which we ordinarily make sense of educational activities do not entail any obvious set of behaviours. The fact that someone has learned something, understands something, or has developed an interest in something normally implies that he or she has developed some new capacity or inclination, but not necessarily that these changes will be manifest in any observable change in behaviour. How could one characterize, for example, the differences that Sharon and her class would expect to find in the physical behaviour of new nurses if their program were successful at fostering critical thinking? How could one intelligibly capture such differences without reference to what the nurses were "trying to do" or some other terms that made reference to their intentions?

Many of the words that are most central to understanding what other people are doing depend for their meaning as much on inferences about purposes and intentions as they do on observable behaviour. Because purposes and intentions are, however, not observable states, they are excluded from behaviouristic analysis. Behaviourists are faced with an unattractive choice: either they accept that much of what we want to understand under the description of educational activity and achievement cannot be captured within their theoretical structure (because the concepts cannot be operationalized adequately) or they conclude that their strictures on what counts as scientific are too rigid. Either many of the questions we most want to understand cannot be addressed or some of the basic premises of behaviourism must be given up.

As a result of these and other problems, behaviourism has fallen from being one of the most dominant psychological theories, especially in the field of education, to having a rather restricted role in explaining learning in which understanding or cognition is thought to play a limited role. Examples would include learning that is limited to rote memorization, repetitive drill aimed at the development of physical skills or the training of those with very limited mental capacity. Nonetheless, behaviourist language and assumptions remain common enough in educational writing that sensitivity to these issues is required if one is not to adopt them unwittingly.

The history of behaviourism is typical of many of the more positivistic theories, especially in the human or social sciences. Most current philosophers and theorists hold that there is no clear way of separating logical and empirical claims from questions of intention and value. Thus, there is no way to establish a completely neutral, value-free method for establishing the truth. This kind of realization, however, can give rise to concerns that there is no such thing as knowledge in general. This is commonly referred to as *relativism*. It suggests that all claims to knowledge or truth are relative to the purposes, interests and intentions of whomever is making the claim. But this suggestion seems to raise possibilities that run strongly against some basic intuitions, intuitions that many people do not want to give up. For instance, some have taken it to mean that there is no reality, only versions of it as viewed by different individuals or different social groups. Further, it has been taken to imply that agreement or shared understanding between people with different backgrounds and purposes is unlikely, or even impossible, as they live in essentially different realities. Claims to truth by one individual or group would then have no more force than statements of preferences or opinions.

II. Pragmatism and Analytic Philosophy

Philosophers and others have differed greatly over how seriously to take this problem and its apparent consequences for communication between individuals and social groups. One very important tradition in philosophy, especially in American philosophy, is called *pragmatism*. Pragmatists, as the name implies, treat this and other philosophical issues as practical problems to be worked out in experience. Thus, a pragmatist would be inclined to ignore the problem about the nature of reality and discuss the issue of relativism in terms of its practical consequences in human communication. If, in fact, it turns out that we can successfully communicate with others with very different interests and experiences, if we can translate from language to language and obtain reasonably coherent reactions on the basis of our translations, then the worst fears raised by the issue of relativism can be put to rest.

John Dewey, mentioned earlier in the discussion of learner-centred curriculum, was little troubled by the issue. Dewey was one of the most important of the pragmatists, especially for those in the field of education, with a strong faith in human nature, in democracy and in science. He believed that, if human beings were given the freedom to pursue their own interests within a supportive environment, human knowledge and understanding would flourish. A dominant metaphor in his work is the notion of education as growth. This metaphor has great merit in some respects, especially when contrasted to metaphors of production and consumerism that have come to dominate much educational discussion. However, a common objection to this idea is that people's mental lives, unlike plants and other things that grow, have no natural or predetermined shape. Allowing the uneducated person's own interests to guide the educational process is, according to this objection, an abrogation of the educator's responsibility.

One of the sources of this objection is the *analytic* school of philosophy of education. These philosophers believe that many educational theories and programs are based on misunderstandings of the concepts with which we make sense of educational activities and achievements. But, rather than arguing for the development of a new, more scientific language in which to formulate educational theories, as the positivists did, analytic philosophers have argued that we should pay very close attention to the structure of ordinary language and the way we ordinarily use certain concepts. They point out, for example, that the notion of a person's interests, which is central to Dewey's arguments, is ambiguous in an important way. People's "interests" may refer either to that in which they are interested or to what is in their best interests. It is obvious that people should be educated in a way that advances their best interests, but this is quite different, they claim, from using what they are interested in as the determining factor in what they will study.

R.S. Peters, introduced in the section on subject-centred curriculum, and Paul Hirst, two of the most influential analytic philosophers of education, go on to argue that, on the basis of an analysis of the way that the concept of education is employed, only some of the achievements and some of the activities of educational institutions are truly educational. By being careful with the way we use the term, they argue, we could avoid confusing activities that are indoctrinatory, for instance, with those that are genuinely educational. They also argue that "being educated" implies a certain breadth and depth of knowledge, typically taken to mean that an educated person has some acquaintance with each of the traditional disciplines of knowledge. Thus, according to these philosophers, it is the traditions of the academic disciplines, rather than the interests of students, that provide the most significant guide to planning educational activities.

This point returns us to the issue of whether program planning or curriculum development ought to proceed primarily on the basis of the structure of the academic disciplines and other fields of study, or whether it ought to be determined primarily by the interests of those studying. It may be that individual educators will need to determine the most satisfactory way of dealing with this issue on a situation-by-situation basis. Nonetheless, it seems important that educators do consider some of these issues, because whether or not philosophers come to agreement about which of the possible positions is most reasonable, educators will end up making judgements and decisions that presuppose some position, at least, for a given context. Sharon, for instance, may want to consider some of the ideas of the analytic philosophers in her quest for an understanding of critical thinking. The educational goal of becoming truly knowledgeable, and of being very clear about what is indoctrination and not education, could be related to the goal of teaching critical thought, although traditional academic disciplines seem far removed from the concerns of new nurses and the practical subjects that need to be dealt with in her classroom.

Autonomy as an Example of an Educational Ideal

Presumably none of us would like to have our professional practice based on ideas that are in fundamental conflict with other of our deeply held beliefs about reality, human nature and so on. To provide an example of how an educator's basic beliefs and values might be connected with, or be in conflict with, some of these positions, we will consider the related concepts of *maturity* and *autonomy*. Most of us are committed to the idea that autonomy is an important character trait, one that we ought to foster in ourselves and enhance in others. Maturity is a particularly important notion for adult educators in that it is one of the characteristics that is typically thought to distinguish adults from children. It is on the basis of a presumption of greater autonomy (in the sense of independence of judgement) that adults are entitled and expected to take an active role in legal and democratic processes, for example.

The issue of autonomy is relevant to an evaluation of each of the major positions discussed. It can be argued that behaviourism, for example, obscures our sensitivity to the issue of students' autonomy, focussing as it does simply on observable inputs and responses. In fact, it tends to treat human beings simply as objects of study who react in this way or that, without regard for their purposes and intentions, which are inextricably related to the issue of autonomy. Notice, for instance, that fostering autonomy is not a legitimate educational objective according to the principles of behaviourism, as it cannot be operationalized in terms of any specific set of behaviours. Thus, unless there is reason to doubt one or more of these descriptions of behaviourism, an approach based on behaviourist theory is inappropriate if we agree that issues involving autonomy are critical to the responsible practice of education.

The dispute between philosophers inspired by the pragmatist Dewey and the analytic philosophers can also be understood as crucially involved with the issue of autonomy. Dewey inclines us to think that it is through the practice of autonomy in choosing their educational pursuits that students both express and develop their autonomy. Peters and other analytic philosophers argue that autonomy in its richest sense is closely connected with the ideal of an educated person and that, without a relatively broad and deep understanding of our cultural and academic traditions, the freedom to pursue one's interests is of limited value. It is perhaps like having the freedom to vote in an election without any real understanding of the issues at stake.

The fact that there can be such fundamental differences between sincere and intelligent people concerned with issues in education, people who are equally concerned about virtues of character such as autonomy, is an indication that this is an area in which human judgement plays a significant role. This issue is not likely to be settled by some scientific discovery or by some startling new argument that no one has ever thought of before. More likely, through reflection and study of others' work, we can each develop a deeper appreciation of the connection between our ideals, such as maturity and autonomy, and our various practices. By considering the importance of autonomy, we become more sensitive to the ways in which common educational practices may pre-empt students' autonomy and encourage them to be dependent on the reasoning or intellectual and/or political authority of others. It could be helpful for Sharon to consider how the apparently straightforward goal of teaching critical thinking might be better understood when issues of autonomy have first been explored with her class.

Many kinds of study can enhance our understanding of these issues. Historical and literary texts often provide insight into the ways that other individuals and groups have made sense of them. Another source that is not often included in the study of issues in adult education is the writing of philosophers themselves. Consider these comments by Immanual Kant, one of the greatest of Western philosophers, about the nature of *enlightenment*. Kant understands enlightenment as both an individual and a sociopolitical ideal:

> Enlightenment is man's release from his self-imposed immaturity. This immaturity is man's inability to make use of his understanding without direction from another. It is self-imposed in that its cause lies not in lack of reason but in lack of resolution and courage to use it without direction from another. Laziness and cowardice are the reasons why so great a portion of mankind, long after nature has discharged them from external direction, nevertheless remains in a state of immaturity, and why it is so easy for others to set themselves up as their guardians and kindly assume superintendence over them. It is not easy to be of age. If I have a book which understands for me, a pastor who has a conscience for me, a physician who decides my diet, and so forth, I need not trouble myself.[12]

Even this short passage raises some critical issues for adult educators. Kant links enlightenment and maturity with ideas we have considered under the notion of autonomy. Notice that he thinks that the most crucial factors that interfere with autonomy are "lack of resolution and courage," not the lack of a development of reason or discipline-based knowledge, as suggested by the analytic philosophers. If Kant is right, it may be that educators should devote far more of their attention to fostering these virtues on the part of their students. It may be that these virtues are best fostered in a situation that emphasizes the shared nature of intellectual inquiry, and de-emphasizes the traditional disciplines as established bodies of knowledge. (Given the changing content of knowledge in the disciplines, many philosophers have come to regard them more as traditions of practice that are modified over time, in part through the use of critical practices that form part of a discipline's structure.)

Another crucial point in this excerpt from Kant is the notion that people are apt to slide into a position of either dependence or superintendence. This is a constant danger in the practice of adult education. Many students and educators find it easier to think according to the book or to act on the basis of some theory they are taught, rather than to use their own judgement and take responsibility for their own decisions. Many others may, quite without malicious intent, assume superintendence of them by taking the place of the book, the pastor or the physician in Kant's examples. This draws attention to the danger of adult educators trying to emphasize the place of their professional expertise to the extent of interfering with the autonomy of their students.

Obviously, this is not an argument against the development of knowledge in the field of adult education, any more than Kant's is an argument against books, pastors or doctors. What it does point out is that there is a dangerous link between the development of knowledge, especially in the fields that involve knowledge of people (the human and social sciences), and conditions in which people's autonomy is limited or discouraged. As adult educators, involved with the education of those who are at least presumed to be in a state of relative maturity, we might be expected to be particularly cautious about acting in ways that might discourage maturity and autonomy in Kant's rather rich sense.

Philosophy and the Language of Adult Education

The above was an example of a way in which philosophical writing, like literary and historical writing, can help us to reflect on the practice of adult education. Another way in which philosophical inquiry may contribute to an understanding of this field is in providing what might be called "perspicuous accounts" of central ideas and terms. What is meant by this is that philosophical inquiry may be useful in clarifying conceptual confusions, in showing how certain word uses are related to each other or by providing a more overarching perspective than that obtained by a more specific or narrowly focussed theory.

In order to see what this might mean in a particular case, we will consider one of the most influential concepts in the field, the notion of *andragogy*. This is a particularly useful example, both because of its impact on the field and because of its relation to the concepts of autonomy and maturity, which were discussed in the previous section. By seeing how this concept is applied and by seeing its relation to the more general concepts of adulthood, maturity and autonomy, we will get a sense of the relation between theoretic and more broadly philosophical understanding.

The andragogical perspective, suggests Malcolm Knowles, is significantly different from at least the traditional approach to teaching children, or pedagogy.[13] It is different because adults are more mature than children, and so their experience is more extensive and plays a more significant role in defining their self-concept. Adults are more likely to be self-directed rather than dependent on others for direction. Unlike children, they expect whatever they learn to have quite a direct and immediate application to their daily lives.

This characterization is based broadly on theories of humanistic psychology, and the criteria that are used to differentiate adult learning from children's learning are psychological characteristics of the learners.[14] But the psychological characteristics are only one of the many criteria by means of which we differentiate the activities of adults from those of children in ways that are relevant to understanding education. Thus, it is to be expected that the phrase "adult learning," when employed by Knowles and others who have adopted his criteria, may be applied more specifically than the same phrase would be by other competent language users. Similarly, the "Knowlsian" use would fail to recognize some of the other, non-psychological criteria implied in the ordinary, non-theoretic use; for instance, it will fail to incorporate the distinctive rights and entitlements normally associated with adulthood. But this "value-laden" feature of concepts such as adulthood is also relevant to the practices of education, even if it is not part of the formalized, "operationalized" concepts of a psychological theory.

It is, for instance, important to note that adults are considered to be autonomous agents for legal, political and contractual purposes. Philosophers have pointed out that what it means to act autonomously is that the act is committed freely, in the sense that it is not the result of coercion or compulsion; that it is informed, in the sense that the individual has some idea what is at stake in possible alternative courses of action; and that the individual has a relatively stable set of values or purposes. In our society, barring special circumstances, it is presumed that adults' actions, including those aimed at educational goals, are made under these conditions. In the case of children, it is presumed that these decisions are made under conditions of reduced autonomy.[15] But to make this claim is not only, or even primarily, to point out a set of empirical differences between children and adults, or even about differences in the way they are treated. Adults are entitled to be treated as self-determining agents and only in unusual cases is it acceptable to interfere with this right. It is on the basis of this right that adults are treated differently from children in law, and in many other contexts. Surely educational contexts are one of these.

These considerations are not raised in order to criticize or cast doubt on the utility of Knowles' concept of andragogy. Rather they are used to point out that a concept that is defined in relation to a theoretical framework such as humanistic psychology is necessarily applied according to a narrower and more specific set of criteria than are our ordinary language concepts. This is part of what makes a theoretic concept useful in making claims that can be tested through empirical research. But the price to be paid for this increased precision is the loss of some of the richness of our ordinary, non-theoretic language. Philosophical inquiry may be useful as a means to retain normative or value-laden dimensions of ordinary language and also as a way to clarify the relationship between theoretic concepts and that ordinary language.

Changing Disciplines, Changing World

It has become commonplace to recognize that technological, environmental and economic changes are fundamentally altering people's lives. These changes are difficult to characterize briefly, involving as they do many currents and cross-currents. Some of the most critical trends have been discussed intelligently in Steven A. Rosell's *Changing Maps: Governing in a World of Rapid Change*, a report of a roundtable of Canadian federal government officials.[16] Prominent among the changes they discuss are the effects of global information networks that not only increase the sheer volume of information available but also alter the way in which information is framed and selected. At the same time, there is increased social fragmentation, with more people holding more strongly to specific affiliations connected with race, ethnicity, gender, sexual orientation or political and religious views than to nation states or other larger and more heterogeneous groupings of people.

Concurrently, academic disciplines are being restructured and rearranged. Philosophy, which at one time was regarded as the "queen of the sciences," and often understood to have a role in determining the relations of the disciplines to each other and to knowledge in general, has tended towards one of two poles. Some philosophers, most notably those interested in issues of language, logic and cognitive science, have tended to create a new, highly specialized discipline focussed on technical issues that are, for the most part, outside of common interests and areas of knowledge. Other philosophers, most notably continental European philosophers (such as Michael Foucault and Hans Georg Gadamer), American pragmatist philosophers (such as Richard Rorty) and feminist philosophers (such as Nancy Fraser) have tended to overturn and undermine traditional modern philosophy.[17] While such movements are again difficult to characterize in general terms, the broad tendency of these latter groups of philosophers has been to discount or mock the pretensions of earlier philosophers who claim to have established any kind of objective validity or universality for their views and theories. Rather, they have pointed out that in many ways, the most abstract and purportedly timeless claims to knowledge are closely related to the cultures in which they were developed, the male gender of almost all well-known philosophers, and other contingent and arbitrary facts about the conditions under which such philosophizing has been done.

This approach to philosophical issues has struck a responsive chord among many adult educators who are interested in the field as a way of re-dressing social and economic imbalances of power. Emphasizing as it does the extent to which power is exercised arbitrarily or in the interests of the strongest, and attempting to undermine all efforts to legitimize the use of such power according to standards such as reason or justice, it is seen as supporting the interests of those who have been disadvantaged by existing social and institutional relations. To more traditional philosophers, such a stance is problematic. They are inclined to argue that the undermining of categories that are as fundamental as reason and justice must necessarily undermine charges of inequality or unfairness as well, thus weakening arguments against injustices committed by the powerful against those who are weaker.

As is the case in a serious intellectual dispute, there are sophisticated and thoughtful arguments on both sides of this issue. There is also trivial posturing or adoption of style without the depth of thought of more significant writers. There is an unfortunate tendency on the part of those who see themselves as partisans in this debate to advance their own position simply by trivializing the arguments of those who believe otherwise. Defenders of modernism cast postmodern thinkers as being totally relativistic and therefore incoherent. Critics of modernism fail to do justice to the extent to which the best enlightenment philosophers were aware of the limits of reason and other central concepts.

While there is no doubt that postmodern critiques of modern philosophy have raised important challenges to what had become, at least in some cases, dogmatically held beliefs, it is far from clear that we can or would want to do without some of the central insights that have made possible our relatively open and humane society. Perhaps Michel Foucault has made this point best. In his response to Kant's essay "What is Enlightenment?", Foucault suggests that we "must free ourselves from the intellectual black-mail of 'being for or against the Enlightenment.'"[18] In other words, we should not determine our own views by either accepting or rejecting every-thing that Enlightenment thinkers have to say. As with other elements of our historical heritage, we must sort through and find what speaks to us now and which ideas are irrelevant or even dangerous. This leaves each of us with the difficult and potentially exciting task of sorting through the com-plex and important ideas that make up our philosophical assumptions and form the background against which we make many of our day-to-day decisions.

Endnotes

1. M.S. Knowles, *The Modern Practice of Adult Education* (Chicago: Association Press, 1980), 43.

2. R. Blakely, "The Path and the Goal," *Adult Education* 7, no. 2 (1957): 93-98.

3. P. Freire, *Pedagogy of the Oppressed* (New York: Herder & Herder, 1970).

4. H. Entwistle, *Antonio Gramsci* (London: Routledge & Keegan Paul, 1979).

5. Canadian Association for Adult Education, *A White Paper on the Education of Adults in Canada* (Toronto: CAAE, 1966), 1.

6. C. Griffen, *Curriculum Theory in Adult and Lifelong Education* (London: Croom Helm, 1983), 38, 68.

7. H.F. Munro, "Editorial," *Adult Learning* 1, no. 2 (1936): 2-3.

8. G. Grant, "Philosophy and Adult Education," *Food for Thought* 14, no. 1 (1953): 3-8.

9. N. Frye, *On Education* (Markham, Ont.: Fitzhenry & Whiteside, 1988).

10. A.F. Laidlaw, ed., *The Man from Margaree* (Toronto: McClelland & Stewart, 1971), 83.

11. E.A. Corbett, "Director's Report to Annual Meeting of Canadian Association for Adult Education 1941," in G. Selman, *Adult Education in Canada: Historical Essays* (Toronto: Thompson Educational Publishing, 1995), 124.

12. Version adapted from I. Kant, *Foundations of the Metaphysics of Morals* (New York: The Liberal Arts Press, 1959 [1784]), 85.

13. M.S. Knowles, *The Modern Practice of Adult Education* (Chicago: Association Press, 1980), 43.

14. As Sharan Merriam has pointed out, this is one of three types of criteria used in the field to make this differentiation. The other two are "the adult's learning situation" and "changes in consciousness." None of these approaches, as characterized by Merriam, identify adult learning as distinctive according to socio/political and legal criteria, although the "change in consciousness" approach is a part of explicitly political approaches to education, such as Freire's. S.B. Merriam, "Adult Learning: A Review with Suggestions for the Direction of Future Research" in *Building Tomorrow's Research Agenda of Lifelong Learning*, edited by R.A. Fellenz and G.J. Conti (Montana: Kellogg Centre for Adult learning Research: Montana State University, 1989), 9.

15. For a more detailed argument of this point, see Mark Selman, "Learning and Philosophy of Mind," *The Canadian Journal for the Study of Adult Education* 2, no. 2 (1988): 39.

16. S.A. Rosell, *Changing Maps: Governing in a World of Rapid Change* (Ottawa: Carleton University Press, 1995).

17. There are also modernist European philosophers (such as Jurgen Habermas), American pragmatists (such as Hilary Putnam) and feminist philosophers (such as Onora O'Neil and Sabina Lovibond).

18. Michel Foucault, "What is Enlightenment?" in *The Foucault Reader*, edited by Paul Rabinow (New York: Pantheon Books, 1984), 45.

4

Theory Building in Adult Education: Questioning Our Grasp of the Obvious

Donovan Plumb and Michael R. Welton

It is a typical Sunday afternoon in an ordinary country home in England. A man and his wife, as they have done for years, sit down for afternoon tea with strawberries and cream. Each pour their tea to their liking, one putting the cream in the cup first, the other taking the tea without. The wife, as she has done for years, assembles the strawberries, spooning them into small bowls. They talk, sip their tea, savour their farm-fresh berries. To the visible eye, this event in English life is scarcely worth noticing. What needs to be said? This man and wife still enjoy each other's company after all these years; the tea tastes the same as it always has. Yet the scientific eye would see something terribly wrong. Research laboratories studying the cream produced by the country cows have revealed that a radioactive substance is present in the milk. This substance, quite damaging to one's health, is present in both the tea and strawberries. This cannot be detected by simple observation, or from experience. The ability to see what the visible eye cannot detect is made possible only by the particular knowledge of the chemical structure of substances and the technological sophistication to study them.

Experience cannot always be trusted. Think for a moment of the prevalent view of the relationship between the earth, sun, and moon in the Middle Ages. The conventional view was that the earth was fixed and that the sun rose and set, as this is how it appeared to the naked eye. Later, in the heat of the Copernican revolution, this cosmology was turned upside down. Men like Galileo were put on trial for their views. The great theological minds of Europe defended the view of the earth as the centre of God's universe. People were very upset. They clung to their views like barnacles to rocks.

Today, when philosophers discuss events like strawberries and cream, or Galileo and his magical telescopes, they usually tell us that we human beings never see the world as it is. Human beings distinguish themselves in the world by their use of language. We do not simply invent private languages; languages are shared symbolic worlds. Language occupies our perception and conditions how we apprehend our world. It is like a lens through which we peer at all the wonderful things outside and inside ourselves. Change the lens and a different world appears. The chemist's detection of the presence of strontium 90 in cow's milk and Galileo's attempt to revise the picture of the cosmos changed our perceptual lenses. They undermined common-sense perception, giving people a choice as to how they viewed both cream and the stars.

These examples may help us to consider the way adult educators often take ways of thinking about the role of the adult educator and the meaning of adult learning for granted. The term *adult educator* is applied to a person who engages in a particular kind of activity, but we cannot assume that everyone knows what the term means. For instance, if I think that adult educators are those who teach in formal classroom settings, then I will obviously not include teaching activity occurring in informal, community settings. The term *adult learning* is even trickier. Learning is defined in quite different ways within our culture. Some think that only individuals can learn; others speak of the learning organization. Language is not as fixed as we sometimes like to believe. To further complicate matters, theory comes to us all wrapped up in language that claims to be a more certain base for our action than is common sense. Theory may threaten our certainty, but it also holds out the promise of taking us deeper into how things work and what they mean. Like Alice in Wonderland, one has to risk the plunge, testing one's own perceptions with those who may offer us different lenses to see various dimensions of the world. In this chapter, we will provide a practical method of challenging our taken-for-granted assumptions about the role of the adult educator as well as offering three conceptual paradigms as useful theoretical tools to help us understand the different forms of adult learning in society.

The Role of the Adult Educator

People have different beliefs about the purpose, role or function of adult education. Very often, these beliefs reflect a person's deeply held values about learning, about people and about society. For example, someone who believes in the importance of individual freedom might hold the view that adult education should foster people's ability to be self-determining. Someone else who believes in the importance of a strong economy might hold the view that adult education should nurture people's ability to produce efficiently in a work organization.

The intellectual history of adult education is filled with examples of adult educators' attempts to come to terms with the purpose of adult education. In the nineteenth century, for example, Sir Josiah Stamp suggested that the function of adult education is to help the adult "to earn a living, to live a life and to mould a world" (Selman 1991, 16). In the early 1960s, Coolie Verner (1964) attempted to summarize the different functions of adult education by using terms such as *expansional* (developing new knowledge and skills), *participational* (fostering citizenship), *integrational* (combining new knowledge and skills), and *personal* (enhancing the development and maturation of the individual).

With a keener eye to the social place of adult education, Peter Jarvis (1987) lists the different functions of adult education: (a) maintenance of the social system and reproduction of existing relations, (b) transmission of knowledge and the reproduction of culture, (c) individual advancement and selection, (d) leisure-time pursuit and institutional expansion, and (e) development and liberation. Casting an even wider net, Darkenwald and Merriam (1982) summarize commonly held views about the purpose of adult education: (a) cultivation of the intellect, (b) individual self-actualization, (c) personal and social improvement, (d) social transformation, and (e) organizational effectiveness.

This is indeed a wide range of possible purposes. As you read these lists, some of the purposes may have been more to your liking than others. Now it is time to explore your own view of what the purpose is of adult education. You may wish to keep track of your answers because we are going to pose some questions. These writings will be helpful later for constructing a personal adult educator mission statement.

Step One: Your First Encounter with Adult Education

When did you first become interested in the field of adult education? Where were you working or what were you doing at the time? We recall thinking that adult education was connected with "something important." My co-author Donovan remembers working as a young social worker, trying to help young mothers cope with the stresses of single parenting, when he first became interested in adult education. I recall teaching Bible classes to adults to help them make spiritual discoveries. Can you recall incidents similar to ours? Was it something you read that first introduced you to adult education? How strong was its appeal? What was it you liked about it? What did adult education seem to offer that was important to you? What did you think it could achieve for you? Your answers likely reveal important things about your initial understanding of the purpose of adult education. Did you become interested in adult education because of something it could do or achieve? What was it that you believed adult education could or should do? On a piece of paper, under the heading, "My Initial View of the Purpose of Adult Education," capture your memories of this purpose.

Step Two: Multifaceted Adult Education

One thing that many adult educators learn early on is that their field is multifaceted. People have very different views of what adult education should be and do. On your piece of paper, under a new heading, "Alternative Purposes of Adult Education," list at least three of these different views. Try to express each of these views as concisely as possible. Have any of these views impacted on your own understanding of adult education's purpose? Have any of them helped to change your view of the purpose of adult education since its initial formulation? If so, can you remember what the impetus was for this change? Did someone present you with a view of adult education that broadened your understanding of its purpose? Did you encounter new things that you believed adult education might help accomplish?

Step Three: Your Current View

How do you currently view the purpose of adult education? Under the new heading "My Current View," write a sentence that captures your present beliefs about adult education's purpose. Do you have any underlying values or beliefs about society, people or adult learning that impact on your understanding of this purpose? What are some of these values? You have fairly definite ideas about what adult education can and should do. It may be, however, that you find yourself with mixed feelings about the purpose of adult education. Perhaps you have experienced adult education in a number of different contexts in which it achieved diverse ends. In this case, you might have difficulty identifying only one purpose. If this is your situation, take the time to list the various views that inform your particular perspective. Can you rank the different items in order of importance? Can you identify a favourite view, one that rises above the rest? Are there conflicts or contradictions among the items on your list?

In recent years, experiential learning theorists have recognized that when people attend to their own learning processes they become better able to learn from experience. David Boud and David Walker (1991) identify three different aspects of the learning experience of which the adult learner should be aware. First, it is important for the learner to pay attention to what is actually happening in the learning experience. Learners always approach a new experience from a perspective shaped by their "personal foundation of experience." Learners commonly impose their conventional perspective on the experience, screening out aspects that challenge this perspective. Second, how we feel impacts greatly on our ability to learn from new experiences; our emotional reactions can cause us to shut out learning from new experiences. Paying attention to how we feel in learning situations provides insight into the way our emotions are impacting on our ability to learn. Third, remaining in contact with a learning experience and attending to feelings will influence our ability to acquire new and deepened understandings.

Boud and Walker suggest that learning from experience takes place along four different dimensions: (1) the learner associates new information with things they already know; (2) the learner attempts to seek out relationships among different aspects of the experience; (3) the learner tries to validate that their new ideas and/or feelings are authentic; and (4) the learner appropriates new understandings as their own.

People have very different ideas about what adult educators should be and do. Try a mini-brainstorm and scribble out metaphors that come to mind when you think of what adult educators do. Once again, people's beliefs are shaped by a host of underlying values about society, about humans, and about adult learning. For example, those such as famous adult educator Malcolm Knowles (1975), who believe in individual autonomy and who contend that the adult learner should direct their own learning, suggest that adult educators should be "learning facilitators." Their role should be to support the adult learner in clarifying learning needs, seeking resources and evaluating outcomes.

Brazilian adult educator Paulo Freire (1974) has a somewhat different view. Like Knowles, he believes adults should determine their own learning. Unlike Knowles, however, Freire believes that adult learners are caught in oppressive social situations that prevent them from realizing their full learning potential. For Freire, it is not enough for adult educators to facilitate adult learning. They must also take on the difficult task of helping adults see through, and then to challenge, the oppressive social structures that keep them from directing their own learning future. The Nova Scotian adult educator Moses Coady (1939) thought very much like Freire. He believed that adult educators were like miners whose task it was to detonate the dynamite. Adult educators had the task of dynamiting the encrusted minds of their learners to awaken them to their potential to be masters of their own economic fates.

Other adult educators, such as organizational development theorist Leonard Nadler (1970), view the role of the adult educator from a very different perspective. Nadler is less concerned with values such as autonomy and social equality. He is more interested in fostering the capacity of adult learners to function efficiently in work organizations. Nadler believes that the role of the adult educator should be to create a rich learning environment where adults can successfully acquire new knowledge, skills and attitudes needed in today's fast-paced economy.

These are very different views. Each of them is linked to deeper values. What is your view about the role of the adult educator? What values inform your perspective? Think for a moment about your beliefs about society. Are you positive about our society's future? Do you believe that our society is developing in the way it should? In what ways does our society need to change in order to make it better? Do you think that adult education should be involved in this change? Keeping these thoughts in mind, try to write down what you believe to be the role of the adult educator. A radical adult educator such as Paulo Freire might write this: "I believe that adult educators should work with oppressed communities to problematize oppressive social relations and to foster democratic forms of collective learning." Keep the sheet of paper containing this and your previous responses. You will need them to help develop your personal mission statement.

Now, given what you believe to be the role of the adult educator, what do you think are the most important things adult educators need to learn? This, of course, is a complex question. Take out a clean piece of paper and divide it into three columns. Head the first column "Skills," the second, "Knowledge," and the third, "Attitudes." Return for a moment to the sheet of paper on which you wrote out your beliefs about the role of the adult educator and ask yourself what the qualities would be of the person who could carry out this role. Begin by thinking about the things an adult educator must be able to do. As you come up with answers to this question, jot them down in the "skills" column. It might be helpful for you to visualize an adult educator in action. In your mind's eye, what do you see them doing in a typical day?

Next, think about the things adult educators must know to carry out their role. With what bodies of knowledge must they be familiar? Do they have to have a broad base of knowledge? What might be particularly important for them to know? Do they need to be content experts? What do they need to know about society, about people or about how adults learn? Again, keep track of your answers by filling in the "knowledge" column. Think, finally, about the attitudes you believe adult educators must possess to carry out their role. Imagine an ideal adult educator. What is this person like? What attitudes does this person have about her or his work, the world and other people? List these qualities in the "attitudes" column. When you examine the different items you have written down, do any of these items stand out as particularly important attributes of a good adult educator? Try to identify the "top five" qualities. Are the qualities you identified something people innately possess? What might be the process for acquiring these attributes? Survey the three columns. Which, of all of the attributes you have noted, do you think most need to be learned by one wishing to become a better adult educator? Are any of these among the top five you identified earlier?

All too often adult educators neglect the task of reflecting on the basis of their actions. The reasons for this are many. Strong currents of anti-intellectualism flow through our contemporary culture, reinforcing personal insecurities about thinking "philosophically." Adult education itself is dominated by an "action" ethos. Far more emphasis is placed on "doing" adult education than on thinking about what is done or why. Thus, the advantage of a personal mission statement is that it makes explicit the values underlying your actions. It provides a basis for thinking about why you do what you do as an adult educator. It gives you an opportunity to improve your practices. Developing a strong personal adult education mission statement can regenerate your interest in and commitment to your vocation. It can serve as a reminder as to why you became an adult educator and why you value the field. It is a useful way to become a reflective practitioner. Writing your mission statement is the beginning step in doing theory.

Doing theory, then, begins when we question the language we are using to name different aspects of the world. As soon as we adopt this critical position towards our language use, the question of what we mean by particular phenomena (say, adult educator) arises. We are forced to craft definitions of phenomena that are not self-contradictory and that cover the phenomena under question. In the social sciences, definitional clarification is the first step towards theory building.

Having worked through the previous exercises, you are now in a position to develop your own "personal adult educator mission statement." The writer of the following fictional example of a personal adult educator mission statement is an agricultural extension worker in rural Saskatchewan named John MacKinnon:

> I, John MacKinnon will do my best to foster forms of adult education which help people cope with rapid changes in rural community life. In my role as an adult educator, I will foster the emergence of grassroots community agencies, clubs and organizations that involve rural people in efforts to preserve the family farm. In order to carry out

this role effectively, I will commit myself to learning more about how to facilitate group discussions and how to acquire community development funding. I will also commit myself to becoming more familiar with the history of co-operative agricultural movements in Saskatchewan. My hope is that I can develop further as a caring, listening, politically active person.

John does a good job of summarizing many of his most important values and aspirations in his mission statement. Notice how he opens with a sentence highlighting his commitment to what he believes is an important purpose of adult education. John does not appear to be overly interested in being an adult educator who teaches in a classroom. His notion of the adult educator is of one who enables learning through community building. Finally, he lists some of the key things he thinks he needs to learn to become better at his role.

Conceptual Paradigms

Boud and Walker (1991) contend that each of us encounters new experiences from the unique perspective of our "personal foundation of experience." This observation is important because it highlights the many differences adult educators discover in learners. It reminds us to respect the uniqueness of each person and to tailor our educational efforts to the specificity of the individual. This may seem like a commonsensical statement, but it must also be observed that our personal foundation of experience is not all that personal. It is important to recognize the role culture plays in shaping the cognitive frameworks that enable us to make sense of our lives. None of us lives or learns in isolation. From our earliest moments, we find ourselves wrapped in a pervasive shared blanket of culture. We do not develop the meaning schemes Jack Mezirow (1991) writes about in isolation; rather, they emerge in us as part of our living, and sharing meanings with, others. Our talk, our daily routines, our encounters with power and so forth lead us to internalize the stories, advice, beliefs, prejudices, assumptions, attitudes and values of our culture.

Educational theorists such as Michael Apple (1979) suggest that the cultural milieu in which we find ourselves is never neutral. Drawing on the work of earlier cultural theorists such as Antonio Gramsci (1971), Apple argues that culture is a battleground on which powerful interest groups wage a struggle for people's minds and imaginations. The meaning schemes we internalize (Apple calls these "ideologies") are deeply influenced by the consequences of broad social struggle. In his ground-breaking study *Knowledge and Human Interests*, German philosopher Jurgen Habermas (1971) suggests that the social struggles of the modern age have produced three distinct conceptual paradigms, which, for the sake of simplicity, we would like to label the *technical paradigm*, the *humanist paradigm* and the *critical paradigm*.

It is difficult to identify overarching cultural patterns in the complex cultural landscape of contemporary society. For some thinkers, the very idea that we can discern these patterns from within the horizons of our own meaning frames is a bit preposterous. How is it possible to step outside of our own cognitive frameworks to see how they are constructed? Something about the whole process really does seem contradictory. Stephen Brookfield (1992), the popular writer on the teaching of adults, suggests that formal theory can play a notable role in helping us to reflect on premises underlying our meaning schemes. Theoretical reflection enables us to entertain new ways of thinking about what we know about our world and ourselves. It is another important lens with which to view our experience in the world.

With this in mind, let us examine the three conceptual paradigms derived from the work of Jurgen Habermas. Habermas helps us to think about the forces influencing our understanding of adult education. In our view, adult educators can make far better decisions when they are able to reflect on the premises underlying their practices. We, and many other adult educators, have found Habermas very helpful in this regard.

I. The Technical Conceptual Paradigm

Habermas (1971) argues that one of the chief concerns of humanity is the efficient control of the material world. Human survival is dependent on our ability to acquire accurate knowledge about the world and to act in ways that can bring about desired changes in it. Given its importance, it is little wonder that our interest in controlling the world underlies the first cognitive paradigm Habermas identifies, that of the technical paradigm. From within the technical paradigm, the human subject is perceived as solitary and self-interested. The primary value guiding the subject's actions is efficient control of an objectified reality. For knowledge to be deemed valuable, it must accurately depict world relations (be true) so that the subject can effectively assert his or her control over material objects or processes. Habermas observes that the physical sciences are the prototype institution for the technical paradigm. Over the last century, though, this paradigm has penetrated almost all aspects of human existence (witness the intrusion of technology and technocratic values into our daily lives).

Increasingly, adult educators feel the pressure to efficiently transfer knowledge and skills to their students. We live in a competitive and fast-changing world where adults must learn rapidly to adapt to new economic and social conditions. Vast technological changes constantly revolutionize the workplace. But it is not only at work that adults are challenged to learn; the growing diversity of our communities and the changing structure of family life also challenge adults to learn new ways of living. It is little wonder, given the intense pressures of contemporary life, that adult educators have increasingly viewed adult learning and adult education from the perspective of the technical paradigm. This is especially true in our time when all things seem subject to "economic" evaluative criteria (productivity, efficiency, cost-effectiveness).

The technical paradigm opens an important window onto the field of adult education. It enables adult educators to understand and to act in ways that make them more effective at what they do. It helps them become more efficient at assessing needs and stimulating adult learning. It enables them to control the learning process better to achieve specified ends. It leaves them capable of providing a clear account of their activities and of justifying outcomes. However, like all paradigms, the technical paradigm is also restrictive. Its tight focus on efficient control can cause adult educators to overlook crucial moral and ethical questions. Adult educators in the technical paradigm view the adult learning process as a technical problem to be solved. They ask the question "How can I best achieve a desired outcome?" The question they often fail to ask, though, is "What ought to be the desired outcome?" Indeed, adult educator Michael Collins (1991) observes how, over the past three decades, adult education has become obsessed with what he calls the "cult of efficiency." The technical conceptual paradigm is most visible in the tendencies of modern adult education to control the learning processes. One of its favoured methods is competency-based learning.

II. The Humanist Conceptual Paradigm

Habermas (1971) observes that, as social creatures, humans have an ongoing need to maintain harmonious relations. Through language, people are able to communicate their mutual needs, reach understandings and establish binding agreements. Habermas contends that this second human interest, the interest in establishing harmonious relations through understanding others, underlies another important cognitive paradigm, that of the humanist paradigm. From within the humanist paradigm, the human is viewed as a being-in-society who is committed to community and group. In this case, the primary value that guides an individual's actions is the achieving of mutual understanding and intersubjective agreement. For knowledge to be deemed valuable, it must accurately depict social norms (be right) so that the subject can live harmoniously and respectfully with others. Whereas in the technical paradigm the primary concern is with questions of "what is," in the humanist paradigm the principal concern is with questions of "what ought to be."

Habermas observes that the humanities (philosophy, history, art and literature, which teach us lessons about how we live together) constitute the prototype institution for the humanist paradigm. Humanists are also often associated with the Romantic movement of the eighteenth and nineteenth centuries. The primary concern of the Romantics was for human beings to express their full potentiality in all dimensions of life. However, over the last century, this paradigm has waned in importance. Recent historical events that have placed the efficient production of wealth above almost all other concerns may spell an even further erosion in the prevalence of the humanist paradigm in contemporary society. Despite its fading visibility, this paradigm has deeply influenced adult education. The humanist conceptual paradigm is most visible within two strong tendencies in modern adult education practice: the valuing of the unfolding of the person's capacities through the life cycle, and the autonomy of the adult learner.

Adult education's long-standing concern for moral and ethical questions reveals its great indebtedness to the humanist paradigm. History is replete with examples of adult educators who questioned, not only how to be more efficient in their practices, but also how to be more ethical, more just and more humane. Perhaps one of the finest instances of the presence of the humanist paradigm in adult education is the notion of self-directed learning. While self-directed learning is often touted as the most efficient and effective way of educating adults, its importance in adult education cannot be reduced simply to a matter of efficiency. Adult educators such as Malcolm Knowles and Carl Rogers believe that it is important to treat adults as autonomous and responsible beings because it is the moral thing to do.

It is quite easy, from the perspective of the technical paradigm, to offer criticism of the humanist paradigm's "soft values." We are all well aware of the growing demands in our society to be accountable, to be objective, to be realistic and to be efficient. As much as values such as humility, honesty, fidelity, propriety, dignity and fairness still motivate us in interpersonal contexts, the growing demands of a competitive economy increasingly lead us to shape our actions according to the more "technical" criteria. The struggle between the technical and the humanist paradigms is manifest in almost all aspects of our lives. To some extent, we are all familiar with the arguments in favour of and against each.

While it is fairly easy to take shots at self-directed learning from within the horizons of the technical paradigm (in a sense, playing one value scheme off another), this is not the only position from which to understand the limits of self-directed learning. The assertion that adults should direct their own learning presumes something about the relative status of adults in our society. To truly assess whether or not self-directed learning should be a basis for contemporary adult education practices, it is important to ask who benefits from this ethical position and who does not. From within the horizons of the humanist paradigm, though, we are under no obligation to make this assessment.

III. The Critical Paradigm

The third paradigm identified by Habermas is slightly different than the previous two. It springs from the recognition that human knowledge is subject to the distorting influence of power. Power can distort our efforts to understand both what is and what ought to be. The third cognitive paradigm, the critical, is undergirded by an interest in minimizing the distorting influences of power. From within the critical paradigm, the human is viewed as a communicative agent who should be free to participate as an equal in society. In this case, the primary goal that guides an individual's actions is to free communication with others from the distorting influences of social power. For knowledge to be deemed valuable, it must be achieved through communication unhindered by coercion (be just).

Habermas (1971) observes that critical social science (for example, critical sociology and some forms of psychoanalysis) is the prototype institution for the critical paradigm. Over the last century, this paradigm has waged a tight battle against many forms of social domination. In recent years, the critical paradigm has received attack from all sides. Most significant, perhaps, has been the decimation of the socialist project and the emergence of cybercapitalism and the global economy. The influence of the critical paradigm on adult education has been profound. For much of its early history, adult education endeavoured to foster the capacity of adults to see through the distorting ideologies of traditional and industrial society in order that they could assume responsibility for determining their own fates. In recent years, the critical conceptual paradigm is most visible in the tendencies of modern adult education to spawn critical thinking and reflection. In this paradigm, adult education practices are evaluated according to their ability to overcome oppressive social relationships. Critical awareness and transformative action are seen as most desirable.

Even in the realms of adult education practice traditionally dominated by the technical paradigm, notions such as critical thinking and reflective action are becoming more prevalent. For example, adult educators interested in workplace education, such as Donald Schon (1983) and Peter Senge (1990), assert that critical reflection is growing in importance. Rapid technological and organizational changes demand that adults possess increased capacities for active and creative learning. Postmodern organizations need workers capable of more than just reacting and adapting to changing circumstances. Increasingly, they need workers capable of thinking ahead, critically intervening in their environment and creating completely new ways of getting things done. Still, Schon and Senge's insights only begin to tap the contribution that the critical paradigm can make to our understanding of the potentials and pitfalls of contemporary adult education practice. We can gain a clearer understanding of the critical paradigm by thinking for a moment about the nature of critique.

Jack Mezirow (1991) is helpful in this regard. As part of his theory of perspective transformation, for instance, he differentiates several levels of critique. He maintains that we understand the world through an integrated framework of meaning schemes that function as a lens or filter through which all new experience must pass. These meaning schemes develop in complexity and comprehensiveness throughout childhood and adulthood. They form a structured and highly organized experiential backdrop through which we incorporate and make sense of new experience. Mezirow suggests that, for the most part, we take for granted our particular backdrop of meaning schemes (in his words, our meaning perspective). When we use the phone, for example, we do not think about how we are dialling. We simply proceed according to our taken-for-granted views of the world. However, if we injure a hand, we are forced to be conscious of how one tiny aspect of our meaning perspective actually works. Mezirow calls this level of critique content or process reflection.

Mezirow observes how a life crisis or "disorienting dilemma" occasionally renders problematic so much of our meaning perspective that we begin a very different kind of reflection. Rather than being critical of one aspect of our meaning frame, we begin to call the whole thing into question. For example, perhaps one day I am told that I have to carry a cell phone with me so that my workplace can contact me at any time. I begin to wonder about the whole notion of modern telecommunications and the way it invades our privacy and locks us into the workplace. I begin to question if telephones and other communication technologies are as commendable as I once took for granted. Mezirow calls this kind of critique premise reflection. More than surface issues are being criticized in such an instance. Fundamental assumptions, beliefs and values are being held up to scrutiny. Critique at this level can lead to vast transformations in the way we view the world and live our lives.

But here Mezirow stops. Other adult educators, such as Paulo Freire, for instance, suggest yet another level of critique. Freire (1974) argues that the frame of meaning schemes that influences how we perceive and understand the world is not neutrally derived. Rather, our perceptions of the world are shaped by social relations of power. To be truly critical, Freire argues, one must become sensitive to the way power impacts on how we know the world. Let us return to the example of the telephone. Rather than simply questioning whether telephones and other communication technologies are good or bad, we might go a step further and identify the different ways telephone companies and other vested interests manipulate our understanding of the role of the telephone in our world. To what extent, I might ask, have common people been free to discuss the changes the information revolution has provoked? To what extent has the development of this technology been a democratic process where all affected parties have had equal opportunity to discuss its advantage and disadvantages? And, to what degree has our understanding of telephones been shaped to serve vested interests (make some people rich and powerful and others poor and weak)? This is critique in its strongest and most contentious form. It calls into question not only the premises that undergird our understandings of the world, but also the process by which those fundamental understandings are developed. It attempts to reveal the ways power shapes understanding in the hope of fostering better, more democratic forms of learning and understanding.

The history of adult education is rich, however, with examples of adult education practices that enable critical thinking. Many early instances of adult education–the British Mechanic's Institutes, agrarian adult education movements on the Canadian prairies, Canadian Women's Institutes, the Antigonish Movement, Highlander of Tennessee–encouraged people to question basic attitudes and assumptions. All challenged existing power hierarchies and opposed the limits these power structures placed on people's understanding of themselves and their world. To this day, the critical paradigm continues to both irritate and animate. New critical voices–lesbian, gay, feminist, ecological, aboriginal–continue to appear, challenging us to realize that it is not time to hibernate until the sun goes down on market globalization. While conservative adult educators continue to expend considerable and careful effort in suppressing the transformative effects of critical inquiry, it seems very difficult for them to inhibit critique in a society that is changing as rapidly as our own.

Conclusion

Theory building begins when we critically position ourselves in relation to our everyday language usage. We destablize our relationship with our taken-for-granted assumptions about the world. Once destablilized, we are pressed towards definitional clarity. However, definitions of the terms *adult educator* or *adult learning* require a conceptual framework to give them their full meaning. These three paradigms, technical, humanist and critical, provide us with the necessary framework to understand the multiple roles assumed by the adult educator as well as the different forms of human knowing. This three-paradigm conceptual framework constructs the lens through which we see and name phenomena in the social landscape.

References

Apple, Michael. 1979. *Ideology and curriculum.* New York: Routledge.

Boud, D., and D. Walker. 1991. *Experience and learning: Reflection at work.* Geelong: Australia: Deakin University.

Brookfield, S. 1992. Developing criteria for formal theory building in adult education. *Adult Education Quarterly* 42: 79-93.

Coady, M. 1939. *Masters of their own destiny.* New York: Harper and Row.

Darkenwald, G., and S. Merriam. 1982. *Adult education: Foundations of practice.* New York: Harper and Row.

Freire, P. 1974. *Pedagogy of the oppressed.* New York: Seabury Press.

Gramsci, A. 1971. *Prison notebooks.* New York: International Publishers.

Habermas, J. 1971. *Knowledge and human interests.* Boston: Beacon Press.

Jarvis, P. 1987. *Adult learning in the social context.* Beckenham: Croom Helm.

Knowles, M. 1975. *Self-directed learning.* New York: Associated Press.

Mezirow, J. 1991. *Transformative dimensions of adult learning.* San Francisco: Jossey-Bass Publishers.

Nadler, L. 1970. *Developing human resources.* Houston: California.

Schon, D. 1983. *The reflective practitioner: How professionals think in action.* New York: Basic Books.

Selman, G., and P. Dampier. 1991. *The foundations of adult education in Canada.* Toronto: Thompson Educational Publishing.

Senge, Peter. 1990. The leader's new work: Building learning organizations. *Sloan Management Review* (fall): 7-23.

Verner, C. 1964. Definitions of terms. In *Adult education: Outlines of an emerging field of study*, edited by G. Jensen. Washington, D.C.: Adult Education Association.

5

Perspectives and Theories of Adult Learning

Karen M. Magro

What does learning mean? Understanding the dynamics of learning continues to be of interest to educators, philosophers, psychologists and scientists. Learning has been described as the process of acquiring relatively permanent changes in understanding, attitude, knowledge, information, ability and skill through experience (Wittrock 1977). Learning involves both the acquiring of the new and letting go of the old, whether one intentionally or unintentionally changes awareness, perceptions, behaviour or ways of knowing (Boucouvalas and Krupp 1989). Unique life experiences, barriers, personality traits, learning style preferences and attitudes influence an individual's capacity for and involvement with learning. Technological innovations, the restructuring of the family and sociocultural diversity are a few of the social changes that have, to some degree, influenced how and what adults will learn. An understanding of the social context and the "larger picture" is critical to any discussion of adult learning. Significant personal learning can occur in many contexts, other than in an educational institution (Tough 1979). Through relationships with others, the media, travel, books and other sources, individuals can broaden their perspectives, adapt to or restructure their environment.

The link between learning and experience is a recurring theme in many of the views and theories of adult learning. Learning is often connected to discovery, transformation and the pursuit of making life more meaningful. In his classic work *The Meaning of Adult Education*, Edouard Lindeman (1926) conceptualized adult education as "a cooperative venture in nonauthoritarian, informal learning, the chief purpose of which is to discover the meaning of experience" (p.6). Lindeman viewed intelligence as the ability to learn, the capacity to solve problems and the ability to apply knowledge to new situations. It was the learner's experience that should be "the resource of highest value in adult education" and moreover, "to be educated is not to be informed but to find illumination in informed living" (p.110). Too often educators get caught up in mastering the "techniques of teaching" rather than pausing to reflect on understanding the process of learning—their own and their students. One way that adult educators can reflect on their own beliefs about learning is by more closely exploring what different theorists have to say about the concept and process of learning in adulthood. This chapter will introduce some of the key perspectives and theories of adult learning.

Key Perspectives of Adult Learning

I. A Behaviourist Perspective

The industrialization of the nineteenth century and the emergence of the technological society of the twentieth century shaped the research focus of both the natural and the human sciences. Control or manipulation of the environment through schedules of reinforcement and shaping, observable behavioural changes, prediction and causal explanation are key features of the behaviourist orientation to learning. Researchers such as Watson, Thorndike, Hull, Guthrie and Skinner had a major impact on psychology throughout the twentieth century. The shift of psychology from the "science of mental life" (James 1961) to its frequently cited definition as "the science of human behavior" (Skinner 1956) indicates the transition in the importance of studying the dynamics of images, emotional states and dreams to an emphasis on analyzing behaviour that is observable and quantifiable. Skinner (1956) writes that advances in the human sciences were "steadily increasing our power to influence, change, mold—in a word, control human behavior" (Skinner, cited in Rader 1980, 589).

A behaviourist orientation in adult education focuses on skills development and behavioural change. Computer-based instruction, competency-based education, demonstration and practice, and criterion-referenced testing reflect the behavioural orientation to teaching and learning. Learning is viewed as hierarchical; one step is mastered before the next step is tried. The teacher's role is to manage and control the learning environment by setting specific expectations and then monitoring the learner's progress. Merriam and Caffarella (1991) further note that

> the behaviorist orientation to learning underlies much educational practice, including adult learning. Skinner, in particular, has application of his theory to educational issues. As he sees it, the ultimate goal of education is to bring about behavior that will ensure survival of the human species, societies and individuals. The teacher's role is to design an environment that elicits desired behavior toward meeting these goals and to extinguish behavior that is not desirable (p.28).

In terms of its application to teaching strategies, the behaviourist orientation emphasizes the importance of clearly defined learning objectives and a breakdown of specific strategies that would lead to the desired goal, positive reinforcement in terms of praise, and the teacher being able to provide the learners with frequent feedback with respect to their progress.

II. Cognitivist and Constructivist Perspectives

In contrast to the behaviourist's emphasis on environmental manipulation and observable behavioural change as key elements in the learning process, the cognitivist orientation emphasizes the importance of the learners' mental processes. Interpretation, meaning, perception and insight are recurring themes in the cognitivist approach. Key figures in the cognitivist orientation include Piaget, Kelly, Von Glaserfeld, Ausubel, Bruner, and Gagne and Briggs. The research on cognitive development by Jean Piaget (1972) emphasizes that individuals move through qualitatively different ways of thinking, from sensorimotor to formal operations that include metacognition or thinking how to think (Boucouvalas and Arin-Krupp 1989). George Kelly's (1955) theory of personal constructs emphasizes the idea of the "person as scientist." Individuals understand themselves, other people and the world around them by constructing personal and tentative theories and models. These theories serve as guides to predict and control events. Kelly suggests that any event is open to as many reconstructions of it as possible; as a result, new experiences may lead to changes in individuals' perspectives.

Learning from a cognitivist perspective involves a process of reorganizing experience in order to make sense of new information from the environment. David Ausubel (1978) stressed the importance of teachers being able to help learners connect new ideas to existing cognitive structures and experiences: "The most important factor influencing the meaningful learning of any new idea is the state of the individual's existing cognitive structure at the time of learning" (Ausubel and Robinson 1969, 143). Educators must be able to help their learners "build bridges" by linking new ideas to the learners' prior knowledge and experience. A major challenge for the educator, writes Nuthall (1995), is how to structure activities and guide the learners' mental processes so that an equilibrium exists between the new knowledge and the underlying conceptual structures and anticipatory schemes that the learners use to understand and assimilate their experience. Ausubel (1978) recommends the use of "advance organizers," which are general explanations given in advance of the main source of information. He also emphasizes the importance of "anchors" such as stories, case studies and critical questions as a way of helping learners find reference points for linking prior knowledge to new knowledge. Arseneau and Rodenburg (1998) summarize the key constructivist principles:

- Prior knowledge is key to learning.
- Prior knowledge must be activated.
- Learners need to construct their own understanding of new content.
- Making more, and stronger links between ideas takes time.
- Context provides important links for storing and retrieving information.
- Motivation and anxiety are associated with approaches to learning.
- Teaching should become increasingly unnecessary; that means, the object of instruction is the development of learner autonomy (Arseneau and Rodenburg 1998, 112).

Cognitive and constructivist perspectives of learning emphasize the importance of understanding the process of learning from the learner's perspective. In terms of implications for adult teaching practices, Candy (1991) suggests that educators can use metacognitive strategies such as concept maps, learning journals, summaries and repertory grids to help them develop "deeper" level, rather than surface or more superficial, approaches to learning. Deeper level approaches to learning involve learners trying to understand new material through critical reflection, questioning and discussing implications for how the information could be used in different contexts. Writing summary statements, rephrasing content or formulating questions about new information or material, comparing the new material to what is already known and explaining new material to peers in pair or group activities are ways that educators can help learners develop deeper level processing skills (Candy 1991; Entwistle 1984; Ramsden 1988; Saljo 1988). In contrast, surface level approaches to learning involve memorizing and reproducing information, without critically reflecting on it.

Biggs (1988) links deep and surface approaches to learning with extrinsic and intrinsic motivation. *Extrinsic motivation* involves motivation that occurs from reinforcers, feedback or rewards that are not a part of the learning activity itself (for example, grades, money, rewards, special privileges and so on). *Intrinsic motivation*, on the other hand, is motivation resulting from personal reinforcers and interests that are part of the activity itself (Forsyth and MacMillan 1991; Good and Brophy 1995). Biggs (1988) emphasizes that learning emerges from the students' perceptions of the academic tasks as well as their personality characteristics. Individuals may be motivated by a "hope for success" or a "fear of failure" or "academic interest." Based on research studies focusing on college students' approaches to essay writing, Biggs found that students adopting a surface approach tend to be "pragmatically motivated" in that their motivation to complete a task, be it an essay or report, is viewed as "a necessary imposition" if the longer-term goal (a degree or certificate) is to be attained. "The general strategy to which this situation gives rise is to focus on what are seen as essentials: minimal effort, factual data … and the ability to reproduce this information as accurately as possible" (p.186). According to Biggs, the reproductive nature of the surface strategy bypasses a complex or holistic understanding of the content material. Interrelationships between ideas are not explored. In contrast, learners who adopt a "deep approach" appear to be more intrinsically motivated; they focus on the meaning of the text and on understanding how the parts integrate to form a whole. "[Learners] adopt strategies that are likely to help satisfy their curiosity by searching for meanings inherent in the task. It may be appropriate to personalize the task, by making it coherent with their own experience, to integrate it with existing formal knowledge, or theorize about it, forming hypotheses" (p.186).

Biggs (1988) further notes that if deeper level learning is to be fostered, students must first be aware of "their motives and intentions, their own cognitive resources, and of the demands of the academic tasks; and second, that they are able to control those resources and monitor their consequent performance" (p.187). He suggests that learners need to be given opportunities to interpret and encode information in their own words, develop questions and test themselves to see if they have attained their goals. In short, the cognitivist and constructivist perspectives of learners highlight the importance of the learners' readiness to learn and the relationship between their prior knowledge and the way in which they construct and try to find meaning from new information. The cognitive view also emphasizes the need for educators to understand the way individual students *perceive* or interpret the task at hand; this perception influences the way they approach the task.

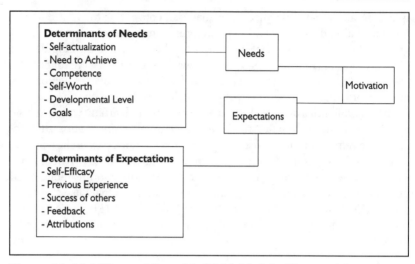

Figure 5.1: McMillan and Forsyth's (1991) Model of Learner Motivation in an Academic Setting

III. The Social Learning Orientation

The social learning orientation integrates many of the ideas and concepts evident in both the cognitive and behavioural views of learning. Albert Bandura's (1977, 1986) social learning theory synthesizes ideas about learning, motivation and cognitive mediation. Bandura sees learning as a reciprocal interaction between cognitive, behavioural and environmental factors. While the behavioural concept of reinforcement remains important, Bandura stresses that learners' anticipations and cognitive mediations of their environments also determine their attention or focus on what they will learn. Drawing on the research of motivational theorists such as Rotter (1966) and Atkinson (1964), Bandura (1977) refers to the concept of *self-efficacy* to explain how the *specific beliefs* that individuals have about their abilities influence their approach to learning and their learning outcomes. Based on his studies, Bandura found that students with a high sense of self-efficacy have high expectations and are more likely to engage in complex learning tasks. These learners seemed more hopeful, relaxed and confident in their ability to solve the problem. In contrast, learners with low self-efficacy tended to have low expectations; they displayed more anxiety, fear and a lack of confidence in their own competence to solve a more complex learning task. Compared to the students with a high sense of self-efficacy, they became more easily frustrated and did not persist as long as the students with a high sense of self-efficacy in completing the learning task. Bandura's research emphasizes the importance of educators being able to understand their students' own beliefs about their ability as learners.

In related research, Weiner's (1984) attribution theory explains how individuals reason the causes of events. With regard to achievement situations, many attributions can be identified: ability, skills, effort, luck, task difficulty, mood, fatigue, attention, knowledge and so on. In their model of adults' motivation to learn in academic situations, McMillan and Forsyth (1991) explain that needs and expectations are two critical determinants of motivation. Academic learning, note McMillan and Forsyth, is influenced by the learners' cognitive and emotional processes and the learners' beliefs in the importance of achieving a goal (see Figure 5.1).

The research studies by theorists such as Atkinson (1964), Bandura (1977), Forsyth and McMillan (1991) and Weiner (1984) suggest that educators can encourage the development of a high sense of self-efficacy if students are provided with learning experiences that foster personal responsibility for success rather than experiences in which learners associate a positive learning outcome with "luck" or an "easy test." Educators need to convey a sense of confidence to learners about their ability to achieve; they also need to uncover learners' "negative myths" about their capabilities and attempt to provide learning opportunities that create a positive orientation towards learning (Candy 1991; Forsyth and MacMillan 1991). McMillan and Forsyth (1991) suggest that educators can foster intrinsic motivation by:

1. Introducing the course and each topic in an interesting, informative and challenging way;

2. Presenting material at a challenging level that communicates respect for the adults' interests and their abilities;

3. Using varied and creative styles of teaching to maintain the students' interests;

4. Focusing on higher-order learning outcomes such as application, analysis, and synthesis, and evaluation;

5. Modelling enthusiasm for the course.

Bandura (1977) also emphasizes that individuals learn through observing others. Social role modelling or vicarious learning is one way that individuals learn attitudes, beliefs and behaviours. The most important dynamic lies in the process of cognitive mediation. Based partly on their social experiences, individuals construct cognitive models of social reality to guide their decision making and thinking about social behaviour. By observing others, individuals also learn about possible actions and their probable consequences (Good and Brophy 1995, 161). Bandura's ideas gain increasing importance as we look at two concepts that in recent years have gained prominence in the development of adult learning theory: the concepts of "situated cognition" and "cognitive apprenticeship."

IV. Situated Cognition

The underlying assumption of the concept of situated cognition is that learning is a process of *enculturation*. That is, if individuals are to learn, they must become embedded in the culture in which knowing and learning have meaning (Brown, Collins and Duguid 1989; Farmer, Buckmaster and LeGrand 1988; Wilson 1993). The context of the learning is just as important as the skill or knowledge to be learned. These theorists suggest that when a skill or concept is used in a specific situation, it acquires meaning that it did not possess before. "From a very early age and throughout their lives, people, consciously and unconsciously, adopt the behavior and belief systems of new social groups. Given the chance to observe and practice in situ the behaviour of members of a culture, people pick up relevant jargon, imitate behavior, and gradually start to act in accordance with its norms" (Brown, Collins and Duguid 1989, 34). Collins, Brown and Newman (1986) maintain that a "cognitive apprenticeship" approach to teaching would involve the following elements: modelling (demonstrating a cognitive task so that students can observe it); coaching (assisting the learner during learning or the performance of a task); scaffolding (providing expert guidance initially and gradually removing it); articulating (reasoning process and knowledge in use); reflecting (comparing students' problem-solving processes with those of an expert) and exploring (encouraging learners to establish their own goals).

Learning that is situated in a practical context may be central to an individual gaining a more in-depth and critical understanding of a skill or content. Brown, Collins and Duguid (1989) argue that the primary concern in many schools seems to be the transfer of abstract and decontextualized formal concepts. More emphasis should be placed on helping learners to see connections between theory and practical applications. Theorists such as Brown, Collins and Duguid assert that it may make educational sense to begin with activities and experiences and then work back to the relevant skills or concepts. Prawatt (1992) suggests that "teachers could also play the role of a disciplinary practitioner modeling the process that a mathematician might go through in solving a problem; or that of a historian in accounting for why a particular event occurred" (p.378). He further emphasizes that "the goal of enculturation is not to produce miniature mathematicians or historians—the purpose is simply to create a more meaningful educational environment" (ibid.). Social role modelling, practical demonstrations and embedding key ideas in "authentic" activities are ways in which learning can be facilitated based on this perspective.

V. The Humanist Orientation

The humanist orientation to learning highlights the importance of the affective domain as it influences learning. Learning is neither solely a behavioural nor cognitive process, but rather a process of personal growth and development. Humanist psychologists such as Abraham Maslow and Carl Rogers emphasize choice, freedom, creativity and self-realization as essential aspects of meaningful learning. In contrast to conceptualizing individuals in a mechanistic or reductionist view, humanistic theorists recognize the complexity of individuals and the importance of an individual's perceptions that are rooted in experience. Maslow (1954) developed a theory of human motivation based on a hierarchy of needs. While he notes some exceptions and reversals of needs, Maslow emphasizes that the fulfilment of "lower level" needs (for example, physiological needs, shelter and belonging) is necessary if "higher level" needs, such as love, self-esteem and the need for self-actualization, are to be fulfilled. He views the need for self-actualization as the individual's desire to actualize to their fullest potential. Similarly, Rogers (1969, 1980) asserts that individuals are born with an "inherent wisdom" to reach their unique potential if certain conditions in the individual's personal and social context are met. Many of Rogers ideas behind "student-centred teaching" developed through his work as a therapist.

In his book *On Becoming a Person*, Carl Rogers (1961) describes significant learning as "learning which is more than an accumulation of facts. It is learning which makes a difference–in the individual's behavior, in the course of action [he] chooses in the future, in [his] attitudes and in [his] personality" (p.280). Rogers maintains that the role of an effective educator is not to teach information but rather to provide the conditions whereby significant learning would be more likely to occur. This would require the educator to possess personality characteristics similar to an effective therapist. These characteristics include empathy, congruence or genuineness, and unconditional positive regard. Rogers (1961) wrote that "the teacher who can warmly accept, who can provide an unconditional positive regard, and who can empathize with the feelings of fear, anticipation, and discouragement which are involved in meeting new material, will have done a great deal toward setting the conditions for learning" (p.288). In this context, learners will be more willing to take risks, explore new ideas, and confront issues and problems that may have inhibited learning. Rogers further emphasized that (a) we cannot teach anyone directly; (b) we can only facilitate a person's learning; (c) a person learns significantly only those things which are perceived as applicable in the maintenance or enhancement of the structure of the self; and (d) the educational situation that most effectively promotes significant learning is one in which threat to the self of the learner is reduced to a minimum (Rogers 1961, 280).

Many of the ideas that surface in the writing of adult educators such as Kidd (1974), Knowles (1980), Freire (1970), Cross (1981) and Mezirow (1981) can be traced to humanistic psychology and philosophy, and more specifically to the work of Carl Rogers and Abraham Maslow. Collectively, these theorists emphasize a collaborative teaching approach that is grounded in the needs and interests of students. Critical thinking, problem solving, self-direction and personal development are emphasized (Conti 1985). The humanistic orientation is an optimistic one, highlighting the goodness of individuals and their innate potential to become self-actualized or fully functioning. Elias and Merriam (1986) state that

> principles from humanistic philosophy and psychology have permeated the field of adult education…. One of the reasons for this popularity … is humanism's compatibility with democratic values…. A second reason for humanism's hold in adult education is that unlike other levels of education, nearly all adult education is voluntary. Educational activities must meet the needs of adult learners in order to survive. [Third], humanistic adult education takes into account adult development…. The notion of growth, development, and change is integral to much of the psychological literature on adult development (pp.135-136).

The humanistic orientation to learning also tells us to pay attention to the way that emotions influence learning. MacKeracher (1996), for example, notes that the values, beliefs and attitudes that we have learned as part of our personal model of reality have emotional or affective states attached to them. New learning situations, competition, tests, teachers, past negative recollections of school and the fear of failure can trigger anxiety reactions in learners. MacKeracher (1996) further explains that "adults have more to be threatened about in learning situations than children do, because their self-concept is already well organized. They stand to lose much of their previous gains in self-esteem and self-confidence if they try to learn and fail" (p.67). Entwistle (1984) also notes that just as it is important to examine the forces that motivate individuals to learn, it is of equal importance to explore the factors that "demotivate" individuals: "It is salutory to consider what form of (de) motivation is built up by repeated failure and humiliation, and to ponder the educational consequence of 'incompetence motivation' or of having no achievable goal in learning" (p.7). Finally, the humanistic orientation to adult learning emphasizes the importance of understanding the learners' beliefs and attitudes and how these may influence their approach to learning and what they will learn.

VI. Patricia Cross's Chain of Response Model

Patricia Cross (1981) integrated important research regarding barriers to adult learning, theories of motivation and participation and developmental stages in adulthood. The two conceptual frameworks that Cross is perhaps best known for are the Chain of Response Model (COR) and the Characteristics of Adult Learners (CAL) (Cross 1981; Hiemstra 1993; Merriam and Cafarella 1991). Cross (1981) emphasized that "participation in a learning activity, whether in organized classes or self-directed is not a single act but the result of a chain of responses, each based on an evaluation of the position of the individual in his or her environment" (p.125).

In Cross's (1981) conceptual framework, the starting point is with the adult's personality and self-perceptions (see Figure 5.2). Individuals who are frightened, anxious and insecure about their abilities based on past educational experiences are unlikely to engage in educational pursuits if they believe that they will be judged or evaluated negatively. There is also a relationship between participation and the individual's perceived expectation of success or failure. Attitudes about education also arise indirectly through the attitudes of family and peer groups that may encourage or discourage further education. Points A and B highlight how attitudes and personality factors are linked to educational participation. At point C of Cross's model, the importance of goals and the expectation that goals will be met are addressed.

Researchers such as Boshier (1977) and Rubenson (1977) have presented extensive data to help understand how emotion, motivation and interest variables influence the individual's sense of learning competence and lead to participation in particular educational programs. Boshier (1977), for example, asserts that participation and drop out in educational activities stem

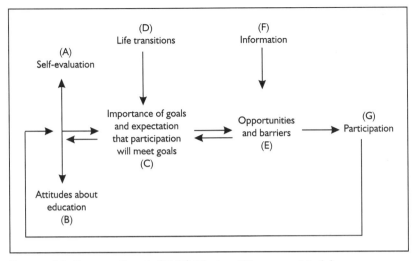

Figure 5.2: Patricia Cross's (1981) Chain of Response Model

from an interaction of internal psychological and external environmental variables. According to Boshier, congruence both within the participant and between the participants and their environment determines participation/non-participation in an educational endeavour. Drawing on the work of theorists such as Boshier and Rubenson, Cross asserts that if the educational goal is not valued or the probability of success is questioned, motivation may decrease. Point D suggests that life transitions such as a job loss or a divorce can also be a catalyst for participation. At point E, those adults who are highly motivated and who are not deterred by any major barriers will likely persist with learning activities. However, if one or more of the barriers that Cross identifies as psychological or dispositional, situational and institutional are strong, the likelihood that the individual will persist in learning will decrease. For instance, if the individual is weighed down by family pressures or financial constraints (situational) and feels insecure and anxious (psychological) and could not attend when the course is scheduled (institutional), participation will be unlikely. At Point F, accurate information about learning opportunities is critical; individuals may not know who to contact for course information, for example, if they live in an isolated area. Cross (1981) maintains that of the three barriers, the psychological or dispositional barriers were the most significant: "If adult educators wish to understand why some adults fail to participate in learning opportunities, they need to begin at the beginning of the COR model–with an understanding of attitudes toward self and education" (p.130).

Cross's (1981) second conceptual framework, Characteristics of Adults as Learners (CAL), incorporates elements of Knowles's (1980) work on andragogy and various stage and phase theories of adult development. Cross (1981) states that the CAL model provides "a mechanism for thinking about a growing, developing human being in the context of the special situations common to part-time volunteer learners" (p.243). She differentiates between two classes of variables involving adult learners: personal characteristics and situational characteristics. Cross (1981) explains that the situational variables of the CAL model are "usually expressed as dichotomies: part-time versus full-time learning and voluntary versus compulsory learning" (p.235). The personal variables refer to the growth or developmental continua along physical, psychological and sociocultural dimensions. Cross emphasizes that while educators can do little to change the "inner code" of physiological changes, they can work to understand how internal and sociocultural changes may affect adults and their experiences of learning. In doing so, educators might maximize learning and capitalize on "teachable moments."

Transformative Theories of Adult Learning

Transformational learning has become a focal point of theoretical and practical study in adult education over the last twenty years. Transformational learning involves deep level changes in the existing values, attitudes, beliefs and ultimately the actions of individuals. The critical education theory of Paulo Freire (1970), Jack Mezirow's (1978, 1981) theory of perspective transformation and Laurent Daloz's (1984) holistic perspective have analyzed different dimensions of transformative learning in adults (Clark 1993). Their ideas have been applied to adult education contexts that include literacy education, social change movements, environmental education, women's consciousness-raising groups, in the workplace and critical media literacy (Aronowitz and Giroux 1993; Berry 1988; Brookfield 1986, 1987; Clover, Follen and Hall, 1999; Fingeret 1984; Grabove 1997; Kozol 1985; Macedo 1994; Malicky et al. 1997; Mezirow et al. 1990; O'Sullivan 1998).

Daloz (1991) emphasizes the need for adult educators to integrate the course content and curriculum to the larger context of learners' lives and the global issues that face them. He identifies seven areas that most affect learners' lives, and which could be addressed at some point in their educational experiences: (1) technological change, (2) nuclear threat, (3) geopolitical shifts, (4) the population explosions, (5) the feminist challenge, (6) environmental degradation, and (7) spiritual longing. Daloz emphasizes that part of education involves helping empower learners to help themselves and to take an active part in improving the world: "We should work hard to help students make the connections between the micro and the macro, between the everyday details of their lives and the broader world in which those details finally do make a difference" (Daloz 1991, 8).

Themes from both the humanistic and constructivist orientations to learning are evident in transformative learning perspectives. Theorists such as Jack Mezirow and Paulo Freire focus on the dynamic interplay of psychological and social factors that explain how and why changes occur in adults. Reflection, dialogue and critical thinking are viewed as prerequisites for meaningful change or transformation on an individual and social level. Clark (1993) states that "transformational learning produces more far-reaching changes in the learners than does learning in general, and that these changes have a significant impact on the learner's subsequent experiences. In short, transformational learning shapes people; they are different afterward, in ways both they and others can recognize" (p.47).

I. Paulo Freire's Critical Pedagogy

Although most often associated with literacy education, Paulo Freire's ideas have had a major impact on the thinking and practice of adult education around the word. Shor (1993) writes that underlying Freire's conception of education is a critique of educational authoritarianism and a commitment to challenge inequality and injustice at all levels.

> From a democratic point of view, Freire sees society controlled by an elite which imposes its culture and values as the standard.... After years in passive classrooms, students do not see themselves as people who can transform knowledge and society.... Uncritical citizens who deny their own intellects ... are the easiest to control, so it is understandable for the mass education system (invented decade by decade by authorities) to underdevelop most students (Shor 1992, 28-29).

While Freire incorporates many of the humanist principles of education, his focus is more radical. Political action is the end result. In Freire's view, education is never neutral; it can either work to oppress or liberate individuals (Freire 1973). Freire believes that, used positively, education has the power to transform existing political, economic and legal oppression in society. However, this education cannot be one that dictates, imparts or prescribes knowledge.

> Democracy and democratic education are founded on faith in [men] on the belief that they not only can but should discuss the problems of their country, of their continent, of their world, their work, the problems of democracy itself. Education is an act of love, and thus an act of courage. It cannot fear the analysis of reality (Freire 1973, 38).

In his books *Pedagogy of the Oppressed* and *Education for Critical Consciousness,* Freire (1970, 1973) emphasizes the crucial role that "critical consciousness" plays in individuals' lives. He maintains that if individuals are unable to perceive critically the themes of their time and intervene actively to change existing inequalities, "they are carried along in the wake of change" and are left vulnerable to being "objects" who passively adapt to situations rather than subjects who create and intervene in situations. Stemming from his work in basic literacy education in Brazil, Freire believed that the greatest psychological barrier to learning among the disenfranchised is the internalization of the self-fulfilling prophecy of failure and self-blame. As a result, a person may become "crushed, diminished, converted into a spectator, maneuvered by myths which powerful social forces create; ultimately they destroy and annihilate the individual" (1973, 6). Freire rejected many traditional literacy approaches that focus exclusively on basic skills development without recognition of the existential reality. Literacy education should go beyond teaching basic skills into helping individuals gain critical awareness of the systems that oppress them; they would then move beyond their "culture of silence."

Freire uses the term *conscientization* to refer to this process of becoming critically aware of one's life world through an in-depth interpretation of problems and through dialogue with others. In Freire's (1970, 1973) view, the educator assumes the role of the co-learner who with empathy and insight understands the existential reality of the learners. Education becomes democratic when educators participate collaboratively with adult learners in "critical and liberating dialogue that varies in accordance with historical conditions and the level at which the oppressed perceive reality" (Freire 1970, 52). Adult learners are actively involved in defining their own needs, interests and goals. Through "praxis" or the interplay between critical reflection and action, individuals are able to transform their world and become "a maker of the world of culture" (Freire 1970, 403).

The teachers' conviction that they can learn from their students' expertise is an important cornerstone in understanding Freire's "problem-posing" process of critical education. Freire's analysis of the role of the educator and the shift from an "expert"-centred to a learner-centred environment reflects the humanistic orientation that he takes. "This teaching can not be done from the top down, but only from the inside out, by the illiterate himself, with the collaboration of the educator" (1970, 404). He criticizes the "banking concept" of educators who view the students as "depositories" who receive, memorize and repeat "deposits" made by the teacher. In contrast, "problem-posing" education enables learners to critically reflect on the way they exist in the world and to develop strategies to transform it.

> In the banking concept of education, knowledge is a gift bestowed by those who consider themselves knowledgeable upon those whom they consider to know nothing. Projecting an absolute ignorance on to others, a characteristic of the ideology of oppression, negates education and knowledge as processes of inquiry. The teacher presents [himself] as their necessary opposite; by considering their ignorance absolute, [he] justifies his own existence....
>
> The *raison d'être* of libertarian education, on the other hand, lies in its drive toward reconciliation. Education must begin with the solution of the teacher-student contradiction, by reconciling the poles of the contradiction so that both are simultaneously teacher and students (Freire 1997, 53).

Freire's (1970) "team approach" emphasizes dialogue, respect, collaboration and solidarity among learners, facilitators, psychologists, sociologists and other community members. Through informal discussions, the thoughts, aspirations and problems of the learners could be identified. Generative words identified by the learners might focus on themes that have existential relevance—poverty, justice, home, work, racism and so on. Teaching materials built around these themes would have the dual aims of teaching literacy and developing critical awareness. In "thematic investigation circles" facilitators and students would investigate, challenge and pose problems on topics raised by the learners. Freire is cautious not to invade or impose predetermined plans or models: "Instead of following predetermined plans, leaders and people, mutually identified together create the guidelines of their action. In this synthesis leaders and people are somehow reborn in new knowledge and action" (Freire 1970, 183).

II. Jack Mezirow's Theory of Perspective Transformation

For Mezirow (1991), learning does not only include the addition of new information; rather, our existing *meanings* (the content of our personal model of reality), *premises* (how we come to know and value what we know), and *perspectives* (the framework and cultural understanding that undergirds our model of reality) can be transformed through a process of critical reflection and action. In his theory of adult learning, Mezirow (1991) differentiates between instrumental, communicative and emancipatory learning. While in instrumental learning, knowledge may be used to control and manipulate the environment in some way, in communicative learning, "the learner actively and purposefully negotiates his or her way through a series of specific encounters using language and gesture and by anticipating the actions of others" (p.79). Social norms provide a frame of reference where individuals seek to reciprocate experiences and understand perspectives: "Reaching an understanding is the inherent purpose of communicative action" (p.96). Problem solving or learning in the communicative domain involves individuals testing the validity of their assertions by a continuous process of consensus. In emancipatory or transformative learning, a critical examination through critically reflective and rational discourse of our assumptions can result in transformed meaning perspectives: "Reflection involves the critique of assumptions about the content or process of problem solving.... The critique of premises or presuppositions pertains to problem posing as distinct from problem solving" (p.105). Mezirow contends that most significant learning in adulthood falls in the communicative rather than in the emancipatory domain.

Mezirow (1981, 1990) asserts that adulthood is a time for reassessing the assumptions of our formative years that may have resulted in distorted self-perceptions and limited perceptions of our "life worlds." In his work with college re-entry women, Mezirow (1978) described the dramatic changes in women's self-perceptions as they began to redefine their identity and challenge culturally prescribed assumptions of what comprises the "appropriate" role for women (for example, the obedient wife, the good mother and so on). Mezirow noted that the women's movement in the 1960s and 1970s provided a supportive atmosphere that encouraged and helped women to re-evaluate their lives and set a "new agenda" for their own life changes and transformations. Rather than conform to narrowly defined roles and passively accept feeling devalued in a patriarchal society, these women began to explore the sociopolitical factors that reinforced their own feelings of oppression. Mezirow et al. (1990) present detailed examples of how the theory of perspective transformation can be applied to social change movements, self-help groups and critical studies of literature and the media.

Mezirow (1990) defines perspective transformation as a process of "becoming critically aware of how and why the structure of psychocultural assumptions has come to constrain the way we see ourselves and our relationships, reconstituting the structure to permit a more inclusive and discriminating integration of experience and acting upon these new understandings" (p.14). Drawing on the ideas of developmental theorists such as Roger Gould (1979), Mezirow explains that perspective transformation can be triggered by a "disorienting dilemma" or crisis such as divorce, the death of someone close, a job loss or a move. These situations challenge individuals to change existing patterns of thought and behaviour to meet the new demands. The crisis or disorienting dilemma may also be triggered by a provocative discussion, book, painting or poem. Mezirow (1981) identifies ten stages in the process of perspective transformation. These include:

- A disorienting dilemma.

- Self-examination.

- A critical assessment of personally internalized role assumptions and a sense of alienation from traditional social expectations.

- Relating one's discontent to similar experiences of others or to public issues–recognizing that one's problem is shared and not exclusively a private matter.

- Exploration of options for new roles, relationships and actions.

- Exploring options for new ways of acting. Planning a course of action.

- Acquisition of knowledge and skills for implementing one's plans.

- Provisional trying and testing of new roles.

- Building of competence and self-confidence in new roles and relationships.

- A reintegration into society on the basis of conditions dictated by the new perspective (Mezirow 1991, 168-169).

Like Freire, Mezirow acknowledges the influence of social, political and cultural forces that may hinder, distort or limit an individual's capacity to progress and gain a sense of agency over his or her life. These distortions may be acquired through the socialization processes and the uncritical acceptance of others' views. Mezirow (1990) identifies three common distortions that can be challenged through rational discourse: epistemic distortions (related to the nature and use of knowledge); sociocultural distortions, which may arise from the uncritical acceptance of belief systems that relate to power and social relationships; and psychological distortions related to internalized feelings and thoughts that may continue to generate fear, depression and anxiety in the individual. According to Mezirow, these distortions can be challenged in an environment where learners can (a) have accurate and complete information; (b) be able to weigh evidence and assess arguments objectively; (c) be open to alternative perspectives; (d) be able to become critically reflective about presuppositions and their consequences; (e) have equal opportunity to participate (including the chance to challenge, question, refute, and reflect and to hear others do the same); and (f) be able to accept an informed, objective and rational consensus as a legitimate test of validity (Mezirow 1991, 77-78).

Mezirow (1990) emphasizes that the development of more sophisticated and discriminating meaning perspectives is a central task of adult development. Moreover, he further explains that "perspective transformation fills an important gap in adult learning theory by acknowledging the central role played by the function of critical reflectivity. Awareness of why we attach the meanings we do in reality, especially to our roles and relationships ... may be the most significant distinguishing characteristic of adult learning" (Mezirow 1981, 11).

Like Freire, Mezirow sees the adult educator as an "empathic provocateur and role model, a collaborative learner who is critically self-reflective and encourages others to consider alternative perspectives" (Mezirow 1981, 206). The adult educator, in Mezirow's view, should be a guide who can establish and encourage "rational discourse" and group support. There is a therapeutic dimension to Mezirow's theory of perspective transformation. Indeed, there is often a fine line between his description of an adult educator and the role of a therapist. He refers to the "psycho educational process" of helping adults overcome internalized sociocultural and psychological distortions: "While psychotherapists make transference influences in a treatment modality, educators do not–but they can provide skillful emotional support and collaborate as co-learners in an educational context" (p.17).

Mezirow's (1981, 1991) perspectives on learning raise numerous concerns regarding the role of the adult educator and the "readiness" of learners to experience a process where their beliefs and values are being critically challenged. He does not seem to account for the complex interplay of factors that may influence the process of perspective transformation: the diversity of personality and learning styles; the level of readiness individuals must possess if they are to understand and apply transformative learning concepts; the goals of the specific curriculum and the skill and interest of the adult educator in promoting transformative learning. Mezirow (1991) also raises questions: Do we intentionally stimulate transformative learning without the full awareness of the learner that transformative learning could result? To what extent do we present our own perspectives? Do we decide on which beliefs and values of the learner should be critically challenged? Cranton (1994) asserts that Mezirow does not address individual differences in his theory. She suggests that transformational learning may be experienced differently among individuals of different psychological types, and that the process dynamics will vary from one person to another: "It may be that some people are less likely to be aware of or to question their values and assumptions or to respond to dilemmas with reflection; the process of transformative learning must be different for them" (p.108). Moreover, not all learning may be transformative, and not all adult educators perceive themselves to be "emancipatory oriented." Cranton contends that educators who view themselves as "subject oriented" see their role as that of one who disseminates and clarifies knowledge. Educators who see learning as being initiated by the expressed needs of individuals tend to view education as "consumer oriented" and their role centres around responding to and meeting those needs. It may be that transformative learning experiences may reside more within the needs, perceptions and readiness of the learner rather than with anything that the educator may do to provoke a transformative experience. Tennant and Pogson (1995) argue that Mezirow does not sufficiently explore the social origins of the life course, which leads him to find instances of perspective transformation in growth events that we would call normative psychological development. They emphasize that adult educators who work in areas where there is a link between personal and social change (for example, migrant education, literacy work, labour education, racism and sexism workshops, programs for the unemployed), and who wish to realize the radical intent of perspective transformation, need to be aware of the ways in which the life course and the norms of adult development are socially constructed both in theory and in the lives of individuals. The views of transformational learning theorists such as Paulo Freire and Jack Mezirow provide an important framework for adult educators who see their role as someone who does more than "dispense" knowledge. Their views on learning challenge educators to consider their own understanding and application of concepts such as critical thinking, collaboration and dialogue. Transformational approaches to learning also emphasize the importance of relating subject matter content to personal, social and global concerns. Learning integrates both affective and cognitive dimensions. No doubt, the ideas presented by transformative learning theorists will continue to provide a rich resource for further developments in adult learning theory. (For another perspective on Mezirow's work, see Welton in this volume.)

Kolb's Experiential Learning Cycle and the Concept of Learning Styles

Kolb's (1984) experiential learning theory can help us to understand the *cyclical* process of learning. Kolb's model of experiential learning was influenced by theorists such as Kurt Lewin, Carl Jung and Jean Piaget. For Kolb, learning is a process whereby knowledge is created through the transformation of experience. Learning occurs through the active extension and grounding of ideas and experiences in the external world, and through an internal reflection about these experiences and ideas. The cycle begins with the learner's personal involvement with an experience; the learner then reflects on this experience from different viewpoints. As a result of this reflection, the learner develops theories and logical conclusions about events. These "personal theories" and constructs influence and guide decision making and further action (see Figure 5.3). While adult learners have different preferences and learning styles, ideally they would have the opportunity to experience activities in all four dimensions of the learning cycle. Kolb asserts that in order to be an effective learner, you have to be able to shift from getting involved (concrete experience), to listening (reflective observation), to creating an idea (abstract conceptualization), to making decisions (active experimentation).

In Kolb's (1984) experiential learning cycle, the two dimensions of the learning task form a dialectic and represent two things that can be done with information. The vertical dimension (concrete experience to abstract

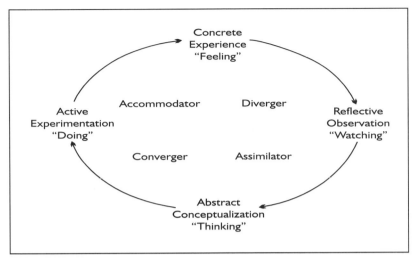

Figure 5.3: Kolb's (1984) Learning Cycle and the Four Learning Style Modes

conceptualization) represents the input of information either from first-hand experience or by reflecting on abstractions. The horizontal dimension refers to the processing of information through the external process of active experimentation or the internalized process of reflective observation (Kolb 1984; Svinicki and Dixon 1987). This process of transforming information in different ways is central to creating knowledge and is critical to understanding that learning is an active process.

Like the developmental psychologist Jean Piaget, Kolb (1984) emphasizes that learning is a process of accommodation and adaptation: "We are thus a learning species, and our survival depends on our ability to adapt not only in the reactive sense of fitting into physical and social worlds, but also in the pro-active sense of creating and shaping those worlds" (Kolb 1984, 47). Learning involves a transaction between individuals' internal characteristics and external circumstances, and between personal knowledge and social knowledge. Learning styles or preferred "possibility-processing structures" are influenced by individuals' hereditary characteristics, past life experience, cultural background, their work or chosen profession and the demands of immediate situations. While Kolb suggests that individual styles of learning are complex and can vary depending on the context, there are unique and consistent patterns of information processing that emerge over time as individuals attempt to "grasp reality." The structural basis of the learning process lies in the transactions among the following four adaptive modes:

- *Concrete Experience* (CE): This mode of learning emphasizes a receptive, experience-based approach relying heavily on feeling-based judgements. Emphasis on specific examples in which each situation can be considered for its unique features is important. Feedback and discussion with other learners is also preferred.

- *Reflective Observation* (RO): This mode of learning emphasizes a careful assessment of understanding the meaning of ideas and situations by observing, reflecting and describing them.

- *Abstract Conceptualization* (AC): An orientation to abstract conceptualization focuses on using logic, ideas and concepts. It emphasizes thinking as opposed to feeling and there is a focus on building theories rather than on intuitive understanding. Individuals with this orientation value precision, rigor and discipline in analyzing ideas.

- *Active Experimentation* (AE): This is an active "doing" orientation where individuals emphasize experimentation and individual projects.

Based on his research and observations, Kolb (1984) identified the characteristics of four basic learning style patterns. He suggests that individuals are also more likely to choose educational and career paths that reflect their dominant learning style mode.

Divergers. Kolb contends that individuals who are more divergent in their learning style are more imaginative and are able to view a situation from many perspectives. Divergers are interested in people and tend to be creative and sensitive to feelings. They have broad cultural interests and they tend to specialize in the arts. In Kolb's analysis of learning style and university undergraduates, those individuals majoring in history, English, political science and psychology tended to have divergent learning styles. Professions such as social work, education and nursing tend to attract "divergers."

Convergers. The convergent learning style mode emphasizes abstract conceptualization and active experimentation. Individuals who tend to have convergent learning styles demonstrate strengths in problem solving, decision making and the practical application of ideas. Professions with a scientific or technical orientation such as accounting, engineering, medicine and management tend to attract individuals with convergent learning styles.

Assimilators. Individuals who express an assimilative learning style have learning strengths in abstract conceptualization and reflective observation. Similar to the convergent learning style, this orientation is less focused on people and more concerned with ideas and abstract concepts. Kolb's (1984) research found that individuals who majored in subject areas such as mathematics, economics, sociology and chemistry tend to express assimilative learning styles.

Accomodators. Individuals with an accomodative learning style emphasize concrete experience and active experimentation. The adaptive emphasis of this orientation is opportunity seeking, risk taking and action. Problems are solved by an intuitive trial-and-error manner with a reliance on other people for information rather than on the individual's own analytic ability. Individuals in business management are more likely to have accomodative learning styles.

Kolb's (1985) Learning Style Inventory may be a useful instrument that educators can use to provide a framework for exploring learning, teaching and counselling with adults. Svinicki and Dixon (1987) demonstrate how Kolb's experiential learning model can provide educators with a framework for selecting a broader range of classroom activities that challenge learners to develop skills in all the learning dimensions of Kolb's cycle. For example, while the reading of primary sources and field experience may give the learner first-hand personal experience with content, activities such as discussion and journal keeping challenge students to reflect on their experiences and the experiences of others. While abstract conceptualization can be fostered by model-building exercises and research papers, active experimentation could be fostered with simulations, field work and projects (Svinicki and Dixon 1987, 142). For further applications of Kolb's (1984) experiential learning model, please refer to Hunt (1987) and MacKeracher (1996).

Conclusion

Despite the attempts to theorize about learning and its dynamics, there remains, as Dirx (1997) notes, an inherently illusive and mysterious nature about the learning process. Wlodkowski and Ginsberg (1995) maintain that all learning activities should be aimed at establishing inclusion, positive attitudes, meaning and competence. The six general observations that Smith (1982) identified concerning the nature of learning are reflected in the different perspectives and theories of learning presented in this chapter. Learning is lifelong; it is personal; it involves change; it is partially a function of human development; it relates to experience and it is partially intuitive. Learning can mean the acquisition of different types of knowledge or it can mean the transformation of existing knowledge to form new insights. The different views and perspectives of learning that are addressed in this chapter can be compared to different lenses or perspectives through which we understand our world. The behavioural, humanistic and cognitive theories of learning have helped create frameworks for better understanding the links between motivation and adult learning, the role of the educator in facilitating the learning process and how the interplay of individual differences and social forces influences learning. One thing is certain: people will continue to learn both in formal educational settings and in the setting of everyday life. In reflecting on our own assumptions about learning, we build a base for understanding, appreciating and incorporating new ideas that may enhance the teaching-learning exchange.

References

Aronowitz, S., and H.A. Giroux. 1993. *Education still under siege.* Toronto: OISE Press.

Arseneau, R., and D. Rodenburg. 1998. The developmental perspective: Cultivating ways of thinking. In *Five perspectives on teaching in adult and higher education,* edited by D.D. Pratt and Associates (pp.82-120). Malabar, Fla.: Krieger.

Atkinson, J. 1964. *An introduction to motivation.* Princeton, N.J.: Van Nostrand.

Ausubel, D., and F. Robinson. 1969. *School learning: An introduction to educational psychology.* New York: Holt, Rinehart, and Winston.

Ausubel, D. 1978. In defense of advance organizers: A reply to the critics. *Review of Educational Research* 48: 251-57.

Bandura, A. 1977. *Social learning theory.* Englewood Cliffs, N.J.: Prentice-Hall.

———. 1986. *Social foundations of thought and action: A social cognitive theory.* Englewood Cliffs, N.J.: Prentice-Hall.

Berry, T. 1988. *The dream of the earth.* San Francisco: Sierra Club Books.

Biggs, J. 1988. Approaches to learning and essay writing. In *Learning strategies and learning styles*, edited by R.R. Schmeck (pp.185-228). New York: Plenum Press.

Boshier, R. 1977. Motivational orientation re-visited. Life-space motives and the educational participation scale. *Adult Education* 27 (2): 89-115.

Boucouvalas, M., and J.A. Krupp. 1989. Adult development and learning. In *Handbook of adult and continuing education*, edited by S. Merriam and P.M. Cunningham (pp.183-200). San Francisco: Jossey-Bass.

Brookfield, S.D. 1986. *Understanding and facilitating adult learning*. San Francisco: Jossey-Bass.

———. 1987. *Developing critical thinkers: Challenging adults to explore alternative ways of thinking and acting*. San Francisco: Jossey-Bass.

Brown, J.S., A. Collins, and P. Duguid. 1989. Situated cognition and the culture of learning. *Educational Researcher* (Jan.-Feb.): 32-42.

Candy, P. 1990. *Self-direction for lifelong learning*. San Francisco: Jossey-Bass.

Clark, C. 1993. Transformation learning. In *An update on adult learning theory*, edited by S. Merriam (pp.47-56). San Francisco: Jossey-Bass.

Clover, D., S. Follen, and B. Hall. 1999. *The nature of transformation: Environmental, adult and popular education*. OISE/University of Toronto: Transformative Learning Centre.

Collins, A., J.S. Brown, and S.E. Newman. 1986. Cognitive apprenticeship: Teaching the craft of reading, writing, and mathematics. In *Cognition and instruction: Issues and agendas*, edited by L.B. Resnick. New Jersey: Erlbaum Associates.

Conti, G. 1985. The relationship between teaching style and adult learning. *Adult Education Quarterly* 35 (4): 220-228.

Cranton, P. 1994. *Understanding and promoting transformative learning: a guide for educators of adults*. San Francisco: Jossey-Bass.

Cross, K.P. 1981. *Adults as learners: Increasing participation and facilitating learning*. San Francisco: Jossey-Bass.

Daloz, L. 1986. *Effective teaching and mentoring: Realizing the transformational power of adult learning experiences*. San Francisco: Jossey-Bass.

———. 1990. Slouching toward Bethlehem. *Continuing Higher Education* (winter): 2-9.

Dewey, J. 1938. *Experience and education*. New York: Macmillan Publishing Company.

Dirx, J. 1997. Nurturing soul in adult learning. In *Transformative learning in action*, edited by V. Grabove (pp.83-92). San Francisco: Jossey-Bass.

Elias, J. L., and S. Merriam. 1980. *Philosophical foundations of adult education*. Malabar, Fla.: Krieger.

Entwistle, N. 1984. Contrasting perspectives on learning. In *The experience of learning*, edited by F. Marton, D. Hounsell, and N. Entwistle (pp.1-18). Edinburgh: Scottish Academic Press.

Farmer, J., A. Buckmaster, and B. LeGrand Brandt. 1988. Situated-specific approaches. *Lifelong Learning* 12 (3): 8-13.

Fingeret, A. 1984. *Adult literacy education: Current and future directions*. (Contract No. NIE-C-400-81-0035).

Forsyth, D.R., and J.H. McMillan. 1991. Practical proposals for motivating students. *New Directions for Teaching and Learning* 45: 53-65. San Francisco: Jossey-Bass.

Freire, P. 1970, 1997. *Pedagogy of the oppressed*. New York: Continuum.

———. 1973. *Education for critical consciousness*. New York: Seabury.

Good, T.L., and J. Brophy. 1995. *Contemporary educational psychology*. White Plains, N.Y.: Longman.

Gould, R. 1979. *Transformations*. New York: Simon and Schuster.

Grabove, V., ed. 1997. *Transformative learning in action*. San Francisco: Jossey-Bass.

Grabove, V. 1997. The many facets of transformative learning. In *Transformative learning in action*, edited by V. Grabove (pp.89-95). San Francisco: Jossey-Bass.

Hiemstra, R. 199). Three underdeveloped models for adult learning. In *An update on adult learning theory*, edited by S. Merriam (pp.37-46). San Francisco: Jossey-Bass.

Hunt, D. 1987. *Beginning with ourselves*. Cambridge, Mass.: Brookline Books.

James, W. [1902] 1961. *The varieties of religious experiences*. New York: Macmillan Publishing Company.

Kelly, G.A. 1955. *The psychology of personal constructs*. New York: Norton.

Kidd, J. R. 1974. *How adults learn*. New York: Association Press.

Knowles, M. 1980. *The modern practice of adult education*. Englewood Cliffs, N.J.: Prentice-Hall.

Kolb, D. 1984. *Experiential learning*. Englewood Cliffs, N.J.: Prentice-Hall.

Kozol, J. 1985. *Illiterate America*. New York: Anchor Press.

Lave, J. 1988. *Cognition in practice*. Boston, Mass.: Cambridge.

———. 1996. Teaching, as learning, in practice. *Mind, Culture, and Activity* 3 (3): 149-162.

Lindeman, E. [1926] 1961. *The meaning of adult education*. New York: New Republic.

Macedo, D. 1994. *Literacies of power: What Americans are not allowed to know*. Boulder, Colo.: West View Press.

MacKeracher, D. 1996. *Making sense of adult learning*. Toronto: Culture Concepts.

Malicky, G., H. Katz, C. Newman, C. Norman, and M. Norton. 1997. Literacy learning in community based programs. *Adult Basic Education* 7 (2): 84-103.

Marton, F. 1988. Describing and improving learning. Chap. 3 in *Learning strategies and learning styles*, edited by R.R. Schmeck. New York: Plenum.

Marton, F., D. Hounsell, and N. Entwistle. 1984. *The experience of learning*. Edinburgh: Scottish Academic Press.

Maslow, A. [1954] 1987. *Motivation and personality*. New York: Harper Collins.

Merriam, S.B., ed. 1993. An update on adult learning theory. *New Directions in Adult and Continuing Education* 57 (spring). San Francisco: Jossey-Bass.

Merriam, S.B., and P. Cunningham, eds. 1989. *Handbook of continuing and adult education.* San Francisco: Jossey-Bass.

Merriam, S.B., and R.S. Caffarella. 1991. *Learning in adulthood: A comprehensive guide.* San Francisco: Jossey-Bass.

Mezirow, J. 1978. Perspective transformation. *Adult Education* 28: 100-110.

———. 1981. A critical theory of adult learning and education. *Adult Education Quarterly* 32 (1): 3-24.

———. 1990. *Fostering critical reflection in adulthood: A guide to transformative and emancipatory learning.* San Francisco: Jossey-Bass.

———. 1991. *Transformative dimensions of adult learning.* San Francisco: Jossey-Bass.

Nuthall, G. 1995. Understanding student thinking and learning in the classroom. In *The international handbook of teachers and teaching,* edited by B.J. Biddle, T.L. Good, and I.F. Goodson. The Netherlands: Kluwer Academic Publishers.

O' Sullivan, E. 1998. *The dream drives the action.* London: Zed Press.

Piaget, J. 1972. Intellectual evolution from adolescence to adulthood. *Human Development* 15: 1-12.

Pratt, D.D., and Associates. 1998. *Five perspectives of teaching in adult and higher education.* Malabar, Fla.: Krieger Publishing Company.

Prawatt, R. 1992. Teachers' beliefs about teaching and learning: a constructivist perspective. *American Journal of Education* (May): 354-395.

Rader, M. 1980. *The enduring questions: Main problems of philosophy.* New York: Holt, Rinehart, and Winston.

Ramsden, P. 1988. Studying learning: Improving teaching. In *Improving learning: New perspectives,* edited by P. Ramsden (pp.13-31). London: Kogan Page, Ltd.

Rogers, C. 1961. *On becoming a person.* Boston, Mass.: Houghton Mifflin Publishing Company.

———. 1969. *Freedom to learn.* Columbus, Ohio: Merrill.

———. 1980. *A way of being.* Boston: Houghton Mifflin Company.

Rotter, J. 1966. Generalized expectancies for internal versus external control of reinforcement. *Psychological Monographs* 80: 11-13.

Rubenson, K. 1977. Participation in recurrent education: A research review. Paper presented at a meeting of national delegates on developments in recurrent education. Paris: Organization for Economic Co-operation and Development.

Saljo, R. 1988. Learning in educational settings: Methods of inquiry. Chap. 2 in *Improving learning-new perspectives,* edited by P. Ramsden. London: Kogan Press.

Schmeck, R.R. 1988. *Learning strategies and learning styles.* New York: Plenum.

Scott, S., B. Spencer, and A. Thomas, eds. 1998. *Learning for life: Canadian readings in adult education.* Toronto: Thompson Educational Publishing.

Shor, I. 1992. *Empowering education: Critical teaching for social change.* Chicago: University of Chicago Press.

Skinner, B.F. [1956] 1980. Some issues concerning control of human behavior: a symposium. In *Enduring questions: main problems with philosophy,* edited by Rader (pp.589-590). New York: Holt, Rinehart, and Winston.

Smith, R.M. 1982. *Learning how to learn: Applied learning theory for adults.* Chicago: Follet.

Tennant, M.C., and P. Pogson. 1995. *Learning and change in the adult years: A developmental perspective.* San Francisco: Jossey-Bass.

Svinicki, M.D., and N.M. Dixon. 1987. The Kolb model modified for classroom activities. *College Teaching* 35 (4): 141-146.

Tough, A. 1979. *The adult's learning projects: A fresh approach to theory and practice in adult learning.* 2d ed. Toronto: The Ontario Institute for Studies in Education.

———. 1997. The future of adult learning. In *The craft of teaching adults,* edited by T. Barer-Stein and J. Draper (pp.237-233). Toronto: Culture Concepts.

Weiner, B. 1984. Principles of a theory of student motivation and their application with an attributional framework. In Vol. 1 of *Research on motivation in education,* edited by R. Ames and C. Ames. Orlando, Fla.: Academic Press.

Wilson, A. 1993. The promise of situated cognition. In *An update on adult learning theory,* edited by S. Merriam (pp.71-79). San Francisco: Jossey-Bass.

Wittrock, R., ed. 1977. *Learning and instruction.* Berkeley, Calif.: McCutchan Publishing Company.

Wlodkowski, R., and S. Ginsberg. 1996. *Diversity and motivation: Culturally responsive teaching.* San Francisco: Jossey-Bass.

II

THE PRACTICE OF
ADULT EDUCATION

6

Needs Assessment

Thomas J. Sork

Needs assessment is a much discussed concept in adult education, but there is little evidence that it has a commonly understood meaning or that it is as widely used in practice as some theorists might suggest. The dominant literature on program planning regards needs assessment as an important element of "good" planning (Sork and Caffarella 1989), but there is no generally accepted view on what a needs assessment is or how one should be conducted. There is also a troubling tendency to label any information-gathering process that is used early in planning as a "needs assessment," even when the information gathered has little to do with educational needs.

Some friendly critics of adult education have argued that needs assessment is too often regarded as a purely technical task devoid of value judgements or political influence (Collins 1991; Davidson 1995). This, they claim, is at best an oversimplified notion of needs assessment that leads to the development of programs that largely maintain the status quo and reinforce existing power relations in society. The approach presented in this chapter recognizes needs assessment as being part technical, part sociopolitical and part ethical. It is dangerous to plan a needs assessment without considering all three of these domains.

Needs assessment is a compelling concept in adult education because it is difficult to argue with the general claim that programs should be based on the education or training needs of adult learners. If we accept this claim, then the ability to conduct a needs assessment is an important skill for practitioners to acquire. Yet not everyone accepts the notion that programs should or can be based on the "needs" of adult learners (Pearce 1998). The concept of "need" itself is open to multiple meanings and interpretations, so that the topic of needs assessment is not as easy to address as some might expect.

This chapter sets out to accomplish several things. First, it presents needs assessment as one of many planning tools that can be used by skilful adult educators to design programs. Second, it describes a general approach to needs assessment that can be adapted to a wide variety of adult education situations and contexts. Third, it alerts the reader to some of the limitations of relying on needs assessment as the primary tool for justifying and focusing planning in adult education. Fourth, it suggests several alternative tools that may be used when needs assessment is not the best choice and it later argues that needs assessment is the best choice in a relatively small number of cases.

In my own planning framework (Sork 1997; Sork 2000), I treat needs assessment as one of several tools that can help to justify and focus planning.

The phrase "justify and focus" captures the two primary uses of the concept "need" in educational planning. One use of need is to *justify* the resources that we put into planning and offering programs. In order to claim that we are using these resources responsibly, we are expected to show that we are planning a program in response to some circumstance that requires action. A second use of the concept need is to *focus* our planning efforts so that we can determine what the form and substance of the program should be. We are expected to make these decisions in a reasoned way by deriving the content of the program from the needs of the learners whom we hope will participate. So needs also provide a rationale for selecting the content and processes of the learning experience.

Defining Need

Although there are many different definitions of the concept "need," the one that is most often found in the literature is the discrepancy or gap definition. Witkin and Altschuld (1995) capture this definition well: "A *need* is generally considered to be a discrepancy or gap between 'what is,' or the present state of affairs in regard to the group and situation of interest, and 'what should be,' or a desirable state of affairs" (p.4).

Thinking of need as a gap or discrepancy between what is and what should be is helpful, but I have found this definition too general for direct use in adult education. Because educators are concerned with helping learners improve their capabilities in some way, I prefer the following definition of educational need: *An educational need is a gap or discrepancy between a present capability* (PC) *and a desired capability* (DC). A capability is any human quality that can be altered through learning. The qualities that we are most often concerned with in adult education are knowledge, skills and attitudes, but these are not the only qualities that may be the focus of an educational program. If we accept the discrepancy definition of need, then an educational needs assessment involves identifying gaps in the capabilities of adult learners. Assessing needs always involves making value judgements, because this and other gap or discrepancy definitions of need include the word *desired*.

Figure 6.1 represents this definition of need with capability on the vertical axis and time on the horizontal axis. Time is included because it is assumed that the present capability exists *now,* but that the desired capability is something that will be attained *in the future*, presumably following participation in some educational activity.

The term *felt needs* is used to label those gaps in capability identified or acknowledged by the learners themselves while the term *ascribed needs* is used to label gaps identified by someone other than the learners (Houle 1996, 260). This distinction is useful because programs based on needs identified or acknowledged by learners themselves are typically more attractive to those learners than programs based on needs identified by others. Through laws, policies and social pressure, adults can be coerced into attending programs, but unless they recognize a gap between their present and desired capabilities that the program addresses, they are unlikely to be enthusiastic,

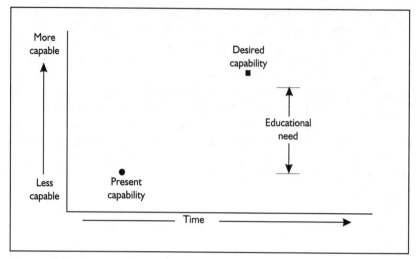

Figure 6.1: Educational Need as Gap in Capability

engaged participants. It is also important to realize that learners are often "rendered needful" by society by changes in technology, by demands of the workplace, by new expectations in the community and so on. In other words, what it means to be a capable person/employee/citizen/parent is constantly changing. As expectations change, needs are made (Davidson 1995). In this needs-making process it is important to ask whose interests are served by the way needs are stated. There are many good examples of cases where the way needs are stated serves the interests of someone other than the learners. This political and/or ethical dimension of needs making is often ignored in the process when needs assessment is regarded as a technical task.

It is possible for a need to be both felt and ascribed as suggested in needs numbered 1, 2, 5, 6 and 7 in Figure 6.2 (Beatty 1981). From a planner's perspective, it is ideal to work with a need that is both felt and ascribed since the validity of the need would not be open to question; however, there may be some disagreement between the owner of the need and others about where the present and desired capabilities should be located on the continuum. Needs that are only ascribed (such as need number 3 in Figure 6.2) may be problematic for the planner unless a strategy can be developed to convert them into felt needs. If the potential participants do not acknowledge that a need exists, then convincing them to participate in programs may be very time consuming and expensive, not to mention a waste of time and money if the learners end up participating without a commitment to the objectives of the program. If needs are only felt (such as need number 4 in Figure 6.2), then it may be difficult to marshal the resources required to offer a program because it is often the others who control resources.

Whether felt or ascribed, value judgements must be made before a need exists. First, someone must conclude that a present capability is inadequate.

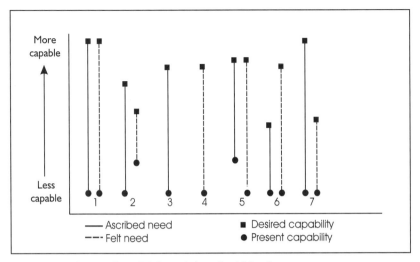

Figure 6.2: Examples of Felt and Ascribed Needs

Second, someone must describe the desired capability. In both cases these decisions are influenced by the value system of the person or persons making them. Values can not and should not be divorced from needs assessment: they provide the basis for judgements about what is desirable. This can make reaching agreement between the owners of the need (the learners) and others on desired capabilities a challenge, because they may be operating from different value positions. For example, needs numbered 2, 6 and 7 in Figure 6.2 all indicate that the owners of the need and others disagree on how capable the learners should be. These differences are not easy to resolve because they are based on different value positions. And yet it is important to resolve them—whenever possible—before a program is planned, for otherwise it may be difficult to successfully recruit or retain participants because they will question the relevance of the program. Differences of opinion about present capabilities as found in needs numbered 2 and 5 are easier to resolve. We can use familiar tools such as observations, tests, simulations and so on to gather additional information to confirm or validate present capabilities. Using these tools does not guarantee that agreement will be reached, but it is more likely that agreement will be reached between learners and others about present capabilities than about desired capabilities.

Purpose and Timing of Needs Assessments

Before presenting a specific approach to needs assessment, a few words need to be said about when a needs assessment is conducted and the relationship to its purpose. Needs assessment is often discussed without first clarifying when the needs assessment should be done. Some describe a process that is intended to provide information that will be used to develop the basic structure of the program—what I call a pre-program needs assessment.

Others describe a process that is well suited to an instructional setting in which the structure of the program has been determined, the program has been marketed and the participants recruited—what I call a within-program needs assessment.

I. Pre-Program Needs Assessment

A pre-program needs assessment is always completed prior to the offering of a program. Its purpose is to determine what should be included in the substance of the program. There are two subtypes of pre-program needs assessment: one in which the topic is known and one in which the topic is unknown. An example of a *topic known* needs assessment would be a needs assessment for a mandated program on sexual harassment. The focus is on sexual harassment and this is non-negotiable; a needs assessment is done to determine what people know and don't know about sexual harassment. Once the gaps in knowledge, attitudes, skills and sensitivities are known, a suitable program can be designed. An example of a *topic unknown* needs assessment would be when the staff of a new community learning centre conduct a needs assessment of the people who live in the area to determine the gaps in capabilities that should be addressed in the centre's programs. There are no preconceptions about what will be included in the program. The purpose of the needs assessment is to gather information that can be used to develop the overall program structure.

II. Within-Program Needs Assessment

A within-program needs assessment is conducted once a program begins. Its purpose is to confirm the needs of the participants and to fine-tune the structure of the program so that it is maximally responsive to the needs of the participants. Within-program needs assessments are usually incorporated into the instructional plan. They are important to conduct for two (and maybe more) important reasons. First, those who participate may be different from those whose needs were assessed in the pre-program assessment. Second, participants' needs may have changed between the pre-program and within-program assessments. Within-program needs assessments may also be used to "place" learners in a program; they can serve a diagnostic function to determine gaps in capabilities so that participants can be placed in the most suitable program or at the appropriate level (i.e., beginning, intermediate, advanced). Although the process described below can be adapted to both pre-program and within-program assessments, it works best for developing a pre-program needs assessment.

A Question-Based Approach to Needs Assessment

There are many available texts on needs assessment that provide guidance about the technical aspects of the process. Most of these describe the merits of and procedures for using various information-gathering techniques such as surveys, interviews, focus groups and so on. Although the technical aspects of needs assessment certainly require careful attention, my main concern is with raising questions that will be helpful in thinking through the design of the needs assessment. This question-based approach to developing a needs assessment is intended to prompt those involved to consider a variety of factors and options of which they might not otherwise be aware. The list of questions presented below is not the ultimate or necessarily the best set of questions to guide this task, but it is a starting point from which other questions can be developed that are better suited to particular contexts, learner groups, organizational settings and personal planning styles. There is also no right or wrong order in which the questions should be answered. Following each question is a brief explanation of issues that may be important to consider when answering the question. When all questions have been answered, the product is a plan for a needs assessment that is consistent with the gap or discrepancy definition of need.

What characteristics of the context and learner community will be especially important to consider as you design the needs assessment and why?

The context is the complex milieu in which planning takes place. Factors in the context influence what is possible and what is preferred. There might be many factors in the context that are especially relevant to the needs assessment or there might be only a few; however, some that are potentially important include:

- Mission, aims and purposes of the organization or planning group;
- Internal and external political considerations;
- Authority and accountability relationships;
- Philosophical and material conditions that influence what is possible;
- Co-operative and competitive relationships (internal and external).

The learner community is the group of adults whose needs you hope to identify. The word *community* means simply that the learners have something in common—where they work, where they live, a condition or circumstance they share, certain demographic characteristics such as age, income, education level, first language, gender and so on. Certain characteristics of the learner community will have important implications for how you design and carry out the needs assessment. The challenge is to identify those characteristics and to keep them in mind as you go through the process. Ignoring certain key learner characteristics, such as reading ability, can render a print-based needs assessment meaningless, if only a small number of the learners can understand your questions.

What is the purpose of this needs assessment?

A well-written, concise purpose statement clarifies why the assessment is being done and provides a reference point to return to if the task begins to become unmanageable. I recommend that this statement be written without using the word *need* because circular purpose statements such as "The purpose of this needs assessment is to identify the training needs of managers" are not very useful. A more useful version would be, "The purpose of this project is to identify the gaps in knowledge and skills among managers in the areas of conflict resolution, diversity and teamwork so that work-relevant training programs can be offered during the next two months."

Who should be involved in designing and carrying out the needs assessment?

In theory, all those with an interest in the learner community should participate in designing and carrying out the needs assessment, but there is rarely enough interest, time and resources to involve all stakeholders. There is usually someone who takes primary responsibility for the needs assessment process. This person may form a committee to provide assistance or may do most of the work and submit the plan to others for their suggestions or approval. Subject matter experts, learner representatives, supervisors, union representatives and representatives of professional or regulatory bodies, among many others, may have important roles to play at some point in the needs assessment. Making the process as democratic and participatory as possible is an important value in adult education (Cervero and Wilson 1994). Identifying who will be involved, when, and the role they will play in the needs assessment should occur early in the process.

Will the assessment identify only felt needs, ascribed needs or both?

Remember that felt needs are gaps between present and desired capabilities identified or acknowledged by the learners themselves whereas ascribed needs are gaps identified by someone other than the learners. A needs assessment focused on identifying felt needs would collect information only from the learner community and one focused on ascribed needs would collect information only from those outside the learner community. Most needs assessments focus on either felt needs alone or on a combination of felt and ascribed needs. One benefit of a combined approach is that it ensures the participation and perspectives of both the learners (who will presumably attend the programs) and the important "others" (who often control the resources available for offering programs). However, combined approaches do require more time and energy, because you are collecting more information and may also face the task of reconciling conflicting or contradictory ideas about the needs.

What existing information might be useful in the needs assessment and where is it located?

There is often a great deal of information available that can be useful in identifying present and desired capabilities. Because it is expensive and time consuming to collect new information, it is good practice to use existing information whenever possible. Examples of information that is often available include job standards, test scores, performance appraisals, incident reports, quality audits, complaint reports, evaluations, strategic plans, mission statements and so on. Any of these that are relevant to the learner community should be thoroughly analyzed to extract any useful information related to present and desired capabilities. It is not likely that they will directly identify education or training needs, but they may help in understanding either what capabilities are desired (by the learners, employers, regulatory bodies, professional bodies, clients and so on) or what capabilities currently exist.

Will you use a continuous strategy, a one-time strategy or a combination?

Too often needs assessments become complex projects that take extraordinary efforts to complete. Although these might yield quite useful information, they require such effort and commitment that there may be little enthusiasm for doing them again. My advice is to consider a more modest but continuous needs assessment process in which information gathering is woven into the usual routines of the setting. For example, annual performance reviews are good opportunities to ask some questions about present and desired capabilities from the perspective of the person being reviewed and of supervisors, managers or peers.

One-time needs assessments are suitable when there is no routine into which the process can be inserted or when there are other benefits to doing a time-limited assessment such as motivating and/or involving a broad-based learner community. A combined strategy is one that begins with a highly visible, time-limited information-gathering phase, but later incorporates continuous information collection into the routines of the group or organization.

How will you determine present capabilities (PCs)?

Since we are using the gap or discrepancy definition of need, this question and the next are the essence of the process. This is where knowledge of various information-gathering tools and techniques—and of their advantages and disadvantages—is important. Examples of the tools that can be used to determine present capabilities include self-assessments, tests, observations, surveys, checklists, interviews, role plays, in-basket exercises, simulations, performance appraisals and practice audits. Detailed advice about how to use each of these can be found in such sources as Witkin and Altschuld (1995), Gupta (1999) and Rossett (1999). The key task at this stage of the needs assessment is to gather information that makes it possible to paint a clear picture of what the current capabilities are of the learner community from the perspective of the learners (if you are identifying felt needs) or of other stakeholders (if you are identifying ascribed needs).

How will you determine desired capabilities (DCs)?

Desired capabilities are not objective conditions out there waiting to be discovered; they are value judgements made by individuals and groups (Davidson 1995). These value judgements may be incorporated into such formal documents as job descriptions, tests, performance standards, competency profiles and even laws; however, they remain value judgements. This explains why people disagree about desired capabilities and why the learner community may disagree with the others about what capabilities are required for certain roles in home and work life.

How can you ensure that the information you collect about present and desired capabilities is credible?

Information about human capabilities is subject to intended and unintended bias or distortion. Descriptions of present capabilities may be inaccurate because people are not necessarily good judges of their own abilities, because assessment tools may not produce valid results or because it is in someone's interest to misrepresent their own or someone else's abilities. Since information about desired capabilities includes value judgements, we must understand the origins of these judgements in order to decide whether they are credible. Desired capabilities may be unrealistic or inappropriate. They should be critically analyzed rather than simply accepted.

There is no simple way to ensure that information gathered in a needs assessment is credible. The likelihood that it will be credible is increased when questionnaires, tests, interviews, focus groups and other information-gathering techniques are used carefully. The literature on each of these contains principles that should be observed when they are used and suggests strategies for reducing the possibility of bias and distortion. It makes little sense to devote considerable time and energy to a needs assessment if the results are not considered credible by key stakeholders.

What process will be used to determine priorities among the needs that you identify and who should be involved?

Priority setting involves deciding which needs will be addressed and in what order. There never seem to be sufficient resources–time, energy, money–to respond to all needs that are identified; some process must be used to decide how these limited resources will be allocated. Most often the process is fast and informal with a small group discussing the needs and reaching agreement on which needs should be addressed. In other cases the process involves multiple stakeholders with differing views on what the priorities should be, and it can become both time consuming and contentious. Detailed guidance on various ways to approach priority setting can be found in the work of Caffarella (1994) and Sork (1998), among others, but the key elements are (a) identifying criteria, (b) applying the criteria to the needs and (c) arranging the needs in order from highest to lowest priority.

What is the estimated cost in dollars and time to carry out the needs assessment?

This question is fundamentally about the feasibility and cost/benefit of doing the needs assessment. Ideally, this question should be revisited periodically, as the needs assessment plan takes shape. It may be that the needs assessment simply becomes too expensive or too complex to justify. Although the type of needs assessment described here is a powerful planning tool, it is not implemented very often, as it requires a substantial commitment of resources. Conducting a simple "interest inventory" requires much less time and money, so it is not surprising that these are often done instead of needs assessments. It is important not to underestimate the cost of conducting a needs assessment and to be convinced that the results will justify the cost.

What are the most important sociopolitical issues you are likely to encounter during the needs assessment and how will you deal with them?

All aspects of educational planning, including needs assessment, are embedded in a sociopolitical context that influences, and is influenced by, the actions that are taken and the decisions that are made. Deciding who will be involved in the needs assessment and whether it will focus on felt or ascribed needs are two examples of actions with important sociopolitical consequences. Key stakeholders may have divergent interests; involving them collaboratively in the assessment may take great skill and sensitivity. A good example to illustrate this point is that of the unionized workplace where some of the interests of "labour" and "management" conflict. An educator conducting a needs assessment in such a setting would have to manage the process in a way that respects the different interests brought to the planning table and recognizes the power relations that exist among those involved (Cervero and Wilson 1996). The key point here is that skilful planners are able to identify and respond to the sociopolitical dynamics of the context. Ignoring these dynamics may shorten your career as an adult educator.

What are the most important ethical issues you are likely to encounter during the needs assessment and how will you deal with them?

Ethics is concerned with how we should act in relation to others. There is no generally accepted code of ethics in adult education; however, there is a growing body of literature dealing with the ethics of practice (Brockett and Hiemstra 1998). Needs assessment involves gathering sensitive information and identifying gaps in human capabilities, so there is clearly potential to do harm. Revealing information about gaps in capabilities of particular individuals to the "wrong" person could have dire consequences. Ignoring the views of less powerful stakeholders because they are at odds with the views of more powerful stakeholders raises questions about the ethics of the assessment. These are only two of many ethical issues that might be encountered in a needs assessment. Skilful adult educators are vigilant about the ethics of practice and can provide convincing moral justifications for the actions they take.

Which of the alternatives to needs assessment might be reasonable substitutes for your plan and why?

Although this question is discussed last, it should normally be asked early and often in planning. It is last here because sometimes it is only after the form and complexity of the needs assessment is clear that an alternative becomes attractive. It is probably obvious by now that needs assessments designed to reveal gaps between present and desired capabilities are neither straightforward nor unproblematic. They are powerful planning tools, but they should be reserved for use only when a powerful planning tool is needed. Other tools can be used to justify and focus planning that are much less resource intensive. Although these alternatives are not as powerful, they may fit the circumstance better and provide quite adequate guidance for planning purposes.

Alternatives to Needs Assessment

What follows are brief descriptions of several alternatives to needs assessment with their relative advantages and disadvantages.

Interest inventory. The interest inventory is often considered to be a type of needs assessment but it involves fundamentally different processes and produces very different products. In the typical interest inventory, potential participants are asked to indicate the degree of interest they have in each item in a list of topics, titles or program ideas. In one version of the interest inventory a listing of potential program topics is provided and respondents are asked to check those that "are of interest." Other versions are somewhat more sophisticated, asking respondents to indicate the likelihood–usually on a rating scale of some sort–that they will participate in programs offered on the topics listed. Interest inventories provide the planner with an idea of the current level of interest in topics or ideas that might be developed into programs to be offered to the learner community.

Ironically, when learners are asked to identify their learning needs, they usually tell us their interests or wants. They may have been conditioned to do this by the many surveys they have received labelled "needs assessment" that ask them to indicate which programs they would like to have offered.

Information produced by interest inventories is quite different from that produced in a needs assessment; this alone is good reason to distinguish between them. Interests are expressions of preference for certain topics or programs; needs indicate present and desired capabilities. Needs do not provide direct information about the kind of program that might be offered; interests tell us how attractive certain program titles or topics are to potential participants.

Level of "interest" is a notoriously poor predictor of participation. It should not be a surprise when a high level of interest does not translate into a large number of participants. This is understandable when we realize that people need more detailed information about the cost, dates, length, content, location, instructor and so on before they decide to participate. However, as a method to help planners decide which potential program topics might be worth developing into programs, the interest inventory is better than guessing. It is inexpensive, quick, and it provides planners with information about the preferences of those in the learner community.

Market test. The typical market test involves developing a small quantity of a new product, offering that product in a carefully selected "market" that is representative of the target consumer group and analyzing the response to the product (usually how many people buy the product and what they think of it when they use it). A variation of this process seems to be in common use in adult education. Program planners–often with the help of potential instructors–generate a program description, specify a location, set the fee, dates and times, and then offer the program to the "market" by advertising it, usually along with many others. If enough people register for the program, the instructor is responsible for fleshing out the details before or shortly after the program begins. Since some institutions cancel a significant proportion of programs because of insufficient enrolment, it seems that market testing is in widespread use.

It can be argued that market testing is an inexpensive way to (a) offer a wide range of courses to the learner community without devoting significant resources to needs assessment and (b) give the learners the opportunity to decide what will and will not be offered by voting with their chequebooks. The market-test approach allows institutions with limited planning resources to offer a wide range of programs, providing they have a pool of potential instructors who do not mind entering into contracts contingent upon the number of registrations.

Using the market test as an alternative to needs assessment would involve developing a program idea into a more or less detailed program proposal that might contain any or all of the following information: program title, expected outcomes or objectives, topics to be covered, instructors, who the program will benefit, day and time the program will be offered, where it will be offered, the general schedule of the program, fees and how to register or enrol in the program. To determine the potential demand for the program, it may be advertised to the learner community to see how they respond. Alternatively, one or more focus groups or other small group meetings may be formed to obtain learners' reactions to the program proposal. In either case, the final product of a market test is reliable information about the actual or potential demand for the program, based on presenting it to the learner community with detailed information about the structure, the costs and the timing of the program. Since learner response is based on much more detailed information about the program than is the interest inventory, the market test is generally a much more reliable predictor of participation.

Problem analysis. A typical approach to problem analysis involves working through several well-defined steps: (1) clarify the problem, (2) generate alternative solutions to the problem, (3) evaluate the solutions and pick the one that is the most promising, (4) implement the solution, and (5) evaluate the results. Problem solving is similar to needs assessment in that both are concerned with gaps. In the case of needs assessment, the gap is between present and desired capabilities; in the case of problem analysis, the gap is between a present condition (a problem exists) and a desired condition (the problem is solved). Most solutions to substantive problems have an educational component; it could be argued that educational needs are embedded in every substantive problem. In those cases where there is general agreement that a problem exists, it makes sense to address the problem directly rather than resorting to a needs assessment. By carefully analyzing the problem, it should be possible to separate the educational and non-educational components of the solution. Once the educational components of the solution are identified, it will likely be clear what learning will be necessary to solve the problem. My point is that it seems unnecessary to layer a needs assessment on top of a problem analysis unless it will provide invaluable information for addressing the educational components of the problem.

A possible advantage to doing a problem analysis rather than a needs assessment is that it can be used to address complex situations that may require both educational and non-educational solutions. Another advantage is that most people have a better intuitive understanding of "problems" and how to approach solutions than they do of "needs" and how to assess them. A disadvantage to using problem analysis is that a situation must be labelled a problem by the parties involved before it can be analyzed. There may be resistance to characterizing something as a problem when it has to do with human capabilities or performance. It may be more acceptable politically to use the language of needs than the language of problems when discussing human capabilities.

Trend analysis. One of the weaknesses in using needs assessment to focus planning is that it is (by definition) a reactive strategy. If we accept the definition of need as a gap or discrepancy between present and desired capabilities, a need does not exist until there is some dissatisfaction with present capabilities. However, consider a situation where present capabilities are quite satisfactory, but if an analysis were made of social, economic, technological and other changes, it might be clear that one or two years from now the capabilities people have will not be adequate. Some educational intervention would be useful *to prevent* a need from developing in the future although no need exists at the present time. A trend analysis requires that we have information about past and present developments in order to *anticipate* what needs might emerge in the future. We can then develop programs that improve capabilities before they are judged undesirable or inadequate. By tracking a trend over time and projecting it into the future, we might be able to anticipate the emergence of educational needs. Projecting trends can be a highly technical process involving sophisticated mathematical models, but it can also be a common-sense process whereby an analyst tracks a development over time, determines what is likely to happen if the trend continues and identifies necessary changes in human capabilities implied by the trend. This is a proactive rather than a reactive stance, since emphasis is placed on anticipating and avoiding undesirable developments rather than reacting to them once they exist.

There are several limitations to trend analysis. One is that trends are notoriously unpredictable. What may first seem like a clear trend may suddenly reverse, or what may seem like a modestly growing trend may suddenly take off for the stratosphere. Another problem is that it is not always clear what the educational implications are of some trends. For example, it was clear in the early 1990s that the World Wide Web was becoming an important means of delivering information, but five years ago it would have been difficult to predict what the implications of the trend would be for educational institutions, businesses, governments and other segments of society. It is still not clear what the ultimate impact of the Web will be on these institutions and what kind of learning will be necessary to use the technology responsibly. Even if you do a good job of predicting the educational implications of a trend, you may be too far ahead of the curve to attract participants into an educational program. The learner community you serve must recognize the benefit of learning ahead of the curve, otherwise your programs will not be attractive.

Combined approaches. Combinations of several approaches may produce a better result than would any single approach. Combining these alternatives with one another or with needs assessment can yield very powerful tools for justifying and focusing planning. For example, an interest inventory might help the planner narrow the range of topics or program ideas to a more manageable number, then a needs assessment could be conducted for each topic or idea. A trend analysis could yield several program ideas that could be market tested with various learner communities. A problem analysis could be used to isolate the educational component of a problem, then a well-focused needs assessment could be done to identify gaps in capabilities for that component.

Combining these methods can produce powerful tools for planning, but they must be used with an understanding of their strengths and weaknesses. Each requires time and money, and some require specialized knowledge. Skilful adult educators know the strengths and weaknesses of these tools and how to decide when they are appropriate to use. There are undoubtedly other alternatives to needs assessment that have not been mentioned above. The point in discussing these is to suggest that needs assessment is not the be-all and end-all of program planning. Justifying and focusing the planning process can be accomplished in a variety of ways, and knowing what some of these are will prevent planners from falling into the trap of believing that needs assessment is the only responsible way to justify and focus planning. Deciding which approach or combination of approaches to use should be based, not on some misplaced belief in the utility of needs assessment, but rather in careful consideration of the options available and their suitability given the task at hand and the resources available.

On Keeping an Open Mind about Needs Assessment

I was once a true believer in needs assessment and felt guilty whenever I planned a program without doing one. However, I realized many years ago that it was not productive to view planning as such a rigid process. I have developed a question-based approach to planning because it seemed much better suited to the highly diverse settings in which adult educators practice. I have presented the set of questions above to help you think through some of the choices you can make if you decide to do a needs assessment, and I have provided some alternatives for consideration if needs assessment does not seem like the best tool for the job. This chapter ends with a different set of questions—a set that does not assume that needs assessment is the preferred tool. It is similar in many ways to the questions discussed above, but it encourages the planner to keep an open mind about the best ways to justify and focus planning. As before, the order of the questions is not set, but rather should be determined by the circumstances and the preferences of those involved in planning.

- Which characteristics of the planning context and learner community will be especially important to consider as you justify and focus planning?

- To whom do you have to justify the resources required to plan and offer this program and what kind of information will satisfy them?

- What existing information or research that is already available to you would be useful in justifying and focusing planning?

- Which approach(es) to justify and focus planning might be suitable for the task?

- What are the advantages and disadvantages of each approach?

- Which approach will you use to justify and focus planning, and why is it the best choice?

- What will be the final product of the approach that you use? (When you complete the process, what information will you have that will help you justify and focus planning? Define any terms you use such as *needs, interests* and so on.)

- What specific tasks will be required to implement the approach that you propose to use, what special skills will be required to complete these tasks, and who will complete each task?

- Will the approach provide continuous information for planning purposes, or will it provide information for planning only one program?

- What is the estimated cost in dollars and time to complete the process you have described, and is it "affordable" given the money and time available?

- What important sociopolitical issues are you likely to encounter when justifying and focusing planning, and how will you address them?

- What important ethical issues are you likely to encounter when justifying and focusing planning, and how will you address them?

I do not presume that these are the best questions to guide you through the process of justifying and focusing your planning activities, but they may provide a starting point for you to develop a set of questions suited to your context, philosophy of adult education and personal style. Proposing the adoption of a question-based approach to planning is a moderately radical departure from conventional wisdom. It may be awkward and confusing to use at first, but it promises to keep the process much more open and less likely to become dominated by rigid technical procedures or "cookbook" planning models. My hope is that you will always keep an open mind about the best way to plan programs, and that you will constantly challenge yourself to consider all reasonable options before deciding how to proceed.

References

Beatty, P.T. 1981. The concept of need: Proposal for a working definition. *Journal of the Community Development Society* 12 (2): 39-46.

Brockett, R.G., and R. Hiemstra. 1998. Philosophical and ethical considerations. In *Program planning for the training and continuing education of adults: North American perspectives*, edited by P.S. Cookson. Malabar, Fla.: Krieger Publishing Co..

Caffarella, R.S. 1994. *Planning programs for adult learners: A practical guide for educators, trainers, and staff developers*. San Francisco: Jossey-Bass.

Cervero, R.M., and A.L. Wilson. 1994. *Planning responsibly for adult education: A guide to negotiating power and interests*. San Francisco: Jossey-Bass.

———. 1996. What really matters in adult education program planning: Lessons in negotiating power and interests. *New Directions for Adult and Continuing Education* 69. San Francisco: Jossey-Bass.

Collins, M. 1991. *Adult education as vocation: A critical role for the adult educator*. New York: Routledge.

Davidson, H.S. 1995. Making needs: Toward a historical sociology of needs in adult and continuing education. *Adult Education Quarterly* 45 (4): 183-196.

Gupta, K. 1999. *A practical guide to needs assessment*. San Francisco: Jossey-Bass/Pfeiffer.

Houle, C.O. 1996. *The design of education*. 2d ed. San Francisco: Jossey-Bass.

Pearce, S. 1998. Determining program needs. In *Program planning for the training and continuing education of adults: North American perspectives*, edited by P.S. Cookson. Malabar, Fla.: Krieger Publishing Co.

Rossett, A. 1999. *First things fast: A handbook for performance analysis*. San Francisco: Jossey-Bass/Pfeiffer.

Sork, T.J. 1997. Workshop planning. In New perspectives on designing and implementing effective workshops, edited by J.A. Fleming. *New Directions for Adult and Continuing Education* 76. San Francisco: Jossey-Bass.

———. 1998. Program priorities, purposes and objectives. In *Program planning for the training and continuing education of adults: North American perspectives*, edited by P.S. Cookson. Malabar, Fla.: Krieger Publishing Co.

———. 2000. Planning educational programs. In *Handbook of adult and continuing education*, edited by A.L. Wilson and E.R. Hayes. San Francisco: Jossey-Bass.

Sork, T.J., and R.S. Caffarella. 1989. Planning programs for adults. In *Handbook of adult and continuing education*, edited by S.B. Merriam and P.M. Cunningham. San Francisco: Jossey-Bass.

Witkin, B.R., and J.W. Altschuld. 1995. *Planning and conducting needs assessments: A practical guide*. Thousand Oaks, Calif.: Sage Publications.

7

Program Planning in Adult Education

Atlanta Sloane-Seale

As a novice program planner in the field of adult education, I often wondered what I was required to do, what was meant by program planning, whether I had accomplished it and whether I could define what I had done. Program planners engage in *andragogy*, that is, in the art and science of helping adults learn (Knowles 1980), and it is their job to identify, develop, design and implement learning activities for adult learners. Program planning is a central activity in the adult education enterprise for which program planners are responsible.

Both new and experienced program planners must confront a number of interrelated and dynamic issues, including the values (organizational, environmental and personal), beliefs and norms that govern their practice; the procedures, policies and rules that guide the program planning process; and the collection and analysis of data to facilitate critical decision making. How these various components are negotiated among often competing and conflicting needs and interests is central to the practice of "good" program planning (Cervero and Wilson 1994).

The goal of professional program planners is to help their clients learn, and they struggle to choose methods, materials and content that best serve this goal. By analyzing what they do as program planners and why they do it, they may conceptualize their practice in new and more comprehensive ways, as well as discover how context influences and is influenced by practice.

Program planning is an interactive, dynamic, interdependent process where everything happens at once; it is not a step-by-step process. Each component of the plan is viewed as a circle that fits together with the other components to form a set of interlocking circles. At the centre of each circle are planners' knowledge, skills, abilities, and core values and beliefs about learners, education, learning and program planning (planning context, focus of concern, needs assessment, curriculum development, collaboration, marketing and ethics and evaluation), and about the commonplaces (learners, content, instructors, context). These core values and beliefs are integral to the planning process.

Professional practice requires program planners to have, understand and use–implicitly or explicitly–a framework of practice, or a model, to plan programs for adult learners. A model is a general representation of reality that allows planners to diagnose what is to be done, what works or does not work and why. It helps to validate their personal knowledge, skills, abilities and judgements at every decision point of the planning process (Kowalski

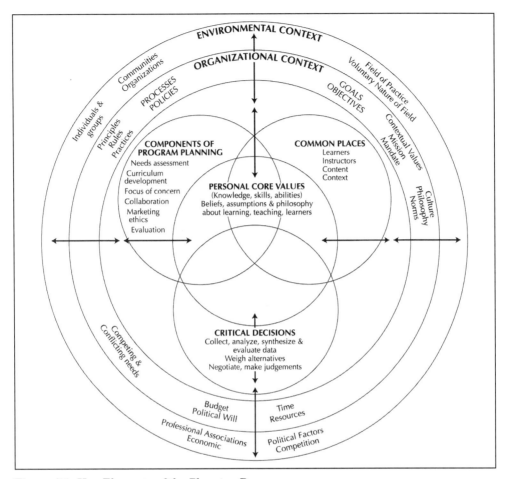

Figure 7.1: Key Elements of the Planning Process

1988). Using a model also helps planners to meet the high expectations of learners, organizations, client groups and communities, as well as to clarify, justify and validate their practice. Figure 7.1 illustrates the key elements in the planning process that are discussed in this chapter.

Before a discussion of the elements of program planning, some key terms need to be defined.

Adult education. Houle (1972) defines adult education as the process by which men and women (alone, in groups or in institutional settings) endeavour to improve themselves or their society by increasing their skills, knowledge or sensitivities. Darkenwald and Merriam (1982) view it as a process whereby people undertake systematic and sustained learning activities to bring about changes in knowledge, skills, attitudes and values. In general, adult education is a process by which individuals, groups, institutions or communities try to assist people to improve their knowledge, skills, abilities or sensitivities.

Program. Schroeder (1970) defines this as all the educational activities provided in a community, or what is provided by a given agency, or what is designed for segments of the population. Verner and Booth (1964) view it as a series of learning experiences designed to achieve, in a specific time period, certain instructional objectives. More recently, program has been broadly defined to incorporate not only curriculum or a structured series of intended learning outcomes, but also all the programming activities planners must engage in to identify, design and implement learning opportunities for adults.

A program is also seen as a plan for educational activity (Houle 1972; Knowles 1980); thus, it is any deliberately organized activity for adults in which the primary intention is to learn (Sloane-Seale 1994). Bergevin, Morris and Smith (1963) view program and program planning as intimately related, since planning and implementing programs involve the same activities.

Program planning. This term is used interchangeably with program development. Houle (1972) and Pennington and Green (1976) define it as a series of decision points in which program planners complete clusters of activities and then move to the next set of activities or decision points. Boyle (1981) sees it as a deliberate series of actions and decisions through which representatives of those affected by the potential educational program are involved with the programmer to plan the program. Kowalski (1988) defines it as a dynamic, interactive process in which the concept of a discrete step is rarely a reality and where planning decisions are deliberately manipulated to affect intended learning outcomes. It is thus a complex process of interdependent actions, judgements and behaviours that takes place in situations that are complex, uncertain and unique (Sloane-Seale 1994).

Program planning is defined here as a deliberative, reciprocal process of mindful interaction and action in a specific situation that considers both the commonplaces (learners, content, instructors, context) and the planning components (needs assessment, curriculum development and so on) in order that appropriate decisions can be made among the educational alternatives in planning programs for adult learners (Sloane-Seale 1994).

Program Planning Models

Sork and Buskey (1986) outline three types of program planning models found in the literature. First, a small number of analytical models provide a "theoretical" framework or a set of interrelated ideas, principles or practices on which the model is developed. Boone (1985), Boyle (1981), Freire (1970), Houle (1972), Kidd (1973) and Knowles (1980) offer examples of these. Second, a very few descriptive models represent how planning was actually done in a particular context; these models include the works of Lauffer (1977), Pennington and Green (1976) and Schon (1983). Finally, many models are prescriptive and normative "how-tos" of program planning, presenting the authors' practical recommendations for how to go about the tasks of program planning. Examples include the Continuing Education Instructor Development (1980), the Program Planning Guide for Health Professionals

(1977) and Renner's Ten Step Model (1983). In practice, program planners rarely use one model. Instead, they appear to be guided by a personally held set of beliefs, values and principles, and by contextual factors. Given this, planners must be fully aware of their own implicitly held knowledge base and of the context of their practice in order to more accurately define their practice model.

Sork and Buskey (1986) identify a generic planning model that provides a framework for program planning practice. There are nine dynamically interrelated, interdependent components: (1) analyzing planning content and the client system; (2) assessing learners' needs; (3) developing objectives; (4) selecting and ordering content; (5) designing and ordering instructional processes; (6) selecting instructional processes; (7) formulating a budget and an administrative plan; (8) designing a plan to assure participation; and (9) designing a plan to evaluate the program. These planning components, however, are framed by the larger aspects of program planning, such as environmental and organizational context that underlie the planning process. Program planners need comprehensive knowledge of these larger aspects in order to be efficient and effective in their practice. The components of the generic planning model are thus structured into six broad categories, which are discussed and analyzed using the following example of a program planning process.

I. Example of the Generic Program Planning Model

Practitioners, educators and consultants approached a program director in a Continuing Education Division (CED) to develop a program in Child Welfare Practice, a highly specialized field in which expertise is usually developed through on-the-job training, in-house training initiatives, workshops and advanced study and skill development. The practitioners and the key stakeholders involved have concluded that specialized training and educational and skill development opportunities for child welfare workers are severely lacking. Although training in the core competencies of basic child protection work has been provided, specialized areas of child welfare work are not being currently addressed in any organized, systematic or comprehensive way.

Child welfare practitioners include case workers, treatment providers, support workers, foster parents and collaterals, such as group home workers and residential care workers. The almost one thousand child welfare workers in the case study's geographic area are the target audience for the new program. Many are not interested in pursuing an advanced degree program due to time constraints, lack of energy, prohibitive tuition costs, the inability to meet admission requirements to degree programs or a lack of educational opportunities focusing on child welfare issues.

A planning model for the proposed program in the case example will now be discussed and analyzed using several broad categories.

A. The Planning Context

To identify and understand the nature and characteristics of the planning context, several interrelated aspects of it must be examined.

Focus of concern. This can be determined either by potential learners or by key stakeholders in a learning situation. In the case study, a resource group of educators, practitioners and consultants identified the focus of concern as a lack of specialized educational opportunities to meet the needs of child welfare practitioners. Based on their discussions and consultations with key stakeholders, they approached a program director in a CED to discuss this concern.

Personal values and beliefs. To facilitate an efficient and effective planning process, program planners must explicitly state their values and beliefs. In the case study, those involved believe in lifelong learning and that a structured series of learning opportunities is required to address the focus of their concern.

Organizational factors. Knowledge and understanding of the culture, mandate, values and beliefs involved in the planning process are critical for program planners. Internal and external organizational factors, including economic and political values, provide the planning context.

In the case example, the CED's mandate is to offer accessible, reasonably priced programs that recover operating costs and generate revenue, as well as meet the specific needs of the target market and attract a new one. The mandate of the child welfare system is to meet the many challenges of those in care and to have knowledgeable and skilled employees. Building and increasing community partnerships is seen to be both desirable and politically expedient.

Environmental constraints. The program planning process is affected by factors such as the availability of instructors, ease of content delivery, time and budget constraints and political will. Planners must also take into account the fact that adult learners are voluntary learners who vote with their feet. They want learning opportunities that are flexible, current and open to change, and programs that are practical, relevant and useful.

In the case example, although support from key stakeholders in the child welfare system appears to be in place, several questions need to be answered. Are content specialists available to develop and offer the program within the set time frame? Are there reasonably priced materials for delivering content? Do administrative procedures and policies allow for speedy program development? Is the format designed to serve the needs of the majority of the potential learners?

B. Needs Assessment

Needs and needs assessment involve a cluster of interdependent activities, including defining needs, developing strategies for assessing needs, identifying needs and making critical decisions about the needs to be addressed. Needs assessment is the method or strategy used to determine if a need exists. French Bell (1978) discusses the pros and cons of eighteen techniques, including advisory groups, analysis of charts, personal interviews, program assessment and survey use.

Defining needs. The concept of need is central to the practice of program planning and is defined as a condition or situation in which something necessary or desirable is required or wanted. It is described as a measurable discrepancy between a present state of affairs and a desired state of affairs as asserted by the owner of the need or an authority on the need (Beatty 1981; Boone 1985; Sork 1986). (For a detailed discussion of this topic, see Sork in this volume).

Monette (1977) outlines four types of needs that programs address. A "basic" need is a deficiency that motivates the learner to participate in order to relieve a bio-physiological condition, for example, the need for food and shelter. A "felt" (or expressed) need is identified by the owner of the need and motivates the learner to remove the need, for example, by registering for a remedial math class in order to pass an accounting course. A "comparative" need is determined by comparing the services of group A with the services of a similar group B. If group B is not receiving the same services, then group B is said to have a need. A "normative" need is a gap or deficiency between a desirable standard and the existing standard (as measured or defined by someone), for example, professionals who must take courses to keep up-to-date in their field of expertise.

In the case example, the needs are normative because they are expressed as deficiencies or gaps in the knowledge, skills, abilities or sensitivities of a group of child welfare practitioners. The needs are also ascribed, as they were determined by the key stakeholders, educators and practitioners rather than the potential learners. In the needs assessment, core and specialized competencies of basic child protection work were assessed through a formal competency-based instrument that was developed, tested and administered to all child welfare practitioners. The need for proficiency in other more specialized areas was confirmed informally through consultation with key stakeholders and discussions with advisory committee members, educators and trainers. An analysis of current training opportunities established the need for a comprehensive curriculum delivered in a structured series of courses.

Identifying needs. Needs exist because we create and define them. The process of identifying the needs to be addressed is framed by personal values and beliefs and by the politics, economics, organizational constraints and mandate of those involved in the planning process. In the case example, the data collected during the needs assessment phase of the planning process were analyzed, synthesized and evaluated by those involved in the planning process. The evaluated data were categorized and prioritized, based on feasibility and importance criteria (Sork 1986). The planners then weighed the alternatives according to the perceived needs and decided which particular needs to address.

Making critical decisions. Even the most sophisticated needs assessment will not ensure that learners will take part in a planned educational event. Their participation may vary according to their self-evaluation and attitudes towards education; their experience of life transition factors (such as divorce or death of a loved one), which might accelerate their need to learn; the importance of their expectations that participation will help them to meet their goals and the information they have about opportunities and barriers to participation (Cross 1981).

Davidson (1995) and Scissons (1985) argue that needs do not exist but are constructed and inferred on the basis of evidence that planners and educators collect and analyze. No one best method exists to assess needs, and the final decision-making process is filtered through many screens, such as planners' values and beliefs, organizational philosophy, budget constraints, human resource issues and learners' willingness to participate. In the case example, the implementation of the program and the actual registration in it will determine the measure of success of the needs assessment process.

C. Curriculum Development

This entails a number of dynamically interrelated activities: identifying objectives, selecting and prioritizing content, delivering content, nurturing instructors, evaluating learners and instructors and developing course outlines. These activities are analyzed in the context of learners' characteristics and needs, values about learning and teaching and the role of learners in the program planning process.

Identifying objectives. Objectives are determined based on the nature of the course, learners' characteristics and how people learn. Bloom's (1956) taxonomy of educational objectives is helpful in determining the nature and the level of the objectives. In the case example, learners need to acquire specialized knowledge of child welfare practice and then apply the theory and learned skills to their individual practices. Learners may have several years of experience in child welfare work, and many have a bachelor's degree. Thus, middle to high order educational objectives will be appropriate for the proposed program.

Selecting and prioritizing content. This activity builds upon the needs identified by the core competency-based training instrument and upon the informal needs assessment conducted by key stakeholders in the planning process. In the case example, the advisory committee has a pivotal role in determining the knowledge of greatest value to learners, that is, not what would be "nice to know" but what learners "must know" to be effective and proficient child welfare workers.

Delivering content. Numerous techniques can be used to deliver content, such as lectures, tutorials, demonstrations and study assignments. Tapper (1977) provides a helpful guideline for assessing the pros and cons of instructional methods and their application. The most appropriate technique, however, will be determined on the basis of available resources, instructors' knowledge, skills and abilities, the nature of the content, learners' characteristics and how people learn. In the case example, the methods selected to deliver content include lecturette, small and large discussion groups, role play, case studies and assignments.

Kolb's (1971) inventory is a tool for helping learners' assess their style of learning and instructors select content-delivery techniques to match these styles and facilitate the learning experience. "Concrete experience" characterizes those who prefer learning with their peers in small-group situations where they can become involved in the learning process. Learners who show a tendency for "abstract conceptualization" learn best in a lecture-based environment where theory and systematic analysis are emphasized. "Active experimentation" learners learn best by engaging in group projects and group discussions. A high score on "reflective observation" indicates learners who prefer passive learning situations, such as lectures. In the case example, learners may display one or more of these learning styles.

Nurturing instructors. Providing professional development opportunities, such as workshops on effective teaching styles or micro-teaching courses, facilitating meetings with colleagues, holding instructors' meetings to discuss programs and their relevance and offering other non-monetary benefits and rewards for teaching are some ways to let program instructors know they are appreciated. In the case example, the program planner will establish a formal structure to facilitate a nurturing process.

Evaluating learners and instructors. Curriculum development must also include evaluating learners' work and the evaluation of the quality of instruction in the program. Both formal and informal methods can be used. In the case example, learners will be evaluated using a number of methods such as (but not limited to) role plays, experiential exercises, written assignments and in-class presentations. Their work will be graded according to the university letter grade system. Quality of instruction will be determined by (a) formal, standard, end-of-course evaluation forms designed to collect data about the relevance of learning objectives, content-delivery methods, instructors' teaching styles and usefulness of the content and by (b) ongoing, informal debriefing discussions with instructors. This information will be used to make re-hiring decisions.

Developing course outlines. The curriculum will be supplemented with a course outline, which includes the course name and description, course hours, the target audience, prerequisites (if any), course goals and objectives, delivery format, course materials, course details by topic and evaluation methods. In the case example, the program planner, in conjunction with the advisory committee members, will develop the course outline.

D. Collaboration

Co-operating with internal and external individuals, groups, agencies, organizations and professional associations has become common strategy for continuing educators. Collaboration involves identifying the nature of the collaborative effort, analyzing its benefits and costs, determining the extent of the arrangement, working with advisory committees and defining successful collaboration.

Beder (1984) identifies four types of collaboration: "co-sponsorship"–where a CED jointly offers a program with another agency; "referral"–where other organizations and individuals refer learners to a CED;

"donor-receiver"–where other organizations make outright donations to a CED for charitable or promotional purposes; and "co-ordination"–where CEDs agree to co-ordinate activities to maximize efficiency, reduce competition and mutually assist each other's efforts. In the case example, the CED program planner co-ordinates program development with practitioners, educators, consultants and key stakeholders in the child welfare system. Through this joint arrangement, each party expects that the mutual benefits will outweigh the costs.

Nature of collaboration. Cervero (1984) presents a framework of questions to help program planners determine the nature of a collaborative relationship: What resources does the unit seek from its environment? What type of co-operative relationship does the unit form with its environment to obtain these resources? What factors help explain the extent to which the unit has formed co-operative relationships? What are the benefits and costs of this relationship to the unit?

Benefits and costs. In the case example, the CED expects to benefit from an increased number of students, and thus, increased income. Child welfare agencies are expected to support the program by encouraging their staff and providing incentives for them to take the program; these agencies have also had input into its design and implementation without incurring delivery costs. Agency workers will have an up-to-date, structured and comprehensive program to meet their needs. A successful program will accrue intangible benefits such as recognition, visibility, prestige and domain for all parties.

The costs of co-operation include: some lost autonomy by those involved in the planning process; what may be a prohibitive and frustrating amount of time spent on the decision-making process; and the negative impact of cancellation of the program or partnership.

Extent of collaboration. The extent to which organizations engage in collaborative efforts may be explained by factors such as compatibility in organizational goals, resource security, type of instruction, domain and environment. In the case example, the CED and the child welfare agencies have compatible goals–to provide or facilitate the training of child welfare practitioners. All parties want resource security: the CED must recover costs and generate profit, while the agencies must ensure workers receive adequate training and education within the limitations of the agencies' scarce resources. The type of instruction provided by the CED is consistent with the agencies' needs, and the CED is legitimately empowered to provide this instruction. In terms of environment, CEDs are constantly in search of resources in order to survive. By co-operating with child welfare agencies, the CED may obtain vital resources, as well as increased public support.

Advisory committees. Program planning is conducted by an individual program planner or by a group. Group members require some orientation and background information about the goals, mandate, structure, policies and procedures of the organizations represented in the group. A formal committee structure, including terms of reference to operate the committee, should be established. In the case example, an advisory committee was formed to facilitate the program planning process. It is a representative group consisting of key stakeholders, educators, content specialists, practitioners and the program planner. The group was small and manageable, and it quickly developed cohesiveness as members had the same focus of concern and common goals.

Successful collaboration. Beder (1984) identifies themes that characterize successful interorganizational collaboration, including reciprocity, system openness, trust and commitment and compatible organizational structures. Reciprocity refers to the mutual benefits that organizations will accrue from the relationship. System openness allows interaction between the organization and its external environment (Kowalski 1988). The more open an organization, the more capable it is of coping with conflict and change created by internal and external environments. Trust and commitment among organizations are based on ongoing working relationships that have developed over time, and compatible organizational structures facilitate the attainment of mutual goals.

In the case example, reciprocity for the CED involves gaining new learners and increased income while the child welfare agencies gain a structured, comprehensive program to meet their employees' needs. All parties have a degree of system openness that has allowed them to join forces to address the changing needs of learners. The CED has earned the trust and commitment of key stakeholders in the child welfare system over many years, and all those involved in the planning process have compatible educational goals and the organizational structures to accomplish them.

E. Program Marketing

Kotler and Fox (1985) define marketing as the analysis, planning, implementing and control of carefully formulated programs designed to bring about the voluntary exchange of values with target markets to achieve institutional objectives. Program planners use a marketing strategy that creates conditions whereby learners exchange their time, tuition fees and good opinion of the learning opportunity for the acquisition of knowledge and a worthwhile learning experience. Marketing is dynamically related to the needs assessment, curriculum development and evaluation components of program planning. It entails identifying markets, developing a market plan, implementing the plan and the issue of marketing ethics.

Identifying markets. Successful program planners identify their markets and the characteristics of their learning audiences. A "market" is a distinct group of learners who have the resources to exchange for the benefits offered by a program; audiences are actual and potential learners with an interest in or an impact on the program.

In the case example, the target market includes anyone who works in and with the child welfare system in either a paid or volunteer position, such as case workers, group home workers, foster parents or mental health workers. Participants in volunteer positions who are admitted to the program must provide evidence of supervised practice opportunities. Most of those in the target audience have a bachelor's degree in Social Work, Arts or Education. They are twenty-four- to fifty-four-year-old women—with an income ranging from $24,000 to $46,000—who are socially conscious and goal-oriented. They may be described as lifelong learners who participate in educational programs to keep up-to-date in their field and to increase their knowledge and skills.

Developing a plan. A good marketing plan is framed within an organizational strategy to determine the needs of its various target markets and to satisfy them through the design, communication, pricing and delivery of appropriate, competitive and viable programs and services (Kowalski 1988). Strategically manipulating the four Ps of the marketing mix (product, price, place and promotion) will achieve the organization's objectives of providing the right program at the right place, time and price to the right clientele and of effectively communicating information about the learning event to that market segment. The marketing cycle also includes situational analysis, setting objectives, developing an action plan and evaluating and revising the plan. In the case example, the product is a comprehensive, specialized program of four courses, or 110 hours of instruction, that will address the needs of the target audience, be competitively priced and be delivered in an accessible location.

Implementing the plan. The current situation must be assessed in order to begin implementing the plan. If necessary, a situational analysis of the internal and external environment and of any problems or opportunities surrounding the program may be conducted. Goals must be established to determine which direction the marketing plan will take, and strategies must be identified for achieving these goals, such as program positioning, identifying target segments, offering incentives to attract learners, manipulating the marketing mix and effectively communicating program benefits to the target audience.

An action plan should be generated to ensure that the marketing goals are achieved. The activities necessary to achieve each goal must be identified, as well as who is responsible for each activity, a timeline, and potential tangible and intangible outcomes. A budget needs to be developed. Costs and benefits must be calculated, including resources, time, money and people. Marketing controls need to be established, including an annual report, revenues and costs associated with the plan, and the strategies used in the plan to promote the program (newspapers, flyers, brochures, journals, direct mail, exhibits, education campaigns, public relations campaigns, radio spots and so on). Techniques for evaluating and revising the marketing plan must be created.

In the case example, the program is promoted by using paid advertisements in newspapers and journals and through the free publicity offered by in-house newsletters. Information sessions to key stakeholders are organized to market the program. An advisory committee comprising representatives from key stakeholders was established by and reports to the Program Area. The purposes of the committee are to provide an advisory liaison function between the program and the community; to ensure continuous development and revision of the program; and to advise on the development of any other programs in the area of child welfare that may impact the delivery of the program. The committee functions include contributing names of potential registrants to the mailing lists; suggesting names of potential instructional resources; promoting the program to colleagues and organizations who may benefit from participation in the program; advising on the need to revise the program; identifying the need to develop seminars, workshops or conferences in the field of child welfare; and providing advice on program evaluation. In short, the advisory committee is involved in the marketing, needs assessment, curriculum development and evaluation of the program.

Marketing ethics. Considerable debate exists about the ethics of the marketing strategies and practices used in adult education. Ethics applies to any situation in which there is actual or potential harm to an individual or group. Business ethics is the process of determining what are (and are not) reasonable standards of moral conduct in order to resolve actual or potential conflicts of interest. Resolving ethical dilemmas often involves moral, social and economic trade-offs that require sacrifice and tolerance. Moral reasoning skills must be part of the fundamental skill set of all program planners in order to ensure marketing ethics in program planning.

Manuel Velasquez (cited in Cooke 1990) provides seven questions for evaluating and resolving an actual or potential moral dilemma:

1. What are the relevant facts? Program planners must identify the key factors shaping the planning situation and any associated ethical issues.

2. What are the ethical issues? Some may be broad systemic issues, others may be business issues and still others may be personal issues.

3. Who are the major stakeholders in the decision-making process? A variety of individuals, groups or organizations may be affected by decisions made in the planning process.

4. What are the possible alternatives? Program planners must identify all the alternatives that were considered and justify the chosen course of action.

5. What are the ethics of the alternatives? Each alternative must be evaluated.

6. What are the practical restraints? Practical factors that limit the organization's ability to implement the alternatives (lack of knowledge or resources, internal or external politics and so on) must be outlined.

7. What actions should be taken? After weighing the alternatives, the practical constraints and the ethics of the alternatives, the steps to implement the action must be selected.

Riggs (1989) also identifies a number of potential ethical issues that may occur under the marketing mix (product, price, place and promotion).

Given the pressures of practice to recover costs and generate profit, these issues may be a reality for many program planners, and an ongoing discussion and review of these issues is important.

In the case example, several ethical marketing issues exist. Does the promotional material make explicit all costs associated with the program's application and registration procedure? Does the published program description meet the learners' and stakeholders' expectations of high standards and quality? Have the key stakeholders who will be affected by the CED's program pricing decision been identified? Does the program planner have the requisite knowledge or ability to conduct certain program planning activities? Is elitism, ethnocentricity or parochialism of those involved in the planning process inhibiting the inclusion of certain target groups (for example, foster parents)?

F. Evaluation

Understanding the concepts, principles and strategies of evaluation is critical to professional practice. Evaluation is the process of inquiry into the performance of a program (Dignan and Carr 1992; Sork 1991). Program planners can use the evaluation results to make improvements or changes, or to defend planning decisions. Evaluation can occur at the beginning, middle, or end of a program. Evaluation may be summative and/or formative. Summative evaluation normally occurs at the end of a program and focuses on the impact of the program. Formative evaluation focuses on improvements while the program is in progress.

Program planners need to address the following issues when structuring a program evaluation: identification of the program; an evaluation plan; including its purpose; a design proposal; data collection; and critical decision making.

Identification. The program name must be clearly written in the program description along with details of program purpose, goals and location. Its structure and content must be outlined (including the involvement of other partners or organizations and the names of staff assigned to it), as must the standards for successful program completion. In the case study, a detailed proposal outlines the program content, objectives and goals, the assessment process, content-delivery methods, program admission criteria and completion requirements, and a budget for internal purposes.

Evaluation plan. The purposes of an evaluation may be to contribute to decisions about program installation; to make decisions about program continuation, expansion, deletion, modification or certification; to measure whether goals have been achieved and so on. There are both formal and informal evaluation strategies. Standardized course evaluations administered at the end of a course are formal evaluations that normally occur on an ongoing basis after the program has been offered at least once. Informal strategies (such as meetings with advisory committees and instructors) are also used to collect data about the program.

Program planners must address several issues when developing an evaluation plan. What is the purpose of the evaluation? Who will receive the evaluation results? What questions or issues will be raised in the evaluation? Who will conduct the evaluation? What resources are available and/or needed to conduct the evaluation? What information sources are available?

In the case example, the purpose of the evaluation is to assess whether the goals and objectives of each course in the program have been achieved and to aid in making decisions to improve the course and/or re-hire instructors. Because the program is new, the formal evaluation will not take place until after all four courses in the program have been offered at least once. At that time, summative evaluation will be implemented; students will complete standardized evaluation forms to determine if they feel goals and objectives have been met. In the meantime, ongoing, informal discussions with students and the debriefing of instructors will be part of the formative evaluation.

Design proposal. This must take several factors into account. What data should be collected and from whom (students, program graduates, instructors, employers)? How will data be collected (participation count, questionnaires, interviews and so on)? How will data be analyzed (using a statistical software program, for example)? How and when will data be reported? Who will receive the results (different results go to different audiences)? Has the evaluation plan been approved by all those involved in the program planning? Has a management plan been developed, detailing a co-ordinator, available resources, a timetable and a budget?

Strategies for conducting evaluations are included in a design proposal. The three basic methods are: (1) examining records and documents of what people have done or said, such as minutes of meetings, annual reports, program descriptions and so on; (2) observing what people do, through class visits or calculating attendance or how much printed material has been disseminated; and (3) asking people questions in person, by telephone or in writing. Gardner (1977) describes the basic assumptions and distinguishing characteristics of five evaluative models and discusses the pros and cons of each.

Data collection. Devlin (1994) and Kowalski (1988) identify four categories of variables for program planners to consider in this phase of the evaluation process. Contextual factors, such as location and facilities, class times and size, program format, tuition fees, registration and admission, and quality of facilitators must all be examined. Learners' characteristics, such as age, sex, education, occupation and income, as well as reasons for taking the program, details of employment and expectations are also important to know. Program implementation factors, such as effectiveness of program design or format, facilitators' delivery of content, value of content and learning activities, pacing of instruction, availability of reading and library materials and relevance of assignments must all be considered. The final category is program outcomes, including achievement of stated goals and objectives, consistency with program promotion and learners' reasons for participating, stakeholder satisfaction and future offerings.

In the case example, learners will be asked to complete an end-of-course evaluation at the appropriate time. Participants will be asked if the learning objectives of the program were clearly stated and if the course met their personal learning objectives and expectations. Responses will also be solicited on course content, instruction and administration. Questions will include: Did the instructor create a stimulating learning experience? Did the instructor draw on learners' life experiences to enrich classroom learning? Was the material well organized? Learners will also be asked about staff attitudes and about class facilities, size and location.

Critical decision making. Program planners must constantly make decisions around various program planning components, including evaluation. They begin the process by collecting data about the specific planning component, which they then analyze, synthesize and evaluate, after taking into account the contextual factors, that is, the values, norms, politics, economics and social elements of the situation. The next step is to weigh the alternatives, which requires making judgements about them, in order to select the most appropriate alternatives and take action. Often these decisions concern learners, content, instructors and context, and must be made in the face of competing and conflicting needs and economic, political and social trade-offs. Thus, negotiation and critical decision making are key elements of the planning process and essential skills for program planners.

Conclusion

Program planners make decisions, alone or with others, about many things, such as achieving learning objectives, ensuring positive learning experiences for learners, content and content delivery, educational alternatives for adult programming and meeting learners' needs in the face of competing and conflicting interests of various groups. Some programmers use rules to guide their practice—usually a brief, clear statement of what to do and how to do it in frequently encountered practice situations. Others use practical principles, a more inclusive and less explicit statement of purpose than a written rule (Elbaz 1983). However, to be effective and efficient, all program planners need a systematic framework to guide their practice.

A systematic framework provides the basis for rational decision making, helps identify the program planning components that need to be addressed and makes explicit the knowledge, skills and abilities program planners need to undertake and conduct an effective and efficient practice. Program planning is both an art and a science; the planning process is not a step-by-step process, and the decision-making process that underlies program planning is often muddled. Nevertheless, professional practice requires that program planners critically reflect on their practice, be knowledgeable about the various models of practice and apply the most appropriate model to the situation.

References

Apps, J.W. 1985. *Improving practice in continuing education*. San Francisco: Jossey-Bass.

Beatty, P.T. 1981. The concept of need: Proposal for a working definition. *Journal of the Community Development Society* 12: 39-46.

Beder, H. (1984). Interorganizational cooperation: Why and how? In Realizing the potential of interorganizational cooperation, edited by Hal Beder (pp.3-22). *New Directions for Continuing Education* 23. San Francisco: Jossey-Bass.

Bergevin, P., D. Morris, and R.M. Smith. 1963. *Adult education procedures: A handbook of tested patterns for effective participation*. New York: Seabury Press.

Bloom, B.S. 1956. *Taxonomy of educational objectives: The classification of educational goals*. New York: Longmans, Green & Co.

Boone, E.J. 1985. *Developing programs in adult education*. Englewood Cliffs, N.J.: Prentice-Hall.

Boshier, R. 1973. Educational participation and dropout: A theoretical model. *Adult Education* 23 (4): 255-282.

Boyle, P.G. 1981. *Planning better programs*. New York: McGraw.

Cervero, R.M. 1984. Collaboration in university continuing professional education. In Realizing the potential of interorganizational cooperation, edited by Hal Beder (pp.23-38). *New Directions for Continuing Education* 23. San Francisco: Jossey-Bass.

———, and A.L. Wilson. 1994. *Planning responsibly for adult education: A guide to negotiating power and interests*. San Francisco: Jossey-Bass.

Continuing Education Instructor Development. 1980. Vancouver, B.C.: Centre for Continuing Education, The University of British Columbia Press.

Cooke, R.A. 1990. *Ethics in business: A perspective*. Institute for Business Ethics, De Paul University. South Carolina: Arthur Anderson & Co.

Cross, P.K. 1981. *Adults as learners*. San Francisco: Jossey-Bass.

Darkenwald, G.G., and S.B. Merriam. 1982. *Adult education: Foundations of practice*. New York: Harper and Row.

Davidson, H.S. 1995. Making needs: Towards a historical sociology of needs in adult and continuing education. *Adult Education Quarterly* 45 (4): 183-196.

Devlin, L.E. 1994. *Program planning in adult education*. Victoria, B.C.: The University of Victoria, Division of University Extension and the Faculty of Education.

Dignan, M.B., and P.A. Carr. 1992. *Program planning for health education and promotion*. 2d ed. Philadelphia: Lea & Febiger.

Elbaz, F. 1983. *Teacher thinking: A study of practical knowledge*. London: Croom Helm.

Freire, P. 1970. *Pedagogy of the oppressed*. New York: The Seabury Press.

French Bell, D. 1978. Assessing educational needs: Advantages and disadvantages of eighteen techniques. *Nurse Educator* 3: 15-21.

Gardner, D.E. 1977. Five evaluative frameworks: Implications for decision making in higher education. *Journal of Higher Education* XLVIII 5: 571-592.

H:\mpcp\programs\mdw\reports\program planning in adult education.doc

Henneman, E.A., J.L. Lee, and J.I. Cohen. 1995. Collaboration: A concept analysis. *Journal of Advanced Nursing* 21: 103-109.

Hiebert, M.B., and W.N. Smallwood. 1987. Now for a completely different look at needs analysis: Discover the pragmatic alternatives to traditional methods. *Training and Development Journal*: 75-79.

Houle, C.O. 1972. *The design of education*. San Francisco: Jossey-Bass.

Ishler, R.E., and M.F. Ishler. 1980. Developing desirable teaching behaviors. In *New directions for teaching and learning: Improving teaching styles* 1, edited by Kenneth E. Eble and John Noonan (pp.69-80). San Francisco: Jossey-Bass.

Kidd, J.R. 1973. *How adults learn*. Chicago: Follett.

Knowles, M.S. 1980. *The modern practice of adult education: From pedagogy to andragogy*. Chicago: Follett.

Knox, A.B. 1986. *Helping adults learn: A guide to planning, implementing, and conducting programs*. San Francisco: Jossey-Bass.

———. ed. 1980. Teaching adults effectively. *New Directions for Continuing Education* 6. San Francisco: Jossey-Bass.

Kolb, D.A., I.M. Rubin, and J.M. McIntyre. 1971. *Organizational psychology: An experiential approach.* Englewood Cliffs, N.J.: Prentice Hall.

Kotler, P., and K. Fox. 1985. *Strategic marketing for educational institutions.* Englewood Cliffs, N.J.: Prentice Hall.

Kowalski, T. 1988. *The organization of planning of adult education.* Albany, N.Y.: State University of New York Press.

Lauffer, A. 1977. *The practice of continuing education in the human services.* New York: McGraw-Hill.

――. 1978. *Doing continuing education and staff development.* New York: McGraw-Hill.

Monette, M.L. 1979. Needs assessment: A critique of philosophical assumptions. *Adult Education* 29 (2): 83-95.

――. 1977. The concept of educational need: An analysis of selected literature. *Adult Education* 27 (2): 116-127.

Percival, A. 1993. *Practising theory: A guide to becoming an effective adult education programmer.* Saskatoon, Sask.: Extension Division, University of Saskatchewan.

Pennington, F., and J. Green. 1976. Comparative analysis of program development processes in six professions. *Adult Education* 27 (1): 13-23.

Pratt, D.D. 1998. *Five perspectives on teaching in adult and higher education.* Florida: Krieger Publishing Co.

Program planning guide for health professionals: U.B.C Health science model. 1977. Vancouver, B.C.: Centre for Continuing Education, The University of British Columbia Press.

Renner, P. 1983. *The instructor's survival kit: A handbook for teachers of adults.* Vancouver, B.C.: Training Associates Ltd.

Riggs, J.K. 1989. Determining an effective market mix. In *Handbook of marketing for continuing education*, edited by R.G. Simerly (pp.125-137). San Francisco: Jossey-Bass.

Schlossberg, N.K. 1989. Marginality and mattering: Key issues in building community. *New Directions for Student Services* 48: 5-15.

Schon, D. 1983. *The reflective practitioner: How professionals think in action.* New York: Basic Books.

Schroeder, W.L. 1970. Adult education defined and described. *In Handbook of adult education*, edited by R.M. Smith, G.F. Aker, and J.R. Kidd (pp.25-43). New York: Macmillan.

Scissons, E. 1985. Needs assessment in adult education. *Adult Education Quarterly* 35 (2): 106-108.

Sloane-Seale, A. 1994. *Program planners' practical knowledge.* Vancouver, B.C.: The University of British Columbia Press.

Sork, T.J. 1986. *Yellow brick road or great dismal swamp: Pathways to objectives in program planning.* Proceedings of the twenty-seventh annual Adult Education Research Conference (pp.261-266). New York: Syracuse University.

――. 1991. Tools for planning better programs. *New Directions for Adult and Continuing Education* 49, 89-94.

―― and J.H. Buskey. 1986. A descriptive and evaluative analysis of program planning literature, 1950-1983. *Adult Education Quarterly* 36 (2): 86-96.

Tapper, M. 1977. Teaching methods & techniques for staff development. *The Journal of Continuing Education in Nursing* 8 (3): 72-74.

Tyler, R. 1949. *Basic principles of curriculum and instruction.* Chicago: The University of Chicago Press.

Verner, C., and A. Booth. 1964. *Adult education.* New York: The Centre for Applied Research in Education.

8

University Continuing Education: Traditions and Transitions

Anne Percival

Without the stories of university continuing education, the history of adult education in Canada would be far less inspirational. To illustrate, one need only look as far as the Antigonish Movement (1920s-1950s) and the National Farm Radio Forum (1940s-1960s), two of Canada's most celebrated adult education projects. Both projects were rooted in efforts to promote social change by helping Canadians deal with conditions of economic depression, immigration and geography. In the case of Antigonish, St. Francis Xavier University was the backbone of the project (Lotz and Welton 1987); in Farm Forum, universities played secondary, supportive roles (Faris 1975). These ventures earned international recognition and served as models for community education in Canada and around the world (Brookfield 1983; Lovett, Clarke, and Kilmurray 1983).

More recently, growth in the number of adult education providers and changes in the economics of universities have altered the role and, some would argue, lessened the impact of university continuing education (UCE). That change has occurred is unquestioned; what is less clear, and the subject of considerable debate in the literature, is what these changes mean for the practice of adult education and for adult learners in this country. This chapter examines the features of UCE in Canada from several interrelated perspectives: terms and functions, institutional context, programs, organization, staffing and finance. The chapter ends with the consideration of key challenges and opportunities facing UCE as it strives to remain an influential force for adult education in Canada.

Discussions of university continuing education typically begin with cautions about the limits of generalization. The history of this area of practice, like that of adult education generally, is not well documented (Selman 1994). Incomplete records and selective description create pictures of the collective enterprise in its early years that warrant careful interpretation. Even now, diverse organizational arrangements and program types make generalization problematic. Not only are comparisons between UCE units difficult, but attempts to understand the scope and character of practice are confounded by its ubiquitous nature. In many universities, academic units–other than the unit specifically designated to provide programs for adults–retain varying degrees of administrative and programming responsibility for continuing education (Potter and Morris 1996). The extent of this activity varies by institution but, as it tends to be underreported, its real magnitude is unknown.

Terms and Functions

For newcomers to the field, adult education can present a confusing maze of terms and ideologies, purposes and providers. This confusion is as apparent within the practice of UCE as it is within the broader field of adult education. Terms associated with UCE abound–extension, continuing education, credit and non-credit, certificate and diploma, formal and non-formal education, cost recovery and so on–and the meanings associated with these terms vary from one institution to another. Two designations commonly used to describe this area of practice, and that help to illuminate its underlying rationale, are *extension education* and *continuing education.*

Extension education is grounded in the value of extending the traditional knowledge and resources of the university to those who are not part of the traditional university audience. The term was first applied to early examples of British university-based adult education. The earliest appears to have started at Cambridge University in 1873, when a group of professors began delivering lectures in classical studies off campus (Hatfield 1989). The Cambridge model was imported to North America in the late 1880s, but neither its classical content nor its traditional format was well suited to the requirements of nation building. A few Canadian universities became involved in extension at this time, notably the University of Toronto and Queen's University (Blyth 1976). Queen's University, in fact, lays claim to having the oldest department of extension in North America based on a founding date of 1889 (Baker 1993). However, it was not until the University of Wisconsin's model of extension hit a responsive chord in the early 1900s that universities across Canada began creating extension departments (Kidd 1956). The Wisconsin model, built on a philosophy of service to the state, married the concept of extending the resources of the university to non-traditional audiences to the imperative of meeting community needs and gave birth to a new form of university-based adult education.

By 1935, Kidd notes that there were nine university extension units in Canada. This number had increased to twenty-two by 1956. In 1993, forty-four member units responded to a survey conducted by the Canadian Association for University Continuing Education (CAUCE), an organization representing largely English-language universities. When the francophone institutions represented by the l'Association Canadienne d'education des adults (ACDUELF) were included, Morris and Potter (1996) observed that "almost every university in Canada could report some form of activity in extension and continuing education" (p.ix).

The concept of extension remains central to the mission of UCE, but the term itself, once closely linked to agricultural education, is less popular. By the 1950s, rapid growth in disciplinary knowledge had generated a new awareness of the need for professional upgrading and ongoing education. The term *continuing education*, with its implication that learners are building on or carrying on their education, had an up-to-date, modern appeal to many extension workers (Baker 1993). Moreover, as a descriptor, continuing education was less restrictive and could accommodate a programming direction that departed from the extension model. Whereas conventional extension relies on the university's instructional resources to meet external community needs, the continuing education model, in some institutions, has also come to include non-degree and non-credit instruction on topics outside the interests or expertise of university academics.

In the 1950s, continuing education began appearing in the titles of university extension units. Today, continuing education, and variations such as continuing studies, remain the most popular unit descriptors (for example, the University of Manitoba's Continuing Education Division; University of Toronto's School of Continuing Studies); however, a minority of institutions continue to use the term extension (for example, University of Saskatchewan's Extension Division; St. Francis Xavier's Extension Department) (CAUCE 1998). Although continuing education is often used as a synonym for adult education, a term popularized in the 1920s (Hart 1927), by 1985, the term *adult* was no longer used in the title of any UCE unit in the country (Brooke and Morris 1987).

For many UCE practitioners, the terms *extension* and *continuing education* retain their historical connotations, but it would be a mistake to infer differences in institutional philosophy or programming direction on the basis of unit titles alone. Today, for example, continuing professional education is as much within the purview of units labelled extension as those labelled continuing education. Similarly, programming directions that permit or necessitate the recruitment of community-based instructors are found in extension units, and continuing education units typically offer programs that fit the extension model.

Institutional Context

The importance of context to practice is a dominant theme in the adult education literature (see, for example, Brockett 1991; Cervero 1989; Cervero and Wilson 1994; Kowalski 1988). UCE, as with other areas of adult education practice, reflects the influence of newly emerging communication and information technologies, the ascendance of individualism as a cultural value, and globalization and the growth of mass society. However, it is the mission of the modern university and its response to shifting social, political and economic conditions that have most directly influenced the course of UCE. This section considers the influence of the university context on the scope and nature of UCE practice by examining the institution's mission, core functions and values and its reaction to continuing education in the face of ever-increasing resource constraints.

According to Selman and Dampier (1991), "many of the most outstanding projects in Canadian adult education were distinctively Canadian in origin and character" (p.36). Nonetheless, it is also the case that UCE in Canada owes much to American influences. The rationale for UCE, as exemplified by the University of Wisconsin's philosophy of extension, exists in the link between extension education and the university's public service goals. The provision of learning opportunities to individuals who might not otherwise participate in university programs publicly demonstrates the university's civic responsibility and its commitment to serving community interests.

This link between extension and the public service mission of the university created a programming environment open to addressing a multiplicity of educational needs and laid the groundwork for the broad programming mandate that came to characterize UCE across North America. Self-development, vocational preparation, citizenship education, skills training, degree study, continuing professional education and community education were all—and many remain–important program areas (Baker 1993; Campbell 1977; Marcus 1989). Kulich (1991) observed that, even in the face of changing economic circumstances and shifting programming priorities, Canadian universities have continued to distinguish themselves in their broad provision of programs when compared to their European and British counterparts.

Current descriptions of the purpose of university extension and continuing education, as illustrated by Thompson and Lamble (2000), continue to reflect this broad mandate:

> The knowledge development process–from creation and integration to dissemination and practical application–has been extended to a broad range of personal, professional, and social issues, problems, and concerns in the community at large, such as in personal, community, organizational, economic, social, cultural development and technology transfer (p.53).

Despite this seemingly important institutional purpose and widespread recognition of the need for lifelong education, the university community remains ambivalent about the role of continuing education. This is largely due to the common perception that continuing education's contribution falls under the university's service function, a set of duties that academics tend to regard as subordinate to the primary functions of teaching and research. When, as often happens, terms such as continuing education, public relations, public service, service, and community service are used interchangeably, the effect is confusion about, and devaluation of, continuing education's role within the institution (Thompson and Lamble 2000).

An alternate view sees public service as less a component of the service function than an overriding principle or goal that guides teaching and research activity (Mawby 1987). This position, as elaborated by Thompson and Lamble (2000), holds that "the fundamental characteristic of university extension is its focus on the needs of the external community and a commitment to utilize institutional resources and expertise to respond appropriately to those needs" (p.72). In responding to community-based needs, continuing education gives rise to a third category of teaching along with traditional undergraduate and graduate teaching. Continuing education teaching includes certificate, diploma and non-credit courses and workshops, as well as degree credit courses offered off campus or by distance education. Similarly, continuing education research, which has an external focus, creates a class of research that is distinct from traditional university research. Continuing education research includes program evaluation, applied research, consulting and contract research. Service, from this perspective, is also understood in terms of whether the focus is internal (for example, university service including membership on committees within the institution) or external (for example, service to academic or professional organizations and service to individuals or community organizations) (Thompson and Lamble 2000).

When university continuing education is understood in terms of the mission of the university and its principal scholarship activities, its real value to the university becomes evident. Drawing on institutional resources and expertise to respond to community needs, continuing education does more than address a key institutional mission. By linking the university and the community, continuing education also creates essential opportunities for institutional adaptation, renewal and transformation.

The influence of institutional values and priorities on practice is also evidenced by UCE's endorsement of the movement to professionalize adult education. Prior to the 1950s, university extension staff were actively involved in the Canadian Association for Adult Education (CAAE), an organization devoted to citizenship and community education, but, in the 1950s, interest in a university organization and in adult education as a professional practice grew. The predecessor to CAUCE, known as the Canadian Association of Directors of Extension and Summer School (CADESS), was formed in 1954. In the 1950s and 1960s, provincial adult education associations were founded, often with the support and involvement of university continuing educators (see, for example, Starosilec 1997). In 1957, the first degree program in adult education was offered at the University of British Columbia. In 1959, Kidd published *How Adults Learn*. In recapping the decade, Baker (1993) concluded that "in general, adult education 'took off' as a field of study during the 1950s" (p.42). Within UCE, one consequence of this movement was a shift in programming emphasis away from the social change orientation characteristic of citizenship and community education.

The issue of whether adult education should be viewed as an emerging profession or as a broadly based movement for social change has tended to polarize adult and continuing educators. On the one hand, the majority of practitioners support Houle's (1956) call for established standards of practice, professional training for adult educators and research into adult learning. For university continuing educators, professionalism also promised to lessen institutional marginality and to move continuing education closer to the centre of the university establishment. Baker's (1993) account of CAUCE from the 1950s to the early 1990s suggests that, despite continued ambiguity about the role of continuing education, this strategy has been largely successful.

On the other hand, critics argue that professionalism has institutionalized adult education within the formally established system of schooling. The visibility of non-formal adult education, the field's traditional core, has decreased, and this has devalued the role of those working outside the formal system (Cunningham 1989, 1992). Critics also maintain that professionalism has turned adult educators into technicians concerned with the "how tos" of needs assessment, program planning, marketing and evaluation (Selman 1985). The emphasis on felt needs, which gives learners responsibility for defining their needs, has led adult educators to abdicate their responsibility to address broader social issues and problems (Mezirow 1984). From this perspective, professionalism has encouraged a free market, felt needs, technical approach to adult and continuing education that has all but displaced its social change, "communitarian" traditions (Selman and Dampier 1991).

Of course, professionalism is not solely responsible for the change in program focus—or for the ideological discord that has developed among continuing educators. As suggested earlier, changes to the format and content of continuing education programs have been reinforced, indeed necessitated, by other events affecting universities. While the 1960s and 1970s were years of growth and innovation for universities and university continuing education in Canada, the 1980s and 1990s ushered in hard economic times. The demand for continuing education has remained high; however, as university budgets have tightened, the view that continuing education programs should be self-supporting has also gained hold. As Baker (1993) reported, recent decades have seen an end to much of the non-credit, informal continuing education for community leaders and non-profit groups and, instead, "commercialization and privatization" (p.55) have become the new trends.

Ideological tensions within UCE have magnified as the focus of programs and services has shifted away from those with low revenue-generating potential (for example, programs with social change objectives that serve audiences with limited resources) to those with higher revenue potential (for example, professional upgrading or career advancement programs that serve audiences with adequate resources to pay for programs). UCE's success in generating revenue has earned reproach from social change advocates who argue that university continuing education has become a business whose purpose "has shifted from that of serving community learning needs to that of bringing in money" (Cruikshank 1994, 77). This criticism is myopic in its implication that only certain programs have social value or promote good social order, and cavalier given a review of current continuing education program calendars. Traditional approaches to social change programming are difficult to sustain financially, but the numerous programs targeted to women and women's issues, aboriginal people, care givers and others with high-accessibility needs demonstrate clearly that social purpose programming is not dead. Still, social change proponents highlight a present-day reality, and a potential risk, for university continuing educators. Ongoing budget cuts and increased reliance on tuition revenues have limited continuing education's ability to address the needs of individuals and community groups with limited resources. Unless guarded against, this trend could jeopardize UCE's broad educational mandate and its potential to contribute to the university's mission.

Programs

Campbell (1984) categorized university-based continuing education programs into five major segments: part-time courses for university credit, professional and paraprofessional studies, liberal and general studies, community development and community services. The typology reflects continuing education's diverse mandate and its commitment to the personal, economic, vocational and social needs of its adult constituency; however, as Campbell noted, "the reality is that university continuing education provision is biased towards the development of marketable skills and the attainment of certification" (p.44).

Supporting Campbell's contention, the usual approach to classifying continuing education courses and programs is in terms of whether or not they are credit bearing. For example, two major studies of continuing education policies and practices in Canada have defined a course as degree credit if the course and/or program is awarded academic credit towards a degree, diploma or certificate; they have defined a course as non-degree if no such credit is issued (Brook and Morris 1987; Morris and Potter 1996). Another common distinction is between credit (i.e., a course awarded credit towards a degree only) and non-credit (i.e., all other courses) (Campbell 1984). Yet another common convention, and the one used here, distinguishes between degree credit, where a course is taken for credit towards a degree, non-degree credit, where a course is taken for credit towards a certificate or diploma, and non-credit, where no credit is issued towards a credential awarded by the institution. This last usage differentiates between a course taken for credit towards any credential (i.e., degree, diploma or certificate) and a non-credit course. Across universities, continuing education units have varying responsibilities for these three types of programs; some offer all three, whereas others offer only one or two of these program types.

Part-time degree credit study, traditionally a core feature of university-based adult education, expanded significantly during the 1960s and 1970s (Campbell 1984). In many institutions, increasing numbers of part-time learners were simply absorbed into existing organizational arrangements; however, at York University and the University of Toronto, separate colleges were established to cater to part-time degree students (Selman 1994). By the early 1980s, Deveraux (1984) noted that almost one-half of all courses offered by university continuing education units consisted of academic instruction. The resources required to serve this population strained university budgets and led some institutions to conclude that non-credit, general interest programming should be left to other providers. At the same time, as suggested earlier, the notion that the non-credit component of continuing education should be financially self-supporting gained strength across the country (Baker 1993).

Certificates and diplomas, two other mainstays of UCE credit programming, also provide those who complete program requirements with a credential—a testament to learning in a specific, almost exclusively job-related sphere of knowledge or practice. Beyond this there is little agreement, in either the literature or in university practice, about how these program types are to be defined (Holt and Lopos 1991; Waalen and Wilson 1991). Major differences exist in the criteria and practices associated with certificates and diplomas. There are also differences in jurisdictional control. In 1990, Waalen and Wilson found that less than 20 percent of certificates were controlled by continuing education units. Most were controlled by academic departments, as is the case with degrees, or by professional associations and other external organizations. University continuing education units, on the other hand, managed approximately two-thirds of these programs.

While certificate programs in particular have become an important component of university-based continuing education—in 1990, over six hundred certificates were offered by forty-three Canadian universities—it is also important to note that this format is utilized more in some institutions than in others. In 1990, less than 20 percent of universities offered over 50 percent of the certificates. The average number of certificates offered by an institution was twelve; the actual number ranged from zero to eighty-one (Waalen and Wilson 1990).

Non-credit programs are characterized by a wide array of formats including courses, workshops, seminars, conferences, lecture series and symposia. They tend to address either job-related needs or needs for personal development. Non-credit offerings in liberal studies were "the initial thrust, the 'raison d'être' of adult education in Canada" (Campbell 1984, 53); however, by 1993, less than 25 percent (N=43) of UCE units reported offering non-credit liberal studies courses. The most common category of non-credit programs was "business and professional, with language programs, computers, personal development, and writing and communication as frequently used program categories as well" (Morris and Potter 1996, 61).

The variety of formats used in continuing education programming attempt to accommodate the needs of part-time learners. Programs may be offered in summer school, during the evenings or on weekends, off campus and at the workplace. Distance education, once limited to correspondence courses, has become an increasingly sophisticated multimedia delivery mode. With the advent of audio-teleconferencing in the 1960s, the first in a series of new interactive telecommunications technologies, distance education grew rapidly, particularly for the delivery of degree credit programs. *The Canadian University Distance Education Directory 1998-1999,* an annual publication of CAUCE, lists several hundred degree credit, non-degree credit and non-credit courses from forty-six Canadian universities in over forty subject categories (McFarlane 1998). Included are some initial forays into computer conferencing and on-line Internet course delivery, technologies that herald a new generation of distance education and untold future learning opportunities for adult learners. With today's technology, Garrison's (1989) decade-old prediction is becoming reality: "In the near future, distance learners not only will be able to study where and when they like, but they will be able to choose how they wish to learn and to have all the guidance and support they require or request, thereby acquiring maximum control of the educational transaction" (p.225).

Organization and Staffing

The debate about how best to organize continuing education within the university is long standing and, as reflected in the variations in structural arrangements that characterize continuing education, resolutions tend to be institutionally specific. The fundamental issue centres on whether a centralized or a decentralized organizational design best facilitates academic and administrative decision making in continuing education. In practical terms, discussions focus on the relationship between the continuing education unit and other faculties and departments and on their roles in determining program needs and design, staffing, financing and a myriad of other academic and operational matters. As an ideal type, a centralized approach gives the continuing education unit full responsibility for all academic and administrative decisions related to the continuing education activities of the institution; a fully decentralized model does not maintain a designated continuing education unit but locates the responsibility for continuing education within existing faculties and departments. In reality, most institutions fall somewhere along the continuum separating these two extremes.

Morris and Potter (1996) found that, based on forty-two responses, 76 percent of institutions reported utilizing a centralized approach for administrative functions of continuing education, while 62 percent reported that academic responsibility for continuing education was decentralized. Breaking these responses down further, 50 percent of institutions reported that academic responsibility was decentralized, whereas administrative responsibility was centralized. The next most common organizational design, reported by 26 percent of institutions, had both academic and administrative responsibility for continuing education centralized. These data, which provide only rough outlines of UCE organization and management, impart some sense of the difficulties involved in drawing meaningful institutional comparisons. When structural differences are combined with variations in the size and scope of programming portfolios, the differences between units are further complicated.

Most deans and directors of continuing education units hold academic appointments in their respective institutions. On the other hand, only a minority of institutions extend academic appointments to professional programming staff, the largest professional staff component in UCE, or to professional instructional staff (Morris and Potter 1996).

The educational backgrounds of UCE management and professional staff, whether or not they hold academic appointments, vary more than is the norm for traditional faculties. This stems from the fact that, although the emphasis is on hiring programming staff with advanced degrees, a graduate degree in adult education is not a requirement for employment in university continuing education.

The issue of whether hiring preference for programming positions should be given to candidates with adult education training or, alternatively, to those with subject matter expertise has been much debated. Still, the tendency remains to hire subject matter specialists (for example, someone with a nursing background is hired to develop continuing professional education programs for nurses). Ideal candidates would have both adult education and subject matter expertise; however, when applicants with both qualifications cannot be found, an adult education background is likely to be seen as desirable but not essential. The initial ease with which subject matter specialists can gain entrance into relevant community groups and, in today's lexicon, take off running, is seen as a greater advantage than the disadvantage of having to learn program planning on the job. This hiring practice might seem ironic given the movement to professionalize adult education. However, there are other pragmatic considerations that support the hiring of subject matter specialists. First, program planning practice is acknowledged to be highly context specific, raising questions about the efficacy of formal training. Second, whereas opportunities to acquire specific content expertise might not be readily available, continuing education staff have ready access to professional training opportunities in adult education (for example, the Certificate Program in Adult and Continuing Education by Distance Education, offered by a consortium of universities in western Canada). Whatever the reasons for this hiring practice, the result is typically a UCE staff complement with a diverse mix of educational orientations and experiences—something of a mixed blessing since diversity can be a source of potential program enrichment but, at the same time, a hindrance to the development of a shared professional identity.

Finances

The criticism that university continuing education has become a business and, in the process, has lost its social conscience, points to serious contentions surrounding the financing of UCE. As with other dimensions of UCE, however, there is considerable variation in financial operations and expectations across continuing education units.

Revenue for continuing education comes primarily from two sources: (1) tuition fees from degree credit, non-degree credit and/or non-credit courses; and (2) core budgetary allocations from universities. Grants, as well as contracts with external agencies for the provision of continuing education programs and services, are principal sources of funds for a small minority of units (Morris and Potter 1996).

Within UCE units, it is not uncommon for the financial expectations to vary by program type. For example, the expectation may be that non-credit programs will be financed entirely from tuition fees while credit programs (degree and non-degree) will be supported to some level by budgetary allocation. In 1993, 44 percent (N=38) of units surveyed indicated that their credit operations were 100 percent financially self-supporting (i.e., through tuition fees), while 25 percent indicated that this component of their operation was entirely financed by budgetary allocation from their respective institution. By comparison, 47 percent (N=38) of units reported that their non-credit operations were fully self-supporting; further, no unit indicated that this component of their operation was fully subsidized by their institution (Morris and Potter 1996). When these data are compared to similar data collected in 1985 (Brooke and Morris 1987), the trend towards decreasing reliance on university allocations and increasing reliance on tuition fees to cover program costs, particularly in non-credit programs, is readily apparent.

Continuing education units have adjusted to continued budgetary pressure and an increasingly competitive provider market, in part by assuming business-like practices. Marketing and budgeting, two key management functions, have become standard program planning functions. Their importance to practice is reflected in current models of planning (see, for example, Caffarella 1994), in many recent practitioner-oriented publications, in the hiring of marketing and financial specialists and in the creation of functional subareas within continuing education units. Marketing and financial topics are popular subjects for CAUCE conference sessions and professional development events targeted to UCE practitioners and adult educators generally.

But what of the idea that university continuing education is a business? The term is frequently associated with UCE, possibly as often by champions of its entrepreneurial spirit as by critics. However, the promotion of business-like approaches to program planning and management does not make UCE a business. UCE's mission is adult education, not commerce; its constituency is the adult learner, not the customer or the consumer; its provision is educational programs, not products. Unfortunately, careless use of language is not without cost. For UCE, danger lies in the erosion of its fundamental educational and social values and, ultimately, in the loss of institutional relevance–except, perhaps, as the university mascot (i.e., the cash cow).

Challenges Facing UCE

For UCE practitioners, change has become the constant. Yet, paradoxically, many of the issues and problems facing UCE have been around for a long time.

The mission of UCE and its role within the institution. The problem of how best to link UCE to the mission of the university has dogged continuing educators for years. That the answer remains illusive can be seen in commonplace perceptions that UCE is a revenue-generating, ancillary service and/or a public relations opportunity. If UCE is to be seen as a core activity of the university, continuing educators must find ways to effectively articulate UCE's educational mission, demonstrate UCE's contribution to the academic functions of the university and evidence the institutional benefits of UCE's external community focus.

Program issues. The question of how best to provide programs (i.e., degree, certificate, diploma, non-credit) is also familiar to seasoned continuing educators; however, the issues have become more complex over time. Demands for credit transferability and recognition of learning, no matter where or how acquired, are forcing continuing educators to re-examine their assumptions about the purposes, criteria and linkages between program types, and to consider such innovations as prior learning assessment (PLA). Calls from community groups and organizations for greater control over curriculum, and for degree credit recognition for negotiated curriculum, signal more changes to come for UCE programming. As the numbers of providers and the options available to learners have increased, these and other issues of program quality have become paramount for continuing educators.

Finances. Given the resources available to universities, the trend towards cost recovery programming in UCE will no doubt continue. Until now, UCE practitioners have responded in ways that have enabled them to maintain a reasonably broad program base. Through grants, contracts, in-kind contributions, allocations, surpluses and other creative financing, accessibility to university-based education continues to be provided to underserved individuals and groups (for example, aboriginal people, women, the unemployed and low-income workers, geographically isolated communities and so on). UCE has also established its credibility in more competitive, job-related program areas by offering high quality credit and non-credit courses and programs. To the greatest extent possible, UCE must remain committed to maintaining balance in its program portfolio. If UCE loses its social conscience, its stature within the university and the field of adult education will rightfully diminish.

Teaching and technology. New technologies create imperatives for adult learning and, as demonstrated by the success of many UCE units in offering micro-computer courses, programming possibilities for continuing education. Technology also promises to enhance design and delivery options for flexible learning at a distance. But, along with opportunities, technological innovation brings uncertainty and, due to high initial program development costs and competition from a host of new providers, substantial risk. University continuing educators are struggling with questions about where distance learning technology, in particular, is heading, what opportunities exist for UCE and how continuing educators and their external partners can work together to share expertise and risk.

These are not recent challenges, but in a world where change is as predictable as death and taxes, they represent keys to the future of UCE. If continuing educators can effectively manage these challenges, UCE will remain an important force for change in Canada in the new century. If not, UCE may well become little more than a colourful footnote in the history of adult education in this country.

References

Baker, H.R. 1993. A history of CAUCE: Its formation, development and role. *Canadian Journal of University Continuing Education* 19 (2): 37-65.

Blyth, J.A. 1976. *A foundling at varsity.* Toronto: School of Continuing Studies, University of Toronto.

Brockett, R.G., ed. 1991. Professional development for educators of adults. *New Directions for Adult and Continuing Education* 51. San Francisco: Jossey-Bass.

Brooke, W.M., and J.F. Morris. 1987. *Continuing education in Canadian universities: A summary report of policies and practices–1985.* Ottawa: Canadian Association for University Continuing Education.

Brookfield, S.D. 1983. *Adult learners, adult education and the community.* Milton Keynes: Open University Press.

Caffarella, R.S. 1994. *Planning programs for adult learners: A practical guide for educators, trainers and staff developers.* San Francisco: Jossey-Bass.

Campbell, D. (1984). *The new majority: Adult learners in the university.* Edmonton: The University of Alberta Press.

Canadian Association for University Continuing Education. 1998. *Handbook 1998.* Ottawa: Author.

Cervero, R.M. 1989. Becoming more effective in everyday practice. In Fulfilling the promise of adult and continuing education, edited by B.A. Quigley (pp.107-114). *New Directions for Continuing Education* 44. San Francisco: Jossey-Bass.

Cervero, R.M. and A.L. Wilson. 1994. *Planning responsibly for adult education: A guide to negotiating power and interests.* San Francisco: Jossey-Bass.

Cruikshank, J. 1994. Cost-recovery: The current challenge. In *University continuing education in Canada: Current challenges and future opportunities,* edited by M. Brooke and M. Waldron (pp.74-83). Toronto: Thompson Educational Publishing.

Cunningham, P.M. 1989. Making a more significant impact on society. In Fulfilling the promise of adult and continuing education, edited by B.A. Quigley (pp.33-46). *New Directions for Continuing Education* 44. San Francisco: Jossey-Bass.

Cunningham, P.M. 1992. University continuing educators should be social activists. *Canadian Journal of University Continuing Education* 18 (2): 9-17.

Deveraux, M.S. 1984. *One in every five: A survey of adult education in Canada.* Ottawa: Statistics Canada and Department of the Secretary of State.

Faris, R. 1975. *The passionate educators.* Toronto: Peter Martin.

Garrison, D.R. 1989. Distance education. In *Handbook of adult and continuing education,* edited by S.B. Merriam and P.M. Cunningham (pp.221-231). San Francisco: Jossey-Bass.

Hatfield, T. M. (1989). Four-year colleges and universities. In *Handbook of adult and continuing education,* edited by S.B. Merriam and P.M. Cunningham (pp.303-315). San Francisco: Jossey-Bass.

Hart, J.K. 1927. *Adult education.* New York: Crowell.

Holt, M. E., and G.L. Lopos, eds. 1991. Perspectives on educational certificate programs. *New Directions for Adult and Continuing Education* 52. San Francisco: Jossey-Bass.

Houle, C.O. 1956. Professional education for educators of adults. *Adult Education* 6 (3): 131-141.

Kidd, J.R. 1956. *Adult education in the Canadian university.* Toronto: Canadian Association for Adult Education.

———. 1959. *How adults learn.* New York: Association Press.

Kowalski, T.J. 1988. *The organization and planning of adult education.* Albany, N.Y.: State University of New York Press.

Kulich, J. 1991. Current trends and priorities in Canadian adult education. *International Journal of Lifelong Education* 10 (2): 93-106.

Lotz, J., and M.R. Welton. 1987. "Knowledge for the people": The origins and development of the Antigonish movement. In *Knowledge for the people: The struggle for adult learning in English-speaking Canada, 1828-1973,* edited by M.R. Welton (pp.97-111). Toronto: OISE Press.

Lovett, T., C. Clarke, and A. Kilmurray. 1983. *Adult education and community action: Adult education and popular social movements.* London: Croom Helm.

Marcus, A.L. 1989. *Contextual variables associated with continuing education programs based in private research universities.* Unpublished doctoral dissertation, Teachers College, Columbia University.

Mawby, R.G. 1987. "Public Service." In *The Green Sheet,* edited by G.F. Hudgins. Washington, V.C.: National Association of State Universities and Land Grant Colleges.

McFarlane, C., ed. 1998. *Canadian university distance education directory 1998-1999.* Ottawa: Canadian Association for University Continuing Education.

Mezirow, J. 1984. Review of "Principles of good practice in continuing education." *Lifelong Learning: An Omnibus of Practice and Research* 8 (3): 27-28.

Morris, J.F., and J.P. Potter. 1996. *Continuing education policies and practices in Canadian universities: An overview.* Ottawa: Canadian Association for University Continuing Education.

Selman, G. 1985. The adult educator: Change agent or program technician. *Canadian Journal of University Continuing Education* 11: 77-86.

———. 1994. Continuing education and the Canadian mosaic. In *University continuing education in Canada: Current challenges and future opportunities,* edited by M. Brooke and M. Waldron (pp.4-18). Toronto: Thompson Educational Publishing.

Selman, G., and P. Dampier. 1991. *The foundations of adult education in Canada.* Toronto: Thompson Educational Publishing.

Starosilec, S. 1997. Continuing education at the University of Manitoba: Responding to change. In *Adult education in Manitoba: Historical aspects,* edited by D.H. Poonwassie and A. Poonwassie (pp.157-174). Mississauga: Canadian Educators' Press.

Thompson, G., and W. Lamble. 2000. Reconceptualizing university extension and public service. *Canadian Journal of University Continuing Education* 26 (1): 51-76.

Waalen, J., and L. Wilson 1991. *Policies and practices in certificate and diploma education in Canadian universities: Final report.* Toronto: Ryerson Polytechnical Institute.

9

Facilitating Adult Education: A Practitioner's Perspective

Anne Poonwassie

In *The Craft of Teaching Adults*, Draper (1993) asks: "Practitioners we are, but what is our craft?" (p.256). Many of those who teach adults have probably pondered that question; I know I have. It seems quite overwhelming at first to reflect on what it is that we do, what guides our practice, and–the most challenging part–how to explain all that when put on the spot. About three years ago, I was faced with that challenge as I prepared to instruct the Facilitating Adult Education course for the Certificate in Adult and Continuing Education (CASE) program at the University of Manitoba. This task required not only condensing the literature and my practical experience into a coherent instructional plan, but also "doing as I preached." I realized then that the one thing more challenging in adult education than teaching is teaching *about* teaching.

Teachers of adults are expected to be effective in the following general areas: (a) preparation for instruction, (b) instruction and (c) evaluation. This chapter will focus specifically on some of the key concepts and aspects of instruction of adults, often referred to as facilitation. At first, writing about facilitation may seem somewhat simpler than the actual face-to-face interaction in the classroom, but of course it is not; reading about something is not as effective as experiencing it. In order to make the information in this chapter more meaningful, every attempt will be made to bridge the theory with practical aspects and applications in the field.

First, the chapter will explore some general principles of effective facilitation of adult education in order to set the broader context. Then it will address general teaching approaches and their development, followed by an examination of the main roles, skills and characteristics of teachers of adults. The chapter will also introduce some of the key concepts and applications in facilitating adult education: critical thinking, self-directed learning and motivation. Finally, the chapter will briefly reflect on ethical issues in facilitation.

As in most literature, the terms *teaching, facilitation* and *instruction* are used interchangeably and in the context of adult education throughout this chapter. Adults involved in educational activities will be referred to as learners, students and participants.

Principles of Effective Facilitation

The aims often associated with adult education are those of empowerment, self-actualization and, ultimately, social change. In order to achieve these aims, facilitation must be based on mutual respect and collaborative efforts (Brookfield 1986; Brundage and MacKeracher 1980; Cross 1981; Draper 1993; Knowles 1980; Percival 1993; Renner 1994). The process of facilitating adult education involves discussion and critical reflection of experiences, collective questioning, interpretation and exploration while the objectives, methods and evaluation criteria are continually negotiated. Brookfield (1986) refined this process into six principles of effective practice:

1. Facilitators must recognize that adults participate in learning on a voluntary basis; the decision may be prompted by external circumstances, such as loss of job, change in family situation, etc., but it is ultimately theirs. Learners can easily withdraw their participation, but facilitators should avoid coercion, bullying, or intimidation; instead, they should utilize participatory and collaborative learning techniques and design activities relevant to the participants' experiences and learning needs.

2. Effective practice is characterized by mutual respect of participants' self worth. Any behaviours or statements that embarrass, belittle, or otherwise abuse others should be avoided. Although challenges and criticisms are important components of facilitation, they must be presented in a helpful and respectful manner which does not take away from the participant's dignity or self-esteem.

3. Facilitation is based on the collaborative process. Facilitators and learners should work together in identifying learning needs, setting objectives, developing curriculum, identifying methodologies, and evaluating progress; exploration, discussion, and renegotiation of these aspects should be an on-going and integral part of the group process.

4. Praxis is key to effective facilitation. Exploration, action, and reflection placed in the context of the participants' past, present, and future experiences help them interpret ideas and/or facilitate changes in their consciousness, attitudes, or beliefs.

5. Facilitation aims to encourage critical reflection. An effective facilitator will provide opportunities for learners to understand that their values, beliefs, behaviours and ideologies are culturally constructed and that alternative structures and practices may exist.

6. Facilitation strives towards the development of nurturing, self-directed, and empowered adults who will have the ability to continually re-evaluate, renegotiate and reinvent their personal relationship, work situations, and social structures (pp.9-20).

Brookfield emphasizes that the above principles apply to the aspects of facilitation that support teaching-learning encounters, including teaching-learning transactions, curriculum development and planning and selection of instructional methods; they do not apply to marketing, budgeting or administration of adult education. The spirit of these principles will re-surface in each section of this chapter, as the key concepts and their practical applications are discussed.

The complexity of the principles of effective practice implies a unique set of circumstances that present a formidable challenge to facilitators of adult education. As Renner (1994) points out,

> not unlike myself, participants bring unique attitudes, interests, and abilities; each comes for a different reason, and with separate expectations. As a facilitator, my task was to devise learning opportunities that would enable individuals to meet their specific learning needs (p.2).

How do facilitators fulfil such a demanding and complex mandate?

General Approaches and Styles

Teachers with formal credentials have not always been effective in the classroom, while many non-credentialed teachers do an excellent job (Apps 1991). This provides the basis for a convincing argument that neither formal qualifications nor their absence determine the effectiveness of a teacher, begging the question–what does?

The instructional or facilitation process involves many different types of skills, certain personal traits and characteristics and a well-grounded philosophy about learning and teaching adults. All of these factors contribute to facilitators' teaching styles and to how well they relate to the learners. Apps (1991) provides us with interesting metaphors that describe a variety of approaches:

- *Lamplighters*. They attempt to illuminate the minds of their learners.

- *Gardeners*. Their goal is to cultivate the mind by nourishing, enhancing the climate, removing the weeds and other impediments, and then standing back and allowing the growth to occur.

- *Muscle Builders*. They exercise and strengthen flabby minds so learners can face the heavyweight learning tasks of the future.

- *Bucket Fillers*. They pour information into empty containers with the assumption that a filled bucket is a good bucket. In other words, a head filled with information makes an educated person.

- *Challengers*. They question learners' assumptions, helping them see subject matter in fresh ways and develop critical thinking.

- *Travel Guides*. They assist people along the path of learning.

- *Factory Supervisors*. They supervise the learning process, making sure that sufficient inputs are present and that the outputs are consistent with the inputs.

- *Artists*. For them teaching has no prescription and the ends are not clear at the beginning of the process. The entire activity is an aesthetic experience.

- *Applied Scientists*. They apply research findings to teaching problems and see scientific research as the basis for teaching.

- *Craftspeople*. They use various teaching skills and are able to analyze teaching situations, apply scientific findings when applicable, and incorporate an artistic dimension into teaching (pp.23-24).

Apps suggests that "master teachers are challengers, travel guides, gardeners, craftspeople, or some combination of these" (p.25). These approaches are reminiscent of Brookfield's (1986) principles of effective facilitation discussed in the last section of this chapter. Lamplighters, Muscle Builders, Bucket Fillers, Factory Supervisors and Applied Scientists clearly fall short in facilitating and/or creating adequate and appropriate opportunities for self-directed learning, cross-cultural inclusion and critical thinking in the facilitation process. As such, these styles may have a negative impact on the participants' motivation to learn and may compromise ethical practice.

Teaching styles of effective facilitators evolve over time and are greatly influenced by the individual's philosophical orientation. In adult education, effective practice is most closely linked to the humanist philosophy. This approach is focused on encouraging people to explore the depths of their feelings, building self-concept, and valuing human life. The goal is to maximize human potential, building on the innate goodness of the individual, with the support of empathetic teachers who are themselves on a quest of self-discovery—as partners in learning (Draper 1993, 61).

Effective facilitators may not always be fully aware why they do what they do, but at the core of their practice is the belief that people are basically good and that they can grow and change. In adult education, a master teacher's goal is to help facilitate that process.

Roles, Skills and Characteristics of Effective Facilitators

An important aspect of the humanist approach in facilitating adult learning is the belief that adults will take responsibility for their own learning, providing the psychosocial environment is conducive to do so. According to Knowles (1980), effective facilitators create a climate of "mutual trust and respect, mutual helpfulness, freedom of expression, and acceptance of differences" (p.57). They model these values by respecting the participants, their feelings and their ideas and work along with the students "in the spirit of mutual inquiry" (p.57). Instructors who are consistently empathic, genuine, accepting and respectful generally develop a more open and trusting relationship with students and facilitate the opportunity for students to develop more open and trusting relationships with each other; the result is usually a climate of collaboration and mutual exchange in the learning process.

Factors such as comfortable room temperature, appropriate lighting, availability of required materials and equipment and the seating arrangement are all carefully considered by experienced facilitators. A circular seating arrangement—as opposed to rows of desks all facing the facilitator seated in the front of the room—generally enhances the sharing and exchange among all group members, including the facilitator. Seating arranged in a circle, or even a square or a rectangle, implies equality and inclusion of everyone in the group and enhances the motivation to fully participate in the learning experience.

Skilled instructors also consider factors such as the participants' age, previous educational experience, level of skills, preferred learning style, motivation and cultural factors. They continually assess—and attempt to address—learners' needs and interests; however, they are also charged with responsibilities such as analyzing, and often challenging, learners' definitions, assumptions, beliefs and values (Apps 1991; Brookfield 1986; Cross

1981; Knowles 1990; Knox 1986; Renner 1989). They must also be willing to question and critically examine their own beliefs, values and assumptions and to provide opportunities for critical reflection in their classrooms.

Critical Thinking

Brookfield (1986) argues that "the criteria of success regarding good teacher performances relate to techniques of effective group management rather than the prompting of critical awareness on the part of learners" (p.135). He suggests that, in order to create a meaningful learning experience, facilitators must "include activities in which adults are encouraged to consider alternative ways of thinking and living and in which they are prompted to scrutinize critically the extent to which supposedly universal beliefs, values, and behaviours are in fact culturally constructed" (p.143). This process of action and reflection in adult education is often referred to as *praxis* (Friere 1970).

Facilitators who encourage critical reflection recognize and support both positive and negative emotions presented in class by (a) being aware of any nuances in the communication process, (b) constantly scanning for verbal and non-verbal clues, (c) inviting and supporting emotions as part of the learning process, (d) encouraging emotions in a non-intrusive way, (e) being genuine and self-sharing, and (f) being non-judgemental and non-defensive in dealing with emotions as part of the learning process (Menlo 1979). Critical reflection is an experience that is often sparked by emotional events in learners' lives; as a result, emotions are an integral part of the process (Brookfield 1987).

The process of critical thinking is not linear, but it generally consists of a number of components: (a) becoming aware of existing values, assumptions or behaviours and the context within which they exist and influence our lives; (b) exploring alternatives and perhaps challenging the status quo; (c) working through an often emotional transition to a new understanding or perspective; (d) strategizing to integrate the new ideas into our lives; and (e) taking action in some way, sometimes by starting the process all over again (Apps 1991).

Critical thinking needs to be integrated into classroom activities by selecting experiential instructional methods such as group discussions, seminars and consciousness-raising activities. Facilitators can also encourage the process by modelling critical reflection and by their willingness to receive criticism without becoming defensive (Apps 1991; Brookfield 1987; Renner 1994). In challenging participants' values, beliefs and behaviours, facilitators must be prepared to experience resistance, anger and other emotions as part of the learning process and to openly recognize and validate them. Controversial or emotionally charged issues such as racism, gender bias, homophobia and so on must be handled with great care; "the truth must be presented as bearable" in order for the participants to enter into discussions about these issues, consider alternative ways of thinking and shift their views, attitudes or opinions on such topics. In other areas, such as ethics or cross-cultural issues, there may be many truths and each may be equally valid within its particular context. For example, it is important that the facilitator be equally willing to, on one hand, accept that his or her cultural construct is neither the only one nor the "correct" one and, on the other hand, skillfully challenge a racist view expressed by a student.

Clearly, facilitators who successfully promote critical reflection in the classroom are knowledgeable; possess excellent interpersonal and communication skills, including the ability to deal with conflict openly and effectively; are willing to take risks; believe in the resilience of the human spirit; embrace the group process in teaching and learning; advocate for social change; know when to be flexible and spontaneous in order to move beyond the curriculum; continually affirm participants' self-worth in their struggles with challenging issues; and recognize that not all questions lead to definitive answers and that the process of questioning may be equally or more valuable than the outcome. Above all, such facilitators are genuine, non-judgemental and very patient. They have faith in the adult learners' capacity for change, and they love the opportunity to join them in the adventurous, and often precarious, process of discovery. Their students often leave the classroom with a sense of accomplishment beyond the knowledge and the understanding of the curriculum and the attainment of a course grade; they have gained a sense of empowerment and independence that may positively influence many aspects of their lives.

Self-Directed Learning

Teaching students about the possibilities and benefits of learning beyond the classroom has become one of the main goals of education. As Knowles (1975) points out, adult educators' role has changed from that of transmitters of information to facilitators of learning. They are faced with setting aside their secure positions of authority and bringing forward their authentic self, including their strengths and weaknesses. The focus has shifted from implementing their agendas to responding fully to the students' experiences in and out of the classroom. It has become clear that learning takes place anywhere and at any time, far beyond adults' planned and organized educational experiences, and the development of self-directed learning has become a priority and "a prerequisite for living in this new world" (Knowles 1975, 17).

The literature is in agreement about proactive learners: they pursue educational experiences with a sense of purpose, seem to be more motivated, tend to learn more and faster and retain a greater portion of what they have learned (Brookfield 1986; Knowles 1975; Renner 1989; Thomas 1993; Wlodkowski 1999). On the other hand, many students experience a great deal of anxiety and frustration when faced with self-directed learning challenges. Contrary to what some facilitators expect, self-direction is not an instant by-product of adult status in our society. Students may, in fact, be at different stages of readiness for independent learning activities. For example, when a facilitator invites the students to be involved in the planning process for their course, some will embrace and enjoy the opportunity to participate, others will feel that they have been unfairly saddled with what is really the instructor's responsibility, some may consider the exercise to be a complete waste of time, wishing that the instructor had prepared ahead so that they could get on with the "real work," while others conclude that they have complete control over their learning experience and that the instructor is relieved of all responsibility. How do facilitators bring everyone on board and pulling in the same direction?

First, students need to understand the facilitator's reason(s) for implementing self-directed learning activities, and both the challenges and the benefits need to be clearly articulated. It is equally important to attend to the students' concerns about their perceived lack of abilities to work independently. They need to be reassured that they will not be abandoned by the facilitator and/or set up to fail; the facilitator will be available as a resource, coach or mentor throughout the process. To build the participants' confidence and to introduce the concept of self-directed learning to those who remain sceptical, it is often helpful to begin with group activities in which students have the opportunity to lean on and to learn from each other. At times, it may become necessary to meet with some students individually to reassure and encourage them and to normalize the anxiety they may be experiencing. Finally, it is important to be very clear about the scope of the activity, the learning objectives and the evaluation criteria. Students must understand exactly what is expected of them, as well as be encouraged to welcome and value the unexpected as part of the learning process.

Facilitators who implement self-directed learning activities in their classrooms face the difficult challenge of ensuring a relative safety in the learning process without sacrificing their students' full potential for growth and development. Apps (1991) wisely chose the words of poet Guillaume to illustrate the tenacity required of facilitators in helping students pursue their dreams:

> *Come to the edge, he said,*
> *They said: we are afraid.*
> *Come to the edge, he said.*
> *They came,*
> *He pushed them ... and they flew (p.1).*

Perhaps one of the most rewarding experiences that facilitators encounter are the times when their students accept the invitation to spread their wings and fly without the push; maybe in many of those instances, the exciting benefits presented to them by a motivating facilitator outweigh their fears.

Motivation

According to Kroehnert (1995), "motivation is the urge to have a need filled" (p.116). This urge can be based on either negative or positive consequences; for example, students may be motivated to learn because they will receive a failing grade if they do not meet the instructor's expectations, or they may be motivated to learn because they enjoy learning. Congruent with the principles of effective practice of adult education, the literature generally describes motivation as a positive factor in the learning process. Nevertheless, many teachers continue to utilize negative motivation strategies at the peril of their students' self-esteem, perhaps discouraging many of them from entering other learning experiences in the future.

Wlodkowski (1999) points out that "motivation is important not only because it apparently improves learning but also because it mediates learning and is a consequence of learning as well" (p.5). He presents two important assumptions: (1) anything that can be learned can be presented in a motivating manner, and (2) a motivational plan needs to be an integral component of any instructional plan. He suggests that any facilitator can develop or improve these skills.

Motivation is not an outcome of something that facilitators simply put in place at the beginning of an educational experience; rather, it a process that is ongoing throughout its duration and must be well planned, monitored, altered and sustained as the learning journey continues to unfold. Motivating facilitators understand that meeting the needs of their students is the cornerstone of helping to create a motivating experience for adult learners. The challenge involves skilful juggling of the needs of the group as a whole, the needs of individual students and the integrity and the quality of the curriculum. Flexibility, the ability to listen and the ability to read body language, openness and curiosity about feedback, an endless supply of energy, expertise, empathy, enthusiasm, clarity, cultural responsiveness, and an unwavering sense of ethical responsibility are some of the key skills and characteristics of motivating instructors.

When motivational strategies are well integrated into the classroom activities, the learners often perceive motivation as something that happens because of the spontaneous and energetic personality of the facilitator. This is only one side of the coin; the other side of the same coin involves a great deal of serious planning, strategizing and structuring of classroom time in order to create a blueprint for a motivating learning experience. Such a plan often begins with psyching out the students (What do we know about them before they get there?) and checking out and expanding the information base when the class begins (Who are they? What are their expectations?).

Involving students in the ongoing planning and negotiating some of the course content helps them take ownership of their learning experience. At some point, it may become clear that not all of the individual needs will be met, and it is important to be honest about what can realistically be addressed within the scope of the course. Facilitators often collaborate with students in compiling a list of what will be covered, what may be covered if time allows and what will not be covered and why (time constraints, covered in another course, a specialized topic requiring specialized expertise and so on). Motivating facilitators are genuinely excited about all the topics and ideas that their students suggest and encourage and/or assist them in independently pursuing those interests that are beyond the scope of the course.

Process needs, which are also important to the motivation of most learners, are sometimes ignored. These may include a sense of safety and competence in the learning process, as well as social needs or, for example, a need to get a promotion in the workplace. Facilitators often explore these needs by asking the "What brings you here?" question; they recognize that learning experiences occur within the larger context of adults' lives. Students' motivation hinges, to a great extent, on how well the learning experience fits into that context. Effective use of motivational strategies at the beginning of the learning experience results in creating a positive rapport between the students and the facilitator, heightening students' interest and commitment to the content and the learning process and laying out a clear and achievable set of steps for a successful learning venture.

Motivational strategies implemented during the learning experience focus on, first and foremost, ensuring that learners' needs continue to be met as the course unfolds. Ongoing evaluation and assessment are key to successfully maintaining students' motivation throughout their learning experience. Course-end evaluations come much too late in the game. A variety of tools can be used to elicit the information required on an ongoing basis to maintain a motivating atmosphere:

- Utilizing daily or weekly journals (depending on the length of the course) in which students describe what was most helpful, what was least helpful and any suggestions on how the course might be improved;

- Periodically reviewing course topic and/or objectives that have been covered to date and those that remain to be covered, as well as eliciting any other topics of interest suggested for future classes;

- Implementing a mid-course evaluation that provides comprehensive, up-to-date information about what is going well and flags out any areas of concern;

- Being approachable and/or available to individual students to discuss specific activities and/or concerns about the course, eliciting feedback and suggestions;

- Managing facilitation problems effectively as soon as they arise;

- Encouraging students' interaction and participation in learning activities, assessing their interest and involvement in the learning process and addressing any difficulties in a timely manner;

- Monitoring and safeguarding the psychosocial climate of the group as well as the emotional well-being of individual students to ensure that emotions are welcome as part of the learning process and are safely and thoroughly debriefed;

- Creating opportunities for critical reflection by modelling and challenging;

- Creating opportunities for self-directed learning by building in independent learning activities throughout the learning process;

- Checking for readiness as students progress through the curriculum and assisting those who are experiencing difficulties;

- Affirming the students' abilities and achievements throughout the learning experience to help them build confidence and positive self-esteem.

Wlodkowski (1999) provides a comprehensive list of 68 motivational strategies that can be applied from the beginning to the end of a learning experience.

Finally, it is important to note that no facilitator will be successful in creating motivating experiences for all students all of the time. Those who are forced or coerced into attending educational programs or courses—often referred to as "prisoners"—present a particular challenge for a motivating facilitator. It is most helpful, in that instance, to express genuine empathy and validate such participants' anger and resentment rather that trying to talk them out of those feelings: "Yes, I see that you are not here by choice, and I understand why you would be angry about that." It is then worthwhile to challenge resistant or reluctant students to benefit from the opportunity, although they may not have chosen it: "And now that you are here, what might we come up with to make this worthwhile for you in some way?" Most of the time this works, with varying degrees of success.

Other instances where attempts to motivate learners sometimes fail occur in cross-cultural situations where the sociopolitical factors affecting students of different cultures have been ignored or not understood. Students who do not feel included by the facilitator and/or by other students often find course content irrelevant or even offensive and the learning climate and/or process disrespectful. It is unethical and inexcusable when facilitators stick their heads in the sand like the proverbial ostrich in their interactions with students of different cultures, even when they are motivated by the best of intentions to avoid stereotypic assumptions and/or prejudices. Such actions often alienate those students; they feel that their sociopolitical reality has been denied or devalued—this in itself may constitute an act of racism.

Facilitators need to understand and openly acknowledge that their students' life histories, experiences, languages, communication styles, values and goals may differ, based on their cultural background and/or identity, and that these factors impact on their daily lives in and out of the classroom. Neither education nor the educators are value-free; facilitators need to examine their own biases, welcome cultural differences as valuable learning opportunities for everyone and strive to create relevant and inclusive learning experiences for all students in their classrooms.

When it comes to motivating adult learners, facilitators often get very creative about the methods and strategies they use to make learning experiences more relevant, exciting, challenging and rewarding for the students. Incentives, positive reinforcements, use of new technology, games, energizers and many other motivation-enhancing activities and teaching aids help to create a vibrant classroom environment.

Generally, the rule of thumb is: do whatever works, as long as it is ethical. The problem is that making ethical decisions in facilitating adult education is not a simple task because many of them involve subjective thought; the line between "right" and "wrong" often tends to be very thin and, at times, almost invisible.

Ethical Issues

Ethical conduct for facilitators of adult education implies a set of standards for practice based on professional values. Generally, ethical guidelines for adult educators parallel, to a large extent, to ethical guidelines for practitioners in the counselling field. First and foremost, learners must be unconditionally respected and their dignity protected throughout the learning process. The three main skills that facilitators rely on in these areas are attending, responding and understanding (Brockett 1988). In fact, facilitators are often called upon to utilize these skills in providing guidance and assistance regarding problems related to their students' personal issues or situations. Apps (1991) points out that this is a particularly sensitive area, as it may require skills and expertise beyond those of a facilitator. He suggests that facilitators have an ethical responsibility to assist students with personal problems in identifying appropriate help, but he cautions them not to break confidence without the respective participant's permission and to avoid giving advice. In some situations, a referral to a qualified counsellor may be appropriate.

Facilitators are also constantly faced with making decisions in their relationships with colleagues and employers, and with respect to the honesty and integrity of teaching materials, promotional materials and social issues such as personal values, beliefs, biases and feelings (Apps 1991). These decisions are generally guided by the key aspects of the practice of ethics: (a) promotion of self-determination and autonomy, (b) promotion of the well-being of others, (c) avoidance of doing harm, (d) equal treatment of all, (e) keeping promises and honouring commitments, and (e) honesty with self and others (Meara, Schmidt and Day 1996). Apps (1991) refines these values into the following six criteria of ethical decision making for teachers: a fundamental concern for people, respect for justice and human rights, love for the earth, quest for quality, search for truth and an appreciation of beauty (p.113). He concludes that applying these guidelines is not an easy task: "Ethical decision making is often a lonely, individual task for each of us as we search our beliefs and values, trying to make a decision that we can live with and believe is ethically appropriate" (p.120).

Conclusion

This chapter focused on the key concepts and aspects of facilitating adult education, coming from the premise that "the purpose of facilitation is to assist individuals to exercise control over their own lives, their interpersonal relationships, and the social forms and structures within which they live" (Brookfield 1986, 291). As eminent as this task may seem, there is no one method of practice that guarantees success in achieving these important goals. The literature in the field is vast and varied, providing many different viewpoints on the roles, skills and characteristics of effective facilitators and on other aspects that constitute effective practice.

The key competencies of facilitators of adult education generally fall into the following main areas: interpersonal skills, expertise in content and skills in instructional methods and techniques. These competencies are firmly grounded in the humanist philosophy and implemented within the guidelines of ethical practice. Each facilitator develops, over time, a unique teaching style that is the synthesis of his or her special blend of personal and professional characteristics, values and beliefs, as well as knowledge, skills and experience in the field.

Most importantly perhaps, effective facilitators take very seriously their responsibility to encourage and promote the process of critical reflection; they also challenge students to apply that process independently throughout their lives in order to achieve their full potential, fulfil their goals and realize their dreams. Cited in von Oech (1990), the educator Niel Postman suggests that "children enter school as question marks and leave as periods" (p.23). Maybe the challenge for facilitators of adult education is to encourage and guide adults to finding their way back to being question marks.

References

Apps, J.W. 1991. *Mastering the teaching of adults.* Malabar, Fla.: Krieger.

Brockett, R.G., ed. 1988. *Ethical issues in adult education.* New York: Teachers College.

Brookfield, S.D. 1986. *Understanding and facilitating adult learning.* San Francisco: Jossey-Bass.

———. 1987. *Developing critical thinkers.* San Francisco: Jossey-Bass.

Brundage, D.H., and D. MacKeracher. 1980. *Adult learning principles and their application to program planning.* Toronto: Ministry of Education.

Cross, P.K. 1981. *Adults as learners: Increasing participation and facilitating learning.* San Francisco: Jossey-Bass.

Draper, J.A. 1993. Advice and empathy: Teachers talking with teachers about adult education. In *The craft of teaching adults,* edited by T. Barer-Stein and J.A. Draper (pp.239-259). Toronto: Culture Concepts.

Freire, P. 1970. *Pedagogy of the oppressed.* New York: Continuum.

Knowles, M.S. 1975. *Self-directed learning: A guide for learners and teachers.* New York: Cambridge.

———. 1980. *The Modern practice of adult education: From pedagogy to andragogy.* Rev. ed. Chicago: Association Press.

———. 1990. *The adult learner: A neglected species.* Houston, Tex.: Gulf Publishing.

Knox, A.B. 1986. *Helping adults learn.* San Francisco: Jossey-Bass.

Kroehnert, G. 1997. *Basic training for trainers.* Sydney: McGraw-Hill.

Meara, N.M., L.D. Schmidt and J.D. Day. 1996. Principles and virtues: A foundation for ethical decision, policies, and character. *The Counseling Psychologist* 24: 4-77.

Menlo, A., et al. 1979. *Teaching educators of adults how to facilitate participation in adult learning groups.* Unpublished paper. Ann Arbor, Mich.: University of Michigan, School of Education.

Percival, A. 1993. *Practicing theory: A guide to becoming an effective adult education programmer.* Saskatoon: University of Saskatchewan Extension.

Renner, P.F. 1989. *The instructor's survival kit.* Vancouver: Training Associates.

———. 1994. *The art of teaching adults.* Vancouver: Training Associates.

Thomas, A.M. 1993. The new world of continuing education. In *The craft of teaching adults,* edited by T. Barer-Stein and J.A. Draper (pp.21-38). Toronto: Culture Concepts.

von Oech, R. 1990. *A whack on the side of the head: How can you be more creative.* Menlo Park, Cal.: Warner Books.

Wlodkowski, R.J. 1999. *Enhancing adult motivation to learn.* San Francisco: Jossey-Bass.

10

Prior Learning Assessment: Looking Back, Looking Forward

Angelina T. Wong

Prior learning assessment (PLA) is a concept that has relevance to many different types of learners in diverse contexts, including education, training and work. Since the mid-1970s, PLA has provided adults with opportunities for admission into and advanced standing in colleges and universities. When applied to post-secondary education, PLA can be defined as a systematic process to evaluate and accredit learning gained outside formal educational institutions, by assessing relevant learning against the standards required by post-secondary courses and programs. The process enables students and potential students to obtain recognition for learning that they have achieved through both formal and non-formal means. Formal learning is usually organized by professional educators and leads to a credential or qualification. Non-formal learning includes learning achieved via work experiences and other life experiences such as self-directed learning, artistic and cultural pursuits and volunteer community activities. It is also commonly known as experiential learning. PLA as a process can be applied beyond an academic setting. It is gaining acceptance as a tool for assessing and recognizing knowledge and skills for the purposes of occupational or professional certification and employment entry. The focus of this chapter, however, is on PLA within post-secondary education systems.

In the last decade, there has been a growing demand for colleges and universities to implement PLA systems. It is a reflection of a global phenomenon where falling job expectations and a general longing for something better are driving increasing numbers of adults to return to post-secondary education. New information technologies and corporate re-engineering have enabled companies to let go of thousands of workers and to collapse layers of management. Studies such as the background surveys for the review of social programs in Canada show that the public is placing an increasingly heavy emphasis on the need for education and training as a means of overcoming the prevailing economic uncertainty (HRDC 1994). Adult learners, employers and governments, all have practical and financial incentives to implement a system of prior learning assessment so that learners with verified knowledge and skills can be exempted from taking specified courses that offer similar content, thereby shortening the time required to obtain a degree or other credential.

PLA has gained wide acceptance as a means of assessing and granting recognition for experiential and workplace learning in countries such as the United States, the United Kingdom, Australia, New Zealand and France.

The implementation of PLA programs in Canada, however, has been limited in scope; government financial support for the development of materials and training activities has been uneven across the provinces. In general, there is greater acceptance of PLA processes among colleges and more resistance among universities. To understand the challenges and opportunities that can be provided by a system of prior learning assessment, knowledge of the historical background of PLA and how the concept is applied in practice is beneficial.

Historical Background

The PLA movement grew out of a concept that is hundreds of years old. As Peruniak (1993) points out, experiential learning has been prevalent in Europe since the dawn of Christianity. The most dominant initial modes included apprenticeship training by craft guilds, "chivalry training" in courts and private learning in monasteries and abbeys. These modes were slowly replaced by more formal systems as industrialism developed and modern occupations took the place of crafts. Even in the nineteenth century, the need for concomitant experiential learning was recognized, as medicine and other professions looked to real-world demonstrations and clinical practice to supplement prescribed textual learning.

In the 1930s in North America, Dewey (1938) emphasized the need for experiential learning or "discovery learning" in the natural sciences. It was the returning veterans from World War II who put pressure on the formal education system in the United States to recognize alternative sources of learning. This pressure resulted in the development of standardized examinations to facilitate admission into higher education programs, namely, the College Level Examination Program or CLEP (Lamdin 1992). Following the recommendations of the 1971 Commission to Study Non-Traditional Education, a small number of universities and colleges in the north-eastern United States co-operated with the Educational Testing Service in Princeton, New Jersey, to investigate a variety of means for the valid and reliable assessment of experiential learning.

Since the late 1970s, the Council for Adult and Experiential Learning (CAEL), a non-profit organization, has taken a leadership role in promoting experiential learning as an important part of higher education. The academic and administrative standards of PLA developed by CAEL have guided practitioners and institutions for a decade (Whitaker 1989). CAEL has also spearheaded PLA professional development activities and the development of resource materials for educators (1998). Parallel to CAEL's initiatives, a number of influential books were published during this period, including those by Keeton et al. (1976), Chickering et al. (1981), Kolb (1984) and Boud, Keogh, and Walker (1985). These publications provided a useful theoretical framework for experiential learning.

In the United Kingdom, PLA is known as Accreditation of Prior Experiential Learning or APEL (Evans 1990, 1994). In 1986, the British government established the National Council for Vocational Qualifications (NCVQ) to promote the assessment of competency-based vocational qualifications. The incorporation of polytechnics and some large colleges into chartered universities in the years since 1988 has dramatically accelerated APEL into mainstream degree programs. Over 50 percent of undergraduate studies in Britain are taken under the umbrella of the Council for National Academic Awards (CNAA).

In Australia, the Australian Vice-Chancellors' Committee unanimously endorsed a set of guidelines for the Recognition of Prior Learning (RPL) as a means of improving access and equity for Australian students (Cohen et al. 1993). The committee recognized that, when selecting students for admission from backgrounds other than Year 12, universities should consider a range of prior learning experiences, including experiences other than those credentialled by a university or college of technical and further education (TAFE). Another study commissioned by the committee found that eighteen out of thirty Australian universities gave standing recognition to industry-based training conducted beyond universities and TAFEs, with credit given across fifteen discipline or professional areas (Topley and Clinch 1992). In 1995, the commonwealth government established the Australian Credit Transfer Agency (ACTA) to conduct assessment and grant recognition for prior learning.

In 1995-96, the Canadian Labour Force Development Board (CLFDB), a national advisory body comprising labour market partners, initiated a national consultation that resulted in the development of national standards for prior learning assessment and recognition or PLAR. The "R" was added to ensure the recognition of prior learning and to emphasize the potential of using prior learning assessment tools to address issues of social justice, labour force development and reforms in education and training. The Canadian Association for Prior Learning Assessment (CAPLA) was incorporated in 1997 and has taken on an advocacy role for continuous learning opportunities and formal acknowledgement of previous learning experiences.

The term *prior learning* was originally used by American educators in the 1970s to refer to learning that had been acquired before college attendance. In the 1980s, British educators expanded the concept beyond the act of accrediting prior learning achievements to the provision of guidance and counselling and the evaluation of evidence in support of claimed achievements. In Canada, the 1997 national forum on prior learning assessment adopted the slogan "Learning Has No Boundaries." PLA presents both challenges and opportunities for post-secondary institutions, which will be discussed in greater detail later in this chapter. The sources of prior learning and the issues that educational institutions must confront are summarized in Figure 10.1 (Wong 1996).

PLA and Adult Education

The assumptions and values of prior learning assessment are congruent with the foundations of adult education, particularly in the recognition that, (a) as individuals grow to adulthood, they tend to learn in a variety of ways, and (b) as adults, they will seek to join educational programs when they

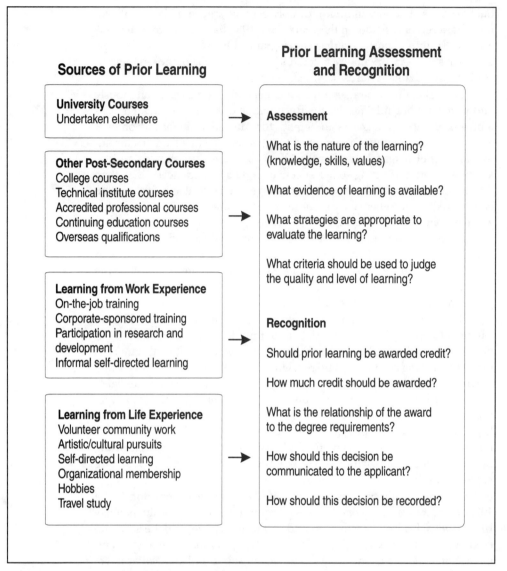

Figure 10.1: Sources of Prior Learning

need to know more about a subject or develop more skills in a specific subject area.

Various organizations and institutions have developed different definitions of prior learning assessment, but they tend to share a common set of assumptions and values, including:

1. Individuals can and do learn throughout their lives in a variety of ways.

2. Adult students who return to formal learning have had a variety of life experiences, which can (but do not always) result in learning that is equivalent to university- or college-level learning. Within

reasonable limits, such learning has an appropriate place in the post-secondary curriculum.

3. Formal learning that occurs in schools, colleges and universities is not necessarily of a higher quality than non-formal learning gained through life and work experiences.

4. Adult students, when provided with the appropriate guidance, can articulate and document the learning they have gained through life and workplace experiences.

5. Their learning (but not their experiences) can be reliably assessed and related to the expected learning outcomes of formal courses to determine whether or not credit should be awarded.

6. By being more flexible and responsive educational providers, post-secondary educational institutions contribute to a society that is better able to accommodate itself to the demands of an increasingly complex world.

The Practice of PLA

Colleges and universities, when selecting students for admission from backgrounds other than the completion of Grade 12, normally have policies and procedures for granting recognition to learning that the applicants have acquired elsewhere. This recognition has traditionally been extended to formal learning that has been accredited by other colleges and universities recognized by the admitting institution.

Institutions that offer PLA services usually make use of three types of assessment methods. The first two types are similar to the traditional processes of assessing formal learning for the purpose of admission into a course or program, obtaining transfer credit from one program to another, or for gaining advanced standing in a program. The third type is increasingly used to assess non-formal learning from work and/or life experiences. The three types can be summarized as: examinations (standardized, challenge); equivalencies (course, program); and documentation and demonstration of achievement via a portfolio (which can be supplemented by interviews, oral and/or written tests and demonstrations).

I. Examinations

Standardized exams are recognized by most colleges and universities in the United States, but they have not gained widespread acceptance in Canada. Over 150 titles exist in the areas of arts and sciences, business, nursing, computer science, education, technology and in a range of occupational areas. Standardized examinations have been found to be most appropriate for introductory-level and highly theoretical courses.

The ones that are the most widely accepted for PLA purposes include the College Level Examination Program (CLEP); the Program on Non-Collegiate Sponsored Instruction (PONSI); and the Defense Activity for Non-Traditional Examination Support (DANTES).

Challenge exams have traditionally been available to students in higher education, but the number of cases is usually limited because it is a time-consuming process. A challenge exam is usually prepared especially for the learner by the instructor of the course being challenged. When offered as an option of PLA, the exam should ideally reflect consensus among instructors of the department offering the course as to what constitutes the accepted body of knowledge and skills that are being examined.

II. Equivalencies

Course equivalencies are also known in the traditional post-secondary education context as "transfer credit." They are commonly granted by the registrar's office of the accrediting institution based on input from the academic department that is offering the course for which transfer credit is requested. When a learner initiates a request for course equivalency, the prior learning reviewed could be for formal learning gained in another institution or for credentialled learning verified by a professional body. Where there is one-to-one correspondence or a close match between the prior learning and the course content, credit for specified courses may be granted.

Like returning adult learners, many traditional university-age students have to cope with varying standards for credit among different post-secondary educational institutions. A course from University A may not be accepted by University B when a student changes institutions. The level of mathematics skill that enabled a student to pass Math 101 at University C may not give her the background skills to pass Math 202 at University D. These problems intensify when adults are involved in the system, especially when they bring prior learning that has been acquired outside the traditional classroom.

In the case of non-formal or experiential learning, the learner requesting PLA bears the responsibility for documenting and providing evidence of learning that matches the expected learning outcomes of the course. Many American institutions with PLA programs have staff who counsel potential students about program areas that may have courses that can be equated to their own areas of experiential learning. Binders of course descriptions are available for review before the learners commit themselves to preparing a portfolio. Some colleges in Canada have adopted the American model of providing a portfolio development course that guides adult learners in the development of a portfolio and at the same time orients them to the institutional culture.

Program equivalencies are also known as "block credit." Institutions with linkages to other institutions, professional bodies or industry may grant advanced standing to a learner who has successfully completed a recognized course, program, professional license or professional certificate. A block of "unspecified credit" is sometimes given towards the elective component of a program when it is difficult to closely match the prior learning with a specific course within the curriculum, but the learning is nevertheless judged to be relevant to significant aspects of a variety of courses within the program. Strictly speaking, when compared to exams and portfolios, program equivalencies do not assess learning. It is the instruction that was delivered that is being evaluated and recognized.

The American Council on Education's (ACE) Center for Adult Learning and Educational Credentials has done evaluations of several hundred corporate training programs as well as a number of union and governmental programs. Since 1974, it has offered the Program on Non-Collegiate Sponsored Instruction to assist adult learners seeking advanced standing for prior learning. ACE accredited programs are widely accepted among universities and colleges in the United States.

In Canada, there is increasing awareness that the recognition of foreign credentials is vital to the socioeconomic integration of immigrants. Many immigrants who have acquired post-secondary level education and professional training in their native countries have great difficulty finding work that matches their qualifications because employers are unfamiliar with their credentials. There are currently three provincial agencies that provide foreign credential assessment services, a form of program equivalency: the Service des équivalences of Quebec, the International Qualification Assessment Service (IQAS) of Alberta, and the International Credential Service (ICES) operated by the Open Learning Agency of British Columbia.

III. Portfolio-Assisted Assessment

A *portfolio* is a collection of information and artefacts that demonstrates the depth and breadth of what a learner knows and can do. It is used to back up the learner's claims that, through various learning experiences, he or she has met the expected learning outcomes of specific credentialled courses. When a portfolio is combined with other means of assessing learning (such as an oral interview or a performance), the method is called *portfolio-assisted assessment.*

Portfolios are especially useful for documenting non-formal learning achieved in uncredentialled contexts. An individual engaged in the process goes through three phases that can be termed "the three Rs of portfolio development": recall the past, review the present and reflect on meanings. A completed portfolio indicates the learner's ability to reflect on and to analyze learning experiences, to apply learning from specific experiences to new contexts and to identify the relationships between the experiential learning and the formal courses. The process of writing and organizing a portfolio is developmental; it can lead to a deeper understanding of personal strengths and weaknesses and assists the learner in prioritizing personal and academic goals.

If PLA credit is claimed for specific courses, the assessment should determine if the applicant has achieved the theoretical and practical learning objectives of the designated courses. If unspecified credit is sought, the assessment should determine whether the applicant's learning achievements are at an appropriate level of depth and complexity for the level of the credit sought. Recognition of this latter type may be credited towards the elective component of a program. The applicant should ideally receive further counselling about the academic areas under which this credit could potentially be applied.

Many universities and colleges in the United States, particularly those that were created to serve adult learners (for example, Empire State College in New York, Thomas Edison State College in New Jersey, University of Maryland University College), offer portfolio development courses for learners. In some cases, these courses are a major access point for traditionally disadvantaged groups who would not normally participate in higher education (Mandell and Michelson 1990). Participants in a portfolio development course usually spend several weeks and sometimes a whole semester preparing and organizing a portfolio before submitting it for evaluation by one or more faculty assessors. Portfolio development courses are also offered at some Canadian institutions on a more limited scale.

Components of a portfolio. Portfolios can be viewed as both a process and a product. The process of developing a portfolio can be a valuable learning experience for the learner, who follows an approved format in systematically organizing and recording relevant learning experiences. As a well-organized product, the portfolio enables an individual to "showcase" relevant achievements in a discourse style that is familiar to the academic assessor(s). Different institutions may vary in their guidelines for portfolio development, but the learner is usually expected to go through the following steps:

1. Reflect on significant life events and activities that have been influential (for example, personal experiences, work experiences, community service, artistic or cultural pursuits).

2. Summarize these achievements in a written "autobiographical narrative."

3. Prepare a statement of educational, career and personal goals.

4. Identify learning outcomes from the autobiographic narrative and cluster them into areas of competencies.

5. Review institutional calendars and course outlines for comparable expected learning outcomes and competencies.

6. Relate personal learning to specific courses or to the elective "block" or area within a program.

7. Describe or delineate each cluster of learning, summarizing what knowledge, skills and values have been acquired and how they have been acquired.

8. Collect and assemble the materials that will be used as evidence of learning, including direct evidence (for example, samples of work done) and indirect evidence (for example, letters of verification, certificates of completion).

9. Compile all of the above items in a binder (two or more copies may be required by the institution).

10. Submit the portfolio to the designated institutional representative.

IV. Types of Evidence of Learning

It is important to remember that PLA credit is given for verified learning, not for experiences per se. Applicants usually submit a combination of direct and indirect evidence.

Direct evidence. There are four types of direct evidence of learning: (1) a product evaluation, in which the faculty assessor evaluates the student's previous work (for example, articles, essays, written reports; musical score composed; design plans; artwork); (2) an oral interview, in which, by means of a conversation, the faculty assessor determines the extent of the student's knowledge and ability to construct valid arguments; (3) a written test, which provides an opportunity for the student to demonstrate an understanding of the subject by using concepts of the discipline to reflect on his/her practical experiences; and (4) a performance test or observation, in which the student demonstrates knowledge or skills by "doing," such as playing the piano, using designated instruments to conduct a test and explaining the findings.

Indirect Evidence. The following types of indirect evidence are commonly submitted in varying combinations: description of job requirements; letters from supervisors and employers verifying job duties and performance; description of license or certification requirements; letters of corroboration from clients served or co-volunteers; programs from performances; newspaper or magazine clippings about applicant's work; awards, citations and commendations.

In general, the method of assessment will be influenced by the circumstances under which it is sought and the purpose for which it is sought. Applicants of PLA, however, need to remember that it is not the intention of PLA to equate amount of experience with prior learning credit. PLA evaluates an individual's learning outcomes from a variety of experiences in relation to the learning outcomes expected in specified courses or programs. Recognition, if granted, will be given on the basis of validated learning, or demonstrated knowledge and skills.

Challenges and Opportunities

The PLA movement is growing as increasing numbers of adult learners, employers and community leaders forcefully articulate the need for educational services that are more responsive to the circumstances and needs of adults. Colleges and universities are being asked to put their proclaimed support of lifelong learning into action by providing continuous learning opportunities and formal acknowledgment of previous learning. The experiences of countries such as the United States, Australia and the United Kingdom have shown that, while governments can play a significant role in kick-starting the adoption of PLA, the integration of PLA into post-secondary teaching-learning systems requires the support of the faculty, staff and senior administrators of the institution.

As mentioned, when compared to colleges, whose programs tend to be vocationally oriented and competency based, universities in Canada have been much more resistant to PLA processes. In many universities, the curriculum is traditionally structured according to the overall architecture of the major disciplines. Curriculum development begins with a focus on what faculty ought to teach in terms of the major concepts, subject matter and methodologies of the academic area and the discipline. It is based on a tradition that has flourished and survived for several hundred years. The first challenge for an adoption of PLA within universities is to have faculty accept that non-formal, experiential learning beyond the classroom can be of comparable quality and can be assessed reliably.

To prepare for an implementation of PLA, faculty need to reconsider existing curriculum content, structure and processes to realign it with the intent and spirit of PLA. Most academic programs have an order in which subject matter (structured as course units) is usually taken. Faculty need to review issues by asking such questions as:

- Are there alternative routes through the program other than the currently prescribed sequence?

- Are a subject's content and process absolutely dependent on the prerequisites stated, or are they merely a continuation of tradition?

- Are the courses described in terms of expected learning outcomes, and are there clearly stated criteria for assessing levels of achievement?

- What options are there for students who successfully demonstrate mastery of skills commonly taught in advanced courses but who do not possess the theoretical underpinnings?

These issues, in addition to questions about alternative evaluation practices that are fair and reliable, need to be discussed and addressed if PLA is to achieve its potential in the long term. All this, however, takes time—a precious commodity when most faculty members across the nation are trying to cope with multiple demands in a period of institutional budget cuts and downsizing.

The second challenge to the adoption of a PLA system is the lack of institutional policies and support structures to integrate PLA into the institution's student services. Even among those institutions that have developed PLA policies, there are continuing difficulties in implementing the policy broadly and consistently, usually because of a scarcity of resources. There is an advantage, however, in being a newcomer to the PLA movement, as there are valuable lessons to be learned from the experiences of other countries. An institutional policy on PLA should reflect the overall goal of minimizing barriers to student access to and mobility in higher education while maintaining the integrity of academic programs and accreditation (Wong 1996). The development of an institutional policy on assessing prior learning for credit should include the following actions:

1. Make clear the basic values and principles held by the institution regarding credit for prior learning.

2. Provide explicit guidelines as to what is considered college-level or university-level learning.

3. Make clear that credit may be awarded only for demonstrated or college or university-level *learning*, not for *experience* per se.

4. Specify which forms of request for credit the institution is prepared to consider, for example, course equivalency, challenge exams, portfolio-assisted assessment of non-formal learning.

5. Specify which degree requirements may be met by prior learning and the limits of PLA credits.

6. Specify how credit for prior learning will be recorded.

7. Define the roles and responsibilities of all staff connected with the assessment process.

8. Develop clear, descriptive information for students, faculty, administrators, and other staff and external audiences such as employers and professional bodies.

9. Develop procedures to ensure that the evaluation of learning is undertaken by qualified individuals who are knowledgeable about both the subject matter and prior learning assessment methods.

10. Develop procedures to monitor fair and consistent treatment of students within the assessment process.

Simosko (1995) has pointed out that, twenty or thirty years ago, postsecondary education programs were developed on premises that reflected a particular paradigm of education and training that met the mass market needs of growing numbers of homogenous groups of young people. The diversity of today's learners, changes in the economy and the labour market and the need to make learning more relevant to meet the particular needs of individuals–including members of designated equity groups–have all served to challenge some of these premises.

Many of the administrative policies and structures that once worked now limit access and constrain flexibility. For example, most universities offer the majority of their classes during the day, when most faculty want to teach but when most adult learners are obligated to work at their jobs. Many student support services such as academic advising, counselling and registration are not available at night or on weekends. However, as more learners become more assertive "consumers" of education and training, institutions will likely experience more pressure to shift away from traditional modes of providing services.

Conclusion

The development of an institutional policy on PLA can provide the impetus for a review of curriculum design, course and program delivery and administrative systems that are truly supportive of lifelong learning. This exercise may lead to opportunities for attracting new groups of learners and to increased retention of existing groups of learners. It may also lead to beneficial partnerships with other institutions and corporations from the private sector who are also supportive of flexible learning.

Individual adult learners can prepare themselves for the benefits and opportunities offered by PLA by embarking on a continuous process of looking back and looking forward–that is, taking inventory of personal achievements, reflecting on personal goals and values and developing a plan for bridging the gap between where they are currently and where they want to be in the future.

References

Boud, D., R. Keogh, and D. Walker. 1985. *Reflection: Turning experience into learning*. London: Kogan Page.

Chickering, A. W., et al. 1981. *The modern American college*. San Francisco: Jossey-Bass.

Cohen, R., R. Flowers, R. McDonald, and H. Schaafsma. 1993. *Learning from experience counts: Recognition of prior learning in Australian universities*. Commissioned report for the Credit Transfer Working Party on Credit Transfer and Recognition of Prior Learning, Australian Vice-Chancellors' Committee. Canberra: Australian Government Publishing Service.

Dewey, J. 1938. *Education and experience*. Kappa Delta Pi.

Evans, N. 1990. Pragmatism at work in Britain: Some reflections on attempting to introduce the assessment of prior experiential learning. *Studies in Continuing Education* 12 (2): 122-130.

———. 1994. Experiential learning in higher education: Peripheral or central? *CAEL Forum and News* 17 (2): 31-34.

Excel course guide. 1995. University of Maryland University College: Office of Prior Learning.

Human Resources Development Canada. 1994. *Improving social security in Canada. A discussion paper*. Ottawa: Ministry of Supplies & Services.

Keeton, M.T., et al. 1976. *Experiential learning: Rationale, characteristics, and assessment*. San Francisco: Jossey-Bass.

Kolb, D.A. 1984. *Experiential learning: Experience as the source of learning and development*. Englewood Cliffs, N.J.: Prentice Hall.

Lamdin, L. 1990. *Earn college credit for what you know*. Rev. ed. Chicago, Ill.: Council for Adult and Experiential Learning.

Mandell, A., and E. Michelson. 1990. *Portfolio development and adult learning: Purposes and strategies*. Chicago, Ill.: Council for Adult and Experiential Learning.

Peruniak, G. 1993. The promise of experiential learning and challenges to its integrity by prior learning assessment. *Canadian Journal of University Continuing Education* 19 (1): 7-29.

Simosko, S. 1995. *Prior learning assessment & educational reform: A vision for now*. Victoria, B.C.: Ministry of Advanced Education, Training and Technology.

Topley, J., and G. Clinch. 1992. *Recognition by universities of education and training offered by industry and private providers*. Commissioned report for the Credit Transfer Working Party on Credit Transfer and Recognition of Prior Learning, Australian Vice-Chancellors' Committee. Canberra: Australian Government Publishing Service.

Whitaker, U. 1989. *Assessing learning: Standards, principles and procedures*. Philadelphia, Pa.: Council for Adult and Experiential Learning.

Wong, A.T. 1996. *Prior learning assessment: A guide for university faculty and administrators*. Saskatoon, Sask.: University of Saskatchewan University Extension Press.

11

Adult Education in the
Community Colleges

Anthony Bos

This chapter provides a general picture of the adult learner in Canada's community colleges, and describes the extent to which the community college system is shaped by the needs and interests of this growing segment of the student population. Community colleges exist across the nation, and they have much in common. Yet they also have a distinctness that reflects the provincial jurisdictions within which colleges operate. This chapter extracts the common characteristics of the adult learner and describes how these have influenced colleges in general; it avoids reference to the provincial particularities of the colleges. Capturing the common elements of the adult learner in Canada's community colleges provides insights into the future challenges faced by the college sector, and helps the reader to develop a point of reference for understanding the actions a college may take in response to today's rapidly changing educational context.

The Canadian community college system has its beginnings in adult education. During the 1960s, the provinces created community colleges across Canada. Also in that decade, the federal government made available significant funds for the creation of a national skills training infrastructure to be placed within community colleges. The colleges were seen as the federal government's provincial training partners to support labour force development. Under the provision of the 1966 *Adult Occupational Training Act* (AOTA), the federal government was committed to purchasing institutional training from community colleges for its non-job ready clients. As a result, across Canada the local Canada Employment Centres (CEC) sponsored many adults in taking academic upgrading and skill-training programs in response to identified local and regional skill shortages. Not only did these federally sponsored training programs provide one of the defining features of the college system in terms of infrastructure development, but they also did much to shape the character of adult learning that has become such a proud trademark of the college system. Federally purchased training programs were open only to adult learners, and as such, they provided a learning context wherein adult education practices became anchored. The instructors for these programs were recruited mostly from the industrial and business sectors. Adult education theories served as a beacon for these new professionals as they gained skill as educators.

During the 1970s and early 1980s, there were two distinct programming solitudes in a typical Canadian community college: the re-training division referred to above, and the post-secondary division. The post-secondary side of colleges provided secondary school graduates with an educational alternative to university. The economy's insatiable demand for technicians, technologists and practitioners of various kinds spawned a mushrooming of post-secondary college programs across Canada. Recruited directly from the secondary schools, students entering post-secondary programs were typically about eighteen years of age and, almost without exception, enrolled on a full-time basis. Over the last fifteen years, however, the restructuring of Canada's economy, and the changing social values of our society, have blurred the separation between the re-training and post-secondary divisions and between full-time and part-time students. Adult learners now enter post-secondary programs to such an extent that it is not uncommon to see as many adult students as traditional college students in a typical post-secondary classroom or laboratory.

This transformation in the college system caused a significant challenge to instructors, who were faced with a mix of adult and traditional students in their classes. The different life points of the younger and older students gave rise on occasion to frustration and tension in the classroom. The adult learners' career focus, greater sense of accountability, assertiveness and pressure to return to gainful employment were not necessarily shared by the eighteen-year-olds, who were more likely experimenting with their first taste of independence. Fortunately, the blending of adult and traditional students in one learning setting has been eased by, among other things, the increasing availability of educational technology and high-quality learning software. There is a new excitement in today's colleges, brought about by the ever-increasing opportunity to apply new electronic technology to learning. The new technology is making possible the development of a new learning culture, which truly embraces the principles of adult education. It will enable colleges to customize learning opportunities, allowing students to proceed independently in achieving their individual learning goals (Barrett 1995; Bunderson and Inouye 1987). The long-elusive goal of rendering irrelevant the constraints of time and place in the learning process seems finally to be at hand. Community colleges will be among the chief pioneers of this new learning reality. Shifting the educational paradigm from teaching to learning is a new market imperative that colleges must meet in order to continue to be seen as effective agents for providing education and training in support of Canada's economic and social future in the global economy.

The Formation of Adult Education in the Colleges

Adult learner enrolments in colleges across Canada have increased steadily over the years. According to a Human Resource Development Canada (HRDC) survey of adult participation levels in education and training in Canada, it was estimated that, by 1993, nearly one-third of Canadians aged seventeen or over, or 5.8 million individuals, were participants in some form of adult education. The largest provider of institution-based education to this group of learners was the college system, with 38 percent of the institutional market share (Canada 1997). This strong acceptance of the colleges is, in part, a reflection of the maturation of the college system and demonstrates how it has gained public confidence and recognition as a significant learning resource in the post-secondary education continuum. The increased enrolment of adult learners has also resulted from changing social values and expectations. Society now recognizes that lifelong learning is key to maintaining productive employment in a dynamic and global economy. For today's worker, changing careers and re-entering the learning continuum is a common expectation. Increasingly it is seen as an expression of personal growth and a proud testimony to personal effectiveness and resilience in a climate of unprecedented change.

During the early days of the college system this was not so much the case. Education was generally perceived to be a stage of pre-adult life, and adults who were referred to a college re-training program by the Canada Employment and Immigration Commission (CEIC) were lacking in requisite skills. The typical person referred for re-training was unemployed, unskilled and deemed non-job ready. Unlike today, when the economy has created labour market complexities that may leave many a skilled worker unemployed, in the 1960s, 1970s and early 1980s, unemployment was assumed to be more predictably linked to a lack of skill. Hence, new clients of CEIC were often assessed for re-training eligibility.

The training partnership between college and CEIC created a large, federally funded academic upgrading and skill-training network in Canada's community colleges. The typical adult student's learning plan provided for the attainment of academic skills required for the successful completion of a specific skill-training program, selected during a counselling process. The counselling process practiced in CEIC was consistent with traditional approaches to employment and career counselling, and used appraisal instruments such as the General Aptitude Test Battery and the Kuder Occupational Interest Survey to confirm a client's referral for re-training or employment (Isaacson 1985). Subsequent to a client's referral for re-training, the local community college would perform an academic assessment to establish a client's academic functioning level, and estimate, if required, the number of training weeks needed for the client to achieve the threshold academic skills required for a particular skill program. The academic upgrading programs were typically operated as self-paced, individualized courses, focused on the acquisition of skills in language (English or French), mathematics and some science. Students were required to work independently through curriculum modules, obtaining assistance as needed from an instructor and writing unit tests when the instructor deemed a student to be ready to proceed to the next level. Elements of mastery learning underlay this program. Time was a variable in achieving mastery, and students were required to achieve 80 percent in order to be allowed to proceed to the next level of the curriculum (Ryan 1979). As a rule, students were enrolled in academic upgrading programs just long enough to prepare for entry into specific job-focused courses such a welder-fitter, machinist, secretary and bookkeeper. The typical skill course length was forty weeks, and classes ran five hours per day. The training was viewed as a form of employment, and trainees were paid a stipend. The success rate in these skill programs was high. The focus was on a quick return to productive employment. Strict attendance tracking and one-to-one teaching were part of the recipe for this high success rate. CEIC purchased entire, continuous intake, year-round programs, and colleges were accountable for maintaining a high utilization of seats purchased.

At a number of colleges, expert staff members often devised in-house methods for assessing academic functioning levels and linked these to the entry requirements of various skill programs. Prior learning assessment, the inclusive and affirming model of assessing skills previously acquired in order to optimize an adult learner's initial placement on a curriculum, had its roots in these earlier assessment methodologies, aimed at predictable admissions. (For a full discussion of PLA, please refer to Wong in this volume.) This adult re-training system worked well, and produced significant economic benefit to Canada. In retrospect, if there were a fault in this system, it was the fact that implicit in the purchased programs was the notion that the training, if successful, would obviate the need for future formalized training. Lifelong learning was not a conscious value in this system.

Another area where community colleges played a major role in the provision of adult education to support the industrial and economic development of Canada was in the national apprenticeship program. At the time of writing, Canada's colleges continue to offer the in-class training components of various apprenticeship programs under purchase agreements with the provincial governments. This training is prescriptive and rigorous and offered either in blocks of about eight weeks or on a day release system. The curriculum is tightly monitored for adherence to requirements of the trade syllabus and for the achievement of prescribed training standards. In fact, the examinations that apprentices are required to write at the conclusion of the in-class training phase are produced either provincially or nationally. Apprentices who maintain a required level of achievement in their trades training are eligible to be awarded an inter-provincial seal, which allows them to work anywhere in Canada in their particular trade (Canada 1984). The in-class components of apprenticeship programs are concerned primarily with teaching the theoretical components of a particular trade and how these are linked to its practical applications. The in-class portions of apprenticeship training typically require an apprentice to demonstrate his mastery in integrating the theoretical underpinnings with the trade's applications. The curricula of apprenticeship feature a blend of applied academic skills (communications, mathematics and physics) and "hands on" trade applications. In order to succeed, apprentices have to maintain a prescribed grade level.

In the 1980s the federal government developed a new labour market training strategy by working through a new Labour Force Development Board. The Board comprised voices from provincial governments, the business sector, organized labour, social action groups and private training providers (Canada 1991). A major change to the federal government's method of purchasing training was introduced when it allowed private trainers and community groups to compete with colleges for the provision of federally sponsored training. This new reality spelled the end of an era for Canada's community colleges and, in the short term, exercised a devastating impact on many colleges, leaving them in a desperate scramble to find compensating revenues. This development did not, however, diminish the role of Canada's community colleges in providing adult education. A combination of make-up funding from Canada's provincial governments and the creation of new, quality training opportunities allowed colleges to compete successfully in this de-regulated training market. The increased participation rate in adult education in Canada in general, and the greatly increased demand from the corporate sector for customized training, created room in the adult education market for an increasing variety of training providers.

In the past twenty years, increasing numbers of adults entered or re-entered the workforce, either as second wage earners or as newly single wage earners. This shift in Canadian society's labour force habits closely mirrored the transformation taking place in the traditional family structure within most Western societies. Families with one wage earner and the mother at home quickly gave way to double-income families and to a greatly increased number of single-parent families. Large numbers of adults, and particularly women, entered post-secondary programs of all kinds, demanding education for careers in a technologically exploding economy (Canada 1983). The two levels of government responded with a variety of initiatives to support the successful entry of women into technology and trades programs. As well, provincially funded college preparatory programs and other bridging programs were created to compensate for the phase-out of the federally sponsored academic upgrading programs. Canadian provinces dealt differently with the challenges resulting from the phase-out of direct federal funding of programs, and to this day, a variety of funding approaches for adult academic preparation remain in place across Canada.

Different points of view about the appropriateness of offering adult academic preparation in the colleges has engaged college educators, college administrators and government bureaucrats across Canada in a lively debate for a number of years. For some, offering adult academic preparation in the colleges relates as much to social justice as it does to academic development. A strong and articulate lobby within the college system maintains that adult education at all levels should be the mandate of the colleges. In this view, colleges embody a unique and comprehensive learning resource, where adults find respect, understanding and support in achieving their personal growth and career goals. The continued public investment in this role for colleges is both efficient and effective for society and builds on the enviable reputation that colleges have maintained from their days of infancy in the 1960s. The secondary school system, on the other hand, was designed with the needs and behaviours of adolescents in mind. A number of the adults who came forward to enrol in the colleges did so as a result of their lack of success the first time around in the secondary school system. And so the argument continues.

For others, the colleges exist primarily as engines for economic growth, providing advanced training in the technologies and business. Shrinking public funds, according to these proponents, necessitates the allocation of resources, first and foremost, to the priorities of programs that strengthen the role of colleges in the development of the economy in an increasingly competitive and globalized context. Failure to do so will weaken the reputation of the college sector as a reliable and effective trainer of choice vis à vis the increasing competition from private trainers. Of course, both arguments are compelling. These diametrically opposed perspectives about adult education underline the strength and diversity of the contribution of community colleges in Canadian society today.

A less contentious, yet universal program from the early days of the colleges was that of part-time studies, in which adults could sign up for evening and weekend courses in a virtually endless variety of non-credit subjects: crafts, hobbies, fitness, academic subjects, trades, personal growth and so on. In many jurisdictions in Canada, such courses received a government subsidy at the outset and generated handsome profits for investment in the development of other program areas in the colleges. The demand remained strong until the loss of government subsidies in the 1980s caused a steep increase in course registration fees. Nowadays, full-cost recovery courses are still offered by most colleges, but in light of the higher fee, they are now fewer in number in most college markets and they generally focus on special interest subjects.

Adult Education for the Twenty-First Century

Programming for adults in the community college system has developed into a rich and varied array of learning opportunities that cater to the learning needs, interests and availability of a broad spectrum of the adult population. From modest beginnings in the 1960s as a provider of adult re-training programs and part-time evening courses, colleges have blossomed into prolific and innovative creators and purveyors of adult learning. Adult enrolments grew at phenomenal rates as the colleges created course offerings to suit the changing learning needs of the 1970s, 1980s and 1990s. The federal government's withdrawal from the direct funding of programs, and the provinces' increasing priority on educating for the new economy, has led to community and college partnerships for the provision of adult literacy training, life-skills training and academic preparation. The desire of colleges to provide easy access to adult learners has resulted in interesting innovations and partnerships for the delivery of adult basic education. At some colleges, for example, adult secondary schools operate on the college campus, but they are credentialled and partially funded by a neighbouring secondary school jurisdiction. Creative arrangements such as these provide adults with the appropriate support to acquire necessary academic skills while allowing them easy exposure to intended career programs available at college.

The contributions and successes of college graduates throughout Canada's workplaces have strengthened the reputation of the college system in

Canada. A number of these graduates are returning to college for additional learning, not out of deficiency or potential job loss, but as part of a regular life routine, where "just in time" learning has become a fact of modern career life. Learning is now strongly endorsed by the corporate and business sectors as a strategy to maintain an adaptive and vital work force. Employers sponsor their employees' work-related learning in a variety of ways: in-service training, on-the-job training, tuition assistance, education leaves and others. This heightened recognition for learning in the corporate sector has been a boon for those colleges that have maintained effective corporate relations and consistently invested in program and technology innovations within their institutions. The impact of this kind of investment not only benefits the programs and technology infrastructure of an institution, but, over time, such investment encourages innovation, adaptability and leadership at a college. It turns colleges into models of the learning organization, where the contributions of motivated and informed people lead to the achievement of excellence in performance and reputation.

Colleges have also noticed that part-time adult learners are increasingly choosing to attend college during the day, rather than just in the evenings. Although this attendance pattern is likely a reflection of today's world of work, it does give part-time learners access to a wider variety of learning opportunities. Shifting college curricula from a program to a course base may better accommodate the adult learners' growing demand for access to regular post-secondary programs. This shift will give the part-time adult learner greater opportunity to customize learning to suit individual purposes, in lieu of following an established track towards diploma graduation. Access to learning will, of course, continue to become easier as delivery options using new access technologies are integrated into the course delivery structures of colleges. Adult learners will be able to combine learning from a variety of sources, such as public colleges, universities, private trainers and personal study, to reach their goals. Through the creation of on-line learning via the Internet and the use of interactive distance education technology, the distribution and packaging of learning has forever changed. The new technologies will allow more adults to engage in learning as their needs dictate and their schedules permit.

One of the major challenges facing colleges today is the ability to attract the professional adult learner. The professional adult learner chooses to enrol in college to achieve specific goals and expects to be supported in the self-directed pursuit of learning. He or she expects, therefore, to have a role in determining the learning conditions (including evaluation methods), time requirements, the nature of assignments and other related issues. Clearly, packaging and presenting learning opportunities to suit the expectations of the consumer are key to continuing to attract adult learners. Adult learning will truly have come into its own in the context of the new interactive technologies when control and definition, formerly in the hands of the institution, have become responsibilities fully shared with the learner.

Another critically important sector of the adult education enterprise is market-driven training (Lenz 1980). This is the sector of colleges where contract training, customized to the needs of specific corporate or community clients, is arranged. This market has been lucrative particularly for colleges located in the more heavily populated areas of Canada. Colleges have demonstrated their ability to compete effectively with private trainers. In many cases, college reputation in terms of teaching expertise, technology, curriculum and facilities have resulted in high customer satisfaction in this aggressive marketplace. The relationship between a college's market-driven training division and its academic delivery division is critically important in guaranteeing both product quality and competitive pricing for corporate clients. Although price is always an issue with a client, product quality is a stronger factor in shaping a long-term relationship between a college and a corporate client. Colleges that have invested in creating this level of corporate trust have been well rewarded.

Many colleges also offer a number of continuing education programs in conjunction with professional organizations, such as the Purchasing Management Association of Canada and the Certified General Accountant Association. Executive-level training is also increasingly a feature of continuing education divisions. As greater numbers of college graduates reach executive scope in their careers, they will look to the colleges as much as to the universities to meet their professional training requirements. Depending on the college, and on the nature of the training request, a college may opt to produce the required training "in-house" or to broker a training service. Although the production of executive-level training is costly for an institution, responding to the learning demands of executive or professional adult learners invigorates a college. It generates an institutional expectation of high competency, enhances an institution's reputation and produces substantial revenue. Catering to the needs of the professional adult learner exacts from a college an unwavering commitment to quality of instruction, the effective provision of technology supports and the highly effective execution of event management.

Adult education has become a sophisticated, technologically mediated professional development service to business and industry. Colleges are now hosting continent-wide simulcast presentations to business and industry clients, featuring renowned authors and business gurus such as Alvin Toffler, Tom Peters, Stephen Covey and Tom Naisbitt. Some colleges are also becoming professional development specialists for smaller private enterprises. By bundling the needs of various businesses, colleges can facilitate professional growth activities that would not normally be affordable to a small independent firm.

Another important segment of adult learning focuses on recreation and wellness. Many colleges operate institutes, conferences, workshops, colloquia, seminar series and summer schools of all kinds covering personal growth endeavours in areas as diverse as fine arts, holistic health, sports of various kinds, computer graphics, poetry, music and drama, and any other personally enriching pursuits for which a market demand exists. If the product offered is appropriate for the market in terms of price, schedule, product, quality and relevance, the adult learner response can be quite strong. In addition to providing a modest financial contribution to the institutional budget, these recreational programs also enrich the cultural and spiritual fabric of an institution. Today's educated adult leads a stressful life and is keenly aware of the importance of continuing personal growth as a means for creating mental health. Colleges are ideally suited to respond to this part-time learning demand; they have the commitment to adult education, the expertise, the resource networks and the institutional systems to respond quickly and effectively in a rapidly changing market.

A growing and attractive new program option is the post-diploma or post-degree certificate. This programming area is aimed at the specialized learning interests of university or college graduates who require advanced level training in skills and applications, aimed particularly at career entry into the new economy. These one-year certificate programs may feature entirely new curricula, created specifically for learners who are able to function at a graduate level. They may also consist largely of compressions and re-combinations of curriculum components of existing programs. Adults who enrol in these programs have already graduated from an academic program and can easily adapt to self-directed study. The fast-tracking feature of these programs makes them attractive to college graduates who wish to broaden their previously applied skills through bridging with related program areas, and to university graduates who seek to integrate new state-of-the-art applied skills with a previously acquired academic foundation. Post-diploma or post-degree programs are usually one year in length, offer certificate graduation only, and are taught in a variety of ways to accommodate the constraints of the adult learner, that is, on-line learning, distance education, group study and compressed formats. These new programs bring into the colleges a new population of learners, who are successful, academically strong and committed to achieving further growth. They raise the level of academic rigour in the colleges and strengthen the colleges' image as challenging, multi-purpose centres for adult learning.

Canada's aboriginal population is growing at a faster rate than that of the rest of the country's population. Additionally, aboriginal people lag behind other Canadian groups in terms of economic prosperity and health. Clearly, aboriginal leaders have espoused a deliberate strategy to pursue education and training as a means of creating economic strength, cultural renewal and pride among aboriginal people and in First Nations communities. Many aboriginal students enrolling in post-secondary institutions must relocate to do so. Adult students relocating to institutions from their home communities usually do so with their families. Such relocation places great stress on families, and without the proper support, this pressure often exacts a heavy academic toll. Support systems need to be linked with both the home community, the new community and with the college program area so that proper life and education planning may occur. It is essential to have aboriginal staff members available to support aboriginal adult learners, to build trust and to function as encouraging role models. The presence of Aboriginal Centres, the support for traditional cultural practices on campus, the provision of elder services and the respectful celebration of cultural events will ease the difficult bridging that students from remote communities must undergo.

Institutional commitment to the needs of aboriginal learners is also demonstrated by the investment an institution makes in gaining a better understanding of the learning styles of aboriginal students, and in building into the curriculum the appropriate anchors to the aboriginal life experience. Another proven strategy for supporting aboriginal student success at a college is for an institution to offer community-based programming jointly with First Nations education authorities. The opportunity to begin his or her adult education journey through a community-based program allows an aboriginal adult student to develop confidence and familiarity with the academic curriculum of the intended institution prior to relocation. In this regard, exciting joint ventures between public colleges and First Nations are now being forged across Canada. Implicit in the notion of self-government is an expectation that education for aboriginal people will fall, as much as possible, within the jurisdiction of First Nations. This expectation must be respected in the actions of colleges if they hope to generate the trust requisite to forging long-term educational partnership with Canada's First peoples.

Creating Learning Environments That Work for Adults

Adult students thrive in educational environments that have well-defined and transparent operating procedures for providing learner empowerment and input. The opinions of adult learners about the structure of their programs or courses and about the nature of their learning experiences are important to the development of institutional knowledge and should be sought out. Adult learners must recognize that their participation in a democratic institutional process also implies their need to respect that institution's constraint in its ability to act. Being able to balance institutional openness and student-college dialogue while avoiding the criticism of empty consultation requires sustained effort and judicious follow-through on the part of an institution. There are a number of excellent vehicles for maintaining an effective and structured dialogue with adult learners. Properly carried out, these can create genuine institutional responsiveness to the needs and expectations of adult learners while balancing these with the structural constraints of an institution. Adult student associations are ideal mechanisms for airing the opinions of adult learners and for the testing of trial balloons. Being able to express one's point of view or expectation and having these assessed within a reference group before advocating publicly for a point of view is also an important growth opportunity. There are various other effective vehicles to engage adult learners in the affairs of an institution, including suggestion boxes, course evaluations, town-hall meetings, appointments to program advisory committees, appointments to boards of governors and to ad hoc academic committees. In most jurisdictions in Canada, colleges provide opportunities for students to serve on boards and committees, with full voting privileges.

Adult learners require supports that enable their self-directed learning. Adult education in its purest sense would have the learner set his or her goals and then receive support in his or her achievement, including the adjustment of time and space to suit the constraints of the learner (Piskurich 1993). Realistically, institutions can accomplish these goals only some of the time. Self-directed learning, in which students are provided with the tools and supports to achieve their learning on their own terms, is the ideal solution for people who have varied circumstances. The use of individualized and unitized curriculum, small-group work, problem-based learning, instructional technologies such as learning software applications, CD ROMs, on-line learning, e-mail with instructors and chat rooms for courses are some of the ways to individualize learning within an established frame.

Course evaluations are essential to the conducting of effective adult education. Adult learners need to be able to express their opinions on their experience. Doing so not only provides for institutional feedback and discharge of negative energy in the class, but it also maintains an appropriate balance of power in a learning setting in which the learners may well be older than their instructors.

There is a host of learner support services that enhance the effectiveness of an adult education environment. The provision of study and note-taking skills classes to persons who have been away from formal education for a significant time is a strong support for the successful re-integration of adults. Study skills classes often use a commercially prepared curriculum, though some institutions have distilled their own curricula based on their best practices. Counselling services are also an integral component in the provision and design of a strong adult learning context. Counselling plays a major role in the initial reception of an adult learner and in the confirmation of his or her program choice, career stream decision and learning plan development. In addition to such start-up supports, counselling is also required to support learners in their adjustment to the new and often daunting challenge of being a student again. Individuals who are undergoing personal transformation, while also needing to juggle a variety of issues in their personal lives, including at times a lack of support, need to have a safe place to voice their challenges and to receive objective feedback (Cross 1981; Galbraith 1990; Long 1990).

Adult Learner Admission and Assessment

One of the most important and difficult issues in adult education is the admission of adult students who are dealing with self-esteem issues or who do not have a realistic idea of their goals, aptitudes and academic functioning skills (Cross 1981). Implicit in admission is the placement of a student at the appropriate point on a particular curriculum, be it in a preparatory or a post-secondary program. Because adult students often present themselves at a college without an academic skill set as defined by a provincially approved secondary school curriculum, they must be assessed for placement on the curriculum. This process varies from one institution to the next.

However, every adult learner's admission process ideally incorporates at least the following actions or values:

- A staff person skilled in personal and academic counselling facilitates the process.
- An adult learner's need for initial privacy is respected.
- The institution recognizes the uniqueness of the learner, and attempts to understand the learner's particular life circumstance.
- The institution ensures that the learner has access to information or professional resources to arrange her or his personal affairs so as not to constrain the learner's potential for academic success.
- The administration of academic and vocational aptitude assessments is fully explained as to purpose, process and implication.
- The learner is furnished with adequate information to make decisions about the financial realities of being in school, the time required to achieve a certain goal, the academic rigour of a chosen program and salary expectation upon graduation.
- The learner becomes linked to a support system that will be available throughout his or her academic experience at the college.

In my experience as an administrator in community colleges, adult learner admission and placement assessments are among the most difficult and least understood processes of the college academic community. Assessments for vocational aptitude, vocational interest and academic functioning level are usually accomplished by means of either commercially available test batteries or by "home-grown" tests that have been distilled within an institution over years of learner assessment experience. Ideally, an institution has on staff or has access to a psychometrist for the selection of assessment tools, the interpretation of test results and the identification of appropriate learning options within an institution. Academic staff members often express dissatisfaction with the assessment tools used, and one of the prevailing criticisms is the perceived lack of fit between the profile generated by the assessments and the discriminators needed to make effective curriculum placement decisions.[1] Assessments may include a variety of activities, including the demonstration of mastery of actual curriculum materials and challenge examinations. These innovative approaches to enhancing the relevancy of admissions assessments to an adult learner's particular situation and to the curriculum of the chosen program have received great momentum from the prior learning assessment (PLA) movement, which has now become well established in college jurisdictions across Canada. The PLA process removes some of the frustration from the assessment and placement process, and increases an organization's level of sensitivity to adult learner assessment. However, legitimizing and allocating time to individualized admissions to reflect the unique nature of the adult learner has proven more costly for some colleges than was originally anticipated. This has led to only partial adoption of the PLA process in some institutions and the abandonment of the portfolio option, which was recognized by PLA proponents as a cornerstone in the PLA process.

Another alternative to the administration of formalized adult learner admission assessments is the practice of achieving the curriculum placement as part of a more protracted academic orientation, where a new student simply demonstrates his or her place in a particular curriculum by doing academic work within the group. A couple of special circumstances are needed for this method to work well. The program should be operating on an individualized delivery format, and the institution must be able to provide full assurance to the student that his or her admission to the program is not at issue, only his or her academic placement. Hence, this approach lends itself well to academic development programs, where the counselling and teaching functions may be effectively blended and where time is not at issue as much as is the provision of a strong start for the learner on the learning path. An effective beginning to one's second learning path sets the tone for the entire experience and gives the learner a much-needed sense of self-confidence as he or she ventures into the new and difficult challenge of preparing for a world of work in which lifelong learning is the only constant.

On-line academic assessment is still an emerging capability for colleges at the time of writing. Such learner-driven access places control and decision making in the hands of the potential student. Most institutions have yet to determine an appropriate response to such a level of learner autonomy.[2] In the foreseeable future, institutions will be approached with offers from commercial assessment services to have on-line assessments of all kinds conducted for them. This will potentially remove a difficult psychometric challenge from colleges. However, the humanistic values that underlie effective adult education must be safeguarded despite this technological liberation in order that adult learners continue to derive from their institutional experience a sense of enhanced self-understanding and esteem.

Partnerships

Community colleges have prospered and grown out of being connected with their political, educational, social and economical surroundings. Through practicality and adaptability, colleges have been able to form partnerships for the creation of powerful learning opportunities. Innovation and practical vision have made the college system in Canada what it is today: a connected, well-respected and adaptive resource for learning, social development and economic growth. Partnerships have created opportunities for institutions to extend their margins of effectiveness well beyond institutional boundaries in providing students with a breadth of learning opportunity. This kind of entrepreneurship is particularly important at a time when learners' needs grow ever more diverse, the financial capacity of institutions is demarcated by government cutbacks and the path of economic globalization is unstoppable.

Partnerships are also opportunities to transfer out of an institution those programs or services that have been marginalized by changes to funding or institutional mandate and may therefore fit better within another jurisdiction. In the case of academic preparation programs for adult learners, as cited above, the cutbacks have been so severe in many college jurisdictions in Canada that innovative partnerships to retain an effective level of adult academic preparation have been initiated with school divisions and community partners. Another invaluable college partner, the new federal Human Resources Development Canada (HRDC) department, is seeking community partners for the provision of some of its traditional client services, such as vocational assessment. Although colleges are obvious candidates to provide such services, the delegation of this work will not consistently go to colleges. The availability of other service providers in the community, the strength of institutional relationships and other factors will shape the outcome of such service redistribution. This underscores for colleges the reality of operating in a linked and competitive environment.

Articulation arrangements between colleges and universities are of significant benefit and interest to adult learners in that they provide access to degree education concurrent with training in the practical applications for which colleges are renowned. Being able to perform a significant part of the degree work in a college setting and benefiting from the lower college tuition rate and the typically lower student-teacher ratio is attractive to adult learners. College academic work is making steady gains in achieving formal recognition within related university curricula. Such recognition is usually made on a course-by-course basis, but in special circumstances, targeted college programs may be articulated with a particular university program resulting in block recognition for skills and knowledge achieved, rather than courses completed. In this scenario, however, time spent and credits gained in college study do not equate to credits awarded in a university program.

Another and even more compelling arrangement currently gaining favour in Canada is the joint diploma-degree program, offering diploma or degree exit. For such programs the stated curriculum features a blend of college and university level courses, as identified and offered by two or more partner institutions.[3] Such programs provide a useful blending of applied skills training and theoretical knowledge, and this is a powerful combination for adults who demand career preparation and degree credentialling in the shortest possible time. Increasingly in Canada we see a reverse trend of university graduates enrolling in colleges to acquire the applied skills they were not taught in university. This underscores the growing demand for applied degree programs, which integrate the strongest aspects of applied and theoretical education.

Reductions in direct college funding for the provision of literacy, adult basic education and life-skills programs, coupled with an increasing public expectation for the provision of advanced level programming, have had a steering effect on the program mix of colleges. In response, many of Canada's community colleges began working with community partners to strengthen the community-based adult education networks that provide programs for socially and economically disadvantaged adults. Building on the ideals and obligations of individuals, governments, corporations, service clubs and community volunteer groups, a great number of human growth projects, involving colleges as partners, continue to operate across Canada.

Colleges are also looking aggressively for program partnerships outside the traditional education sector. Virtually any new program considered for introduction at a community college today will be structured, when possible, as a partnership program with a corporation, a private trainer, a professional organization or an institute. Typically in such partnerships, the creation of curriculum content, the delivery of instruction and the provision of internships are negotiated with the partner. Co-operative education programs and programs that offer significant workplace components are often linked to several partners. Such cutting-edge programs may also be offered as post-diploma programs, thereby heightening the potential for student success and reducing the risk to the partner's professional credibility. Partnership programming is ideal for adult learners. Adults already have the motivation to achieve success, and in the right partnership program, they will garner an added opportunity to establish their profile in the profession of their choice while they are still engaged in receiving their training.

Funding

The federal funding for adult re-training was a source of tremendous infrastructure development in Canada's community colleges during its earlier days. With the phase-out of direct federal program purchases this has changed dramatically over the past decade. A number of adult education initiatives, ranging from literacy to adult academic upgrading and a broad variety of skills programs, received direct federal support. Finding alternate sources of funding to compensate for the federal withdrawal of funding, though difficult for colleges, has resulted in innovation and renewal. The provinces have felt compelled to fund a greater share of the programs formerly funded by the federal government. Colleges have also had to accept greater risk by offering some of their programs as cost-recovery ventures. To be financially viable, the classes in such programs typically enrol a blend of students: those who have at their avail the funds to pay the full individual program cost and those who are sponsored by a social agency, a government department, a workers' compensation council, a First Nation or other public or private source. The accountability placed on colleges to deliver effective programming is substantial in this circumstance.

Innovative arrangements of all kinds will characterize the future of Canada's community colleges as private corporations continue to embrace education as a commercially viable activity. Increasingly, good curriculum developed by private companies will become available in the electronic marketplace. Some colleges may adapt to this emerging new market condition by becoming hosts for learning and offering their expert services to adult learners. By facilitating the links between content providers and learners, colleges may arrange access to their learning facilities and their expert learning support services without necessarily being the originator of the curriculum being followed or assigning academic credit to the learning being achieved. Creating communities of learning and establishing a reputation for supporting adults in the achievement of their learning goals–this is one of the future roles for colleges in a competitive educational market, where content will reign and institutional opportunity will result from ingenuity and competence.

Considerations for the Future of Adult Education in Canadian Community Colleges

A number of adult education issues will need ongoing development in Canada's community colleges. The leadership provided on these issues will have a major impact on the future role of colleges in the rapidly changing adult education marketplace. The leadership will not come only from inside the institutions, for community colleges are creations of governments, and their purpose is to build social and economic capacity. Their strategic paths must, therefore, reflect the priorities of governments and of interest groups (Dennison 1995). The challenge to colleges is to maintain a reputation for quality, adaptability, relevancy and responsiveness in their program offerings. This will require that colleges have access to, not only content expertise and excellent instructional delivery, but also state-of-the-art infrastructure, such as computers, specialty laboratories, technical equipment and first-rate meeting facilities. Public funding alone will not likely enable colleges to compete successfully in this privatized education world. Creativity in seeking revenues will be required.

With the pre-eminence of technology in modern society, there is also a growing risk of an ever-widening gap between rich and poor. Colleges have an opportunity to marshal their resources to contribute solutions to building a better, stronger and more equitable society. The sustained dialogue regarding the level of institutional support for socially relevant adult education programs will be part of socially conscious and richly diverse institutions.

Colleges will embrace and lead the on-line learning revolution. Freeing students from the constraints of traditionally delivered program curricula and allowing them to proceed at their own pace, independent of time and place, will make college programs accessible and attractive to adult learners. Colleges that can transform themselves into supporters and facilitators of learning will be able to occupy new roles that the education market is just beginning to create–the provision of learning in a virtual environment.

Colleges have moved from their early days as trainers for literacy and skills to become the most resourceful instruments for the creation of wealth, social mobility and lifelong learning. Canada's community colleges occupy a unique and enviable role in the adult education spectrum: they have broad customer loyalty, they have the greatest discretion to innovate new programs, they are in a position to provide a strong role model for lifelong learning and they have demonstrated their ability to adapt and thrive in a context of rapid social change. The strongest prospect for the future of Canada's colleges lies in their ability to be seen by society as valued and dynamic hosts for learning for people of all ages and all walks of life.

Summary

This chapter has traced the history of adult education in the Canadian community college system. The development and delivery of adult education has been one of the significant achievements of the Canadian community college system. From modest beginnings as a provider of academic upgrading and skill-training programs, the colleges have grown into dynamic catalysts for the learning society of the beginning of the new millennium. Through an unremitting commitment to program development, curriculum delivery innovation and the integration of new educational technology applications, community colleges have earned a strong reputation in the Canadian adult education market. Colleges have protected this market position through effective program packaging, the design of learning for life and workplace relevancy, the support of social justice issues, the setting of competitive tuition rates and the building of innovative partnerships. One of the hallmarks of colleges has been the expression of support and respect for adult learners through the maintenance of a wide range of learning and life-support services and the offering of diversity in both the level and breadth of programs. The participation rate of adult learners in college-based programming has enjoyed steady expansion over the first thirty years of community college history in Canada. It is expected that this trend will continue as our society's reliance on lifelong learning gains greater acceptance.

Endnotes

[1] A good overview of assessment issues in adult basic education is provided by Stan Jones (see references below).

[2] Increasingly, educational websites allow applicants to communicate on-line about admissions requirements, associated academic assessments and even to take full programs, for example, the University of Phoenix (www.embark.com) and British Columbia's Open Learning Agency (www.ola.bc.ca).

[3] A number of innovative partnerships have been forged between colleges and universities, whereby students are able to combine courses from a university and a college in proceeding towards either a college or university graduation. One such co-operative relationship exists between Nipissing University and Canadore College in North Bay, Ontario, in the area of Environmental Protection Technology; another is a Bachelor of Education Program offered jointly between Red River College in Winnipeg and the University of Winnipeg.

References

Barrett, E. 1995. NEOS and the development of the electronic classroom at MIT. In *Computer mediated communication and the online classroom,* edited by M.P. Collins and Z.L. Berge. Vol. 2, *Higher education* (pp.111-121). Cresskill, N.J.: Hampton Press.

Bunderson, V.C., and D.K. Inouye. 1987. The evolution of computer-aided educational delivery systems. In *Instructional technology: Foundations,* edited by P. Gagne (pp.283-318). Hillsdale, N.J. and London: Lawrence Erlbaum Associates.

Cross, K.P. 1981. *Adults as learners.* San Francisco: Jossey-Bass Publishers.

Canada. 1983. *A statistical portrait of Canadian higher education from the 1960s to the 1980s.* Ottawa: Statistics Canada.

———. 1984. *Apprenticeship training in Canada: A theoretical and empirical analysis.* Ottawa: Economic Council of Canada.

———. 1989. *Canadian Labour Force Development Board.* Government pamphlet. Ottawa: Employment and Immigration Canada.

——. 1997. *Adult education and training in Canada: Report of the 1994 adult education and training survey.* Ottawa: Statistics Canada.

——. 1999. *Gathering strength. The Government's response to the Royal Commission on Aboriginal People.* [On-line]

Dennison, J.D. 1995. Values in the Canadian community college. In *Challenge and opportunity: Canada's community colleges at the crossroads,* edited by J.D. Dennison (pp.169-183). Vancouver: University of British Columbia Press.

Galbraith, M.W. 1990. Attributes and skills of an adult educator. In *Adult learning methods: A guide for effective instruction,* edited by M.W. Galbraith (pp.3-22). Malabar, Fla.: Krieger Publishing Company.

Isaacson, L.E. 1985. *Basics of career counseling.* Newton, Mass.: Allyn and Bacon.

Jones, S. 1989. Tests for adult basic education and adult literacy. In *Adult literacy perspectives,* edited by M.C. Taylor and J.A. Draper (pp.217-226). Toronto: Culture Concepts.

Lenz, E. 1980. *Creating and marketing programs in continuing education.* New York: McGraw-Hill Book Company.

Long, H.B. 1990. Understanding adult learners. In *Adult learning methods: A guide for effective instruction,* edited by M.W. Galbraith (pp.23-38). Malabar, Fla.: Krieger Publishing Company.

Piskurich, G.M. 1993. *Self-directed learning.* San Francisco: Jossey-Bass Publishers.

Ryan, D.W. 1979. *Mastery learning: Theory, research, and implementation.* Toronto: Ministry of Education.

A UNESCO View of Adult Education and Civil Society

Marshall Wm. Conley and Élisabeth Barot

Over the course of a lifetime, people may experience changes in their family, home, city, region, country and the world. More and more people are aware that changes in their own life—the air they breathe, the water they drink—can be affected by decisions taken elsewhere. Many individuals are required to make decisions that will impact upon others and which may resonate for several generations to come. In facing such challenges two attitudes are possible. First, overwhelmed by the challenges ahead and the flux around them, individuals may approach their role passively, considering themselves disadvantaged and powerless. Second, attuned to external challenges, individuals may assume an active role, whether to safeguard vital aspects of the community or to cultivate social dynamism.

Assuming an active citizenship role requires self-confidence supported by an understanding of the broader social sphere and the limits, possibilities and avenues of appropriate action within it. For educators, this means that any opportunity to give this sense of purpose to their students should be embraced and developed.

This chapter will give the reader a perspective on the role of adult education as a contributor to civil society. It will do this by suggesting that democracy is the key element to developing a viable civil society. The role of the United Nations Educational, Scientific and Cultural Organization (UNESCO), through its various international conferences, declarations and action plans will be highlighted in order to show the relationship of adult education to the concepts of civil society and democracy.

Adult education is growing in importance in Western industrialized countries as the population ages. Increasingly, the concept of lifelong learning is discussed. Furthermore, the trends of long-term unemployment and early retirement, the decline of manual labour and high-tech developments create new demands in a changing work world. Although the complexity of social and political change seems to outstrip our ability to keep pace with it, many of these changes provide opportunities for participation in learning, leisure and social activities. Rapid social change in the late twentieth century has challenged the individual's capacity for critical reflection and for discerning the place of the individual within it. Thus, a pressing question for Western democratic states is how to educate in a society where there is an excess of information.

* This paper would not have been possible without the significant research done by Judy Ettinger. We thank her for her contribution.

It is important that educators adopt a holistic approach to education in the present social context. A holistic approach to education and the value of knowledge as active and developed social agents in civil society[1] is crucial in a knowledge-based economy where the mere technical or instrumental ability to carry out a task is no longer sufficient. For example, issues of bioethics, environmental degradation, applications of new information technology and genetically-enhanced food products all reverberate far beyond the parameters of their realization. In this context it is vital for educators to be aware of, and active in defining, their re-contextualized professional role. This requires a shift from teaching tangible and technical skills to infusing learners with an awareness of the new knowledge context within which an individual agent acts while relating that larger context to more accessible local experiences. Adult educators must impart similar skills to facilitate an environment where the critical skills that must accompany such an awareness and govern the performance of various social roles are learned. In addition, this requires a re-emphasis on broader liberal arts educational ideals. For this we need to create an educational climate wherein critical thinking and philosophical and communicative skills geared towards sifting through exchanged experiences and broader encounters in the world are enabled.

Such ideas are elaborated on in *Whose Human Rights?* (1997) by Margherita Rendel. In the chapter entitled "The Users and Uses of Education," Rendel assesses different attitudes and arguments both for and against varying educational approaches and policies and determines that "liberal concepts of education, of educating the whole person, are reflected in the attitudes of *enablers* and *sybarites*. These are the concepts that offer the widest rights to a broad education" (Rendel 1997, 73). Such a broad educational platform, and the importance of a critical form of agency[2] are also recognized by UNESCO, which characterizes its philosophy of education as

> personal training in the process of reflection ... never forgetting that the life of the mind is vital too. [And that] we have to do everything at once: promote development, encourage the growth of democracy and foster individual growth. We cannot really view these as independent domains, as separate, clearly delineated compartments. They impinge upon and are constantly modifying one another. An individual is not a closed system (Mayor 1997, 1).

Learning How To Value Democracy

For too many people in our democratic societies, democracy is a given that we have not learned to nurture. A simple definition of democracy is that it is a type of society in which an elected government takes decisions on behalf of the public for the public good. We would argue that our participation and our confidence in the institutions are needed if they are to work properly. Confidence is built on shared values that are far too often taken for granted. Participation, until very recently, was limited to participation in elections, which was considered as a privilege and responsibility based on the same values.

To define the will of the public between elections, consultations on a range of issues are becoming more common in our country. Citizens need to be prepared to participate in public debates as stakeholders in these endeavours. The complexity of many issues will make it impossible for many individuals to be sufficiently informed on what impacts them locally. More and more, a global perspective will be necessary to understand, and make sense of, what is happening close to home. Democracies are at risk where the rate of participation is low and there is no more confidence in the system. If democracy is to be valued it must be practised–from participation to adopting a culture conducive to democracy. The role for adult education in promoting democracy can be a challenging one. The following section will offer some observations on this relationship.

Exploring the Linkages between Adult Education and Civil Society

The relationship between education and citizenship within the broader social sphere has long been a topic of consideration spanning philosophy of education literature, citizenship studies and political science scholarship more generally. From such early visions of the vital connection between education and the polis expounded in Plato's *Republic* and Aristotle's *Politics*, through the pivotal work of Paulo Freire (1968, 1970) and Michael Oakeshott (1989), to the contemporary writing of Allan Bloom (1987) and Martha Nussbaum (1997), the relationship of education to issues of citizen formation, participation and social responsibility has long been acknowledged. In the Canadian context, Keith McLeod (1989) tells us that the "idea of educating people for their political and social roles was embedded in education even before Confederation. Egerton Ryerson's ... ideas on the subject were that ... education [was] a public good, ... of 'civil interest' and ... a requisite to social well being" (p.9). In a sense, then, the formative influence of education vis à vis the broader practice of citizenship is, in itself, uncontroversial. However, varied conceptions of the ways in which and forms through which education exerts a social influence have expanded dramatically. Authors such as Ken Osborne (1988) and Keith McLeod (1989), as well as many experts writing in the areas of multicultural education, human rights education and anti-racist education have proposed a very broad role for education, one which borders on advocacy. From such perspectives, citizenship education does not culminate merely in civics education; rather, civics education comprises a component of a broader view of citizenship education from which "all aspects of schooling can be seen in the context of citizenship and ... all aspects of schooling can help to form citizens" (McLeod 1989, 5).

Other authors (especially those working practically in the field of education) may affirm the links between education and citizenship, but they increasingly lament how underdeveloped these links are and how little they are understood. Lui Albala-Bertrand (1996) raises such concerns:

> Most educators believe that social adaptation ought to be carried out through education and, in particular, through formal education. This would assume that the teaching

process does have an influence on students through civic and political socialization, and that the role of the school in shaping one's political personality may be of practical importance. Unfortunately, looking at the effectiveness of citizenship education today, things do not seem to be so (p.2).

The concerns of Albala-Bertrand are foreshadowed in the Canadian Report of the Standing Senate Committee on Social Affairs, Science and Technology (1993) in which the narrow approach to citizenship education and to the possibilities of the education-civil society relationship was lamented:

> Citizenship education in Canada has not been much improved since 1967. Given the importance of teaching fundamental democratic values, we were also somewhat concerned that political education in our schools is taught in a "passive sense," limited to the factual description of government structures. Little, if anything, is taught about the actual dynamics of democratic conflict resolution.... There are still areas of neglect and imbalance in terms of attention to the Canadian component of the matter under study. Teaching about Canada is still ... ghettoized. It is taught, not pervasively throughout the curriculum, ... but over here, in this corner, with a flag on it called "Canadian Studies" (p.17).

Many of the long-standing issues and most vibrant debate regarding the relationship between education and citizenship or between education and a broader scope of agency in civil society revolve around questions and disagreements as to the form that relationship ought to take, as well as the extent to which the two environments should be treated as mutually dependent and informative.

Throughout this chapter the term *civil society* is used very broadly to refer to the intricate web of relations that characterize the social sphere. As *Our Global Neighbourhood* (1995) states:

> Among the important changes of the past half-century has been the emergence of a vigorous global civil society, assisted by communication advances ... which have facilitated interaction around the world. This term covers a multitude of institutions, voluntary associations, and networks.... Such groups channel the interests and energies of many communities outside government (p.32ff.).

Many such issues have taken on a new dimension in the wake of technological change–a social development that has, in and of itself, introduced a new realm of questions, possibilities and dangers to contemporary educational considerations in terms of (a) the actual ways and means of technological integration in educational environments, (b) the introduction of new questions concerning the relationship between "community" and the educational environment, and (c) what some see as the possible reduction of educational philosophy in meeting the demands of educational "relevance" in the global economy.

If we agree that these values (the importance of citizenship and democratic participation) and behaviours have to be taught, adult educators must insist on a few basic points. People no longer live in the same place for their entire lives. We cannot count automatically on the family or the school for socialization into a democratic mindset. In large urban areas, reference groups are lost, and it is thus the responsibility of all adult educators (whatever they teach) to give not only the training but also the values that accompany the use of this knowledge in a democratic society. There are three components with which teachers must work: knowledge, skills and attitudes. All three components are important in both the formal and informal sectors of education (Conley and Barot 1996). The adult educator can play a significant role in contributing to a literate and participatory civil society if these three components are dealt with in a comprehensive manner. (See Thomas in this volume.)

A World Perspective on Civil Society

The United Nations (UN) system may be able to give us the world perspective we need to understand what is happening and what is at stake. A world perspective is becoming more and more necessary in order to make sense of what is happening even in our own daily lives. In this context the launch of the annual United Nations Development Program (UNDP) Report on Human Development is an event for the public interest because of the global perspective it provides. Specialized organizations of the UN system such as the International Labour Organization (ILO) or the United Nations Educational, Scientific and Cultural Organization (UNESCO) also provide very valuable data on labour and on education with their specialized reports on these issues. UNESCO has a special role to play and can make major contributions such as (a) providing a better understanding of why creating and maintaining civil society is essential for democracy; (b) giving examples of a role each of us can play as active responsible citizens in our own field of competence; and (c) demonstrating how international networks enhance survival and increase the exchange of information and knowledge.

UNESCO is of particular relevance to educational considerations in the Canadian context, not least because of Canada's continued and active support of, and participation in, the entire United Nations system. The democratic commitments of UNESCO speak to the complex "liberal democratic" base of Canadian citizenship. As the Standing Senate Committee on Social Affairs, Science and Technology questioned, "how we can best promote active citizenship and how can we do so in a way that is compatible with our views of individual liberty and pluralism?" (1993, 22). In this sense, UNESCO's civic educational considerations are of special relevance. Article One of UNESCO's Constitution articulates its mandate to contribute to the peace and security of the world. UNESCO functions to this end by promoting collaboration among nations in the fields of education, science, culture and communication. In the area of education, UNESCO's work is significant in both depth and scope; it is seen as an important reference for those concerned with exploring the links between education and civil society largely because of the practical approach to inclusive debate and information exchange.

In essence, UNESCO carries out its work with concentration in three different ways. The first is through reflection. An example of such work in the field of education (which will be considered in due course) is the Commission on Education for the Twenty-First Century, or the Delors Commission. The second is through the production of normative instruments and conference declarations. Examples of UNESCO's instruments and declarations on education are the Recommendation on the Development of Adult Education, the Recommendation Concerning Education for International Understanding, Co-operation and Peace and Education relating to Human Rights and Fundamental Freedoms (Recommendation 74) and the Forty-fourth International Conference on Education. The final method is networking. This is the process by which UNESCO facilitates and reaches out to vital stakeholders in its varied fields of work to foster dialogue and the exchange of ideas among broad sectors.

The role for adult education in these three areas is profound and challenging. Traditional education seen in its formal K-12 and university levels, dealing with the five- to twenty-five-year-old age cohort, misses the fact that the majority of the population is outside of this group. Adult education, on the other hand, has the potential of educating (or in some cases, re-educating) for civic competence. The end result is a significant role for creating and/or maintaining civil society.

UNESCO's Delors Report

The Commission on Education for the Twenty-First Century, or the Delors Commission or Delors Report, suggests that creating and maintaining civil society is essential for democracy. The balanced approach towards the social awareness and individual growth aspects of education exhibited by UNESCO is evidenced in one of the recommendations featured in the Delors Report. The report specifies that "the socialization of individuals must not conflict with personal development. It is therefore, necessary to work towards a system that strives to combine the virtues of integration with respect for individual rights" (p.12).

From the perspective of the Delors Commission, in order for education to be active in this sense, it must be organized in light of four different types of learning: learning to know, learning to do, learning to live together and learning to be. Each of these is expressly relevant to adult education's relationship with civil society. The Delors Report is predicated upon and focuses its recommendations around the concept of "learning throughout life." Briefly, the four pillars underpinning all aspects of education as set forth by the Commission are as follows:

1. *Learning to know.* This involves "acquiring the instruments of understanding" and includes, but is not limited to, learning to learn, learning to concentrate, learning to exercise the faculty of thought, and involves combining a broad general education with the possibility of concentration in certain areas.

2. *Learning to do.* This is similar to learning to know, but is more closely linked with vocational training in the broad sense of acquiring the competence that enables people to deal with a fluctuating work environment.

3. *Learning to live together.* This involves education directed towards developing an understanding of other traditions and cultures. It is guided by a sense of the growing interdependence of peoples and

is geared towards meeting mutual challenges in a co-operative and peaceful way.

4. *Learning to be.* This pillar derives from the Edgar Faure report entitled, *Learning To Be: The World of Education Today and Tomorrow* (1972). The Commission's Report in particular stresses that none of the talents that are hidden like a buried treasure in every person must be left untapped: "memory, reasoning power, imagination, physical ability, aesthetic sense, the aptitude to communicate with others and ... while education should constantly adapt to changes in society, it must not fail to pass on the attainments, foundations, and benefits of human experience" (Delors 1996, 23-24).

Again, assuming a vital link between education and civil society (Delors 1996, Part 1, Chap. 2), these pillars derive from a symbiosis of the two. For UNESCO, changes in the nature of both national and global civil society necessitate and provide opportunities for new approaches to education at all levels. At the same time, it is education that is seen by UNESCO as the foundation through which social change may be informed, directed and managed. These views are clear in the Delors Commission Report. The Commission expands on this almost dualistic role for education as it relates to the transformative impact of technological innovation:

> Because the next century will provide unprecedented means for communication and for the circulation and storage of information, it will impose on education two demands which at first sight may appear contradictory. Education must transmit, efficiently and on a massive scale, an increasing amount of constantly evolving knowledge and know-how adapted to a knowledge driven civilization, because this forms the base of skills in the future. At the same time, it must find and mark the points of reference that will make it possible, on the one hand, for people not to be overwhelmed by the flows of information, much of it ephemeral, that are invading the public and private domains and, on the other, to keep the development of individuals and communities as its end in view. Education must, as it were, simultaneously provide maps of a complex world in constant turmoil and the compass that will enable people to find their way in it (Delors 1996, 85).

Given UNESCO's view of the symbiotic relationship between education and the broader realm of civil society, one may turn not only to documents, recommendations and commissions specifically tasked with educational matters in a consideration of how education relates to civil society. As elaborated elsewhere by Conley and Barot (1996, 219-224), many other conferences and reports have also helped to sharpen UNESCO's vision of education (including adult education; see Delors, Part 3, Chap. 6) and civil society. The 1990 UNESCO International Conference on Democratic Culture and Development, the 1992 United Nations Conference on Environment and Development (UNCED) and the 1993 World Conference on Human Rights and the resulting Vienna Declaration all had significant educational components relating both to the present state and the future path of civil society. The Montevideo Declaration on Democratic Culture and Governance, which came out of the 1990 conference, recommended "the development of national, regional, and interregional education programs designed, with a view to developing a democratic culture, to enhance the people's awareness of the values of freedom, solidarity, justice, social peace and tolerance" (p.2). At UNCED the role for citizenship education was conceived, in the vein of the later Delors Report, as underscoring a concerted and united approach on the part of global civil society to the shared challenges posed by environmental questions. The conference participants saw the role for citizen education as contributing "to increasing creativity and rationality, the development of problem-solving capabilities and competitiveness needed to foster the increasingly complex cultural, social, political, and technological decisions involved in sustainable human development" (Conley and Barot 1996, 221). In turn, the Vienna Declaration expounded on the importance of incorporating human rights education in all aspects and levels of educational initiatives and, in large part, echoed the commitments of the Montreal Plan of Action, which derived from the 1993 World Congress on Education for Human Rights and Democracy (http://www.unhchr.ch/html/menu5/ wchr.htm).

At the Montreal Congress, education was seen as a vital component in the formation of civil society. The purpose of the Plan of Action was the creation of a culture of human rights and the development of democratic societies that would enable individuals and groups to solve their disagreements and conflicts in non-violent ways. Adult education figured prominently because education was conceived in its broadest sense across the differences of age, gender, class, ethnic, national, religious and linguistic groups and in all sectors of society. Further, the Plan made specific reference to non-formal educational sectors and proposed that education for human rights and democracy in non-formal settings involve groups of adults and young people, including those not attending school or in out-of-school education, through their families, their professional associations, workplaces, institutions and groupings (Conley and Barot 1996, 222).

UNESCO's Tools for Action

There are examples of a role each of us can play as active responsible citizens in our own field of competence. Rules and codes of ethics have to be part of our framework for action. Have you ever been in a country you didn't know and tried to buy a stamp to send a letter to your family? Each country has its own way of distributing stamps, and you may need to be a bit imaginative to find out where to buy one. But did you ever stop to think that, once you have dropped your letter with the proper stamp attached to it, anywhere in the world, it is going to be transported to the destination you have written on the envelope? Have you ever thought of the number of international agreements and arrangements that make this action possible? Most of us don't need to know all the international conventions and agreements that make our way of life possible. To have this global perspective, as mentioned earlier, it will be increasingly important to know at least the international agreements related to our individual profession and our personal commitments. It will not only be of value to us as informed citizens but also as responsible citizens to remind everybody and especially our authorities of their international commitments.

It was as early as the Universal Declaration of Human Rights of 1948 that the United Nations affirmed the importance of education at all levels of civil society. Since that time, UNESCO has been tasked with a specific role in the area of education and has elaborated on the scope and meaning of this commitment. The way in which this early commitment has evolved to include and expand upon the importance of adult education is evidenced as early as the second and third International Conferences on Adult Education (Montreal 1960; Tokyo 1972) and also in the Recommendation on the Development of Adult Education, adopted by the General Conference of UNESCO, at its nineteenth session in Nairobi on November 26, 1976. The Nairobi Recommendation states:

> Recalling the principles set forth in Articles 26 and 27 of the Universal Declaration of Human Rights, guaranteeing and specifying the right of everyone to education and to participate freely in the cultural, artistic, and scientific life and the principles set forth in articles 13 and 15 of the International covenant on Economic, Social and Cultural Rights ... the access of adults to education in the context of life-long education, is a fundamental aspect of the right to education and facilitates the exercise of the right to participate in political, cultural, artistic and scientific life [and that] ... for the full development of the human personality ... education must be considered ... as a life long process.
> (http://www.unesco.org/education/standards/english/recom_cg.htm)

This Recommendation echoes UNESCO's broader assumptions concerning education's profound and far-reaching social and civic influence, makes evident UNESCO's vision of the integral relationship between adult education and civil society and outlines the areas of potential contribution and transformation adult education might assume in the formation of civil society:

> The development of adult education, in the context of life long education, is necessary as a means of achieving a more rational and more equitable distribution of educational resources between young people and adults, and between different social groups, and of ensuring better understanding and more effective collaboration between the generations, and greater political, social and economic equality between social groups and between the sexes.... [A]dult education can contribute decisively to economic and cultural development, social progress and world peace.
> (http://www.unesco.org/education/standards/english/recom_cg.ht)

It is important to note at the outset that UNESCO's sensitivity to the complexity of educational venues and forms is as characteristic of the area of adult education as it is of education more generally. Though this chapter is more concerned with adult education concentrated in formal educational settings, UNESCO's conception of adult education acknowledges the variety of avenues through which adult education may be channelled. Again, as expounded in the Nairobi Recommendation,

> the term adult education denotes the entire body of organized educational processes, whatever the content, level and method, whether formal or otherwise, whether they prolong or replace initial education in schools, colleges and universities as well as in apprenticeship, whereby persons regarded as adult by the society to which they belong develop their abilities, enrich their knowledge, improve their technical or professional qualifications, or turn them in a new direction and bring about changes in the attitudes and behaviour in twofold perspective of full personal development and participation in balanced and independent social, economic, and cultural development.... [E]ducation and learning, far from being limited to a period of attendance at school, should extend throughout

life, include all skills and branches of knowledge, use all possible means, and give the opportunity to all people for the full development of the human personality.
(http://www.unesco.org/education/standards/english/recom_cg.htm)

In this way the wide-ranging vision of educational opportunity envisioned by UNESCO extends also to the area of adult education. The passages from the Nairobi Declaration speak to the potentially symbiotic nature of the education-civil society relationship. Education not only retains positive potential in structuring the individual lives and broad range of interactions that make up civil society, but varying levels of civil society are equally vital in discerning and devising opportunities to increase and facilitate access to educational programs and initiatives for all.

Yet another vital international instrument related to adult educators is the Recommendation Concerning Education for International Understanding, Co-operation and Peace and Education Relating to Human Rights and Fundamental Freedoms, adopted by the General Conference of UNESCO in 1974. Recommendation 74, as it has come to be known, sets out guiding principles by stressing the need for education about contemporary world problems such as the maintenance of peace, disarmament, respect for human rights, development and an awareness of the increasing global interdependence between peoples and nations. It also stresses the duties incumbent upon individuals, social groups and nations towards each other (http://www.unesco.org/education/standards/english/recom_cg.htm).

The Yamoussoukro Declaration on Peace in the Minds of Men (1989) brought together delegates from five continents to discuss peace and human security. The Declaration incorporates a broad view of the range of obligations in the social sphere. The Congress called upon states to include peace and human rights components as a permanent feature in all education programs. It also proposed the promotion of education and research in the field of peace using an interdisciplinary approach aimed at studying the interrelationship between peace, human rights, disarmament, development and the environment, thereby reflecting the broad understanding of contextualized social roles and agency with which adult educators must be concerned (http://www.unesco.org/cpp/uk/projects/yamouss.pdf).

During March 1990 the World Conference on Education for All met in Jomtien, Thailand. The World Declaration on Education for All: Meeting Basic Learning Needs includes certain recommendations on education relevant to our discussion (http://www.unesco.org/education/efa/07Apubl.htm). Article Two of the Declaration is particularly relevant to questions of adult education: "To serve the basic learning needs of all requires more than a recommitment to basic education as it now exists. What is needed is an 'expanded vision' that surpasses present resource levels, institutional structures, curricula and conventional delivery systems while building on the best in current practices."

Article Three specifically mentions adults: "Basic education should be provided to all children, youth and adults. To this end, basic education services of quality should be expanded and consistent measures must be taken to reduce disparities. For basic education to be equitable, all children, youth and adults must be given the opportunity to achieve and maintain an acceptable level of learning." Relevant to citizenship education is Article IV: "Whether or not expanded educational opportunities will translate into meaningful development–for an individual or for society–depends ultimately on whether people actually learn as a result of those opportunities, i.e., whether they incorporate useful knowledge, reasoning ability, skills, and values."

The Declaration ends with a statement that sums up UNESCO's goals: "Only a stable and peaceful environment can create the conditions in which every human being, child and adult alike, may benefit from the goals of this Declaration."

The April 2000 World Education Forum has taken these points and expanded them in "The Dakar Framework for Action" (http://www2.unesco.org/wef/en-conf/dakfram.shtm).

In October 1994 the forty-fourth session of the UNESCO International Conference on Education was held in Geneva, Switzerland. Under the theme "Education for Peace, Human Rights and Democracy," 129 member states met, represented by Ministers of Education. They adopted a Declaration and recommended that UNESCO, at its General Conference in 1995, adopt the Framework of Action negotiated at the same meeting. The Declaration indicated that the Ministers give highest priority to those actions that will encourage comprehension, solidarity, and tolerance between peoples, between ethnic, social, cultural or religious groups, and between nations. The Declaration cites, as a major priority, the co-operation of all partners who would be able to help teachers to link the education process more closely to social life and to transform it into the practice of tolerance and solidarity, respect for human rights, democracy and peace (http://www.ibe.unesco.org/Dialog/decla94.htm).

The UNESCO Fifth International Conference on Adult Education, held in Hamburg, Germany, from July 14-18, 1997, was

> viewed and lived by many participants as a sounding board to construct a new vision, looking at adult learning as an integral part of a life-long and life-wide learning process, promoting family and community learning as well as dialogue between cultures, respecting differences and diversity and thereby contributing to a culture of peace (Esi Sutherland-Addy, Rapporteur-General).

It is interesting to note that the conference participants believed that educational systems must be designed with a perspective of learning throughout life to ensure that adult education contributes to, among other things, the empowerment of individuals and communities.

UNESCO's Strength: International Co-operation

International networks can be seen as a way to navigate an overwhelming exchange of information and knowledge. It is, perhaps, this vital endeavour that makes UNESCO's contributions to the consideration of education and civil society of the utmost importance. Accomplishing much of its work through an engagement with the multitude of actors, organizations (both governmental and non-governmental), and interested communities that make up civil society, UNESCO's expertise on matters of education and civil society is informed by the diversity of that civil society itself. Formed by the benefit of such diverse input, UNESCO's reflections and normative instruments have the benefit of perspectives deriving from wide-ranging and diverse sectors of the educational community and from other interested civic parties. Belonging to professional associations remains a vital linkage in sharing information and knowledge, a practice that is, itself, a continuing educational process. In most international fora, intellectuals from the South seek this kind of invaluable follow-up to their training. The problem is not only international; it is also taking place in countries such as ours, and could be counteracted by the new technologies. This subject, however, is beyond the scope of this current chapter.

Conclusion

In concluding, we would like to highlight some of the rewarding aspects of dealing with a pluralist society of adults to create a renewed democratic society. Adult learners have their own experiences, culturally, socially and with democracy. These may include marginalization, employment concerns and/or difficulties and so on. Canada's sectoral participation rate and lack of variety of participatory forms suggest that political efficacy is low. These considerations, in a student-centred learning model, must be taken into account. As a result, instructors need to be prepared to acknowledge the diversity of social experiences represented in the educational environment, to facilitate interaction between those experiences and to have their own positions and perspectives challenged by these varied experiences. This respect for and validation of the broader experiences of adult students in the formal environment is vital in order to work co-operatively with students. This co-operation is needed in order to make sense of their experiences and to reinvigorate a meaningful sense of agency in the educative environment that can inform participation in the broader social sphere. Broad civil society education must, therefore, be underscored by the awareness that varied individual experiences occur within a larger social whole, an awareness that may assist in sifting through these varied and seemingly removed experiences. Essential, then, in adult education for civil society is attention to context and the interplay of social roles, individual agency and social connectedness. Adult educators concerned with maintaining civil society through education must be aware of the role of social understanding as a crucial facet of individual agency.

Importantly, reinvigorating the "social agent" in education at the adult level also demands consistent attentiveness and vigilance on the part of instructors to similarly contextualize and define their own professional role and to explore possibilities of, and means of creating space for, a student-centred educational model that may inform that professional role within the new knowledge environment. Is the role of the adult educator simply to make information on human rights, peace and democratic institutions available to students? Again, this does not entail the creation of a specific citizenship course per se. The vital role is to demonstrate the embedded nature of various social positions, the broader context of individual experience and the existence of avenues of inquiry and redress available to varying social roles and positions. At the core of these provisions is the need for grounding any meaningful agency-advocacy for those with alternative lived experiences in a broader awareness of social connections and available resources.

An exploration of the possible role for adult educators in relating individual and local experiences to the larger global context is essential. Underpinning this comprehension of levels of community in the world is the idea that an understanding of the reciprocal nature of experience does not constitute a resignation to futility and a devaluation of individual agency. Rather, this broader comprehension can lead to increased self-esteem, a feeling of interrelatedness and a sense of empowerment. UNESCO's work in the education and human sciences sectors promoting civil society dovetails with its work in adult education. The Delors Report is likely the most important UNESCO document of the 1990s because of the impact it will have on concepts of education, and adult education in particular.

Endnotes

1. Throughout the paper the term *civil society* is used in the broad and operational sense set forth by the Canadian International Development Agency in its draft policy on "Human Rights, Democratization and Good Governance" prepared by the Good Governance and Human Rights Policy Division, March 11, 1994. The draft characterizes civil society as referring "broadly to organizations and associations of people, formed for social or political purposes, that are not created or mandated by the government. NGOs, unions, cooperatives, grassroots organizations and professional associations are all part or civil society ... [and] give voice to a variety of interests and perspectives that governments and decisions makers would otherwise never have access to" (p.58). This document may also be found on the CIDA website: http://www.acdi-cida.gc.ca/publications-e.htm.

2. Human agency is used here to refer to a lived way of being and interacting in the world. In other words, it is not a mere state of mind or intention in the Kantian sense. For a further elaboration of human agency as an activity see the chapter "What is Human Agency" in *Human Agency and Language* by Charles Taylor (New York: Cambridge University Press, 1985), 15-44.

References

Albala-Bertrand, L. 1996. Citizenship and education: Towards meaningful practice in prospects. *Quarterly Review of Comparative Education* 100.
    Website: http://www3.itu.ch/ibecitied/publicat.html.

Bloom, A. 1987. *The closing of the American mind.* Toronto: Simon & Schuster.

Canada. 1993. Standing Senate Committee on Social Affairs, Science and Technology Report on Canadian Citizenship: Sharing the Responsibility. The Senate of Canada.

Conley, M.W., and É. Barot. 1996. Human rights education: Present and future trends. *The Journal of Canadian and International Education* 25 (2).

Declaration adopted by the International Conference on Democratic Culture and Development: Towards the Third Millennium in Latin America. 1990. Organized jointly by UNESCO and the PAX Institute, under the auspices of the Government of the Eastern Republic of Uruguay, November 27-30, Montevideo, Uruguay.

Delors, J. 1996. *Learning: The treasure within.* Report to UNESCO of the International Commission on Education for the Twenty-first Century. Paris: UNESCO Publishing.

Faure, E., et al. 1972. *Learning to be: The world of education today and tomorrow.* Paris: UNESCO.

Freire, P. 1970. *Pedagogy of the oppressed.* New York: Seabury.

International Congress on Education for Human Rights and Democracy. 1993. Montreal, March 8-11. *Draft world plan of action on education for human rights and democracy.* Document SHS-93/CONF.402/4, Paris, February 22, 1993.

International Congress on Peace in the Minds of Men. 1989. Held on the initiative of UNESCO in Yamoussoukro, Cote d'Ivoire.

Mayor, F. 1997. Philosophy education: A key to the twenty-first century. in *Newsletter of the UNESCO Division of Philosophy* 5 (p.1). Paris: UNESCO.

McLeod, K.A. 1989. Exploring citizenship education: Education for citizenship. In *Canada and Citizenship Education*, edited by Keith McLeod. Toronto: Canadian Education Association.

Nussbaum, M. 1997. *Cultivating humanity: A classical defense of reform in liberal education.* Cambridge: Harvard University Press.

Oakeshott, M. 1989. *The voice of liberal learning: Michael Oakeshott on education.* New Haven: Yale University Press.

Osborne, K. 1988. *Educating citizens: a democratic socialist agenda for Canadian education.* Toronto: Our Schools/Our Selves Education Foundation.

Recommendation on the Development of Adult Education. 1976. Adopted by UNESCO General Conference at its nineteenth session. Nairobi, November 26.

Rendel, M. 1997. *Whose human rights?* Staffordshire: Trentham Books.

Report of the Commission on Global Governance. 1995. *Our global neighbourhood.* Oxford: Oxford University Press.

Sutherland-Addy, Esi, Rapporteur-General. 1997. The UNESCO Fifth International Conference on Adult Education, Hamburg, Germany, July 14-18. Website: http://www.unesco.org/education/uie/confintea/repeng.html#B. Thematic Working Groups.

United Nations Conference on Environment and Development. 1992. Rio de Janeiro. Website: http://infoserver.ciesin.org/ TG/PI/TREATY/unced.html.

United Nations Development Programme. 1998. *Human development report.* Website: http://www.undp.org/hdro/98.htm.

UNESCO. Commission on Education for the Twenty-First Century, or the Delors Commission. Website: http://www.unesco .org/delors/.

———. International Conference on Education, Geneva, Switzerland. 1994. *Education for peace, human rights and democracy.* Declaration.
Website: http://www.ibe.unesco.org/Dialog/decla94.htm.

———. 1976. General Conference, nineteenth session, Nairobi, Kenya, November 26. Website: http://www.unesco.org/education/standards/english/recom_cg.htm.

United Nations World Conference on Human Rights. 1993. Vienna, Austria, June, and the resultant Vienna Declaration. Website: http://www.unhchr.ch/html/menu5/wchr.htm.

World Declaration on Education For All. 1990. Jomtien, Thailand.
Website: http://www.unesco.org/education/efa/07Apubl.htm.

World Education Forum. 2000. Dakar Senegal.
Website: http://www2.unesco.org/wef/en-conf/dakfram.shtm.

Yamoussoukro Declaration on Peace in the Minds of Men. 1989.
Website: http://www.unesco.org/cpp/uk/projects/yamouss.pdf.

III

ISSUES IN ADULT EDUCATION

13

The Issue of Access in Adult Education: Privilege and Possibility

Dianne L. Conrad

I f access to adult education seems, at first glance, a simple concept about who participates in programs and who doesn't, then the starting point for this chapter should be the pointed statement that the issue of access is not simple at all. In fact, much of the discussion of the entire field of adult education is as messy and complicated as the notion of access to it. Defining adult education, as evidenced in recent literature (Grace 1998; Harris 1987; Selman et al. 1998), is itself an onerous task. Discussion leads not only into politics and pedagogy but also into a broad range of sociological issues. This chapter will address the issue of access to adult education by providing a brief historical overview, a review of current issues and considerations and some ideas about enhancing adults' access to educational programs of their choice.

A Backwards Glance at Access: Historical Considerations

As recently as 1992, the theme of the annual Canadian Association for University Continuing Education (CAUCE) conference centred around the tension between the historical understanding of adult education as a social movement and the perceived evolution of our current adult education enterprises into entrepreneurial ventures.

Historically, Canadian adult education has a rich tradition of devotion to social causes. From the importation of the Mechanics' Institutes from Britain in 1827, to the organization of the Women's Institutes by Adelaide Hoodless in Ontario in 1897, to Alfred Fitzpatrick's founding of the Reading Camp Association (later Frontier College) in 1901, to Moses Coady's championing of co-operatives in the Maritimes, to the Challenge for Change project on Fogo Island in 1966, adult educators have framed their work in the language of social justice, citizenship and participatory democracy. During the years of both World War I and II, calls for attention to citizenship and mindfulness were even more pronounced. Note the urgency in the definition of adult education in *The 1919 Report* to the British Ministry of Reconstruction by its Committee on Adult Education, as quoted in Selman et al. (1998, 17): "All the deliberate efforts by which men and women attempt to satisfy their thirst for knowledge, to equip themselves for their responsibilities as citizens and members of society or to find opportunities for expression."

During these years, the recipients of adult education's social advocacy thrusts were members of identifiable disadvantaged groups: the working poor, immigrants without the skills to use the English language, women without access to information about their rights or venues for expression or farmers who were geographically dispersed and unable to access the agricultural knowledge necessary for their commercial success.

It is worth noting also that the institutions of adult education that hallmarked Canada's past strove to take their educational opportunities *to* those in need in order to ensure access to learning. Moses Coady and his cousin Jimmy Tompkins travelled Nova Scotia to encourage co-operative participation from that province's workers. Fitzpatrick's young labourer-teachers left the comforts of the city to live and work alongside the immigrant men who became their students in the evening, after the toil of long days. The National Farm Forum, supported by Ned Corbett and the Canadian Association for Adult Education (CAAE), broadcast its weekly programs and co-ordinated the flow of information back and forth to its audiences across the nation. In Alberta, Corbett's department of Extension actually drove University of Alberta instructors out across the rutted roads of rural Alberta, their cars loaded up with film strips and books for awaiting students.

Over the years, however, most notably in the boom of the 1960s, adult education in Canada became institutionalized in bricks-and-mortar structures that responded to a different calling: the education and credentialization of the country's expanding youth population. These efforts were supported by the infusion of federal funds for the provision of vocational and technical training initiatives.

Spencer (1998), in describing the history of adult education as a social "movement," questions our current goals:

> If the field of adult education refers to all adult education and training, including vocational and workplace learning, post-secondary provision, vocational and non-vocational, credentialized and non-credentialized, it is difficult to view adult education as a "movement." Today's diverse goals reflect some fundamentally opposed philosophies and values...; it is not at all clear that most adult education today is geared toward emancipation and democracy. Another way of looking at this issue is to consider that adult education today is best understood as a process which can aid other social movements (p.24).

In terms of access, then, Spencer describes a philosophical shift that changes the criterion from need based on observable deficiencies, in language or other areas, to need based on vocational training and professional advancement.

The Question of Access Today: Some Cautions

Human Resource Development Canada's (HRDC) regularly published adult education and training surveys do their statistical best to record the flow of educational activity in the adult education domain. Despite the necessity for the accumulation of these data, attempting to quantify access in this way raises some problematic issues. Who is counted in the surveys outlining attendance? How is attendance defined? How should the data be interpreted? And what knowledge do they ultimately give us about Canadians' access to adult education?

Adult education offerings fall into these categories: formal, non-formal and informal. The effective measurement of participation in adult education ventures is largely dependent on the placement of a particular program or course into the *formal learning* category, that is, courses or programs offered by institutions in a structured manner, often for credit. These are the types of courses in which participation can be measured by enrolment–by counting those who enter or those who pay. Selman et al. (1998) suggest that enrolment "can be thought of metaphorically as a turnstile" (p.121), pointing out that while enrolment is a valid and institutionally necessary way of determining the popularity, worth or success of a course, quantitatively it does not address what is understood by most adult educators to be the underpinning critical importance of the endeavour–the value of the learning that goes on.

Selman et al. (1998) describe the "occurrence of adult learning wherever and however it occurs" (p.122) as *engagement*. Engaged learning can, by definition, occur *outside* of formal institutions, in non-organized, loosely organized or personal and private situations that involve solely the learner and any stimulus–a book, another person or perhaps a reflective moment.

Adult education lore maintains that the majority of adult learning is best described using the engagement approach, and, using Tough's (1979) well-known self-directed learning project research,[1] Selman et al. (1998) explain the seeming discrepancy between statistics that report 20 percent participation levels and those that report 90 percent participation levels in adult learning: the difference, of course, lies in the counting methodology.

With this caution in mind, what do the statistical figures on adult education and training tell us? The first observation here is that the patterns of adult education attendance have not changed substantially in recent years. The first nation-wide data that were gathered in the field, published by the Canadian Association for Adult Education in *From the Adult's Point of View* (1982), indicated trends at that time that are still evident in the recent data published by Human Resource Development Canada in 1997:

- Geographically, the level of adult education or training increases from the east (Newfoundland) to the west (British Columbia).

- The majority of participation is job related.

- Seventy percent of attendees receive some or total sponsorship from their employers.

- Women participate more than men.

- The majority of participants are between the ages of twenty-five and forty-four.

- Individuals with higher levels of education are more likely to participate in *more* education.

- Full-time workers participate more than part-time workers (31 percent to 21 percent) and those not attached to the labour force participated at a level of only 5 percent.

A second and more important observation pertains to the interactivity of the socioeconomic pattern of adult education participation. Higher levels of education generally ensure employment at higher income levels; these positions are often supervisory or management. Individuals filling these positions require ongoing or additional education in order to successfully meet the challenges of expanding and changing markets. In addition, the individuals most likely to occupy these positions have histories of successful learning that include study skills, communication skills and the belief that further education will continue to benefit them both professionally and personally (HRDC 1997). Statistics verify that participation in adult education and training activities correlates positively with previous educational attainment (CAAE 1982; HRDC 1997).

Changes in the Workplace: New Demands for Education and Training

The Canadian workplace has changed dramatically in the last decade. Practitioners and theorists in adult education and in human resources and training have identified the sets of conditions that have effected changes in recent years and have articulated and documented the shape of those changes on Canada's workforce (Beck 1995; Couture 1993; Yerxa 1993). Demographics—an ageing workforce and a workforce comprised of more women and minorities than ever before—and the rise of technology enabling global competition and communication have resulted in broad workplace shifts, described in HRDC's 1994 *Adult Education and Training Survey*:

> The continuous and effective upgrading of Canada's human resources has become an essential condition of ensuring long term growth and success in the global economy. In the coming years, the changing demands of the workforce will put a lot of pressure on Canadian workers. Traditional jobs, with work patterns and skills that remain stable over the worker's entire career, are disappearing. Changes in technology modify the variety of jobs available and skills needed to accomplish them (pp.5-6).

Couture (1993) classifies the structure of new economic demands in the following way:

> The widening gap between rich and poor is related to a growing divergence in how much money people receive for the work they do. That divergence is related to each person's level of education. The American political economist Robert Reich divides workers into three types: routine producers, in-person servers and symbolic analysts (p.14).

In short, Couture (1993) sees our economy valuing and rewarding individuals in positions of high skill value that she terms "symbolic analysts." These are the knowledge workers of the future who will be skilled in decision making, problem solving and strategy. Quoting Reich, she explains that symbolic analysts will "solve, identify and broker problems by manipulating symbols" (p.15).

What Does This Mean for Agencies of Adult Education?

In his 1984 publication *The New Majority: Adult Learners in the University*, Campbell was already heralding changes in adults' learning patterns, attributable at that time to the introduction of silicon chip technology and the Information Age (Beck 1995) and to the rise of the lifelong learning concept in which educational "front-end" loading–Kindergarten to Grade 12 and then off to work–gave way to integrated learning and recurrent learning.

> The range of learning interests of adults has expanded. Adult learners have adopted a format of non-sequential or recurring education to an extent quite unpredictable even a decade ago. It is commonplace today for education to be interrupted for periods of work or travel or reflection. Education and training connected to those interests are not necessarily confined to a single source. Would-be learners tend to move across educational sectors, from provider to provider as, for example, from college to university to technical school to industry-provided in-service training services to museum recreation classes. Today's students seek a mix of educational experiences to maximize "self-actualization" (Campbell, 13).

Campbell's (1984) observations have become even more acute as today's motivating forces of economy and culture fuel a continuing pressure for credentialization and information. Reflecting on the integration of future technological prowess into our lives, author and scholar Umberto Eco predicts a new societal class struggle–not Marxian, between workers and owners,

> but between those who know how to deal critically and actively with the new media and those who will use them passively.... There will be: a nomenklatura, a ruling class able to use all the new instruments; a middle class using them passively, like bank clerks or airline employees; and proletarians, watching TV (Globe and Mail 1998).

Casting an eye backwards over adult education's rich traditions enables us to appreciate the field's contribution to matters of citizenship, national identity and literacy. Clearly, the role of adult education in the continued development of a successful and healthy Canadian society is as important now, at the beginning of the new millennium, as it ever has been. But who will participate in continued learning? Who will benefit from conditions of access? Who will be denied? The question of access is undeniably critical to not only the future of educational endeavours but also, more pointedly, to the social and economic well-being of our society.

Increased Access through Distributed Learning: New Opportunities?

The change in our technological world in recent years has been phenomenal. New hardware and new software work together to link businesses and corporate enterprises around the world in partnerships and collaborative endeavours. Banking transactions on one continent are electronically processed on another; economic ripples from one nation impact every other country world-wide within days. Factors of distance and geographical diversity have disappeared almost overnight, not only in business and industry but also in education.

The emergence of virtual on-line universities such as Athena and Phoenix and Western Governors, made possible and academically viable by the development of sophisticated on-line teaching and learning technologies, has purportedly opened up access to many learners whose vistas were previously curtailed by barriers of time and space. Is this really so? Statistically, it is too soon to tell; however, if the sociological indicators that have continually been reinforced by statistical data remain extant, then certain predictions can be assumed:

- Technological interest will be most apparent in the more educated members of society.

- Training in technology will be undertaken by those in upper-level positions and those already possessing some training in those areas.

- Training in new systems will be made available to those already immersed in associated fields and areas of professional interest.

- Access to learning at a distance using sophisticated technologies will be gained by those already familiar with such technologies and in possession of the necessary equipment.

However, the issue of access and distance education is larger than the technologies that usually accompany distance endeavours and that have attracted much of the attention associated with learning at a distance. Let us first examine what traditionally have been considered the barriers to accessing adult education.

Barriers to Access

Adult education research has identified three overarching categories of barriers that, at first glance, could seem easily to explain adults' non-participation in learning experiences (Cross 1981; Percival 1993). They contain situations familiar to most of us, situations that may have prevented any of us at some time or another from being able to attend a program or a course of our choosing.

1. *Situational barriers.* These barriers, relating to an individual's circumstances at a given time, may include the following: geography, lack of money, fatigue, lack of time, child care considerations and the lack of technology or the training to use it.

2. *Dispositional barriers.* These are concerned with the learner's attitude towards self and towards learning, and they are usually associated with negative experiences in the learner's educational past. Learners with a history of failed educational attempts may harbour grave doubts about their ability to successfully complete any further learning.

3. *Institutional barriers.* These "relate to policies and procedures of the institution that make participation difficult or impossible" (Percival 1993). Examples of such barriers may include scheduling, fees, admission requirements, residency requirements, transfer policies and curriculum decisions.

Distance education, sometimes referred to as distributed learning and open learning, has been heralded in recent years as providing new avenues of access to formalized learning for those previously not able to participate in post-secondary education because of various situational barriers such as those described above. For some learners, most obviously those who live at a distance from institutions providing the required educational services, being able to complete courses at a distance is indeed an improvement in access. However, the categorization above does not "sufficiently emphasize the socially constructed barriers of gender, class and ethnicity" (Spencer 1995) that limit learning opportunities for some members of society.

Beyond Barriers: Inequality of Opportunity

There are other larger and more pervasive considerations about issues of access that look beyond learners' immediate financial or daily situations to their positions in society's social structure. Such perspectives are based on sociological doctrines and philosophies that seek to understand the relationship of individuals to their society and offer explanations of broad structural factors that inhibit certain individuals' participation in adult education (Himelfarb and Richardson 1991; Jarvis 1985). Percival (1993) notes that,

> according to Jarvis, formal education, since it is part of the prevailing social system, exists to maintain that system. To this end, adult education serves a number of functions that help to explain why some people participate and others do not. For example, education exists to reproduce existing social relationships and to transmit the dominant culture. Since adult education is organized by those in the middle class, its content is middle class, its language middle class, and it selects out middle-class participants.

Himelfarb and Richardson (1991), elaborating on these themes, suggest that those who will hold real power—"the real 'priests' of post-war Canadian society"—will be those who can obtain an education that allows them "access to the 'new gods' of technology and computer expertise." More specifically, they see education as playing a critical role in society's "selection process," whereby people are "sifted and sorted" into "various roles in the social hierarchy and, more important, perhaps making people accept as just and proper their position in that hierarchy" (p.289).

Using the more traditional examples of books, Himelfarb and Richardson (1991) highlight the concept of *cognitive poverty* that has contributed to conditions of limited access for some:

> Students from different class backgrounds bring with them to the school different kinds of resources. It has become obvious that children raised in families where there are good books, conversations and discussion ... and so on are likely to have a "head start" over those raised in a more impoverished environment. There is increasing recognition that poverty is not simply lack of money. It is also, at times, a world-view or a subculture which leads to a kind of cognitive poverty—a world with narrowed horizons, limited aspirations and inadequate knowledge and social skills (p.309).

Using the same logic, the introduction of greater dependence on highly selective sets of technological skills presents the possibility of the same type of exclusion from what could become the elitist group—the "nomenklatura" described by Eco (Globe and Mail 1998). Those without access, not only to the purchase of expensive computer equipment, but more importantly, *to the more fundamental understanding of how the world is moving and what forces are driving the conditions of success,* will be even more lost and even less equipped to complete in the new world than they have been in the past. Far from being a type of equalizer, then, the advent of sophisticated systems of learning at distance can even more stridently separate the *haves* from the *have-nots.*

Enhancing Access to Adult Education

Given the preceding discussion outlining some thinkers' views of a deeply ingrained and pervasive societal malaise that predetermines the exclusion of many citizens from an emerging educational elite, one might question what actions, if any, can be taken to promote the level and/or types of access that Canadians have to adult education.

The challenge is both broad and deep; a strong political resolve and economic resources are required to begin to facilitate educational efforts that will result in socioeconomic changes (Coombs 1985). In some parts of Canada—such as First Nations reserves—community development is of key importance. Poonwassie (1993) identifies three major issues in creating wider access to education in such communities: (1) good quality of education, (b) availability of resources, and (c) development of reserves into economically viable communities.

Through whose eyes, then, should we reasonably envision action? Our stake as citizens in adult education is multi-layered: we are taxpayers and thereby funders of adult education; we are participants and thereby receivers of adult education; we are Canadians and thereby integral threads in the societal fabric that frames adult education; and we are providers and thereby professionals. It would be redundant and perhaps even pointless to muse over idealistic remedies for problems that are understood differently by different constituencies through a variety of philosophical lenses. How can the lines between formalized adult education—that which is contained within university continuing education units—and other venues continue to be clearly drawn along the axes of credentialization and cost recovery? The barriers to attendance in these ventures, as described earlier in this chapter, can be attributable to many situational and institutional factors.

Let us consider, then, the question of enhancing access to adult education through a lens both common and accessible to most of us involved in the field of adult education: the sense of the learner. As a thinking adult who is either actively learning or who is already educated in the study of adult education (and is *still* learning), what could your role be in breaking down the barriers that prevent others from coming forward? From eighteen years' experience in the teaching of adults and the provision of adult education experiences in Alberta, I make the following suggestions:

- Uncover for yourself the rich history of Canadian adult education. Come to know the traditions upon which our field is proudly founded. Relate historically to the journeys of those whose successes we continue to celebrate and upon which we continue to build. Let these stories inspire your belief in what you do.

- Know adult education's philosophical underpinnings and understand your own bias. Explore the roots of Knowles' andragogical tradition in your appreciation of adult education's contribution to learner autonomy and self-fulfilment.

- Be cognizant of the evolution of the field as a vocation and recognize the nature of adults' inevitable search for self-development and challenge within the workplace.

- As an adult education practitioner, make yourself and your expertise accessible to those who seek your knowledge and advice, regardless of how informal or tentative the occasion. Life's changes are difficult for all of us, and your thoughtful and informed counsel might provide the necessary catalyst in someone's decision-making process.

- Continue to critically reflect upon your world and your practice. Continue to seek professional development opportunities that enlarge and nurture your abilities.

Can these humanistically oriented, homespun suggestions be useful tools in the march towards fuller access to adult education? Barring government policy changes, radical injections of funding and sweeping social reform, two well-worn adult education notions provide hope. One, articulated by Percival (1993), recalls entrance to adult education as characterized by "back door" routes, a nod to the often circuitous and informal routes that bring people into the field. The other, articulated by Selman et al. (1998), speaks of adult education's responsiveness to the factors that shape it and should encourage us, as practitioners, to assume levels of responsibility within the society: "The enterprise of adult education, like any field of social practice, responds to the nature of the society within which it is functioning" (p.33).

Conclusion

Danish educator, historian and theologian N.F.S. Grundtvig maintained that the adult learning venture should reflect the idea of a "school for life" so that participants would awaken to a "truer and deeper understanding of life, leading to service for a better community and a better nation" (Kulich 1984). Although in recent history it can be argued that the purposes of adult education have focused more specifically on vocational and practical outcomes than on the use of education for social change, the question of who chooses to access and who is *able* to access education is still an issue that deserves society's scrutiny.

Endnotes

[1] Tough researched adults' self-directed learning projects, the definition of which included factors of time, motivation, retention and resultant effects on behaviour, and concluded that the median number of projects conducted annually by an adult is eight. See A. Tough, *The Adult's Learning Projects: A Fresh Approach to Theory and Practice in Adult Learning*, 2d ed. (Toronto: OISE, 1979).

References

Beck, N. 1995. *Excelerate: Growing into the new economy.* Toronto: Harper Collins.

Campbell, D.D. 1984. *The New Majority: Adult learners in the university.* Edmonton, Alta.: The University of Alberta Press.

———. 1977. *Adult education as a field of study and practice: Strategies for development.* Vancouver, B.C.: University of British Columbia.

Canadian Association for Adult Education. 1982. *From the adult's point of view.* Toronto: CAAE.

Canadian Association for University Continuing Education. 1992. *Conference proceedings.* Regina, Sask.: University of Regina University Extension.

Cervero, R.M., and A.L. Wilson. 1994. *Planning responsibly for adult education: A guide to negotiating power and interests.* San Francisco: Jossey-Bass.

Coombs, P.H. 1985. *The world crisis in education: the view from the eighties.* New York: Oxford University Press.

Couture, P. 1993. Lifelong learning and prosperity. *Learning Magazine* 6 (2): 12-18.

Cross, K.P. 1981. *Adults as learners: Increasing participation and facilitating learning.* San Francisco: Jossey-Bass.

Globe and Mail. 1998. Interview with Umberto Eco, Oct. 24.

Grace, A. 1998. Parameters, pedagogy and possibilities in changing times. In *Learning for life: Canadian readings in adult education,* edited by S.M. Scott, B. Spencer, and A.M. Thomas. Toronto: Thompson Educational Publishing.

Harris, F.. 1987. Adult education and community. In *Choosing our future: Adult education and public policy in Canada,* edited by F. Cassidy and R. Faris. Toronto: OISE Press.

Himelfarb, A., and C.J. Richardson. 1991. *Sociology for Canadians: Images of society.* 2d ed. Toronto: McGraw-Hill Ryerson Ltd.

Jarvis, P. 1985. *The sociology of adult and continuing education.* London: Croom Helm.

Kingwell, M. 1998. On the nature of truth and the truth about language. *The Globe and Mail,* October 24.

Knowles, M. 1980. *The modern practice of adult education: From pedagogy to andragogy.* 2d ed. New York: Cambridge.

Kulich, J. 1984. Grundtvig: Education for life. *Learning* 4 (1): 19-21.

MacKeracher, D. 1996. *Making sense of adult learning.* Toronto: Culture Concepts, Inc.

Percival, A. 1993. *Practising theory: A guide to becoming an effective adult education programmer.* University of Saskatchewan: University Extension Press.

Poonwassie, D.H. 1993. Higher education for native students at Manitoba universities: The quest for equal access. In *Issues in the history of education in Manitoba: From the construction of the common school to the politics of voices,* edited by Rosa del C. Bruno-Jofre. United Kingdom: The Edwin Mellen Press.

Selman, G., M. Selman, M. Cooke, and P. Dampier. 1998. *The foundations of adult education in Canada.* 2d ed. Toronto: Thompson Educational Publishing, Inc.

Spencer, B. 1998. *The purposes of adult education: a guide for students.* Toronto: Thompson Educational Publishing.

———. 1995. Removing barriers and enhancing openness: Distance education as social adult education. *Journal of Distance Education* 10 (2): 87-104.

Statistics Canada. 1997. *Adult education and training in Canada.* Ottawa: Human Resources Development Canada.

UNESCO. 1976. *Recommendations on the development of adult education.* Ottawa: Canadian Commission for UNESCO.

Welton, M. 1987. "On the eve of a great mass movement": Reflections on the origins of the CAAE. In *Choosing our future: Adult education and public policy in Canada,* edited by F. Cassidy and R. Faris. Toronto: OISE Press.

Yerxa, J. 1994. *The Yerxa report.* Edmonton: John Yerxa Research, Inc.

14

Labour Education in Canada

Bruce Spencer

This chapter provides an overview of labour education in Canada today. It discusses the range and nature of the provision, gives examples of programs and reviews the effectiveness of this major contribution to non-formal education for working people.

> The largest public contribution to systematic adult education during the early seventies has been the financial support of the Federal Government for labour education.... The expenditures of these organizations (labour unions) on education has also increased, making it possible for thousands of Canadian workers to acquire skills of management, decision making, and knowledge about society that otherwise would have been very hard to achieve.
>
> It is important to note that the money was not given to educational agencies, but to the labour organizations themselves. Most of these latter established their own educational programs, seeking only occasional assistance from the formal educational agencies (Thomas 1993, 35).

Alan Thomas' reference to labour education in the popular text *The Craft of Teaching Adults* alerts Canadian adult educators to an important sphere of adult education little known to them. This may not be so surprising because, as he makes clear, labour unions undertake most labour education themselves without the assistance of professional adult educators. Although the funding by the federal government has now ended, union-controlled labour education remains a major provider of non-formal adult education for working people, probably more significant than companies' "workplace learning" schemes.

This chapter is essentially descriptive. It seeks to (a) describe the scope of Canadian labour education, (b) give examples of union provision, (c) discuss the involvement of educational institutions, (d) explore labour education's contribution to union environmental policy, and (e) review the effectiveness of labour education in Canada.

A main purpose of labour education[1] is to prepare and train union lay members to play an active role in the union. Another purpose is to educate activists and members about union policy and changes in the union environment, such as new management techniques or changes in labour law. Labour education is also used to develop union consciousness, to build common goals and to share organizing and campaigning experience. Unions have a small full-time staff and therefore rely on what is essentially the voluntary activity of their members to be effective at work; the labour education program is a major contributor to building an effective volunteer force.

Most labour union members learn about the union while on the job (what is often referred to as informal or incidental learning). They will learn more and be most active during disputes, but they also learn from union publications and communications, from attending meetings, conferences and conventions and from the union's educational programs. Although labour education only caters to a small number of members in any one year it is "social," as opposed to personal, education. It is designed to benefit a larger number of members because the course participants bring the education to other union members. Labour education has a social purpose—to promote and develop the union presence and purpose so as to advance the union collectively. (The first comprehensive history of Canadian labour education has just been published—*Union Learning: Canadian Labour Education in the Twentieth Century* by Jeffery Taylor, 2001.)

The Extent of Labour Education

It is difficult to present an accurate picture of the extent of labour education in Canada as there is no consistent statistical data on labour education courses offered and there is no clear definition of what constitutes labour education. While labour centrals such as the Canadian Labour Congress (CLC) do collect information on the numbers of courses provided by their affiliates or by themselves and the number of union members attending, they do not have the resources to compile statistical reports. There is also no consistency in the reporting of educational provision by affiliates, provincial labour bodies or independent unions. Courses might be provided by a union local or a labour council or they may be offered collaboratively with local colleges. They may draw on funds provided provincially or nationally. When courses were funded by the Government of Canada Human Resources Development (formally Labour Canada), records were kept and receipts forwarded, but the receipts only provided statistical data for those individuals claiming assistance and may not have included a majority of those unionists in the course.

The CLC accounted for the largest slice of Labour Canada funds. It reported that 1,496 students received assistance for twenty-four provincial schools in 1992-93 (60 percent of Canadian union members belonged to unions affiliated with the CLC in the early 1990s; with the addition of the building trades and other smaller unions merging into CLC unions it was more than 70 percent in 1999). This data was for both week-long "schools," which included several courses, and separate week-long courses or workshops. However, the CLC estimated that between 10,000 to 15,000 union members attended courses in which the CLC was involved (personal communication with CLC staff, April 1994). If figures are added from the educational provision of individual unions and labour councils, these figures can easily be tripled, but there are dangers of double counting. For example, a course provided for an individual union might be offered at a provincial federation of labour school that is partly funded by the CLC. However, the educational provision made by individual unions, union locals and labour councils is probably two to three times that made by the CLC and other union centrals.

There is also the question of what counts as labour education. Does an in-company course offered to union safety committee members, taught by union and management tutors count as "labour education"? If so, does it still count if supervisors and management committee members are present? Does a two-hour union induction program for new starters count as labour education? Given these kinds of problems, it is probably of little value to attempt to pin down an accurate statistic of labour education in Canada. At best we can "guesstimate" based on the returns to Labour Canada, the records of individual unions and assumptions as to what constitutes "labour education." Some of the statistics include the following:

- Labour Canada provided educational funds for the independent, non-affiliated unions in 1992-93 on the basis of a total of 454,000 members. The independents claimed that 15,501 members participated in those funded courses, giving a participation rate of 3.4 percent.

- To take an example of one union, the United Food and Commercial Workers International Union (UFCW) calculates 3,227 of its Canadian members participated in courses over an eleven-month period and another 668 members attended industrial conferences (giving a participation rate between 2 percent and 3.5 percent over one year on a membership of approximately 170,000).

- As another example, the Ontario Nurses' Association (ONA) with 50,000 members educates 2,000 (4 percent) members per year.

Just as we can estimate the extent of labour education, we can also provide a list of items to be incorporated within a working definition of labour education. Mainstream labour education includes the following:

1. Courses lasting at least one half-day (thereby omitting short talks and inductions for new members);

2. All weekend, evening and daytime classes up to and including the four-week residential Labour College of Canada course;

3. Courses essentially controlled by the unions and targeted at their members, union representatives and officials;

4. Courses designed to enhance union effectiveness or develop union consciousness;

5. All courses for union members except specific "job" (vocational) training (but including courses on negotiating vocational training).

Using this definition and the statistical information available, we can guess that some 120,000 union members per year (3 percent of the total) underwent some form of labour education in Canada in the early 1990s. (The participation rate may have been double a decade earlier, when the economy was more buoyant and release time was easier to negotiate.[2]) Although union density–the percentage of the non-agricultural workforce that is unionized–had fallen marginally by the late 1990s, from 37 percent to 32 percent, the workforce had increased in size leaving the actual number of union members fairly constant. The building trades have joined the CLC and their representatives are probably taking more courses as a result. The loss of federal funding has affected the CLC. The Labour College of

Canada was suspended for a while and now operates for only four weeks rather than eight. However, unions are continuing to give education a high priority, so on balance there is no substantial argument for changing the figure of 120,000 union members per year.

Such a "guesstimate" would place Canadian labour education at a similar percentage level of provision to that of the United Kingdom and Australia (although there is probably less study time per student in Canada than in the United Kingdom), but much lower than the level of provision in Scandinavia (10 percent or more) where there are stronger traditions of union and workers' education and different relations between unions and the state.

An Overview of Labour Education

Most of the labour education courses provided by unions in Canada are *tools* courses (for example, shop steward training, grievance handling, health and safety). The next largest category are *issues* courses (for example, sexual harassment or racism or new human resource management strategies), which often seek to link workplace and societal issues. A third group of courses can be labelled *labour studies,* which seek to examine the union context (for example, labour history, economics and politics).

Tools courses directly prepare members for active roles in the union and are targeted at existing or potential union activists. They are provided directly by the unions, the provincial labour federations or the union centrals (such as the CLC), and only rarely placed in educational establishments. This is unlike the situation in the United States and the United Kingdom where colleges and university extension programmes have traditionally provided some tools courses.

Many unions, such as the Public Service Alliance of Canada (PSAC) and the Canadian Union of Public Employees (CUPE), layer their courses; that is, they have introductory and advanced programs. Advanced courses are available to those who have completed introductory courses. Some of these tools courses lead to issues courses (sometimes referred to as "awareness" courses), which are specifically targeted at raising awareness of issues and are available after members have completed basic tools courses.

The union movement also provides more extensive and demanding educational opportunities such as the CLC's four-week residential Labour College of Canada. Four courses are offered–labour history, economics, sociology, politics–at a first-year university level (labour law is now taught as a one-week course in the regions). Although the Labour College uses some university educators, and is placed within the University of Ottawa, it is a separate entity directly accountable to the CLC. This differs from the roughly equivalent Harvard's Trade Union Program or adult residential colleges in the United Kingdom, such as Ruskin and Northern College. Although the Labour College has only sixty places a year, it builds union contacts among labour activists from different unions and has been in existence for forty years.[3]

These more extensive courses are labour studies courses, designed to broaden participants' awareness of the context of labour unionism. While the CLC Labour College of Canada is the flagship program, this category could also include short courses, for example in labour history or economics, offered by labour councils over a number of evenings or by provincial labour bodies (often in conjunction with the CLC) in a week-long school, and Paid Educational Leave (PEL) courses offered by the Canadian Autoworkers (CAW) and Canadian Union of Postal Workers (CUPW) for their members.

While many universities in Canada offer labour studies concentrations to undergraduates as part of their degree offerings, few have dedicated programs of study designed for, and made available to, trade unionists. In western Canada those that do include: Simon Fraser University Labour Program (Bernard 1991); Manitoba's University-Labour Three-Year Certificate Programme (Saturday mornings); and University of Saskatchewan's Labour Studies Programme (three hour-long evening classes per week for three years). In the Maritimes, the principal program is the Atlantic Region Labour Education Centre (ARLEC), run through St. Francis Xavier Extension in Nova Scotia. Other universities and colleges claim their classes are open to trade unionists but in some cases it is unclear if these are dedicated courses intended to provide a coherent program of study or if the programs are co-sponsored by local trade unions. Certificates are granted in some cases but these courses are usually non-credit even if a certificate is awarded.

The intention of the dedicated courses is to supplement trade union tools courses with a broader educational program and to provide a research basis for union activity. Although unions are represented on the "boards of studies" of these programs, they are rarely union controlled in contrast to union-run courses. (To be consistent with our earlier definition these should probably not be considered "labour education" but rather labour studies programs made available to labour unionists. However, in practice, many local unions are funding members to attend and do consider them labour or union education.)

Beyond the university programs mentioned, there are also courses and programs offered by other educational bodies. Toronto's Metro Labour Education Centre provides tools and issues courses and, together with George Brown College, offers a Labour Studies Certificate program. This has spurred similar work in other community colleges. For example, Ottawa and District Labour Council and Algonquin College have established a Labour Studies Institute. The Labour Council, working with individual unions, offers a range of primarily tools training and issues courses, typically of thirty hours duration. Members attending the courses have their hours logged and can register for a labour studies certificate issued by the college when they have undertaken 240 hours of study, including some core courses in labour studies (chosen from courses such as labour history, economics, politics and international affairs). The certificate does not give automatic credit transfer but will be taken into account when members apply for other courses at the college. There have been four of these college-labour council collaborations operating for more than twenty-five years in

Ontario; how many will survive the Harris cuts is uncertain at the time of writing.

In other colleges, such as Capilano (Vancouver), courses are provided to meet the needs of particular unions and again cover the range of tools, issues and labour studies topics over a one- to five-day period. Most courses offered by Capilano are focused on two-day tools training for workplace representatives from particular unions. However, they now also offer public and broader courses with a certificate and credit transfer. In spite of these examples, college and university provision of labour education is not widespread and is threatened by public spending cuts. The kind of service that Capilano offers small unions in the Vancouver area is organized in Manitoba by a committee of the Manitoba Federation of Labour. As small unions merge into larger organizations there could be even less demand for institutional provision as their representative training moves "in-house." Canadian college and university provision of labour education is at a much lower level than that offered in either the United Kingdom or the United States.

Other Labour Education

Arguably a review of labour education should include some reference to union-run literacy courses, many of which are tutored by fellow unionists and act as a bridge linking immigrant or illiterate workers to union concerns and publications. The Ontario Federation of Labour (OFL) sponsors an active "Literacy in the Workplace" program. Similarly, unions are responsible for a number of worker training programs that allow the unions to educate workers about union concerns alongside vocational training. The building trades are particularly active in this area, but other examples are to be found in the sectoral training programs—the CAW involvement in autoworkers' training is a case in point, or within particular collective agreements such as those of the International Ladies' Garment Workers' Union (now UNITE). Unions, including non-craft unions, are becoming much more proactive in responding to company restructuring and deskilling and are arguing for reskilling, skills recognition and skills profiling, as well as challenging employers to live up to their rhetoric on "pay for knowledge." However, these questions of worker training or worker education go beyond the scope of this discussion, which is concerned with labour or workers' education—education to support the labour movement, not education for work. Within our review of labour education, a case can be made for including some worker health and safety training in which unions are involved (this should not be confused with union safety representative *tools* training referred to above). These courses allow unions to argue for a union view (safe workplace) as opposed to a management view (safe worker) of health and safety. In Quebec and Ontario in particular, union-run worker health and safety training has been used as part of union organizing drives. In all of these cases it can be argued that sectoral or company money as well as union funds is being used to support "labour education."

Unions have also had some limited involvement in television productions such as *Work Week*, or in British Columbia, *Working TV*, which clearly have educational objectives. Union representatives participate in television and radio programs in an attempt to present union perspectives, influence public opinion and educate their members. Some unions are also actively involved in encouraging schools to broaden their curriculum to include labour issues and are providing speakers for school visits. Nor should we ignore union-sponsored arts events such as Ontario's Mayfest.

In summary, most labour education in Canada is tools training and issues courses targeted at union activists. In addition, unions and union centrals provide labour studies programs, often reserved for those activists who have been through the tools and issues courses, but sometimes targeted at members generally. A few educational institutions work with unions to provide labour education (more often labour studies) programs for labour unionists across Canada. Unions are also involved in workplace literacy and worker training programs, and in televisual broadcasting and arts events, all of which are targeted at members and do include some elements of labour education.

An Example of Union Provision: CUPE's Five-Level Program[4]

Individual unions offer a range of courses for activists. Although the particular offerings will vary, the kinds of courses offered by CUPE are broadly typical of those of other Canadian unions. CUPE's five-level education program is graded and leads to a certificate of completion for members who have undertaken the five levels of courses–including the CLC Labour College.

Courses in levels one to four are usually offered on weekends or at week-long seminars and are instructed by "peer instructors" or union staff. Broadly speaking, the levels are: (1) New Members and Officers; (2) Steward Training; (3) Collective Bargaining; (4) Specialized Courses; and (5) Labour College Distance Education Course and Labour College Residential Program.

Level One: New Members and Officers

Level one includes a course called "Our Union," which is designed to provide newer members and new local unions with knowledge about CUPE and how it functions. It also shows participants how to set up and run an effective union organization, including union committees. For example, it explains the role of union officers and how to conduct meetings. Another course offered at this level is "Financial Officer Training," which is specially designed for secretary-treasurers and trustees.

Level Two: Steward Training

Level two is divided into two courses. The first is "Effective Stewarding," a basic course which is primarily instructed by trained rank-and-file occasional instructors. The second course is "Advanced Steward Training," which is usually presented by union staff. This second course offers more analysis of contract language and arbitration cases than the "grievance handling" component of the first course.

Level Three: Collective Bargaining

Level three offers three courses to be taken consecutively. The "Introduction to Bargaining" course attempts to demonstrate how many of the negotiating skills used in daily life relate to the collective bargaining process. It also focuses on how to develop an overall bargaining strategy to achieve specific goals. The course includes: how to set and pursue bargaining goals; dealing with the employer; the importance of good communication skills; leadership in bargaining; developing effective tactics; building support for bargaining goals, both within the local and the community; the right to strike; and presenting a settlement to the membership.

The second collective bargaining course provides an overview of the collective bargaining system as it exists in Canada today. It outlines the roles played by the three main participants—employers, unions and governments—and analyses the strengths and weaknesses of the system. It introduces the CUPE standard agreement and deals in detail with a number of contemporary issues.

The third course deals with formulating and substantiating collective bargaining demands and helps participants use research and statistical materials. When the course is given in a seminar setting, a mock bargaining session is a component.

Level Four: Specialized Courses

Level four is divided into three categories: (1) advanced discussions of material already covered, such as advanced parliamentary procedure, arbitration, public speaking and face-to-face communications; (2) courses designed to broaden the understanding of the role of trade union activity in the context of Canadian and world citizenship such as "Political Action," "Understanding Economics," "Labour Law"; and (3) all the special issue courses such as "Health and Safety Training", "WHMIS," "Pay Equity," "Employment Equity," "Contracting Out," "Aids in the Workplace," "Union Counselling."

Level Five: Labour College

The first two categories of level four serve the additional purpose of preparing members for the level-five Labour College Distance Education course and Labour College of Canada four-week residential program.

Most of these courses, in the first four levels, are available at weekend seminars sponsored by the CUPE District Councils. Specific courses are arranged for union locals (or groups of them). In Ontario, the Ontario division sponsors up to three large weekend seminars with from ten to twelve courses and upwards of 350 participants. CUPE National also holds three week-long schools in Ontario. Some of these courses are available on a correspondence basis.

CUPE is also the sponsor of SoliNet, an electronic mail and computer conferencing system, which it makes available to all sections of the labour and social movements. It links Canadians "from sea to sea to sea," and includes some subscribers from the United States, providing a vital exchange of information and ideas at a relatively low cost. It also uses the network to support its educational programs and is offering, in collaboration with Athabasca University, distance learning, university-accredited labour studies courses on SoliNet.

Many aspects of the CUPE five-level program are replicated by other unions at local, provincial and national levels. The mix of tools training and issues courses is common to typical union education programs in Canada; however, in some unions the level-four courses on economics or labour law are left to the CLC-sponsored provincial federation of labour schools. Course offerings also reflect the problems faced by a particular industrial sector. For example, the UFCW includes courses on repetitive strain injury as well as more common health and safety topics. It also has programs on lay-offs and closures and an extensive union-sponsored literacy program.

Professional Unions: Nurses and Teachers

A growth area for organized labour in Canada since the 1960s has been public sector professionals, some of whom are organized within existing unions but more typically are organized independently into provincial unions such as the Ontario Nurses' Association (ONA) or the British Columbia Teachers' Federation. Most of these provincial unions are not affiliated to any central labour body.

Many of the programs run by these organizations are similar to those of other unions but some reflect professional concerns. For example, the ONA has a program on professional responsibility that encompasses the dual accountability of nurses as employees and as professionals. The British Columbia Teachers' Federation include such courses as "Code of Ethics" and "Violence in Schools" within their programs.

Other courses offered reflect the particular situation facing members, such as "Assertiveness Training" for nurses and "Political Lobbying" for both groups. The British Columbia Teachers' Federation, in preparation for a shift from localized to centralized bargaining, extended the availability of their education programs to include more local representatives who may be involved in contract administration.

These unions or professional associations face a number of problems, and while they are not unique to professional unionism, they are common to them. These include: the cost involved in gathering together representatives from scattered workplaces; getting time off and meeting the costs of wages lost or replacement labour; and the problem of developing a "union consciousness" among members. The British Columbia Teachers' Federation would argue that what they are trying to do is to develop a critical consciousness among their members, particularly in offering general courses on educational themes. It is clear that such programs also have an objective of building union identity by encouraging members to identify issues the union should campaign on. Some unions have directly tackled the problem of developing union and class-consciousness through a targeted "membership education" program.

Membership Education: The Canadian Autoworkers (CAW) PEL Program

A number of unions are running membership education courses targeted at the broader membership and not just union activists. The most distinctive and intensive is that offered by the CAW. This program, which is now emulated by the Canadian Union of Postal Workers (CUPW), is not focused narrowly on preparing representatives for collective bargaining but on promoting an understanding of the union's social and political goals (Spencer 1992; Saul 1994).

The CAW and its predecessor, the Canadian section of the United Auto Workers (UAW), have been running extensive educational programs for their members and activists throughout the post-war period. Since the split from the UAW, the CAW has refurbished its Family Education Centre at Port Elgin, Ontario, (on the shores of Lake Huron) and overhauled its educational programs. Central to this refurbishment is the union's PEL (Paid Educational Leave) program. The program is funded by a benefit (2 to 3 cents per member per hour) negotiated in contracts with employers. The money goes into a trust fund and is used to pay for lost wages, travel, accommodation and the educational costs of the program. The bargaining unit (usually a particular local) can send as many members as its contributions allow. The program consists of four week-long residential courses, usually separated by two to three weeks on the job between each week of course work. The program is previewed by applicants at a weekend residential school, to which applicants' partners are invited, and commitments are made to take the full course. A PEL course would typically consist of 130 members subdivided into six groups. The union also offers the program in French. By 1994, more than 4,000 members had completed the CAW's PEL program.

Each week (level) of the course has a separate theme: Level One: the present as history; Level Two: sociology; Level Three: political economy; and Level Four: social and political change. Some study skills (for example, basic math and reading) and union representative skills (for example, reporting and effective speaking) are built into the course. There are also committees established at the outset from among the course members, which mirror the kind of committees operating throughout the union—substance abuse, international affairs, women, human rights, culture and recreation. These committees organize events during the course and make recommendations to the course co-ordinator. The course concludes with a convention (mock-conference) focusing on the wide range of issues addressed during the course and reported on by the committees.

Videos are used extensively and shared by members, but they have not replaced written materials that are sometimes read aloud, using a system of voluntary readers, in each group. (Reading aloud was a technique used in early North American unions. For example, Samuel Gompers, AFL president from 1886-1894 and 1896-1924, began his union work as a reader to cigar makers.) Each week there are a number of plenary sessions with union and guest speakers and an opportunity for questions and discussion from the floor. These can vary depending on the issues of the day and on student requests. For example, topics might include free trade, refugees, Palestine, community politics and coalition building. These sessions complement the work going on in the classroom and in student committees.

Local Union Discussion Leaders (LUDLs) lead the groups. These volunteers are union activists whose release can be negotiated for a particular week (their wages are paid for out of the PEL trust fund) and who have received additional discussion leader training. In addition to training in teaching methods, these lay tutors meet annually to discuss changes in course content and updating of materials.

There is plenty of opportunity for student experience and knowledge to be used within the groups, although the approach used is material and subject based rather than reliant on student experience to provide course content. The union's purpose is to provide a broad educational experience that challenges their members to question social, economic and political structures and to review the role of unions in society. The relationship between national and international questions is discussed as well as those between union members.

It is clear from talking to members that the course is an eye-opener for many participants, particularly for those who conceived of the union as having only a limited role. As a result of the experience, some will move from union card-carriers to activists (Dennis McDermott, a former head of the union and CLC president described his stay at Port Elgin in the 1950s as a turning point in his union activism). The experience is also social; contacts are made and members gain an understanding of different work and community situations. Articles and books are read and videos exchanged; newspapers are gutted and discussed. It is always difficult to evaluate the impact of this kind of course. The CAW contends that a majority of participants leave with a heightened union and social consciousness and that a substantial minority are prepared to take on union positions as a result.

A four-week residential membership education program is a model of the kind of PEL that can be won through negotiations. Its future, though, is dependent on what can be achieved in negotiations. A substantial number of students come from plants in the "big three" auto companies, and those companies can be affected by lay-offs and staff reductions. The union is committed to extending the PEL clauses to all its contracts in all of the new sectors merging into CAW. By the mid-1990s, approximately 75 percent of bargaining units, covering 93 percent of the union's total membership, had negotiated PEL. The biggest threat to the program comes from plant closures and the continuing restructuring of the Canadian economy.

It is important to recognize that the employer has no influence over the PEL program. It is not employer-paid time off as experienced in some joint union-management training courses. Once the contract includes a PEL clause, the money collected goes into the CAW-PEL trust fund, which pays the lost wages and expenses of members who attend the course. The member receives time off without pay from the employer. There is no government influence over the educational program that the union offers its members.

This program is now being emulated by CUPW, who have negotiated a 3-cents-per-member levy. They have used the Port Elgin facility to run a number of PEL classes alongside CAW courses in preparation for mounting a separate CUPW program.

Internationalism: Steelworkers' Humanity Fund Educational Program[5]

The CAW and CUPW PEL program is not the only membership education course to include international issues. A number of unions offer courses specifically on international issues and, given the increasing globalization of capital and the growth of free trade deals, it is important to consider how unions have responded educationally to these developments. One of the most impressive courses is that of the Steelworkers. What follows is a description of a course called "Thinking North-South," developed by the Steelworkers Humanity Fund, which is taught in Steelworkers' week-long schools. Rank-and-file activists, drawn from the 280 bargaining units that have contributed to the Humanity Fund, spend a week together thinking about the workings of the global economy.

Over 110 rank-and-file workers throughout Canada had participated in the course by 1992. Fifteen had also travelled to visit projects in El Salvador and Peru. The course was offered seven times in the two-year period from 1991 to 1992, using participatory educational methods. Participants map out the workings of the global economy, starting with their own workplace, and eventually create a complex map linking structural adjustment in the south with free trade in the north.

The instructor team, which includes worker-instructors who have done the course and travelled to other countries, have experimented with different approaches. One course included a role play of a press conference given by delegations at an international meeting on hemispheric initiatives. The "Peruvian delegation" and "Canadian delegation" made presentations on current economic policies. The "journalists" were divided into labour and mainstream press.

In addition to teaching internationalism, some Canadian unions sponsor international educational activity. The more extensive understanding of broader national and international context is often the focus of institutional labour studies courses.

Institutional Provision of Labour Studies

As discussed above, university and college provision of labour education is sparse but varied. Two of the more established labour studies programmes targeted specifically at trade unionists are at the University of Manitoba and the University of Saskatchewan in Saskatoon.

The Manitoba Federation of Labour-University of Manitoba certificate (Friesen 1993) is a three-year program established more than thirty years ago. Students take one course per term, three hours a week (two courses per year). Course topics include economics, politics, labour law, industrial relations and labour history. Graduating students can proceed to a labour studies degree program.

The University of Saskatchewan Labour Studies Program is run by the College of Commerce and endorsed by the Saskatchewan Federation of Labour. The program began in 1988 and has attracted over 350 trade unionists. Courses range from "Labour History" and "The Role of Labour in Society" through "Labour Sociology," "Labour Economics," "Women and Work," "New Technology," and "Labour Law" and "Occupational Health and Safety." After taking six courses over three years, students obtain a university certificate.

Perhaps more typical of labour studies programs in Canada is that offered by Brock University. This relatively new (ten years old) program in industrial Ontario (St. Catherines) offers a degree program for mainstream students. With part-time students and evening classes, it is possible for labour activists to take classes but it is not targeted at them, nor is there any credit given for union education courses.

Athabasca University in Alberta provides another recent model of university credit labour studies courses, but as an open, distance university, it is able to work directly with unions and the Federation of Labour to provide courses at labour schools (courses have been offered at the AFL Spring School and at the CAW, Port Elgin). Athabasca provides the Labour College of Canada Distance Education course. Typically, Athabasca students are working adults studying part time, and those that are attracted to labour studies have a union background. A current research program is devising a schema for granting university- and college-level credits for labour education courses and for learning resulting from labour activity.

In Quebec, the Université du Quebec à Montreal signed an agreement in 1976 with two labour centrals, the Confederation des syndicats nationaux (CSN) and the Quebec Federation of Labour (QFL), and has been providing labour education and research ever since. It is the only substantial institutional provider in Quebec.

Educational institutions offering longer labour studies courses provide union members with the opportunity to investigate substantive knowledge areas beyond their immediate experience and allow students time to reflect on labour's place in the political economy and within new social forces. As noted above, unions are also addressing some of these questions directly on shorter union provided courses, and as a final example, those recently established by the CLC on the environment will be reviewed. This is an important example because it also illustrates labour education's contribution to resolving a controversy within organized labour.

Unions and the Environment

One of the key aspects of social unionism as defined by Canadian unions is coalition building with other social movements; unions recognize that they need to build links with other social movements if they are to influence public opinion and government policy. This raises an important question. To what extent can organized labour, an old social movement with its own educational practices, adopt the concerns and educational practices of the "new" social movements such as women's groups, peace groups or environmentalists? (discussed theoretically in Spencer 1998a, 73-86). If we look at CUPE's program and those of other unions, we can argue that they have done much in this area. Unions offer a number of courses addressing many "new social" issues such as employment equity and sexual or racial harassment; unions have campaigned for peace and against world poverty; and unions have run campaigns and educational programs targeted primarily at members' behaviour outside the workplace, such as violence against women and substance abuse. The CAW, in particular, runs a number of short courses on these themes and has some separate programs for women, persons of colour and physically challenged members.

Environmentalism, however, provides an interesting test for labour. The clash between conservation and economic growth has generally found labour siding with capital in support of development and jobs.[6] In other cases, unions have been split in their support for conservation or development of a particular resource. In the popular image, loggers and pulp and saw mill workers are lined up against environmentalists and Native groups in demanding access to British Columbia's forests.

This image is too simplistic. Unionized workers and their organizations are also concerned with longer-term employment; they do not support the despoiling tactics used by some corporations involved in resource extraction. Others live as well as work in the locality of a particular plant, be it mill or mine or municipal dump site. It is their families, not those of shareholders and directors, who breathe in the foul discharge from the pulp mills. There can also be a coincidence of interests in that fewer chemicals in the plant improve the health and safety of workers *and* reduce the hazardous waste associated with the production process. Also, the simplistic presentation of these issues in some media often does not allow for the diversity of opinion among union members. Just as environmentalists and Native groups can have differences of opinion on development issues, so too can labour. The split between pulp and paper workers (Communications, Energy and Paperworkers; CEP) and the woodworkers (International Woodworkers of America; IWA) over forest management in British Columbia is a prime example.

Given this framework, we can now look at the following question: How has organized labour set about developing a policy on the environment and what role has union education played? One of the problems for labour in dealing with environmental questions has been what environmental stance it could adopt. It had no well-developed theory to support its action. This situation changed to some extent with the publication of the Bruntland

Commission's report (Bruntland 1987) and the Commission's enumeration of the principles of "sustainable development." Although this was not a labour movement document, it captured many of labour's concerns with simple conservationism and melded with some existing campaigns around ensuring future work and reduction in hazardous substances. For example, the CLC has been holding conferences on jobs and the environment since 1978. (A few unions have a national policy that stands in contradiction to environmental concerns; support for nuclear energy by energy workers and for clear-cutting by the IWA are perhaps the most glaring examples. There can also be splits within unions, for example, the desire of chemical workers–CEP members–to see chlorine used in papermaking, and the determination of paperworkers–also CEP members–to see it phased out.)

Labour has argued for a blended approach to the issue of development and the environment. The following stands illustrate this point:

1. The International Chemical and Energy Workers' Federation stated that "to deny the need for economic growth in a world plagued by poverty and undernourishment for the bulk of its population is as unreasonable as to insist that such growth can continue to destroy the natural habitat of mankind without interruption."

2. The CAW has asserted that "workers must have the right to choose both economic security and a healthy environment for ourselves, our families and future generations."

3. Ted Shrecker (1993) argued in a CLC publication, *Sustainable Development*, that this can be achieved via the sustainable development concept that "requires that growth be revived, nationally and globally, *while conserving and enhancing the resource base* on which growth depends."[7] One of the key elements here is the recognition of the importance of renewable resources.

In order to ensure its perspectives were developed by its own affiliates and their members, the CLC began developing courses for union members. A number of provincial and national conferences preceded course development. In 1993, a one-week course, "Union Environmental Action," was written, to be followed by materials on an introductory nine-hour course, "Workers' and the Environment," and a three-hour unit, "Pollution Prevention," developed primarily for inclusion in other courses. Members attending these courses might also receive a copy of the CLC *Sustainable Development* publication.

Although the publication of these materials suggests a very fixed agenda, the course program allows members to inject their own concerns and examples. However, the goal of the CLC is to get course participants to understand the key issues and struggle with the difficult problems raised. Course participants are expected to read the background information and are supplied with lists of additional readings. Many of the problems raised are open-ended, with a variety of policy options discussed. The CLC lists different environmental groups and notes where there have been disagreements between these groups and different unions. The possibility for establishing contacts is left open.

In many ways these short courses, particularly the week-long "Union Environmental Action" course, are examples of the best traditions of workers' education in which the sociopolitical and socioeconomic context is provided as a basis for consideration of policy decisions and union actions. These courses can be seen as issue-based environmentalism, but are not focused on a specific local concern, as informal learning might be in a local environmental group. They provide context for such "learning" and do not preclude local or provincial union organizations mounting such an educational event. On the contrary, by sensitizing a broader constituency to the issues involved, one would expect these courses to result in more union environmental actions. Such actions may be a reaction to a particular event, a toxic dump site, for example, or initiated by the union membership as a result of heightened consciousness, for example, auditing company environmental practices.

Evaluating the success of these courses is difficult but a number of features can be noted. The material is discussion-based, beginning with students' experience to date. Course members are provided with background material, some of which is "taught" directly in the course, with the remainder provided as background reading. Instructors are rarely professional educators; the courses use lay and full-time officials as instructors and/or facilitators. It should also be noted that labour pays for its own education, including loss of wages. This means that organized labour can take an independent stance on issues whereas some environmental pressure groups may be dependent on government grant assistance to support their activities and therefore may be constrained when dealing with some issues.

In addition to CLC initiatives, a number of unions have been mounting their own campaigns. The pulp and paper section of the CEP have a pamphlet, developed from a Swedish pulp and paper union publication, which argues the case for treating forests as a renewable resource and for zero discharge of chemicals. They have taken this publication to all sections of their membership and run half-day schools explaining union policy.

Conclusion

Union or labour education has been divided into tools training for union representatives, issues courses that connect workplace and society and labour studies, which looks at the broader context of unionism. While these categories overlap, they are nonetheless useful for differentiating between the main purposes of particular courses and how they relate to union organization and goals. Labour education is primarily targeted at representatives or activists in the union and they normally begin with basic tools training courses and then move on to issues courses and eventually to the more extensive labour studies courses and programs. Some unions offer membership (as opposed to representative or activist) education courses and in some cases such courses may more accurately be described as labour studies as they examine and explain the context of labour unionism.

Labour education in Canada, therefore, can be viewed as having three main purposes: (1) to maintain and sustain union organization and diverse union purposes, (2) to promote change of policy and organizational goals, and (3) to develop union consciousness and support social action.

How effective is labour education in Canada? Since unions invest a lot of time and resources in education it is clearly important to them. However, other events in a unionist's life, such as a strike or participation in an actual negotiation, may provide more important learning opportunities than a union course—no matter how carefully crafted—which may be considered once removed from the actual experience. Nevertheless, unions regard education as underpinning the union effort in the workplace and community.

A study sponsored by the CLC in 1990 found that members expected to benefit both themselves and the union by taking union courses; the courses helped members to become more interested in the union; and members were able to make better union decisions as a result of attending union courses (Vector, 1990). Generally, members thought courses were too short, but in other ways were content with the course experience.

While respondents felt the major impact of labour education was on how they did their union work, others included comments on how it changed the way they saw Canadian society (this was particularly notable in respondents from the Atlantic region) and influenced them to become involved in local politics and community actions. On the evidence of this study, the CLC's labour education programs clearly worked as a promoter of "social unionism" and the programs also worked as "education." Most students wanted more educational opportunity, preferably using the same format, but with two out of three also stating that they were interested in taking labour courses at home.

In conclusion, the survey enhances the perception of union officials that education supports union activism. The link between education and activism was also confirmed in the Labour Canada LEP study, which included a survey of Labour College of Canada students (Labour Canada 1990, 75-84). Labour education, organization and activism are linked. The CLC's national co-ordinator of Program Development for most of the 1990s, Danny Mallett, has argued that the diverse educational provision of Canadian unions has been a major factor in the growth and maintenance of labour unionism in Canada during a period of international decline (personal communication, July 1994). For example, in the last fifteen years, unions in Canada have retained a density between 32 and 37 percent of an increasing work force. They have therefore maintained their membership, whereas unions in the United States, United Kingdom, Australia and New Zealand have suffered declines in density and actual members of between at least one-quarter and one-half in the same time period. (For a discussion of Canadian labour education in an international setting, see Spencer 1998b.)

This discussion of labour education in Canada illustrates the diversity and vibrancy of current labour education. This chapter has not dealt with theoretical issues or substantive questions of educational philosophy. It is nonetheless clear that the purposes and methods used in some of the educational programs draw inspiration from social change or community education. Labour education is essentially education for social purpose (Spencer 1998a); it is not undertaken to earn individualized credit or vocational advantage but supports union organizational and membership needs and diversity of opinion within Canadian society (Martin 1995). If non-formal labour education is to be recognized for credit, its central purpose as social education must remain unchanged.

Endnotes

1. The term *union education* can be used interchangeably with *labour education* in this chapter. Union education is sometimes reserved for courses run directly by unions as opposed to labour education courses run for unions by other providers.

2. Comment made by Danny Mallet, CLC national co-ordinator of Program Development, telephone conversation with the author, July 1994.

3. The origins of the CLC's Labour College is discussed in Swerdlow 1990, chap. 10.

4. Thanks to Joe Bouchard, national representative, Canadian Union of Public Employees, Niagara Area office, for the following information.

5. The following is a short summary of Marshal 1992.

6. It can also be argued that some environmental groups are anti-worker; see Shrecker 1994.

7. Many of the examples and general points made in this section are taken from Ted Shrecker's 1993 text.

References

Bernard, E. 1991. Labour programmes: A challenging partnership. *Labour/Le Travail* 27 (spring): 199-207.

Bruntland, G.H. (Chair). 1987. *Our common future: The World Commission on Environment and Development.* Oxford: Oxford University Press.

Friesen, G. 1993. HC Pentland and continuing education in Manitoba. *Labour/Le Travail* 31: 301-314.

Government of Canada Human Resources Development. 1990. *Evaluation of the labour education program* (December).

Marshall, J. 1992. Steelworkers humanity fund education programme. *Briarpatch* (October): 51-52.

Martin, D. 1995. *Thinking union: Activism and education in the Canadian labour movement.* Toronto: Between the Lines.

Saul, N. 1994. *Organising the organised.* Unpublished master's thesis. Warwick University, Coventry, England.

Shrecker, T. 1993. *Sustainable development: Getting there from here.* CLC for the National Round Table on the Environment and the Economy.

———. 1994. Environmentalism and the politics of invisibility. *Alternatives* 20 (2): 32-37.

Spencer, B. 1992. Labor education in the UK and Canada. *Canadian and International Education* 21 (2): 55-68.

———. 1998a. *The purposes of adult education: A guide for students.* Toronto: Thompson Educational Publishing.

———. 1998b. Workers' education for the twenty-first century. In *Learning for life: Canadian readings in adult education,* edited by S.M. Scott, B. Spencer, and A. Thomas (pp.164-177). Toronto: Thompson Educational Publishing.

Swerdlow, M. 1990. *Brother Max: Labour organiser and educator,* edited by G.S. Kealey. St. John's, Nfld.: Canadian Committee on Labour History (CCLH).

Taylor, J. 2001. *Union Learning: Canadian Labour Education in the Twentieth Century.* Toronto: Thompson Educational Publishing.

Thomas, A. 1993. The new world of continuing education. In *The craft of teaching adults,* edited by T. Barer-Stein and J. Draper (pp.21-38). Toronto: Culture Concepts.

Vector Public Education Inc. 1990. *Evaluation of schools and programmes* (for CLC Educational Services).

15

Technical-Vocational Education and Training

David N. Wilson

This chapter explores aspects of adult technical-vocational education and training (TVET), examines the forces driving rapid technological change and discusses how these forces are changing adult education, particularly adult TVET. Although this topic is examined in the Canadian context, it is important to relate it to international factors and forces that affect Canada. Since Canada exports about 60 percent of the total value of the goods and services it produces each year (known as the Gross Domestic Product, or GDP), the economy and all workers are subject to the influences of world markets.

Technical-vocational education and training (TVET) refers to education and training that prepares persons for gainful employment (Finch and Crunkilton 1999, 14). TVET can take place either in formal schools (i.e., Kindergarten through Grades 10-13), or in post-secondary community and/or technical colleges, or informally by means of training in the workplace. It should be stressed that many technical and vocational educators favour the integration of academic and technical and/or technological curricula. The education and training of so-called knowledge workers, which will be explored below, suggest that this integration trend will predominate in the twenty-first century.

The terms *education* and *training* also deserve elaboration. Essentially, the goal of education is "to create independent problem solvers [with] sufficient depth of understanding." In contrast, the goal of training "is to teach people to follow prescribed procedures and to perform in a standardized manner" (Gray and Herr 1998, 159). What appears to be taking place in the changing world of work is a convergence between these two, formerly distinct, points of view. This convergence is quite important for the future of adult education, particularly adult TVET.

The term *globalization* is being used a great deal nowadays, yet most of the people using this term do not bother to define it. It is important to both define the term and to explain how globalization of production, services and trade affects ordinary workers. Globalization is "a process that widens the extent and form of cross-border transactions among peoples assets, goods, and services and that deepens the economic interdependence between and among globalizing entities, which may be private or public institutions or governments" (Lubbers 1998, 1). The effect that concerns us most is the impact of globalization upon TVET in Canada, both historically and, even more importantly, in the future.

The challenges facing every nation in a global economy demand more attention to education and training, since most individuals are likely to change careers three to five times during their lifetimes, with each career change requiring new learning. The globalization of production, commerce and informatics has significantly changed the nature of work during the past decade. The globalization process has been driven mainly by rapid technological change. In turn, both rapid technological change and globalization are exercising significant influence upon education, particularly adult education.

In practical terms, globalization means that money can be moved anywhere in the world in a matter of seconds by means of computer electronic transfers. Similarly, large multinational corporations (MNCs) can move production to countries offering the cheapest labour and often less stringent labour and environmental laws. The nations capable of competing successfully seem to be those who have invested in worker training and in adult and continuing education. This is because many of the Least Developed Countries (LDCs) to which some MNCs have moved production do not have the levels of education and worker training necessary to produce high-value or complex products. In some instances, MNCs are moving jobs back to countries that have the necessary trained labour. Thus far, Canada has been perceived by MNCs as having the type of well-educated labour force that meets their requirements. The task of adult TVET is to ensure that Canada continues to have the desired trained labour force.

The days when a Grade 10 drop out could enter productive lifelong employment in agriculture, fishing, forestry, industry, mining and even the service sectors in Canada and elsewhere are rapidly coming to an end. The transformation of our natural resource sectors means that future farmers, foresters and miners require at least fourteen years of education in order to operate computer-controlled agricultural, fish-finding, mining, manufacturing and timber-cutting equipment. The need for technological literacy in nearly every occupational area in the resource, production, service and information technology sectors also implies greater educational attainment and continuous learning. The introduction of new production technologies appears to be one force driving these trends. Many farmers, foresters, miners and production workers have returned to school as adult students to upgrade and/or update their credentials.

Jacques Delors of UNESCO (United Nations Educational, Scientific and Cultural Organization) writes that "the concept of learning throughout life ... emerges as one of the keys to the twenty-first century." He further notes that the concept "goes beyond the traditional distinction between initial and continuing education [and] meets the challenges posed by a rapidly changing world" (Delors 1996, 22). Another prominent trend is the enrolment of many recent university graduates at community and technical colleges, in order to add occupation-specific credentials to their Bachelor of Arts degree that has not earned them employment (Wilson 1998). Since many of these (mainly liberal arts) graduates are choosing TVET courses in the community and technical colleges, this trend, called reverse transfer, is quite important for adult educators. (See also chapter 11 in this volume.)

The Context of Educational Systems in Canada

Article 93 of the Canadian Constitution has, since 1867, reserved education as an exclusive responsibility of the (now) ten provinces. Consequently, Canada is the last remaining country with no central Office, or Ministry, of Education. In fact, this means that Canada actually has thirteen educational systems—ten provincial and three territorial. However, the similarities outweigh the differences between these systems. The reality of Canadian federalism is that the federal government has encroached upon provincial powers, particularly in education, health and occupational training, since about 1910.

> Since the Constitution also empowers the federal government to promote economic growth, equity and stabilization, federal funds—initially for occupational training, and subsequently for post-secondary education—have been transferred to the provinces under what has become known as Established Programmes Funding, or EPF fiscal transfers (Wilson 1992, 114).

Since 1986, the federal government has reduced EPF transfers for training, education and health from a high of 75 percent of total costs to less than 50 percent, which places greater financial burdens upon the provinces. In addition, current federal policy is to negotiate the devolution of responsibility for training to the provinces. Quebec was the first province to sign an agreement with Human Resource Development Canada (HRDC) to take control of training. The fiscal subsidy reduction and devolution of responsibility for technical education and training constitutes the most important current trend in Canadian adult TVET.

A Brief History of TVET Development in Canada

Vocational and technical education developed slowly at the provincial level, as nineteenth-century curricula stressed academic subjects with limited practical instruction in agriculture, art, home making and commercial studies. Egerton Ryerson (the founder of the "common school") emphasized practical subjects in Ontario schools in 1881, and Newton Wolverton, Canada's first vocational educator, began manual training at Woodstock College in Ontario in 1886. Manual training was not taught in day classes until 1900, although evening classes for working people were available from the 1840s. A federal Royal Commission was appointed to determine technical education needs for Canada in 1910, but its recommended Federal Ministry of Vocational Education was never established.

The 1913 Report of the Royal Commission on Industrial Training and Technical Education also recommended that the federal government allocate funding to the provinces to encourage the provision of vocational education and experimental science in the elementary school grades. This grant was to be divided among the provinces on the basis of population but was not to be used for the construction of school buildings. Implementation of these recommendations did not take place until after World War I. Subsequent federal legislation later extended such grants to secondary and post-secondary education.

Meanwhile, in 1911, the Province of Ontario passed the *Industrial Education Act*, based upon the recommendations of a comparative educator, Dr. John Seath, who studied technical and vocational education in Europe and the United States and subsequently became superintendent of Education in Ontario. The result was that Ontario was ready to take full advantage of federal financial assistance when it became available. The ability of Ontario to garner the largest share of federal funding remains valid to this very day to the chagrin of the other provinces (Wilson 1992, 115). Dennison and Gallagher noted that, "in fact, access to federal funds through the Technical and Vocational Training Assistance Act (TVTA) of 1960 was especially influential on the course that Ontario colleges would take" (Wilson 1992, 35).

Such federal assistance began with the *Agricultural Aid Act* of 1912 and was followed by a successive legislation providing federal assistance to elementary and subsequently secondary and higher education, culminating with the *National Training Act* of 1982. The following precedents were established from 1912: (a) national training needs were to be met by an influx of federal funds, (b) federal funds were contingent upon some type of federal control, and (c) federal funds were either given directly to the provincial governments or to training institutions. These trends have continued to affect adult TVET in Canada to the present.

However, expansion of post-secondary education, and with it an increasing federal government role, did not take place until the 1960s. According to Dennison and Gallagher (1986),

> high unemployment in the 1950s prompted the Diefenbaker government to introduce the Technical and Vocational Training Assistance Act (1960). This legislation placed major emphasis on the vocational and technical training required for workers to adapt to changes in technology and to meet the demands of industry. Eight hundred million dollars was provided for such training by the Canadian government over a ten-year period, under a cost-sharing arrangement with the provinces. A 75% federal–25% provincial formula was developed which applied to capital costs, but under certain conditions to operating costs as well. Another series of legislative changes increased the amount of federal financial support, which culminated in 1967 with the introduction of the Adult Occupational Training Act and The Canada Manpower Training Programme (p.15).

The 1982 *National Training Act* implemented many of the recommendations from two 1981 reports, *Labour Market Development in the 1980's*, produced by a task force within the (then) federal Ministry of Employment and Immigration (now Human Resource Development Canada) and *Work for Tomorrow: Employment Opportunities for the 1980's*, produced by a Committee of Parliament. These publications continued the Canadian "tradition" of in-depth (and often lengthy) study, usually undertaken by Royal Commissions prior to program implementation.

The Canadian Labour Force Development Strategy was promulgated in a 1989 policy document, *Success in the Works*. Policy directions were to mobilize a national effort of training and human resource development and to challenge all labour market partners to increase the skill levels of all Canadians and to find the best combination of policies and programs to ensure that all Canadians could achieve their potential. This national effort was required to address three major themes: (1) the adoption of new technologies, (2) the relaxation of world trade restrictions, and (3) the globalization of world markets.

The establishment of Sectoral Training Councils in key industrial sectors in 1992 paralleled the creation of the Canadian Labour Force Development Board (CLFDB) in 1991. However, these councils focus upon key industrial sectors and are jointly funded initiatives between HRDC and private industry. Sector councils must represent both management and labour. These councils assist the private sector in the development of the infrastructure necessary for long-term human resources planning and development. Their activities include: (a) development of occupational and skills standards, (b) organizing youth internships, (c) maintaining sectoral labour market information, and (d) prior learning assessment. Councils also work in partnership with educational institutions and provincial ministries of education. Funding is initially shared 50-50 between private industry and HRDC, but a sector council must become financially self-sufficient after its third year of operation with 100 percent of funding from private sector sources (Wilson 1998, 136).

Community and Technical Colleges

The 208 community colleges, technical colleges and institutes of technology range from the smallest numbers in Prince Edward Island (1) and Manitoba (3) to the largest numbers in Quebec (48 public cégeps and 25 subsidized private) and Ontario (25). While the Yukon Territory has one community college and the Northwest Territories have three community colleges, they do not have universities. Saskatchewan transformed its rural community colleges into regional colleges.

Prior to the 1960s, when the community-technical college infrastructure expanded, the post-secondary non-degree sector was a potpourri of different types of institutions. During the 1960s, each province began to organize these institutions into provincial post-secondary systems, either by changing existing institutions or founding new ones. The outcome of this restructuring was

> designed to offer a range of advanced programs as an alternative to those traditionally associated with university. The term now describes institutions that offer semi-professional career or technical and vocational programs leading to a diploma. In some instances, the institution offers university transfer programs (Gayfer 1991, 37).

Programs at Canadian community and/or technical colleges are provided in most technical, professional and commercial fields; however, there are geographic variations in program availability, for example, in fishing technologies, mining and forestry technologies, agricultural technologies and petro-chemical technologies. Many community and technical colleges have recently added post-diploma programs to upgrade the knowledge component in many occupations (Wilson 1998, 153).

The Changing Nature of Work

The sweeping changes that have brought about the global marketplace are traceable to what Lewis Mumford (1970) called the *neo-technic revolution*, the conscious creation of new technology through institutional research and development. Delors characterizes such changes as being another aspect of globalization: "the establishment of science and technology networks that link up research centres to major business enterprises" (Delors 1996, 42). Both trends are traceable to the efforts during World War II (and central to the "space race") to apply scientific research to military (and later) product development. These efforts have changed both the nature of work and the form and function of education.

The changing nature of work, particularly in higher technologies, means that many workers will increasingly operate in a *mechatronic* environment where they will work with highly precise mechanical equipment operating under electrical power and controlled by electronic devices, often commanded by means of sophisticated computer programs. The multiple skills and cross-training required by this new mechatronic environment have significant implications for the transformation of the workplace and particularly for the skills, attitudes and knowledge required to operate globally (Wilson 1997, 1).

Cross-training is yet another new important TVET trend, best exemplified in industrial robotics, where an operator and/or technician requires training in both the mechanical and electrical and/or electronic aspects of these industrial robots. Canadian workers are disadvantaged; in Japan there are now four high school courses on mechatronics. Both cross-training and mechatronics were developed in Japan. However, their development arose from concepts originated by W. Edwards Demming (1986) in the United States.

Our schools and community and/or technical colleges have been slow in developing courses on mechatronics. Furthermore, since cross-training also crosses union jurisdictions, the training and employment of cross-trained employees must be negotiated between labour unions that have traditionally represented either mechanical (operating engineers) or electrical and/or electronic workers.

Principles of design and product fabrication are also being completely changed by the new field known as *rapid prototyping*. This is a technology that produces models and prototype parts from three-dimensional computer-aided design (CAD) model data and models created from three-dimensional object digitizing systems, known as computer-assisted manufacturing (CAM) (Flint 1998). This new technology has the potential to replace the tool and die industry. Since the beginning of the Industrial Revolution, most products fabricated from metal (and later plastic) have been stamped or shaped from dies, which are produced by hand by an extremely skilled worker, known as a tool and die maker. Still another trend that will make itself felt in the future is *nanotechnology*, which concerns the micro-miniaturization of machinery. Nanotechnology is based on the manipulation of individual atoms and molecules to fabricate structures to complex atomic specifications (Miller 1999, 1). The nanoscale is one thousand times smaller than micro, with approximately three atoms per nanometer. The field originates from a speech given by physicist Richard Feynman in 1959 to the American Physical Society. The resulting immediate combination of chemistry and engineering will usher in a period of self-replicating and self-constructing consumer goods. However, it is likely that it will be at least two decades before this trend impacts upon production and then upon education and training.

These technological changes are also important for adult educators. Post-secondary educational institutions are only now developing courses on rapid prototyping. The impact of this innovation upon production promises to be widespread. Similarly, the adjustment required throughout the workplace is only now becoming apparent. Of course, this adjustment also includes new learning, mainly on the job, by those involved with these processes.

The worker of the twenty-first century will be more of a *knowledge worker*, using logical-abstract thinking to diagnose problems, to research and apply knowledge, to propose solutions, and to design and implement those solutions, often as a member of a team (Wilson 1997, 2). Such workers are no longer found only in the productive sectors of an economy, but they are also increasingly found in the service and information technology sectors. In 1971, only one in sixteen jobs was knowledge intensive. However, by 1996, the ratio was one job in eight. Moreover, an explosion in labour mobility means that such workers are also no longer confined to one economy in one country, but rather operate globally in many economies and countries.

The impact of the latter trends upon the workplace has been phenomenal, effectively altering previous patterns of employment and unemployment. In Canada, the "flattening" of employment demographics, resulting from both economic downturn and global competition, has increased unemployment among the fifty-plus age group and among the fifteen- to twenty-four-year-old age cohort. It is somewhat ironic that these unemployment trends are occurring almost simultaneously with the demographic decline in new entrants to the labour force. Although there are fewer persons in the fifteen- to twenty-four-year age group than during the preceding four decades, the decline in actual numbers appears to have been offset by longer participation in formal education and by the increasing rates of participation in post-secondary education. Both of these educational trends seem to be associated with the transforming workplace.

Thomas Homer-Dixon of the University of Toronto claims that "modern technologies are ever more intelligent and they are working their way up the skills hierarchy." He observes that "as technologies of production change, the workforce in our modern economy is bifurcating." He labels one group "hamburger flippers" and the other, "symbol analysts." He also writes that today's students "will probably have at least half a dozen different jobs in their lives." His rationale is that jobs that require low or moderate skills are being eliminated at an astonishing rate as firms–intent on maximizing profits–replace labor with machines. Robots have replaced assembly-line workers on the factory floor, computerized answering devices have sharply reduced the number of directory assistance operators in telephone companies, and word-processing technology has largely eliminated traditional secretarial jobs. Experts note that new information technologies are now threatening previously secure middle-management positions. The jobs that are left are increasingly low-paid service jobs in stores and restaurants and high-paid knowledge-intensive jobs in the computer, business and consulting industries (Homer-Dixon 1996, A14).

Homer-Dixon identifies the following desirable attributes and/or competencies as important for lifelong learning:

- Characteristics of mind and personality;
- The mental agility that allows [students] to move rapidly from one problem or task to another;
- [The ability] to apply knowledge from radically different domains to practical problems;
- Keen, analytical problem-solving ability;
- [The ability to] think well [and] write well;
- The flexibility to produce novel solutions to rapidly-changing problems;
- [The ability] to think about and solve problems in an interdisciplinary way;
- [The ability to undertake] conflict resolution;
- Entrepreneurship (Homer-Dixon, 1996, A14).

Finally, it should be recognized that Canada is among the most export-trade dependent nations in the world. At least one in three (and some now estimate one in two) Canadian jobs is trade related. In 1996, about 60 percent of Canada's goods and services were exported and 74 percent of the 1996 economic output originated from those exports (GT Global Mutual Funds). This factor makes Canada extremely sensitive to any global event that affects trade. Delors wrote that "growth in world exports between 1970 and 1993 was on average 1.5 percentage points higher than [the growth] of the gross domestic product (GDP)." He noted that this "world growth" was "largely export-driven" (Delors 1996, 41).

Bruce Spencer of Athabasca University examined initiatives to increase job satisfaction and reduce employers' costs. He notes that "workers feel alienated from their work and, if employers want employee loyalty," there should be improvements in the quality of working life, or QWL. He states that "another driving force is the perceived need to meet competitive challenge," which has led "to just-in-time (JIT) stock control, team production techniques, and total quality management (TQM)." Spencer writes that the "renewed focus on human resources" has redefined "human resource management as central to organizational success." These initiatives have recast "factories and offices as *learning organizations*" (Spencer 1998, 48). This commitment to lifelong learning and adult TVET appears to be a reaction to the increased competition resulting from both globalization and technological change.

Technical-Vocational Education and Training

TVET curricula at Canadian community and technical colleges and institutes are developed both centrally by provincial Ministries of Education and at the college level by department heads and/or individual instructors. Most community and technical colleges have had Trade/Industry Advisory Committees since the 1940s. Unfortunately, the record of participation and levels of viability of some of these committees have varied considerably. While in some occupational areas committees remain viable and continue to contribute to program and curricular reform, in other areas committees have fallen into disuse and often exist only "on paper." Some analysts attribute the decline of Advisory Committees to their failure to have finite terms for members, which has often resulted in the prolonged participation of persons who have either "lost touch" with their areas, or were appointed for political, rather than technical, considerations (Wilson 1998, 147).

The "hottest" community and technical college program in Canada is the Sheridan College of Applied Arts and Technology (CAAT) Computer Animation program in Ontario. This high-technology course was designed by former staff of the National Film Board of Canada, and it has been at the leading edge of technological innovation. A majority of its graduates have migrated to Hollywood and have been at the forefront of film animation.

In two- or three-year programs, community colleges award technician certificates (two-year) and technologist diplomas (three-year) in Technology, Trade, Allied Health and Business/Commercial programs, as well as university-transfer programs in several provinces. For example, in Alberta, Saskatchewan and British Columbia, first- and second-year university courses are provided in community colleges. In contrast, it is not easy for Ontario CAAT Diploma graduates to transfer to universities, because Ontario has a binary post-secondary system. Individual CAATs and universities have developed articulation agreements to facilitate such transfers.

Tuition rates for Canadian community and technical colleges are consistently lower than those for universities. Undoubtedly, this feature makes the pre-university programs available in British Columbia and Alberta attractive to students from lower socioeconomic backgrounds. However, these tuition fees are also increasing. For example, in 1991 tuition fees charged to students attending an Ontario CAAT (currently $1,550) defrayed 11.3 percent of the total cost of their education. By 1995-96, however, the student share of the total cost rose to 18.7 percent and was projected by the Association of Canadian Community Colleges to rise to 23.7 percent in 1996-97 (ACCC 1997, 6).

Statistics Canada (Website) reported that community and technical college enrolment in 1995-96 consisted of 386,930 full-time students, of which 72 percent, or 278,592, were registered in career programs and 108,338 in university transfer programs. The number of diplomas and certificates conferred by community and technical colleges nearly doubled between 1971 and 1991, from 43,336 to 83,180.

The major trends at Canadian community and technical colleges reflect those trends discerned in the economy. The shift in emphasis from the resource extraction and productive sectors of the Canadian economy towards the service, informatics and knowledge-based sectors are reflected in community and technical college enrolments. The development of new high-technology college programs, such as computer animation, also reflects the changing nature of the economy and workforce. The challenges precipitated by these trends are how Canada's community and technical colleges respond to changes in the economy and labour force (Wilson 1998, 150).

Labour Force Training in Canada

Ontario was the first province to enact legislation to govern apprenticeships in 1882. The *Ontario Apprenticeship Act* provided for the training of "minors" between the ages of sixteen and twenty-one in the construction trades of bricklayer, mason, carpenter, painter and plasterer. Additional trades were added as the industrial infrastructure developed. In 1944, compulsory certification was introduced in motor vehicle repair "to protect the public from the consequences of faulty work" (Ontario Ministry of Education and Training 1997, 4). In 1963, the Act was revised to enable apprentices aged sixteen years and older to enter apprentice training programs at the (then) Provincial Institutes of Trades and Technology (PITTs).

The Ontario apprenticeship system was reformed in 1964 upon the recommendations of the Select Committee on Manpower Training at the same time that Ontario developed the CAAT system, which incorporated the earlier six PITTs. Ontario CAATs offer apprenticeship training in forty-three regulated trade areas, and in twenty-six non-regulated occupations. The earlier Act was replaced with the *Apprenticeship and Tradesmen's Qualification Act* which was later re-named the *Trades Qualification and Apprenticeship Act* (TQAA). Ontario is currently reforming its apprenticeship system and examining the roles and responsibilities of the Ministry of Education and Training, definitions of trades and employers, training content, entry requirements, length of apprenticeships and the relationship with the federal Interprovincial Standards Program.

All provinces except Ontario have Apprenticeship Boards, which are responsible for the establishment, regulation and administration of apprenticeships in the certifiable trades. The successful completion of an apprenticeship follows passing the Certificate of Qualification examination with a grade of at least 65 percent. While regulated occupations with voluntary certification do not require certificates, in regulated occupations a tradesperson is not allowed to work without possession of a Certificate of Qualification and Apprenticeship.

In 1959, the federal Interprovincial Standards Program (ISP) established the "Red Seal" trades program to test and certify designated critical-skill trades in order to facilitate labour mobility between provinces. This program includes 28 of the 170 apprenticeable trades in Canada and approximately 70 percent of all apprentices are in Red Seal trades. Apprentices must first obtain (or be qualified to obtain) a provincial Certificate of Qualification in order to be eligible to write a Red Seal examination. A grade above 69 percent entitles the apprentice to the ISP Red Seal designation, which permits the practise of that occupation across Canada without further examination. The examinations are developed by the Interprovincial Standards Program Co-ordinating Committee, composed of directors of Apprenticeship from each province and territory, plus two representatives of HRDC. The examinations are revised every two years, and each province involved with the respective trade must unanimously accept the examination (Wilson 1998, 161).

In 1995, Canada had 159,900 registered apprentices, which constituted a 3 percent overall decline from 1994; however, in spite of this decline the number of new apprentice registrations increased by 8 percent in 1995 to 34,500, according to Statistics Canada (1997). The dynamics of apprenticeship registrations are directly affected by the Canadian economy, in particular by the fluctuations of unemployment. For example, in February 1997 Statistics Canada reported that "youth continued to fare poorly ... with an estimated 22,000 fewer 15-to-24-year-old workers." Canada has consistently had the dubious distinction of having the oldest apprentices of any industrialized country, with an average age of twenty-six years.

The challenge in this instance is how to modernize apprenticeship at the turn of the century, given the widespread change in the Canadian economy and labour force. One aspect of this challenge is that both the mining and manufacturing sectors are not about to disappear, and for this reason, there will always be requirements for trained technical apprentices. While the changing nature of resource extraction and industrial production suggests that more technicians and technologists will be required in the future, it will remain necessary for those quality control and supervisory personnel to have trained craftspersons to perform routine operations. The challenge in modernizing apprenticeship is in upgrading the knowledge component of apprenticeships while maintaining the psychomotor and manipulative aspects of these programs.

The Canadian private sector has also been undergoing significant changes resulting from technological modernization, globalization of competition and the participation of Canada in new international trading arrangements, such as the North American Free Trade Agreement (NAFTA) and the World Trade Organization (WTO). The character and skill requirements of the Canadian labour force in a modernizing industrial and informatics society must reflect these changes, as must the nature, amount and type of training provided to both new labour force entrants and existing workers. Pitman (1993) noted that "the sharply pyramidal formation of the industrial society will shift to a flatter arrangement of human resources, demanding increased knowledge, skill and insight from every employee" (p.2). Already, during the 1990-96 recession, it was noticeable that senior levels of management had been reduced from as many as eight discrete levels to as few as three. The impact of this trend upon labour force training may well be the challenge of the next decade, as fewer levels of management necessitate a related increase in the knowledge and skill levels of supporting employees (Wilson 1998, 162).

Labour Force Participation

In February 1997, the Canadian labour force totalled 15,217,600 and the labour force participation rate was 64.6 percent. The unemployment rate was 9.7 percent with 1,477,400 Canadians unemployed (Wilson 1998, 162). The current rate of youth labour force participation is 62 percent, having declined from 71 percent in 1989, according to the Association of Canadian Community Colleges (1999). The youth unemployment rate is 16.5 percent, compared with 7 percent for twenty-five- to thirty-four-year-old Canadians with university degrees and 10 percent for those with community or technical college diplomas. Although the percentage of youth aged fifteen to twenty-four in the Canadian population declined between 1989 and 1995, post-secondary enrolments increased. University enrolment increased by 12 percent and community and technical college enrolment increased by 23 percent during the same period. This indicates that a major contemporary challenge is how to remedy the disturbingly high trend of youth unemployment.

Between 1990 and 1994, 957,000 jobs were created in the Canadian economy for those with post-secondary education, while 830,000 jobs disappeared for those with lower levels of educational attainment. Ironically, while the unemployment rate fluctuated between 9 and 10 percent, some 250,000 to 300,000 high-level positions, particularly in computer-related industries, remained unfilled annually because of the unavailability of technically trained applicants. The Association of Canadian Community Colleges (1990) indicated that

> the Canadian economy is plagued by a shortage of skilled workers in a number of high technology and new or knowledge-based economy sectors. Recently, both the telecommunications industry and software industry sector councils stated publicly that they are facing a shortage of skilled workers. Paradoxically, Canada is also suffering from a persistent unemployment problem (p.5).

This suggests that current trends of the changing nature of employment present additional challenges for the future of adult TVET in Canada. The major challenge appears to be how the Canadian educational system can raise enrolment and output in telecommunications and computer software programs and, at the same time, reduce enrolment in many programs for which there are few employment prospects for graduates.

Conclusion

It is not difficult to conclude that even in a very "loose" federal state, considerations of economic survival can be combined with pedagogical innovation to reform the education and training of the human resources required to maintain international competitiveness. A pertinent note on which to conclude this examination of adult TVET in Canada was provided by the Association of Canadian Community Colleges (1990):

> As the last decade of the 20th Century commences, a powerful new international economic system is emerging. Our former strengths were characterized by the sale of raw and processed natural resources and by the industrial capacity to transform those resources into value-added products. Competitive advantage in the new informa-

tion-intensive economy is increasingly based on the products of research, science and technology, and knowledge, which itself has become a major resource.... With international competition driving us into the knowledge-based economy of the 21st Century, Canada will need to invest wisely in post-secondary education and human resource development (p.7).

The changing nature of work has been the result of the neo-technic revolution, which has been manifested in a mechatronic environment in which workers will require multiple skills that are acquired by cross-training. New technologies, such as rapid prototyping and nanotechnology, and trends such as globalization continue to change the nature of work and the demands placed on adult TVET to train and re-train the work force.

The transitional nature of the Canadian economy, being transformed from an extractive and/or productive to a more knowledge-based emphasis, challenges adult TVET institutions to respond to the demand for new skills in high technology, knowledge-based industries. Adult TVET must prepare knowledge workers who can use logical-abstract thinking to diagnose problems, to research and apply knowledge, to propose solutions and to design and implement those solutions. Some of these workers may have to prepare for as many as six different careers during their working lifetime.

The response by the federal, provincial and territorial governments has been greater co-operation between the thirteen governments responsible for education and training in Canada, as well as greater co-operation between the public and private sectors. The sectoral training initiatives, and the parallel training board infrastructure, have shaped government-industry co-operation.

After two decades of explosive growth, enrolment at Canadian universities and community and technical colleges has stabilized to the current trend of 1 or 2 percent increases annually. A trend of decreasing federal subsidies to post-secondary, particularly university, education has emerged since 1986. The trend of increased enrolment in TVET during the recent economic recession, particularly by unemployed university "arts" programme graduates, suggests that economic developments do influence student decisions about educational and career choices, albeit belatedly. A significant trend in Canadian post-secondary education has been the marked increase in female enrolment, particularly in courses that have historically been male dominated. The impact of technological change upon Canadian university and community and technical colleges has resulted in the development of programs that did not exist in the recent past.

A final challenge is how to modernize apprenticeship training at the beginning of the century in order to accommodate the impact of technological change upon the workplace. This also concerns how to upgrade the knowledge component of apprenticeship training while maintaining the psychomotor and manipulative aspects of these programs.

The trend of marked reduction of senior levels of management must also be dealt with during the next decade, as fewer levels of management necessitate the concomitant rise in the knowledge and skill levels of supporting employees. This suggests that future skilled tradespeople, technicians and technologists require adult TVET in order to better perform their duties in a changing workplace, as well as to better communicate with senior management. The impact of globalization described in this chapter has, therefore, significantly changed both the nature of the workplace and the nature of adult technical-vocational education and training. The task of adult TVET is to ensure that Canada continues to have the trained labour force that enables it to compete in the global marketplace.

References

Association of Canadian Community Colleges. 1997. *Post-secondary education in the knowledge economy.* Ottawa: ACCC.

———. 1990. *Our futures in technology.* Toronto: ACCC.

———. 1989. *A future that works.* Toronto: ACCC.

Delors, J. (Chair). 1996. *Learning: The treasure within.* Paris: UNESCO.

Demming, W.E. 1986. *Out of the crisis.* Cambridge: Massachusetts Institute of Technology Press.

Dennison, J.D., and P. Gallagher. 1986. *Canada's community colleges: A critical analysis.* Vancouver: University of British Columbia Press.

Finch, C.R., and J.R. Crunkilton. 1999. *Curriculum development in vocational and technical education.* Toronto: Allyn and Bacon.

Flint, R.J. 1998. *Using rapid prototyping technology to create functional engineering prototypes.* Paper read at the Educating the Innovator Conference, Ontario Science Centre, March 4.

Gallagher, P. 1990. *Community colleges in Canada: A profile.* Vancouver: Vancouver Community College Press.

Gayfer, M. 1991. *An overview of Canadian education.* Toronto: Canadian Education Association.

Gray, K.C., and E.L. Herr. 1998. *Workforce education: The basics.* Toronto: Allyn and Bacon.

Homer-Dixon, T. 1996. What to do with a "soft" degree in a hard job market. Toronto: *Globe and Mail.* April 1, A14.

Lubbers, R.F.M. 1998. *Trends in economic and social globalization: Challenges and obstacles.* Website: http://www.globalize.org.

Miller, G. 1999. What is nanotechnology?
Website: www.homestead.com/nanotechnology/things.html.

Mumford, L. 1970. *The myth of the machine: The pentagon of power.* New York: Harcourt, Brace, Jovanovich.

Ontario Ministry of Education and Training. Website: http:/www.edu.gov.on.

———. 1996. *Discussion paper: Apprenticeship reform.* Toronto: Ministry of Education and Training.

Pitman, W. (Chair). 1993 *Task force on advanced training.* Toronto: Ontario Ministry of Education and Training.

Spencer, B. 1998. *The purposes of adult education.* Toronto: Thompson Educational Publishing.

Statistics Canada. Website: http://www.statcan.ca.

———. 1994. *Education in Canada: A statistical review for 1992-93.* Ottawa: Ministry of Industry, Science and Technology.

Wilson, D.N. 1992. *An international perspective on trainer competencies, standards and certification.* Toronto: Ontario Training Corporation.

———. 1997. *Reform of technological education in Canada.* Paper read at National Kaohsiung Normal University, Taiwan, May 30.

———. 1997. *Background discussion paper on the reform of technological education.* Toronto: Ontario Ministry of Education and Training.

———. 1998. Tendencias y retos de la educacion tecnica en Canada. In *La Educacion Tecnologica en el Mundo,* edited by Antonio Argules. Mexico City: Noreiga Editores.

16

The Issue of Professionalization for Adult Educators in Quebec

Paul Bouchard

hortly after a province-wide consultation on education in 1996 called *Les États généraux sur l'éducation*, the Quebec Ministry of Education (MEQ) came out with a proposal to formalize the status of thousands of adult educators in Quebec who had received no explicit training in adult education. This proposal was circulated among school boards, universities and other stakeholders prior to legislating on the certification requirements for adult educators.

This move was prompted by a broad outcry both from organizations that sought to improve the quality of education (for example the ICÉA[1]) and from adult educators themselves. The move to professionalize the role of adult educators, as the reader may be aware, has been a rather contentious issue among the various groups that have an interest in adult education, for example, school boards, adult education associations and groups representing adult learners. On the one hand, the need to protect the public is seen as a good reason to require some kind of gatekeeping certification process for professional adult educators. This would entail a set of rules, probably a prescribed university curriculum for aspiring professionals and a certifying body with the authority to give or withhold permission to practice the profession. The move towards specialization also aims to ensure professional recognition and improved status for adult educators, which explains why some professionals in the field are in favour of such a change. On the other hand, many adult educators see their roots more in line with the local development of community and civic organizations. This requires a great deal of flexibility and dedication rather than the ability to jump through administrative hoops. These adult educators see the trend towards professionalization (i.e., the requirement for accreditation and/or certification) as a threat to the more traditional, grassroots involvement of adult education. From their point of view, adult educators need less regulation, not more.

One of the consequences of this two-fold vision of the current needs of the profession is that a kind of deadlock has been created between the Ministry of Education and its 6,000 adult educators spread throughout Quebec's regional French and English school boards. At this time, it is not clear whether we are moving towards greater government regulation with new norms for the certification of adult educators, or whether some other strategy is at play to satisfy either the needs of adult educators and students or the constraints of a certification process.

Table 16.1: Distribution by Qualification of Teaching Staff
in the Adult Sector (MEQ 1994).

	E1-2*	E3	E4	E5	E6	E7	Total
Brevet	188	1388		371			1947
Permis	0	81	0	182	0	0	698
Autori	3	369	0	100	0	0	472
NLQ	1	43	0	516	0	0	560
QNI	99	556	0	1097	0	0	1752
Total	293	2566	0	2570	0	0	5429

*E1-E2: full time; E3: part-time contractual; E4: full-time hourly; E5: part-time hourly; E6-E7: substitute.

Until now, the standard practice in school boards for hiring adult educators has been first to tap into the pool of certified youth-sector teachers who worked less than a full course load (this is to comply with the teacher's union collective agreement), and then fill any remaining positions by contracting out to non-certified teachers on a part-time basis (hence bypassing the regulation that all full-timers be certified). In effect, this ensured that the majority of adult educators in Quebec had received no training in adult education.

One of the first things the government of Quebec did after the province-wide consultation *Les États généraux*, (whimsically translated "The Estates Generals on Education" by local English newspapers) was to establish that regular teachers at the secondary level–specifically in the youth sector–did not generally possess sufficient mastery of the teaching process, as distinct from the mastery of their own area of academic specialization. Interestingly, that observation was not the result of any kind of large-scale survey on the quality of methods employed by secondary teachers, or even of a general public upheaval about the quality of teaching in Quebec. Instead, what was used as the basis for appraising secondary level teachers' "pedagogical competency" was another, quite distinct problem: the fact that Quebec's secondary school system has one of the highest drop-out rates in Canada (Human Resources Development Canada 1996).

In light of this problem, one immediate implication was the need to question the relevance of the curriculum, which the government proceeded to review from top to bottom, generally ending up with a back-to-basics, "no-nonsense" plan designed to redress some of the "liberal excesses" of the last twenty years. (Whatever the reason "Johnny can't read," in this case *Pierre* would learn to read, and that was that.) However, there was also the perception that overhauling the curriculum would not be sufficient in itself to improve student retention in secondary schools. Teaching skills–that is, the teachers themselves–were also an important part of the equation, being in direct contact with those students who were "at risk" of abandoning their studies (this group in fact represents the majority of students in Quebec schools).

The problem of ensuring quality training for teachers has been a hot issue in Quebec educational circles since the introduction of university training in the late 1960s, after the demise of the previous "écoles normales" (Wagner and Turgeon 1996). But just what could be done to maximize, and in this case, improve the quality of teaching in Quebec schools? Surely more university training was not the answer, since secondary teachers in Quebec were already required to complete a specialized three-year baccalaureate (sixteen years of schooling) in addition to a one-year program in the teaching arts (for a total of seventeen years). Faced with the impracticality of requiring *more* university education, the government decided to require that secondary teachers be trained through a process similar to that of elementary teachers, that is, a four-year baccalaureate in general teaching arts (psychological, relational and organizational aspects of teaching), also loosely covering several academic topics. This also totalled seventeen years of schooling, but was more heavily geared towards relational and/or pedagogical abilities, and less on content. This was perceived as better training for teachers, because it concentrated on teaching skills, rather than subject matter–and it was more in line with the current training of primary level school teachers. (As everyone knows, students aren't dropping out of the primary level.) So, in a nutshell, university pre-service programs for secondary level teachers in Quebec have been changed in the past couple of years to resemble those of primary level teachers.

What does this have to do with adult education, you might ask? Well, several things. First, it is difficult to look at the phenomenon of high school attrition without drawing some inferences about the role of the adult education system, not only in helping drop outs drop back in, but also in preventing them from dropping out in the first place. The reason for this is that the parallel system of education at the secondary level, called "adult education," allows any student who is older than the legal mandatory schooling age (sixteen years) to join the adult sector where classes are scheduled more loosely and students are expected to study on their own to prepare for national (i.e., Quebec provincial) examinations. The method in fact is more akin to programmed instruction than to individualized teaching, but was deemed nevertheless to be in line with the needs of adult learners, at least according to TRÉAQ, a national grouping of adult education directors (TRÉAQ 1992).

However, the procedure goes against a recommendation from the 1981 *Commission d'étude sur la formation des adultes* (CÉFA, or *Commission Jean*) which warned that such a system would simply dump onto the adult sector any problems encountered at the regular secondary level, neither resolving the issue of attrition nor addressing the needs of the "real" adult population in Quebec. As it turned out, the warning was premonitory: in 1991, 51 percent of "adult" students were between sixteen and twenty-five years of age, 37 percent lived at home with their parents and 17 percent were never out of school for a whole academic term (Laprise 1992). Nevertheless, that system is now in place, and combined with the 1988 *Loi sur l'instruction publique* that requires all school boards to provide adult education services (L.Q.

1990, c.8, a.4), it has been responsible for a rapidly increasing demand for adult education services. The school boards promptly complied and opened dedicated centres where adults can pursue a high school degree, usually by taking night classes. This, in turn, required a larger number of adult educators to accommodate the growing student population.

Second, by simultaneously holding a new outlook on teacher training and on the provision of adult education services, the MEQ has put adult educators on the spot. When it replaced the three-year baccalaureate plus one formula with the four-year baccalaureate for youth-sector teachers, the MEQ had intended that aspiring teachers would acquire their subject matter at the same time as their pedagogical training in order to ensure that they would learn, not only their disciplinary content, but simultaneously how to teach it. This was achieved by putting in place new university programs offering a series of yearly internships interspersed throughout the four undergraduate years and replacing the previous single, extensive hands-on stage. Another goal was to enable trainees to become competent in more than one subject area, thereby ensuring greater flexibility when it came to assigning workloads in individual schools. By offering internships in a co-op style program and by integrating the study of several subject matter areas, the MEQ hoped to produce a new crop of well-trained and multi-skilled teachers.

The multiple-subject matter in particular was a new concept for secondary teachers in Quebec. The principle was called *polyvalence*, and eventually came to include another provision with heavy implications for the adult sector: that some trainees who could not realistically be expected to teach more than one subject (for example ESL[2] teachers) should therefore fulfil the polyvalence requirement by also being trained to teach in the adult sector. In fairness, that possibility was also extended to all pre-service trainees, so that they had the choice of training in two or more disciplines or training for service at both levels of the school system. Currently, MEQ is recommending that the polyvalence requirement be fulfilled by either mastering two subject areas or by training to teach at both the youth and the adult sectors.

Third, blending the training process for the youth- and adult-sector teachers obscures the legitimate needs of adult educators in the system. For example, the demographics of the adult-sector teacher population has been used by the government to downplay the need for large-scale training of adult educators. Table 16.1 shows the numbers of teachers employed in the adult sector in the province in 1993, by category of qualification and employment status. They show that the "NLQ" ("not legally qualified") category represents only about 10 percent of those currently employed as teachers of adults in the school boards. It also indicates that a mere 472 teachers are currently enrolled in an adult education teaching certification program by virtue of their status (*autorisation* means they are authorized to teach pending their graduation). Therefore, it has been argued that the need for training adult educators is not particularly pressing.

What the figures don't reveal, however, is that among the remaining 4,397 teachers represented in the table, very few are trained as adult educators, since the dominant practice in the past has been to transfer youth-sector teachers to the adult sector in order to maximize efficiency. The same is true for the "QNI" population (qualification unknown), which represents teachers who are either part time or trained in the youth sector but whose employers failed to respond to the MEQ survey. If we add the numbers in that manner, we could be faced with training needs for adult educators that reach into the 5,000- range, more than ten times the MEQ estimate.

After putting together the new four-year teacher-training program for primary and secondary level teachers in the youth (i.e., non-adult) sector, the MEQ wishes to extend the new philosophy to the adult education centres, hoping to resolve the professional issue of teacher training at two separate levels, while retaining a single—although multiple-track—training program. However, there are several problems with this game plan. On the one hand, the typical profile of the adult educator in Quebec has always been a combination of specialized content area knowledge, a loose collection of competencies acquired experientially and a strong motivation to work with adult learners. Currently, adult educators can receive certification if they hold an undergraduate degree in their area of teaching, have acquired probationary experience and are completing or have completed a thirty-credit university program in adult education. In this manner, their preparation and background almost invariably ensures that they are (a) well-versed content specialists, and (b) dedicated instructors of adults.

The proposed MEQ reform would produce teachers with approximately the opposite profile: weak content specialists who have no particular inclination for adult education other than having completed a minimal set of required courses at the undergraduate level—perhaps as few as six to nine credits in total. The reason adult education has little chance of receiving much attention from program planners is that the four-year program designed for youth-sector teachers is already heavily burdened with mandatory courses that are part of the required "core." There doesn't seem to be much room left for an adult education curriculum.

According to the group of consulting adult education professionals who were assembled periodically at MEQ headquarters over the past three years to review the issue (myself included), the existing adult educator profile is more in line with the needs of their learners than anything that could be achieved with the implementation of a four-year baccalaureate. However, many adult educators are not yet certified (i.e., they are either allowed to teach part time in the adult-sector secondary schools without a teacher's license, or are completing their training with probationary status). If we are to regularize their status by requiring that they undertake some kind of certification and/or qualification process, we could probably do nothing worse than to send them back to university for four years.

The four-year baccalaureate in effect proposes to replace the current profile of adult educators by another that would be much less suited to the profession. Typically, adult educators have come into teaching through a complex combination of life circumstances and interests. They are themselves adults and as such possess a background of life experiences that is more in tune with the role of the adult educator. Compare this with the likely profile of a hypothetical graduate of the four-year baccalaureate in general education: (a) they will be typically between twenty-one and twenty-four years of age; (b) in their four years, they will have spent less than one year studying any single subject matter; and (c) they will probably have been trained as youth-sector teachers, with a complementary six to nine credits in adult education. Obviously, this is a much poorer choice than the training received by our current adult educators (which consists of a thirty-credit certificate combined with a specialized three-year baccalaureate). Nevertheless, the MEQ is pushing to have the four-year baccalaureate become the *only* avenue for certification.

The question is, why? Why is the MEQ so keen on implementing the new teacher-training program for adult educators, even when the plan is so demonstrably flawed? Part of the answer lies in the positions taken by some of the stakeholders in the decision. First, the *government's* interest in the matter is straightforward. It considers the coherence of the teacher-training systems at all levels to be the driving force behind the reform. This means that the push for the professionalization of adult education must eventually yield a training system that resembles as closely as possible the training that teachers receive in the youth sector. In taking that stance, MEQ also ensures that it will receive strategic reinforcement from other stakeholders in the process and respond to the call for better teacher qualifications raised by the *États généraux*.

Second, the *school boards*, which are the actual employers of teachers in both the youth and adult sectors, have been among the most vocal supporters of the same-training-for-all program proposed by the government. Faced with the headache of deploying human resources yearly across various programs according to shifting demands, school boards understandably welcome the move towards increased flexibility that the principle of polyvalence allows. With the new program in place, school boards will have the option of assigning at least two academic subjects to every teacher, as well as requiring some of them to teach in both the youth and adult sectors. This reduces considerably the need to juggle numerous teacher competencies to fit the diversity of student needs.

Third, among other actors are the provincial *teachers' unions*. From their point of view, it makes sense to allow teachers to work in multiple environments, because it reduces the need to hire part-time teachers to fill the gaps created by the "specialist" system. In this way, a teacher whose workload has been reduced because of changes in student population will be able to retain full-time status by either teaching a second subject or by putting in some hours in the adult sector. Since the majority of teachers in Quebec work in the youth sector, the interests of the majority are therefore preserved.

Finally, the *universities* also gain from the reform by increasing their control over teacher qualification in the province. Under the current regulation, part-time teachers do not need to be certified. With the new requirements, however, we can predict a decrease in numbers of part-time jobs, and a parallel increase in demand for university programs from part-time teachers seeking certification. The only difficulty, from the universities' point of view, is that the new four-year program for youth-sector certification is already filled with specific required (i.e., mandatory) courses. How can they possibly fit in an additional half-year of training in adult education, while preserving the programs that were so painstakingly put together to satisfy the new MEQ demands? For this reason, universities have opposed the idea of vertical polyvalence (i.e., the requirement that a teacher be trained to teach both youths and adults), but have yet to come up with a viable proposal.

The reform may resolve a number of administrative issues such as workload assignment and the appearance of equivalence between youth- and adult-sector teacher training, but it omits one important group of people: the students themselves, who, lest we forget, are the reason behind the reform in the first place. Theoretically at least, the intent was never to improve administrative expediency, but that of pedagogical quality. It was not the interests of school boards, teachers' unions or even government agencies that were targeted by the *États Généraux*, but those of the province's population in general, and of students in particular.

Historically, the development of adult education services in Quebec has been aimed at out-of-school environments, such as community groups, employer-sponsored programs and citizens' advocacy movements. With the progressive involvement of school boards in offering GED-type programs to adults came the realization that the adult sector had its own legitimate needs and particular modes of operation. This is what has been called the *specificity* of the adult sector, meaning that it would make sense for the adult system not to be the mirror image of the youth sector (where there is an 18 percent drop-out rate, after all). The recognition of this need has been rooted in community and political action since the 1940s and has been strengthened by several policy statements since 1982 (see CEFA 1982; MEQ 1984; MEQ 1996). The overall expectation has been that future models of adult education in Quebec would acknowledge the diversity of needs and social areas to be addressed. For this to occur, a *non-school* based model was needed. In fact, some interesting initiatives by school boards, such as the CREP (*Centre de ressources en éducation populaire*), and by community groups, such as the MÉPACQ (*Mouvement d'éducation populaire et d'action communautaire),* were welcome innovations in the 1970s and 1980s (for a brief history of these movements, see Greason 1998).

However, if we look back at the efforts made to confer some kind of professional legitimacy to adult educators, what we find is not a process to validate activities outside or at the margins of the school system, but rather the opposite. This is what Wagner and Turgeon (1996) have called the progressive *scolarization* of adult education in Quebec, accompanied by an opposing discourse on *descolarization.* The first model is reminiscent of what is often called "traditional schooling," which requires teachers to be school-based content experts whose activities are limited to sharing or imparting that knowledge almost exclusively in the rarefied atmosphere of a classroom. The second is a progressive model of adult education where teacher-facilitators have acquired multidisciplinary life experiences in various settings, including the workplace and the community, and whose tasks are geared towards the development of an inclusive curriculum and an interdisciplinary approach. The latter is consistent with the historic policy statements by MEQ, CSE,[3] TREAQ and others, but is actually in the process of being obscured by the more mundane considerations of human resource placement and CEQ[4] protectionism.

The issue is not a simple one to resolve. By implementing a parallel schooling structure to respond to the needs of adults, the government is trying to respond to a rather candid demand from adult education groups and agencies, but instead seems to have opened an unforeseen can of wriggling invertebrates. First, the notion of what exactly qualifies a student to be labelled "adult" is at the root of a controversy opposing the needs of sixteen-year-old drop-outs with those of the older (one is tempted to say "real") adult population. Second, the intractable expectation that all teacher training be shaped after the same mould (i.e., youth-sector pre-service college) is in direct contradiction with the most basic premise of adult education, namely, that if it is to exist at all, then it must exist as a specific entity, with its own set of rules and priorities, and *not* as a carbon duplication of the familiar—and failing—youth-sector school system. Otherwise, why bother setting up an adult-education sector in the first place?

The outcome so far is less than exhilarating. The goal of offering specific training and professional recognition to adult educators, because of opposition from employers and the training providers themselves (the universities), seems to have been put on the back burner indefinitely. As a result, the adult-sector jobs are being filled by teachers with no particular training or inclination for working with adult learners. And, tragically, the corresponding reduced demand for qualified adult educators has led both Université de Montréal and Université du Québec to close their thirty-credit programs in adult education, concentrating instead on the newly refurbished youth-sector four-year baccalaureate (which does not at this date include any training in adult education). There remains, however, one glimmer of hope for the quality of adult education programs in Quebec. One of the priorities of MEQ in their quest for the "perfect educator" is the implementation of a continuing education requirement for teachers. This would entail the periodic participation of in-service teachers in various learning activities, either at the graduate or undergraduate levels, perhaps including some kind of specialization in adult education. This does nothing to resolve the issue of the teacher profile produced by the four-year baccalaureate, but may offer an interesting option to teachers who wish to actualize their affinity for helping adults learn. In this manner, one can at least hope that a process of "natural" selection will eventually enhance the quality of teaching in the adult sector.

Another possibility is that the upcoming regulations on teacher training at the technical-vocational level will somehow be linked to adult education. The stated goal in this process is to initiate a rapprochement between the school system and the needs of business organizations in the province (MEQ 1998). This approach is more in line with the "real world" approach advocated by many adult educators, and represents a first step towards an inclusive curriculum that takes into account the realities of employment and community organizations, as well as those of adult learners.

Conclusion

For further reflection, here is a summary of the main issues covered in this chapter, each presented as a double question illustrating two opposing views:

Should adult educators in the public school system be required to hold a similar teacher's license as teachers in the youth sector?	Or:	Should there be more flexibility in recognizing adult educators' personal experience and profile?
Should all adult educators be required to complete a four-year, entry-level undergraduate degree?	Or:	Should adult educators already holding a specialized baccalaureate be eligible for licensing after completing an additional one-year certificate in education?
Should adult educators in the school system be trained solely as classroom instructors?	Or:	Should adult educators also obtain expertise in workplace and community learning/facilitating?
Should the interests of school boards, teachers' unions and universities carry equal weight in the debate surrounding adult educators' required competencies?	Or:	Should the needs of adult learners be recognized as the sole criterion for establishing certification requirements?
Should adult education centres offer services to all Quebec residents who are beyond the age of mandatory school attendance?	Or:	Should there be a one- or two-year waiting period to ensure that high school students do not drop out solely to join the adult-sector schools?
Should youth-sector teachers also teach adults?	Or:	Should the competencies required for teaching adults be considered specific and exclusive?

Endnotes

1. The *Institut canadien d'éducation des adultes* is the francophone equivalent of CAAE (Canadian Association of Adult Education).

2. English as a Second Language: One reason ESL teachers cannot teach another subject is that they are not required to satisfy the French Competency requirement. In other words, they may not speak French well enough to teach geography or history, while nevertheless being excellent English-second-language teachers. This exemption was judged necessary to ensure that good English teachers wouldn't be excluded from the profession because of the language barrier.

3. Conseil supérieur de l'éducation: A consulting agency whose opinion is sought by MEQ in conformity with its statutory regulations.

4. CEQ: Centrale de l'enseignement du Québec (the province's main teacher's union).

References

CEFA. 1981. *Apprendre: une action volontaire et responsable. Énoncé d'une politique gloabale de l'éducation des adultes dans une perspective d'éducation permanente.* Québec: Gouvernement du Québec, Commission d'étude sur la formation des adultes.

———. 1982 *Apprendre: Une action volontaire et responsible. Énoncé d'une politique globale de l'éducation des adultes dans une perspective d'éducation permanenete.* Québec: Gouvernement du Québec, Commission d'étude sur la formation des adultes.

Greason, V. 1998. Adult education in Quebec. In *Adult education in Canada*, edited by G. Selman, M. Selman, M. Cooke, and P. Dampier (pp.83-102). Toronto: Thompson Educational Publishing.

Laprise, J.M. 1992. *Rapport d'enquête. Les populations de l'Éducation des adultes en formation générale dans les commissions scolaires.* Sainte Foy: Centrale de l'enseignement du Québec (CEQ).

MEQ. 1984. *Un projet d'éducation permanente. Énoncé d'orientation et plan d'action en éducation des adultes.* Québec: Ministère de L'Éducation du Québec.

———. 1994. *Distribution par qualification du personnel enseignant formé pour l'éducation des adultes.* Document de travail. Québec: Ministère de l'éducation du Québec, Direction de la formation et de la titularisation du personnel scolaire.

———. 1996. *La formation à l'enseignement à l'éducation des adultes en formation générale. Orientations et compétences attendues.* Québec: Ministère de l'Éducation du Québec.

———. 1998. *La formation des enseignantes et des enseignants de la formation professionnelle au secondaire.* Document de travail. Québec: Ministère de l'éducation du Québec, Direction de la formation et de la titularisation du personnel scolaire.

Human Resources Development Canada. 1996. *School leavers follow-up survey.* Ottawa: GRD Canada. Website: http:www.hrdc-drhc.gc.ca.

TRÉAQ. 1992. *L'enseignement individualisé à l'éducation des adultes les commissions scolaires.* Sainte-Foy: Table des responsables de l'éducation des adultes des commissions scolaires du Québec.

Wagner, S., and M. Turgeon. 1996 *La formation des formateurs d'adultes dans le contexte de la scolarisation de l'éducation des adultes au sein du réseau scolaire.* Unpublished paper. Laboratoire de recherche en éducation et alphabétisation des adultes. Université du Québec à Montréal (UQAM).

17

Women's Empowerment and Adult Education

Margot Morrish and Nancy Buchanan

[Women's] empowerment is a way of feeling, conceiving and relating with oneself and with the world.... Empowerment has to occur at the individual, interpersonal and institutional levels, where the person develops a sense of herself as confident, effective and capable (personal power), an ability to affect others (interpersonal power), and ability to work with others to take action (individually and collectively) to improve their lives and change social institutions (political power) (Heng 1995, 79).

Adult education has contributed to women's empowerment and responded to the social conditions of women's learning experiences. While significant accomplishments and understanding of adult education for women has been achieved, there is still a great need to address gender and feminist concerns and to build women's knowledge in the study and practice of adult education. As adult educators in women's programs, we believe that adult education can play an important role in facilitating personal development, institutional change and social justice for women. This chapter attempts to provide an overview of some of the current issues for women in adult education. The importance of feminist adult education practices, research and theories that support women will be highlighted. Empowerment will be discussed within the social context of women's learning experiences. Women's individual learning and learning in women's organizations will illustrate empowerment for women in community-based adult education. This chapter concludes with a discussion of future directions for adult education for women.

Current Issues and Problems

Feminism can be viewed as a political movement for social change. Feminists from a variety of theoretical positions attempt to redress gender inequity and hence we feel it is important to speak of feminisms rather than a monolithic feminism (CJSAE 8, May 1, 1994, 1).

Feminist adult education can be defined as studies and practices that are centred on women's learning experiences and their personal and social development. Discussion of feminism and adult education includes many complex factors and problems such as marginality, invisibility and representation. Marginality of women's concerns occurs with isolation, limited resources for programming or denial of women's experiences in the learning environment. Many women feel invisible rather than present, silenced rather than heard and isolated in their experiences and thoughts. These felt experiences of subordination and powerlessness stand in the way of women's empowerment (Heng 1995, 80). In order to address these experiences, adult educators need to consider the benefits of women-only programs as well as the integration of women's concerns into existing programs. Invisibility in adult education also occurs when gender is not considered to be an important factor. Gender identity is developed through the socialization of girls and women and through the learning of gender roles and images that are portrayed in society. For example, the majority of women study and work in human services such as secretarial work, sales, nursing, teaching and social work and are influenced to make these career choices from childhood (Normand 1995).

Women's experiences, however, are not homogenous and caution should be taken not to overgeneralize or conclude that the experiences of particular groups of women are common for all women. Women of colour, women of different ages and sexual orientations, women with different abilities, education and social class have diverse personal and social experiences. As a result, it is important to examine inclusiveness and representation in adult education. Students, practitioners and researchers have to consider who participates in adult education and who does not and—while women's experiences are diverse—they must attempt to identify and work for shared learning goals and social justice.

Another problem in adult education is the underrepresentation of women in adult education literature. While women make up the majority of adult education participants and practitioners in the field, there are few women scholars and many gaps in the literature on women (Butterwick 1998; Smith 1992). Hayes and Smith (1994) examined twelve articles in four major adult education journals to identify themes on women and adult education including: limited analysis of women as adult learners; a tendency to present women's characteristics as problematic or deficient; lack of social critique of women's roles or resistance; lack of attention to factors of race, class and culture and the diversity among women's experiences, and the potential of feminist perspectives to make proactive efforts for change. In 1970-71 the percentage of full-time male faculty in Adult Education departments in Canada was 82.7. By 1993, the figure was 79.8 (Burstow 1994). Canadian universities remain a male domain with few female faculty and an even lower number of visible minority persons (Agnew 1996).

Burstow (1994) argues that there is a patriarchal structure to adult education and that the dominant white middle-class male leadership was responsible for the official development of adult education. Male-led professionalization of the field shifted adult education "away from grass roots community organizing toward liberal and competency based graduate (academic) training" (p.5). Burstow (1994) also argues that the official histories of adult education such as works by Knowles (1977), Stubblefied (1988), and Selman and Dampier (1991) are authored by men. While adult education students become familiar with the contributions of the prominent men of adult education, such as the work of E. Corbett, J.R. Kidd, the Rev. Moses Coady and John Grierson, the efforts of prominent women such as Nellie McLung, Adelaide Hoodless and Mary Speechly are less familiar. Stalker (1996) analyzed the theoretical base in adult education research and argued that there is a male bias in the discourse and power relations in the literature. Analysis of the foundation of adult education was undertaken by women to identify and uncover biased assumptions that were made in adult education's attempt to define a unique field of study and practice. The traditional cornerstone of adult education was critiqued for its basis in patriarchal norms. For example, Knowles's (1977) concept of *andragogy* (the art and science of helping adults learn) led to a focus on self-directed learning. The underlying values of his theory of andragogy were criticized for an individualistic bias based on white patriarchal norms that preferred values such as independence (over interdependence or dependence), isolation (over association or connection), and clarity and logic (over ambiguity and subjectivity). While this was a major gain from the top-down teaching models, it formed an underlying liberal and male bias in the study and practices of adult education.

Feminist researchers in adult education have made significant contributions to women's knowledge of the field. Butterwick (1997) argued that women must build new knowledge in order to create a more accurate and inclusive picture of adult education. This is a transformative task that is not simply a matter of adding a token chapter or footnote to an established text, but which requires writing the history of women adult educators, challenging sexism and building new curricula. For example, the contributions of women's voluntary organizations and the stories and voices of women in the nineteenth and twentieth centuries are just beginning to be heard (Welton 1992).

Stalker (1996) proposes a framework that can be used to identify and challenge bias and to broaden understanding of feminist concerns. She advocates exploration of gender and cultural differences and women's private experiences and for gender analysis of educational programs. To challenge sexism in curriculum, Susan Parsons (1990) advocates for a continuously critical consciousness to address: stereotypical attitudes to gender that limit self-understanding, opportunities and possibilities in people's lives; language that reflects or reinforces gender bias and the inclusion or exclusion of women (textbooks or communication); and analysis of the social milieu (patterns of gender relations and the social ordering of power and authority).

Critique of adult education by women has demonstrated the need to value women's experiences, voices, expertise and knowledge as learners, teachers and leaders. Adult educators require skills to identify, challenge and transform sexism and gender bias in many areas of practice and research. Gender issues are the basis for challenging biased assumptions of adult learning and male leadership in the professionalization of the field. This work includes writing women's histories in adult education, constructing learning theories that reflect women's experiences, recognizing women practitioners and academics and questioning how adult education can benefit women in all sectors of society. Feminists work to expand adult education to be more inclusive and true to the adult learning goals of personal and social change. We think of feminist adult education as a continuum from consciousness raising for personal awareness of the social conditions of one's life, to awareness raising that is integrally part of social and political actions for change.

Social Conditions of Women's Learning

Transformation begins with conscious appropriation of one's own reality. Those who are oppressed must recognize their oppression, initiate equitable resource allocation, develop the ability to define and defend the type of society that serves them best and struggle to counter the hegemony of oppressive power relationships (Hamilton and Cunningham 1989, 448).

While it is important to understand a feminist approach to women's issues in adult education, it is also important to recognize that adult education processes are not the only aspects of social change. Empowerment for women through adult education is linked to social, economic and political actions to address sexism. Sexism is an ideology that is historically rooted in values, perceptions and social justifications that women are less than men and, in some cases, less than human. These values are evident is social structures such as women's poverty, violence against women, inadequate child care and inadequate women's health services. While blatantly sexist beliefs may seem exaggerated in the new millennium, women do experience sexism in relationships, groups and institutions where they participate as learners. Stalker (1998) critiques the barriers to women's participation in adult education that exist because of sexism in our society. She examined Patricia Cross's (1981) situational, institutional and dispositional barriers that explained the non-participation of adults. Stalker criticizes explanations of barriers that are gender neutral, focus on the individual's responsibility and fail to address the broad social factors based on sexism. She argues that identification of traditional barriers alone, such as low self-esteem and multiple responsibilities at home, can actually result in women being blamed for non-participation. While it is true that these aspects affect women's personal involvement in adult education, a broader analysis of sexism is required to uncover the beliefs that underlie women's experiences.

According to Stalker (1998), an understanding of the concept of misogyny, or the hatred of women, is more useful in understanding the barriers experienced by women and in working towards change. Misogyny is evident in representations of women that are biologically determined and socially perpetuated. For example, idealized images of women as mothers or virgins with characteristics of modesty, gentleness and nurturance can become a stereotype that is internalized by women (reification). Representations of what men fear in women can be characterized negatively as weakness, seduction or aggression (vilification). Subjugation is the process of controlling women through protection or suppression of activities. How women internalize these views and live up to them and how society perpetuates these views are the basis for understanding barriers that women may experience in pursuing adult education.

Adult educators are obligated to understand social factors in the lives of women that affect learning and learning opportunities. Women's empowerment and social development is limited by poverty, health and violence (United Nations 1995). These factors are also significant for women's participation and success in adult education. Kitchen (1992) argued that poverty in Canada today is not gender neutral and disproportionately affects women and children. Women are poor due to a lack of policies that support women as workers and as mothers. In Canada 20 percent of women live in poverty and make up 70 percent of all people living in poverty. Women working full time in 1996 earned, on average, 73 cents for each dollar earned by men (Greaves 1999, 8). Women also face discontinuities in employment, increased part-time work, the blending of work and child care responsibilities and financial restrictions that limit their pursuit of adult education. The National Organization of Immigrant and Visible Minority Women of Canada argues that visible minority women are among Canada's poorest, due to an unstable labour market for women's earning, cuts to government spending and changes to existing social structures that support women (Saraswati 1996). Inequalities and inadequacies also exist in women's unequal access to education and training. Women have made improvements in educational attainment; however, while women are a majority in undergraduate fields, they are a minority in graduate-level study. As well, women are concentrated in female-dominated fields of study including health, education and the humanities, and are underrepresented in mathematics, physical sciences and engineering (Normand 1995).

Poverty is one of the strongest indicators of poor health (Doyal 1998). Advocates for developing the field of women's health argue that since women constitute 52 percent of the Canadian population, there is a critical need for better understanding of gender (sociocultural) and sex (biological) factors in research, treatment and prevention. Patterns of health and illness have been proven to be different between men and women as are risk factors, access and use of services and effective health education (Greaves 1999). There is unequal and inadequate access to health care and related services for women (United Nations 1995). Ironically, "women constitute the majority of workers in the formal and informal health care system" (Greaves 1999, 8).

Violence against women continues to be a threat to human rights and liberties (United Nations 1995). UNICEF (1997) reported facts of violence against women and girls including world-wide acceptance of rape, genital mutilation, murder, and forced prostitution that go unreported and/or tolerated. Statistics Canada identified that three in ten women have experienced at least one incident of physical or sexual violence by a marital partner (Rodgers 1994). Gender inequality is the root of violence against women, and it is an international violation of human rights that is detrimental to health and social development. The effects of violence in families, communities and workplaces affects the learning experiences and limits the learning opportunities of victims. Poverty, health concerns and violence in the lives of women must be addressed in order to facilitate empowerment for women through adult education.

Empowerment

> *In order to promote women's empowerment, it is necessary to create an environment that will allow women to participate in educational programs and share the benefits.... It is also necessary to develop forms of education that will sensitize people towards gender discrimination and will raise their acceptance of women's promotion (Medel-Anonueva and Bochynek 1995, 7).*

Empowerment has been a central concept in women's learning and women's organizations since the 1970s. The concept was popularized as an adult education practice based on participatory learning for personal growth and social change. The term is used by many different kinds of groups including labour organizations, poverty groups, health educators and adult training programs. This concept can be used at different levels to address individual learning, interpersonal relations and institutional sites such as the family, local neighbourhood or international women's groups. Empowerment as a goal for learning programs can be understood as a process "to change the distribution of power" or a process of acquiring the resources to have control over one's life (Medel-Anonuevo 1995, 8). Empowerment, therefore, is a broad concept that has been analyzed by women adult educators to improve facilitation and programming for women and to work more effectively to create learning opportunities and social equality for women. Stromquist (1995) identifies four components of empowerment:

1. *Cognitive:* increased understanding of the self and of the causes and conditions of women's gender roles and relations.

2. *Psychological:* values, feelings, and actions to improve oneself and to work for change by opposing helplessness learned from personal experiences in the environment.

3. *Economic:* productive capacities with a degree of autonomy that is strengthened by resources.

4. *Political:* the ability to analyze and organize for social change through collective awareness and action.

Women's empowerment is a significant aspect in women's learning experiences and in the role of women's organizations as sites of adult education.

Women's Learning

Women have made significant contributions to adult education in the areas of women's development and learning by critically deconstructing concepts and assumptions widely held in adult education. In the process, women have contributed to a better understanding of the complexity of cognitive and psychological aspects of learning for women and for all adults.

Carol Gilligan (1979) criticizes leading theories of life-development for their preference for autonomy and independence. She argues that an equally strong motive in human development is the need and capacity for intimacy and sharing, and that previous developmental theory ignores the importance of the human ability to share, care and create community. Building on Gilligan's work, other researchers have explored female-based models of development that take into account the ways that women define themselves (Bateson 1989; Hancock 1985; Peck 1986). The following major themes emerged from development studies: interpersonal relationships are central to the self-concept of women; role taking plays a major role in women's development; diverse and non-linear patterns of development filled with role discontinuities and change are the norm for women, rather than a linear set of developmental milestones; and women experience different developmental issues and patterns.

Caffarella and Olson (1993) emphasize that the importance of relationships and feeling connected to others is central to the overall development process throughout a woman's lifespan. There is also a need for women to capture their own spirit of self, to be given recognition not just for who they are, but for individual abilities and competencies (p.143). MacKeracher (1996) presents women's self-development along two paths: autonomy and independent action, and connectedness to others and interdependent action. She argued that these self-systems are gender related but not gender specific and that, while some women prefer connectedness, most individuals use a combination of self-systems to create their own unique selves. Belenky et al. (1986) have also expanded our understanding of learning styles of separate/autonomous and connected/relational learners. Separate learners value independent learning, using analysis and logic as separate from feelings. Connected learners value relationship with others, collaboration in learning and the integration of thoughts and feelings.

MacKeracher explores the relationship between women's development and preferred learning styles. She develops a comprehensive framework that challenges adult educators to consider a continuum of separate and relational learners by distinguishing their learning concerns, learning activities, preferred cognitive styles, views towards truth and evaluation.

> Separate knowers and learners prefer knowledge which presents an objective, generalized and logical version of reality, which holds thoughts and feelings separate from each other; and which can presented by an expert or authority figure through presentation-based techniques, such as lectures.... Connected knowers and learners prefer knowledge which presents a personalized, specific and particularized version of reality, which connects thoughts and feelings; and which can be presented by co-learners through discussion-based techniques such as consciousness-raising (p.82).

MacKeracher (1996) further distinguishes dimensions of women's learning as sources of knowledge and information-gathering processes. Sources of knowledge include subjective and received knowledge. Subjective knowledge values feelings, intuition and an inner voice based on personal experience, while received knowledge includes facts and truths from external sources such as valued friends, families or experts. Facilitators of adult learning can assist women to become aware of two sources of knowledge and to express and assess their own knowledge based on experience and external realities. Adult education can become more inclusive and effective when facilitators can identify (a) learning patterns of women who feel silenced; (b) those who attend to knowledge from authority; (c) learners who derive knowledge from experience; and (d) learning strategies that focus on either separate or connected knowing and full development of integrated ways of knowing using a variety of learning strategies (p.138). MacKeracher argues that strategies that support and encourage relational learning would benefit most learners.

The work of women adult educators and researchers confirms that socially constructed gender roles influence the preferred learning styles of men and women. Caution should be taken in making generalizations from research studies that include small homogeneous samples of women, or studies that include both women and men. As well, patterns of learning should not become predictors of intelligence. Rather, because there is often a mixture of behaviours among men and women of different cultural backgrounds, the most significant caution to highlight is that the use of stereotypes "based on gender or racial factors are likely to have a very adverse effect on learners" (MacKeracher 1996, 141). In addition, approaches to development and learning that reinforce traditional gender stereotypes can maintain gender inequality. Gerber (1995) argues that, as men and women conform to cultural expectations of their gender role, they may also be conforming to relations in which men have more power and control over women. Stereotypical values may be that a "truly feminine" woman expresses warmth, concern and connection and a "truly masculine" man asserts himself and his will on others. One important finding in research related to gender and violence is that violent men and battered women have traits that are the extremes of stereotyped masculinity and femininity. Gerber argues that conforming to traditional gender traits basically supports unequal relationships and potentially sanctions men's power over women. When masculinity or femininity are discussed outside of the power relations in a given society, the socially constructed nature of power relations is ignored.

Women have contributed to our understanding of learning and general learning patterns. Principles of adult learning and facilitation have expanded to include women's experiences and different learning styles. It has also been argued that adult education has to go further towards integrating what is known about women's learning and development and towards modifying traditional adult education principles and practices. The following principles are effective in women's learning:

- Fostering a connected learning environment; utilizing small groups to foster the development of trust and mutual respect (Schneidewind 1983);

- Co-operative and collaborative learning structures to help minimize hierarchical relationships among learners and between learners and instructors (Schneidewind 1983);

- Co-operative communication styles (Belencky 1986; Hayes 1989);

- Holistic approaches to teaching and learning that focus on the broad view of a subject or theme before examining it in detail, and then move back and forth between the whole and the parts (Hayes 1989);

- Opportunities to integrate thoughts and feelings, theory and practice, to bring together and find connections between specific, concrete experience and generalized or abstracted versions of experiences–consciousness raising, journal keeping, group discussions, case studies (MacKeracher 1993);
- Teaching for transformation and empowerment (Weiler 1988; 1991).

Women's Organizations as Sites of Adult Education

Critical theorists also challenge adult educators to be more effective in realizing social change through adult education. Further study is required of the power relationships in personal, social and institutional settings that affect women's learning experiences. Adult educators require a more sophisticated analysis of the structural inequalities of race, class and gender (Griffin 1991). Weiler (1991) argues that Freire's (1970) concept of liberatory education fails to "address the specificity of people's lives" and fails to "analyze the contradictions between conflicting oppressed groups" (p.450). For example, a woman can experience oppression in her workplace while being privileged in her lifestyle.

M. Hart (1990) incorporates a feminist analysis of power in personal and social change in her discussion of women's consciousness-raising groups. She identifies the following principles that characterize consciousness raising for transformative learning: (a) acknowledgement of oppression by addressing power; (b) working with marginalized groups; (c) recognizing the importance of personal experience in the learning process; (d) working with relative homogenous groups with respect to major social differences such as gender, race or class; (e) issues of trust and mutuality in working through experiences of inequality; (f) maintaining equality in group processes and the role of the instructor; (g) gaining theoretical distance in order to analyze the structure of female oppression; and (h) avoidance of an individualized focus or group therapy (pp.59-67).

The concept of New Social Movements is also being examined to better understand the role of adult education in social change. New Social Movements have been defined as attempts to change social relations and structures towards peace, feminism, and economic and personal development (Holford 1995; Welton 1993). Women throughout history have challenged underlying historical and social processes that dehumanize women and have made gains to change sexist attitudes and practices. Consider these achievements: in 1918, the right to vote was achieved; in 1928, women become persons; in 1955, women could work for the federal government; in 1969, it was legal to disseminate birth control information; in 1973, the first women's shelter was opened; and in 1983, Bertha Wilson was the first woman appointed to the Supreme Court. The Women's Movement has made great contributions to the field of adult education. However, the importance of women's organizations as sites of adult learning has been neglected (Welton 1992). Through voluntary organizations, women participated in community education on issues such as farming, schooling, global peace, citizenship and the improvement of local neighbourhoods.

Students and historians are beginning to write the history of women's accomplishments, exploring the complex relationships of adult learning, community organizing and social change (Butterwick 1998; Welton 1992). There is increasing interest in women's knowledge and learning sites. Miles (1989) argues that even though adult education has its roots in social movements, the field can be strengthened further by examination and use of feminist approaches. Women were, and continue to be, leaders in creating alternative organizations based on learning and social action.

In the nineteenth and early twentieth centuries, women's voluntary groups were founded to educate women and to raise the standards of home making and citizenship. Adelaide Hunter Hoodless founded the Women's Institutes in 1897 (Cox 1997). The movement grew as Hoodless lectured on hygiene, health and home economics to rural women. Eventually small household science groups were organized to discuss topics of interest. The networks were formalized into a national Federated Women's Institute of Canada in 1919 in Winnipeg. The Women's Institutes, championed by Hoodless and supported by government, became a means for rural women to improve the quality of their own lives, meet their own needs and develop leadership in society.

The history of the YWCA in Canada also demonstrates the blend of women's learning and action. The Canadian Branch of the YWCA was first formed in St. John, New Brunswick, in 1897. Branches expanded across Canada whose primary concern was to "promote the spiritual, intellectual, physical and social conditions of all young women" (Buchanan 1997). The organization played a significant role in social welfare for immigrant women and the development of classes on reading, shorthand, cooking and china painting. In 1897, Miss Colby, the first president of the Winnipeg Branch of the YWCA, developed programs to assist women industrial workers by encouraging self-development and leadership skills. The YWCA continued to develop and respond to the changing needs of women.

In the 1960s and 1970s, women's learning and action were based in consciousness-raising groups that were part of the feminist social movement. Participants met in informal settings to reflect on their experiences, to examine common struggles and to analyze their concerns related to power relationships and institutions. While consciousness-raising approaches challenged sexism in society, Agnew (1996) argues that, in the 1970s, liberal feminist attempts to liberate women from male-dominated society were based on the principles of individuality and involved mostly middle-class, English-speaking women. Discussion focused on gender roles, socialization, opportunities for education and employment, sexuality and reproduction issues. Working-class women or women of colour did not participate due to language barriers, interest in different issues such as immigration and discrimination, poverty and employment in domestic or supportive services. Agnew (1996) argues that the values and practices of the early Women's Movement in Canada treated gender as a universal category and, as a result, excluded the experiences of women of Asian, African and

Caribbean descent. Inclusion remains a critical issue in women's learning sites today. Women are challenged to explore their own covert power relations, authority issues, representation, accountability and sharing of power. Agnew also argues that gender is not more significant than ethnicity, race or class in developing a sense of self or social identity as a woman, and that women do not constitute a single social category. The diversity of women's experiences and situations is crucial in developing meaningful adult learning opportunities for women and anti-sexist and anti-racist adult education. "Race, class and gender hierarchies in social institutions determine what is known and who knows it" (Agnew 1996, 51).

The National Organization of Immigrant and Visible Minority Women (NOIVM) was formed in 1987 with the purpose of ensuring equality for immigrant and visible minority women in Canada. Education is a part of their mandate to challenge sexism, racism, poverty and isolation. The group links with other women's organizations across Canada—such as the Immigrant Women's Association of Manitoba—to advocate and develop strategies to support immigrant women. NOIVM has addressed concerns of immigrant women, such as credential recognition for previous education and work experience, improved information, child care and work experience, as well as challenging professional bodies and educational institutions to become aware of the barriers within their own system to skilled and educated immigrant and visible minority women (NOIVM 1995). NOIVM provides information to the government on key concerns of women related to training, apprenticeship, prior learning, health issues, child poverty, violence, justice and poverty.

Another feminist organization for women's education is the Canadian Congress for Learning Opportunities for Women (CCLOW). Founded as a committee of the Canadian Council for Adult Education, the organization was formed in 1979 with a focus on "transitional women," that is, mature women who were facing the challenges of moving into paid work after working in the unpaid labour market (Butterwick 1998, 113). This national organization played an important advocacy role in formulating government policies, conducting research and creating women's education and training. The national group was active regionally through its membership, particularly during the transfer of training responsibilities from the federal government to the provinces, the implementation of social services review and the restructuring of Employment Insurance. Many groups were formed provincially. For example, at a local level in Manitoba in 1990, the Coalition for Education and Training for Women was formed to ensure that women's voices were heard in the planning stages for changes to training for women. The group advocated for flexibility in programs, lower costs for training, criteria to enable women to access programs and to meet needs of local women. The members acted as advocates and lobbyists as Manitoba took over federal responsibilities for training. Women such as Mary Scott, Rita Owens, Linda Taylor and Joan Doherty were active in the Manitoba Coalition and were linked to the CCLOW, but felt that the local group was better able to examine the kinds of training required by Manitoba women and the trends in participation of women in training.

Today, women's groups are struggling with limited funding, outreach to new members, inclusion of women from diverse backgrounds and responsiveness to the rapidly changing social conditions that affect women. The CCLOW has closed its national office, discontinued the publication of its journal *Women's Education* and is exploring the use of technology to encourage involvement and revitalization.

Future Directions

Equal opportunity in all aspects of education is essential to enable women of all ages to make their full contribution to society and to the resolution of the multiple problems confronting humanity. When women are caught in a situation of social isolation and lack of access to knowledge and information, they are alienated from decision-making processes within the family, community and society in general, and have little control over their bodies and lives.... Education should ensure that women become aware of the need to organize as women in order to change the situation and to build their capacities so that they can gain access to formal power structures and decision-making processes in both private and public spheres (UNESCO, 1997).

Women's learning and empowerment issues present challenges to both the liberal and the critical approaches to adult education. The liberal or traditional paradigm of adult education, allied with male-dominated theorists and theoretical research on "human" development, failed to consider the different values that women associate with development and learning. In addition, the critical paradigm of adult education, although emphasizing transformation and empowerment, failed to understand the multiple and often contradictory factors involved in oppression and empowerment. Building on these insights, adult education is currently challenged to re-visit and re-vision its commitment to social change and empowerment.

The Platform for Action

Women are using adult education to foster social change through organizations that work to ensure that international agreements that focus on peace, democracy and women's equity are carried forward by governments. The Platform for Action, adopted unanimously at the Fourth World Conference on Women by representatives from 189 countries, reflected an international commitment to the goals of equality, development and peace for all women (United Nations 1995). Building on the Forward Looking Strategies (FLS) document adopted at the 1985 World Conference on Women in Nairobi, the Platform for Action identified twelve areas of concern considered to represent the main obstacles to women's advancement and named strategic objectives and actions to be taken by the year 2000. The critical areas included issues such as poverty, armed conflict, violence and health, which must be addressed to achieve women's equality. It also identified education and training as a critical area and, among its recommendations, called for the development of non-discriminatory education and training, the allocation of sufficient resources for and monitoring of the implementation of educational reforms and the promotion of lifelong education and training for women.

In preparation for Beijing Plus Five, the five-year evaluation of progress made on the Platform for Action, women are working together to monitor governments' promises for action; facilitate the development of feminist analysis of global issues as they affect Canadian women; connect with other feminists in different parts of the world to develop common analysis and strategies for action; develop and facilitate feminist analysis of economic and social rights; and ensure women's participation in decisions regarding the implementation of these rights (United Nations 1995). Women working towards these objectives are integrating feminist approaches to adult education. Representing different social, cultural, economic and educational backgrounds, they come together to share their knowledge and experience with other women who are committed to women's empowerment. Using the tools of feminist analysis, they identify areas for action and effective strategies for change.

The Hamburg Declaration on Learning

Another significant initiative that addressed women's adult education was the Fifth International Conference on Adult Education held in Hamburg, Germany, in 1997. Adult educators world-wide were challenged to make a commitment to critical consciousness, analysis and problem-solving practices that are empowering and transformative in addressing issues such as poverty, exclusion, inequality, conflict and sustainability. The Hamburg Conference developed a Declaration on Adult Learning and developed ten specific themes on adult learning to guide adult educators in working for gender equality, equity and the empowerment of women (UNESCO 1997). In addition, women's concerns were reflected in other agenda items for adult learning including greater community participation; the right to literacy and basic education in order to reduce the illiteracy of women world-wide by half; access to jobs and gender equity in work; gender-specific health programs; access to new media and technologies; accessibility of people who are currently excluded from opportunities to participate (the aged, migrants, refugees, disabled and prison inmates); and ensuring that women's programs have an equitable share in the resources of adult learning (UNESCO 1997).

Conclusion

Women adult educators have expanded the study and practice of adult education to address feminist concerns. Problems in adult education, including the marginality of women's experiences in literature and in academic institutions, are being identified. Feminist adult educators have provided adult educators with the tools to gain awareness and take action on gender biases that affect the personal and social development of women. In order to achieve the goals of women's empowerment, adult educators must be aware of sexism rooted in society that underlies women's experiences and concerns. Adult educators have demonstrated action on women's empowerment by increasing our understanding of women's development and learning, as well as women's learning in social movements and organizations that include adult education as a means for social change. Women's contributions historically, nationally and internationally are a vitalizing force for the future of adult education to work towards social development and social justice.

References

Agnew, V. 1996. *Resisting discrimination: Women from Asia, Africa, and the Caribbean and the Women's Movement in Canada*. Toronto: University of Toronto.

Bateson, M.C. 1989. *Composing a life*. New York: The Atlantic Monthly Press.

Belenky, M.F., B.N. Clinchy, N.R. Goldberger, and J.M. Tarule. 1986. *Women's ways of knowing: The development of self, voice and mind*. New York: Basic Books.

Buchanan N. 1997. Continuing education at the YWCA in Winnipeg. In *Adult education in Manitoba: Historical aspects*, edited by D. Poonwassie and A. Poonwassie. Ontario: Canadian Educators.

Burstow, B. 1994. Problematizing adult education: A feminist perspective. *Canadian Journal for Studies in Adult Education* 8 (1): 1-14.

Butterwick, S. 1998. Lest we forget–uncovering women's leadership in adult education. In *The foundations of adult education in Canada*, edited by G. Selman, M. Selman, M. Cooke, and P. Dampier. 2d ed. Toronto: Thompson Educational Publishing.

Cafarella, R.S., and S.K. Olson. 1993. Psychosocial development of women: A critical review of the literature. *Adut Education Quarterly* 43 (3): 125-151.

Canadian Journal for the Study of Adult Education. 1994. Special Issue: Feminisms in Adult Education: Fostering Visibility and Change for Women. Introduction.

Cox, D. 1997. The Manitoba women's institute 1910-1995. In *Adult education in Manitoba: Historical aspects*, edited by D. Poonwassie and A. Poonwassie. Ontario: Canadian Educators.

Cross, K.P. 1981. *Adults as learners: Increasing participation and facilitating learning*. San Francisco: Jossey-Bass.

Doyal, L. 1998. What makes women sick? Promoting women's health: the changing agenda for health protection. *Australian Journal of Primary Health–Interchanges* 2 (2): 8-19.

Freire, P. 1970. *Pedagogy of the oppressed*. New York: Seabury Press.

Gerber, G. 1995. Gender stereotypes and the problem of marital violence. In *Violence and the Prevention of Violence*, edited by L. Adler and F. Denmark. Westport: Praeger.

Gaskell, J., and A. McLaren, eds. (1997) *Women and education: A Canadian perspective*. Calgary: Detselig Enterprises Ltd.

Gilligan, C. 1982. *In a different voice: Psychological theory and women's development*. Cambridge: Harvard University Press.

Greaves, L. 1999. *Canadian institutes for health research 2000: Sex, gender and women's health*. Vancouver: Canadian Institute for Health Research.

Griffin, C. 1991. A critical perspective on sociology and adult education. In *Adult education: Evolution and achievement in a developing field of study*. San Francisco: Jossey-Bass.

Hamilton, E., and P. Cunningham. 1989. Community based adult education. In *Handbook of adult and continuing education*, edited by S.B. Merriam and P.M. Cunningham. San Francisco: Jossey-Bass.

Hancock, E. 1985. Age or experience. *Human Development* 28 (5): 274-280.

Hart, M. 1990. Critical theory and beyond further perspectives on emancipatory education. *Adult Education Quarterly* 40 (3): 125-138.

Hayes, E. 1989. Insights from women's experiences for teaching and learning. In Effective teaching styles, edited by E.R. Hayes. *New Directions for Continuing Education* 43. San Francisco: Jossey-Bass Inc.

———., and L. Smith. 1994. Women in adult education: An analysis of perspectives in major journals. *Adult Education Quarterly* 44 (4): 201-221.

Heng, C.L. 1995. Women's empowerment: addressing emotional subordination. *Convergence* 28 (3): 78-84.

Holford, J. 1995. Why social movements matter: Cognitive praxis and the creation of knowledge. *Adult Education Quarterly* 45 (2): 95-111.

Kitchen, B. 1992. Framing the issues: the political economy of poor mothers. *Canadian Woman Studies* 12 (4): 10-15.

Knowles, M. 1970. *The modern practice of adult education: Andragogy versus pedagogy.* New York: Associated Press.

Lyons, N.P. 1987. Ways of knowing, learning, and making moral choices. *Journal of Moral Education* 16 (3).

MacKeracher, D. 1993. Women as learners. In *The Craft of Teaching Adults*, edited by Thelma Barer-Stein and J. Draper. Toronto: Culture Concepts.

———. 1996. *Making sense of adult learning.* Toronto: Culture Concepts.

Medel-Anonuevo, C., ed. 1995. *Women, education and empowerment: Pathways towards autonomy.* Hamburg: UNESCO.

Miles, A. 1989. Women's challenge to adult education. *Canadian Journal for the Study of Adult Education* 3 (1): 1-18.

National Organization of Immigrant and Visible Minority Women of Canada. 1995. *Political participation for change—Immigrant and visible minority in action.* Toronto: NOIVM.

Normand, J. 1995. Education of women in Canada. In *Canadian social trends*. Ottawa: Statistics Canada.

Parsons, S. 1990. Feminist challenges to curriculum design. *Studies in the Education of Adults* 22 (1): 49-58.

Peck, T.A. 1986. Women's self-definition: From a different model? *Psychology of Women Quarterly* 10: 274-284.

Rodgers, K. 1994. Wife assault: the findings of a national survey. *Juristat: Service Bulletin for the Canadian Centre for Justice Studies* 14 (9).

Saraswati, J. 1996. *Immigrant and visible minority women: Profile of poverty in Canada.* Canada: National Organization of Immigrant and Visible Minority Women of Canada.

Schneidewind, N. 1983. Feminist values: Guidelines for teaching methodology in women's studies. In *Learning our way: Essays in feminist education*, edited by C. Bunch and S. Pollack. London, England: The Women's Press.

Scott, S.M., B. Spencer, and A.M. Thomas, eds. 1998. *Learning for life: Canadian readings in adult education.* Toronto: Thompson Educational Publishing.

Selman, G., and P. Dampier. 1991. *The foundations of adult education in Canada.* Toronto: Thompson Educational Publishing.

Smith, Edith. 1992. Women's Learning: Implications for adult education research and practice. *The Canadian Journal for the Study of Adult Education* VI (1): 45-66.

Stalker, J. 1996. Women and adult education: Rethinking androcentric research. *Adult Education Quarterly* 46 (2): 98-113.

———. 1998. Women in the history of adult education: misogynist responses to our participation. In *Learning for life: Canadian readings in adult education*, edited by S.M. Scott, B. Spencer, and A.M. Thomas. Toronto: Thompson Educational Publishing.

Stubblefield, H. 1988. *Toward a history of adult education in America.* New York: Croom Helm.

Stromquist, N. 1995. The theoretical and practical bases for empowerment. In *Women, education and empowerment: Pathways towards autonomy*, edited by C. Medel-Anonuevo. Hamburg: UNESCO.

UNESCO. 1997. *The Hamburg Declaration on Adult Learning.* Fifth International Conference on Adult Education. Hamburg: CONFINTEA V.

United Nations. 1995. *Fourth World Conference on Women: Platform for Action.* New York: United Nations Division for the Advancement of Women.

Weiler, K. 1988. *Women teaching for change: Gender, class and power.* South Hadley: Bergin & Garvey Publishing Inc.

———. 1991. Freire and a feminist pedagogy of difference. *Harvard Educational Review* 61 (4): 449-474.

Welton, M. 1993. Social revolutionary learning: the new social movement as learning sites. *Adult Education Quarterly* 43 (3): 152-160.

Welton, M., ed. 1992. *Educating for a brighter new day: Women's organizations as learning sites.* Halifax: Dalhousie University.

18

Adult Education in First Nations Communities: Starting with the People

Deo H. Poonwassie

There is a hive of activity in First Nations communities—there are programs for children, adults, elders and mothers; for economic development, social transformation, cultural retention, assimilation and self-government. There are also many social agencies at work in these communities such as the churches, Indian and Northern Affairs Canada (INAC), the RCMP, schools, business and welfare. Unfortunately, the professionals and trainers come and go, as few make the community their home. Doctors, lawyers, teachers, dentists, accountants, nurses and specialists of every persuasion become "circuit riders."

The federal government allocates and spends large sums of money in the name of First Nations peoples; in reality, however, only a small percentage of this reaches the community. The public perception is that these communities are sufficiently resourced, but this is not the case. Despite Canada's rating as the number one country in the world for quality of life by the United Nations, it has been severely criticized by Amnesty International for its treatment of First Nations peoples. The devastation incurred by a punitive system of welfare, the establishment of reserves, the mental and emotional scars created in residential schools and a foreign educational system have all contributed to the impoverishment of Canada's First Nations peoples.

The purpose of this chapter is to argue that adult education is a force that can foster an environment that will improve the living conditions of First Nations peoples by helping their communities to empower themselves. Adult education initiatives will develop a positive sense of self, provide relevant training and skills and create better conditions for a learning community. Of course, adult education alone cannot meet all the needs of these communities; concurrent and sustainable community economic development must be implemented and jobs must be created so that members of the community can find employment at home.

There is some confusion about the use of such terms as *Indian, Native, First Nations,* and *Aboriginal.* Indian is used in the official federal government document *The Indian Act*; this term has now fallen out of general use and appears mostly in official documents. The term Native replaced Indian and is still used today—for example, Native Studies. First Nations is now in use and refers to the first peoples of this land for whom the federal government has fiduciary responsibilities under the Indian Act. The term First

Nations does not in any way indicate homogeneity; there are many First Nations peoples who have different languages, cultural traditions and geopolitical characteristics. The term *Aboriginal* refers to First Nations, Inuit, Métis and Non-Status peoples as defined in the report of the Royal Commission on Aboriginal Peoples (1996).

Adult education has been defined elsewhere in this volume (see Draper). However, in this chapter, the term will mean all learning activities that persons who are beyond the age of compulsory schooling undertake consciously to bring about changes in areas that are important in their lives. This may be formal, non-formal or informal learning. No distinction will be made in the use of the terms adult education and the education of adults. Although distinctions have been made between education and training (Peters 1972), these terms will be used interchangeably to mean learning what is worthwhile for either intrinsic or extrinsic satisfaction. It should also be noted that education is under the jurisdiction of the provincial governments, but for First Nations, it is the responsibility of the federal government.

Glimpses from History

Prior to the arrival of the Europeans, the First Nations peoples were autonomous, self-sufficient and free to decide their destiny. They had their own systems of government, social values, education and sustenance (Adams 1975; Burns 1998; Wien 1986). While it is correct to say that they did not have a system of schooling as we know it today, it is clear that they had an efficient system of passing on the accumulated wisdom, knowledge and understandings of their people. This was done by methods of experiential learning, apprenticeship, mentoring and modelling. The environment in which they lived was their classroom, and elders, parents, the community and nature were the instructors. This interdependence was a holistic approach in which people and nature were intertwined.

The arrival of the Europeans created many stresses on the survival systems of First Nations peoples. Suffice it to say that this contact with Europeans resulted in a treacherous colonialism. Adams (1975) cites several reasons for the subjugation of the First Peoples of this land. Foremost among these was the shift from an agricultural economic base to one of hunting and trapping. Hunting was facilitated by the introduction of the horse, and trapping was introduced by the Hudson Bay company (and others) so that First Nations peoples could exchange furs for European goods. Hunting, and consequently a nomadic way of life, was also supported by the introduction of the gun. Alcohol was used liberally to make agreements that favoured the colonizers and further the process of domination. The creation of reserves and the signing of several treaties enabled the control and containment of First Nations peoples, and their health, wealth and spirituality began a fast slide on a steep slope to anomie and destruction.

One of the most devastating blows struck by the Europeans was the imposition of their education on a culturally different people. These attempts by the colonizers to "civilize" the natives took many forms; most fatal was the creation of residential schools. The residential schools, organized and administered by Christian groups, wreaked havoc with the minds of the young students who were forced to attend. They were required to give up their language, perform menial tasks and, in many cases, succumb to the sexual and sadistic desires of their "liberators." The scars of this treatment are seen today in parents who have problems parenting mainly because of their experience in residential schools (Hookimaw-Witt 1998). The legacy of residential schools is also clearly visible in the overwhelming psychological and social pressures experienced by Aboriginal peoples. These issues manifest themselves in the high incidence of various addictions, suicide rates of epidemic proportions, family violence, unemployment and other socioeconomic problems.

The creation of the Department of Indian and Northern Affairs (henceforth referred to as the Department) as the bureaucratic arm of the federal government implementing the Indian Act saw the complete control of First Nations peoples entrenched in law (Ponting and Gibbins 1980). The regulation of every aspect of living resulted in a concerted attempt to first annihilate, then to assimilate and dictate the conditions of existence for First Nations peoples. *A Survey of the Contemporary Indians of Canada, Economic, Political, Educational Needs and Policies* (Hawthorne 1966) reveals the assimilative policies of the federal government and the educational requirements as deemed necessary by the Department. Following this report, there were several white papers, red papers, reports and books concerning the plight of First Nations peoples in Canada (see, for example, Burke 1976; Cardinal 1969; Hamilton and Sinclair 1991; Indian Tribes of Manitoba 1971; McFarlane 1993; National Indian Brotherhood 1972; Wuttunee 1971; RCAP 1996). The approach in dealing with First Nations peoples changed gradually from one of assimilation to one of recognition of their need for self-government. Indeed the RCAP (Royal Commission on Aboriginal Peoples) made it very clear that the road to survival for all Aboriginal peoples is a form of self-government; this report even goes on to show how self-government can be achieved and details a requisite price tag. Key to the concept of First Nations self-government is education. While there has been much rhetoric and many commissioned research papers, formal education in First Nations communities remains at a very low level.

Education in First Nations Communities

As already noted, First Nations peoples had an effective system of education for both adults and youth. Considering the demands of their social and economic organizations, their environment and their spirituality, education served the purposes of survival and growth guided by a philosophy of holism and interrelatedness. Unfortunately, the new providers of education saw fit to ignore existing educational systems based on the real needs of the people; the authorities (governments and churches) saw education as an instrument of assimilation and acted accordingly. As pointed out above, students were required to leave their home communities to attend either residential schools, day schools or public schools. These were alien and punitive environments, and First Nations students did well just to survive under the very negative learning conditions of racism, alienation, forced manual labour and instruction in a foreign language (English or French). It is no surprise that the academic performance of these students was seen as substandard; however, the authorities chose to explain these results by using the usual negative stereotypical justifications.

The establishment of schools on reserves, administered by the Department, alleviated these problems in one way: students were able to stay in their own home community for schooling up to Grade 6, then later to Grade 9, and in some communities up to Grade 12. Despite this partially positive move, there are still some communities that have to send their children away for senior high school (Grades 10 to 12) education. The parents in the communities were not part of the decision-making apparatus that affected the lives of their children in reserve schools and definitely not in the public schools. Most teachers were non-Aboriginal and mainly from the south or from another province, teaching an irrelevant curriculum to a classroom of students whose culture and language they did not understand. Furthermore, many of these teachers worked on reserves because they were unable to secure jobs elsewhere. Most of the communities served as a "training ground" for new teachers until a "real" teaching job became available in a southern urban centre.

The scarcity of Aboriginal teachers was seen as a major problem in First Nations education. Chiefs, councils, governments and universities recognized the need for training and certifying Aboriginal teachers. In the late 1960s and early 1970s, several teacher education programs (TEPs) were initiated at universities in many provinces, both on campus and community based. The following are examples of these initiatives: Indian-Métis Project Action for Teacher Education (IMPACTE); Winnipeg Education Centre (WEC); Professional Education for Native Teachers (PENT); Brandon University Northern Education Program (BUNTEP); Northern Teacher Education Project (NORTEP); Saskatchewan Urban Native Teacher Education Program (SUNTEP); Morning Star; Indian Teacher Education Program (ITEP); and Native Indian Teacher Education Program (NITEP). Most of these programs initially offered support for Aboriginal students (some still do) in the essential areas of academics (tutoring, upgrading, course selection); finances (family and living allowances, tuition, books, health needs, transportation, incidentals); and counselling (personal, family, career). With the current apparent financial crunch, many of these programs are restricted in the kinds of support they can offer their students. In addition, many Aboriginal students now entering post-secondary institutions have graduated from high school and do not need as much support as their predecessors. However, the majority of the students who take advantage of these programs are mature students, that is, they are adults who may have had their schooling interrupted, they more than likely have children and they are over the age of 21 years (age for mature student status varies with each institution).

Normal support systems, such as extended family, are not available for students who are away from their home communities. Yet another problem may occur if their first language is not English or French. The details of everyday living can weigh heavily on Aboriginal students when they are faced with living in an urban setting for the first time. Sometimes, on their return to their home communities, they are shunned for having adopted a Euro-Canadian lifestyle. Because of these issues, it is desirable for leaders to establish regional centres for the delivery of university programs or, better yet, community-based programs with local involvement.

Community-based programs, such as BUNTEP, have many advantages. They can tap into the traditional community supports of elders and grandparents. Students do not have to be separated from their immediate family members nor do they have to relocate away from home. The whole issue of racism on campus can be ignored, and they can avoid the trauma of being labelled as second class (Poonwassie 1991). While there are many positive aspects to having university training located in the community, such programs are not without their detractors. The professors and administrators must ensure that, although the course content and delivery may be different, academic rigour and standards are maintained. The students must be challenged just as if they were on campus. In some cases this is a challenge for instructors, because they have to make the materials relevant for the students within a different learning environment.

Along with an increase in the number of trained Aboriginal teachers over the past twenty years, the advent of local control of education in First Nations communities has placed the responsibility for education squarely on the shoulders of local education authorities—or so it seems. Does this mean local control of education? How much control do the local First Nations Directors of Education actually have if the Department is still making decisions about funding? For example, why must First Nations adults (and children) face harmful health conditions while they are in school? There have been several instances of this reported in Manitoba. I suggest that if these conditions pertained in any public institution, there would be riots and civil disobedience and the authorities would hasten to correct the situation. However, the federal government is maintaining a system where they can delegate responsibility without the necessary accompaniment of authority—a truly colonial administration.

Present and Persistent Needs

When compared to the national average, First Nations communities experience high unemployment (as high as 80 percent in some cases). Dependence on social assistance is commonplace in many communities, as is addiction to drugs and alcohol, and illiteracy in the indigenous language, as well as English or French, can be as high as 30 percent (personal communication with Donna Carrier, Sept. 15, 2000). There are many programs that are planned and implemented in these communities. They include adult basic education (ABE) and training in trades such as carpentry, plumbing, painting, motor mechanics and electricity. Areas in which more and better training is needed are personal counselling and healing, health and sanitation, language, addictions (drugs and gaming) and child care.

There is great need for local control of planning and implementation by resource people from within the communities (Carney 1982; Martin 1993). All too often, programs are designed for the people by experts from the outside. Local educators and stakeholders must be part of any planning process that is designed to meet the needs of First Nations people (Poonwassie 1993). In other words, planning needs to start with the people, ensuring a consideration of indigenous knowledge, values, traditions and systems. This does not mean that experts should not be hired as advisors; it does, however, mean that they should not be dictating the activities of the local people. It is not sufficient to have local people on advisory boards simply because in many cases these boards are used as shields from genuine substantiated criticism. In order for local boards to work effectively for the improvement of the community, adults must have the skills to assume these responsibilities. Implementation requires an understanding of the local culture and social values; implementers must also understand the local politics and power structures that will affect every aspect of their work. It is often difficult, if not impossible, for an itinerant outsider to make meaningful contributions for successful implementation of educational programs. For programs to work in any community, certain conditions must be met; critical among these is a desired level of literacy.

Considering the high numbers of young people who do not complete their schooling in First Nations communities (INAC 1998), there is a compelling need for adult literacy training. It is encouraging to see many young adults returning to school in these communities to complete their high school programs through ABE or General Education Diploma (GED) programs. Literacy here is used to mean the achievement of a level of training that will enable the individual to obtain the necessary qualifications to gain desired employment. In other situations, literacy is defined by a level of schooling that must be met, for example, a Grade 7 standing. In other cases, the term refers to the ability to function adequately in a particular society, for example, the ability to read the daily newspaper. Yet other interpretations consider cultural literacy, which means understanding one's culture–language, social structures, power levels, government, arts, sports and history. In order for First Nations people to have the power and influence needed to achieve their goal of self-determination, considerable work must be undertaken to improve literacy levels in all communities.

At present post-secondary education and training are critical for First Nations peoples if they are to reclaim their destiny and re-establish some form of self-government (Poonwassie 2000). Effective leadership and an informed indigenous population can be derived from much-needed academic and professional programs in institutions of higher learning. Participation in university and college programs are increasing but not at a rate that will create parity with the general Canadian population in the near future (see INAC 1998, 32-33). There are Native Studies programs on several campuses designed to teach and promote the history and culture of the

Aboriginal peoples in that geographic location. However, generally, large campuses are hostile environments for Aboriginal students. The creation of special programs designed to meet the needs of Aboriginal students have enhanced educational accessibility on many campuses; they may be found under such names as transition programs, bridge programs and access programs. Indeed, at the University of British Columbia, there is a House of Learning erected by and for Aboriginal peoples; this serves as a focal point for Aboriginal students and others to gather, study, conduct research and promote the culture and causes of Aboriginal peoples. The Indian Federated College and the Gabriel Dumont Institute, both in Saskatchewan, and the Yellow Quill College in Manitoba are examples of post-secondary institutions in which the programs are designed to meet the needs of Aboriginal peoples.

As pointed out in Volume 3 of the RCAP Report (1996), Aboriginal peoples must work towards establishing their own post-secondary institutions in order to develop education and training programs that reflect their values, culture, language and indigenous knowledge. Nunavut, the most recently created territory in Canada, will probably lead the way, since the vast majority of its residents are Aboriginal peoples and since the territory has the legislative power and will to serve the needs of its people.

Community-based models are yet another approach for the provision of education to adults in First Nations communities. Students have the benefit of remaining at home while they attend training sessions organized in consultation with community leaders and delivered by accredited institutions. The benefits are enormous: graduates tend to seek employment locally rather than away from home; new graduates serve as role models; the community saves transportation and living allowances; personal supports are available within the community; instructors are directly challenged to incorporate local values and history into their courses; and community stakeholders are able to influence the direction of the programs. Criticisms of these programs are few but persistent: standards are lower in these programs compared to on-campus offerings; students are better prepared if they are exposed to a heterogeneous group of people on a campus; and learning resources on a campus are much more readily available. These criticisms are easily countered when the well-documented positive outcomes for the graduates and the communities are considered.

Community-based programs have been particularly effective in training adults in several areas of need identified by First Nations communities, such as teacher training, social work, arts, business administration, counselling, computers, family studies, language development, the building trades, auto mechanics and general administration. Many of these programs have been initiated, implemented and administered by the communities and are based on internal needs assessments. Areas that are not conducive to local community-based approaches are health sciences, including Western medicine, dentistry, physiotherapy and nursing; engineering; most of the laboratory-based sciences; and pharmacology. The main obstacle to offering these programs in First Nations communities is the financial cost of implementation, given the economies of scale. For studies in these areas, First Nations students are required to leave their communities and attend post-secondary institutions in large urban centres.

Barriers and Possibilities

Compared to the level of living that the Canadian economy affords the rest of its citizens, poverty in the First Nations communities is inexcusable. However, it persists, and the political will to correct it seems absent in a nation that considers itself a front-runner in the field of human rights and global humanitarian concerns. In September 2000, an international conference was held in Winnipeg addressing the plight of children in war-torn nations. Chaired by the Honourable Lloyd Axworthy, the Canadian Minister of Foreign Affairs, some fifty-two countries were represented. While Canadians were showing their concern for a dreadful international travesty, several First Nations leaders were marching outside the conference facility to draw attention to the deplorable conditions under which they live.

There have been skirmishes on the eastern seaboard between First Nations fishers and federal Fisheries Officers over the right of the First Nation peoples of Burnt Church to harvest lobster in order to survive. We have also witnessed the confrontation at Oka and several other conflicts between First Nations peoples and the federal government. It is in this context that we must examine the barriers to adult education and training in First Nations communities.

The reality of powerlessness among the people diminishes their enthusiasm for further training. Why, for example, are treaty rights not respected? Why are there so many outstanding land claims? The leaders of First Nations are fighting a valiant battle for survival through a protracted struggle for their rights and their peoples' well-being. Adult education can play a vital role in providing people with knowledge that can then become the psychological armour that will protect them from the fall-out of possible defeat. The empowerment resulting from knowledge about one's situation can become the base of innovative solutions. The conscientization process is critical in confronting one's reality (Freire 1971).

People must be able to see the purpose of training. Why enrol in any training program if there are no jobs? Education for philosophical reasons or delayed gratification appears nonsensical to most young adults who desire the same material goods that are available to others in general society. If training is to become meaningful, it is critical that there also be community economic development to provide jobs. The infusion of adequate sums of money directly into the community, accompanied by locally controlled technical assistance, will allow local people to develop their own sense of entrepreneurship.

In several First Nations communities, the majority of the adult population participating in training are women. They bring with them enthusiasm and commitment, especially if the training program is within their grasp or creates employment possibilities. However, many more women do not have the opportunity to undertake further training because of poor self-esteem, lack of day care or abusive living situations. The success of the women who are in training programs or are employed does not assure them a leadership position; this is partly due to the patriarchal nature of the local bureaucracy. Opportunities for First Nations women will increase as they continue to develop viable support groups within the community for the purpose of empowering themselves.

If First Nations peoples are to exercise their right to self-government, it becomes imperative for leaders to undertake intensive and extensive training. Adult education is critical when responsibility for the progress of the people is placed in the hands of local leaders. In anticipation of viable self-government, there is a need to train community members in such areas as policy formation and analysis, administration and financial management, which will incorporate indigenous structures and values. Most First Nations have already started this process and are administering their own educational, social and economic programs within tight federal government restrictions.

There is also a need for prevention and intervention workers, health professionals and counsellors. Local people need community-centred and culturally relevant training in order to deal with the problems created by years of oppression and colonization. A recent article in the *Winnipeg Free Press* ran under the headline, "Suicides plague Northern Ont. reserves" (Sept. 16, 2000, A19). The article describes the First Nations community of Pikangikum where the problem is most serious. The reasons cited in the article by the Chief of Pikangikum, the district treatment supervisor for Dilico Child and Family Services in Thunder Bay, Ontario, and Dan Kooses, deputy Grand Chief for Nishnawbe-Aski Nation are sexual abuse, family breakdown, loss of culture, parental addiction, lack of resources and crowded reserve conditions. Jim Morris, a health advisor for the Nishnawbe-Aski Nation, the region's top Native political organization, points out that Northern Ontario has the highest suicide rate in Canada at three times the national average. He is quoted as saying that, since 1990, there have been 204 suicides on Northern Ontario reserves.

Intervention is a critical first step in dealing with this epidemic, but there must be simultaneous development of effective schools, recreation facilities and the local economy. Locally initiated healing, education and training initiatives of support groups and other relevant services have proven to be instrumental in breaking the destructive cycles brought on by a history of dispossession and abuse. The entire community needs to adopt learning as a primary goal not only for employment but also to create a positive sense of self.

The Role of Adult Education

Market-driven adult education cannot solve the problems created by Canadian governments and experienced by First Nations peoples. A humanistic rather than an entrepreneurial approach will yield better results. The launching of the Canadian Broadcasting Corporation, National Farm Radio Forum, the Antigonish Movement, the Women's Institute and Frontier

College were all Canadian responses to the need for citizenship education and social change. There was a need for action, and it was provided by leaders with commitment and vision. It is now time for a revolution in adult education that will focus on the rise of concern for First Nations peoples. It must begin with skilled First Nations people who can provide the vision and direction for socioeconomic development in their communities. Understanding and recognition of indigenous structures and systems are essential if adult educators are to be successful in partnering with First Nations peoples in relevant and meaningful adult education initiatives.

While many First Nations have control of their education, the funding is still controlled by the federal government. Unless there are more resources available to develop better programs for improving the quality of life in these communities, Canada will continue to be criticized for its treatment of Aboriginal peoples. There is a major role for adult education–formal, non-formal and informal–in supporting this revolution. Livingstone's (1999) article on the findings of the first Canadian survey of informal learning practices included only those who speak English and French. This excluded many First Nations peoples, especially if they did not have a telephone. If people in First Nations communities had been included, the results would have been different. There is a need for more basic information about adult education activities in these communities as a first step in the effort towards working with them to improve their quality of life on their own terms.

What is the role of training in First Nations communities? At present most training programs are short term and appear as a reaction to crisis situations. The training of adults to meet the needs of the people requires a firm grounding in the cultural values of the participants. In addition, programs for young adults must embrace their aspirations and goals for a better life in an increasingly global society. The question of who gets trained and why demands that the power structures (internal and external) be examined closely. Cevero and Wilson (1999) state that "adult education always happens in places that have material existence, where socially organized relations of power define both the possibility for action as well as the meaning of the learning for all stakeholders" (p.34). The outcomes of training derive meaning from the possibility of practice within the community. If the power relations within the local bureaucracy are based on internal struggle, training and education become a very low priority, and all stakeholders are adversely affected. In addition, external agencies recognize the conflict and manipulate the variables to their advantage. First Nations training programs have suffered from this type of problem ever since their systems of government were undermined. The idea that education and training are not neutral (Freire 1971) must be re-examined in the context of First Nations aspirations for self-government.

Adult education and training are critical in creating a learning community. Popular education, liberation theology, communal talking circles, traditional teachings and formal schooling are all forms of adult education that can foster and promote the desire to learn. Adults as parents and role models are key to establishing and popularizing learning as a basic indigenous value. While there are adverse living conditions in some communities, significant improvements can only come when the people themselves have again taken charge of their own destiny. First Nations philosophy defines education as preparation for total living as well as a tool for improvement of the peoples' social and economic conditions. "To be effective, education must be nurtured in relevancy, commitment, motivation, and identifiable purpose. Furthermore, education must be a part of community activities and community progress" (Indian Tribes of Manitoba 1971, 116).

The contributions of First Nations peoples are becoming apparent in many aspects of Canadian life. Indigenous practices are finding their way into the medical profession through the integration of traditional healing approaches and methods; into the judicial system through the adoption of community sentencing circles and other restorative justice dispositions (Hamilton and Sinclair 1991); into educational facilities through the inclusion of implicit learning and/or teaching transactions; into business through the transformation of pyramidal structures to fluid circular models, and even into spiritual life by the adaptation of some indigenous beliefs, teachings and celebrations. Similarly, non-Aboriginal adult educators can benefit from their direct interactions with Aboriginal peoples in formal or informal educational settings by picking up new tools and ways of teaching and/or learning while sharing their own (Jordan 1992). They must also re-examine their involvement in Aboriginal education and be prepared to participate as collaborators, facilitators and resource people and not as directors and decision-makers. It is imperative that they recognize that the expertise on what is needed and how it should be implemented lies within the Aboriginal communities themselves. "One of the basic elements of the relationship between oppressor and oppressed is prescription" (Friere 1971, 31). By sharing with First Nations in the critical examination of problem situations, adult educators can participate in the transformation of those situations through a common struggle towards a meaningful resolution.

In recent times there has been a major thrust in the movement towards self-government for First Nations peoples (McFarlane 1993). The resilience of the culture in the face of Western media and technology proves that First Nations peoples are adaptable and flexible; this will ensure their survival in spite of governmental restrictions. There are First Nations leaders who contribute, in traditional and non-traditional ways, to all aspects of Canadian life, including politics, business, drama, film, music, academics, architecture, art, spirituality and the professions. Adult education will assist in this movement as the first priority becomes the aboriginal peoples' own vision of their destiny.

The Royal Commission on Aboriginal Peoples (Vol. 3, 500-525) addresses the need for adult education. It explores fundamental areas such as academic upgrading, adult basic and literacy programs, access to university or college preparation programs, location of program delivery, credit for Aboriginal language competency, educational services for Aboriginal adults, Aboriginally controlled post-secondary institutions, funding in its many forms and preparation for the job market. The emphasis is placed on training adults using indigenous values, traditions and vision in anticipation of self-government. Clearly the aim of this section of the report is to use the education of adults for achieving a comfortable lifestyle. The role of adult education is seen as a vehicle to produce marketable skills and the "good life"; this is consistent with the goals of adult education in any society.

From my experience and knowledge of the First Nations' situation, as a participant, observer and a researcher, I envisage adult education playing important roles in the following key areas: (1) training programs; (2) sustainable community economic development; (3) political conscientization; and (4) cultural and civic renaissance.

Enough has been said about training programs but not enough has been done. Training programs for First Nations adults must produce an entire range of productive persons, from skilled artisans to educated professionals, from sanitation workers to musicians and actors. For training programs to work properly, First Nations peoples must be involved in their planning, implementation and evaluation as directors, consultants and researchers. This is not to say that non-Aboriginal peoples should not participate; however, it does mean that they should be invited, not imposed by funding agencies. The role of adult education at all levels is undeniably critical in providing trained First Nations peoples to lead in their own development.

Sustainable community economic development is the engine that will drive the First Nations programs to successful completion. Adult education programs can develop local planners, business developers, and entrepreneurs. Designated persons can be commissioned to gather ideas that will work in the community, such as small manufacturing, co-operative business ventures and marketing local art and crafts. Again, the role for adult education is unlimited.

Political conscientization must begin with a critical understanding of one's reality. Some questions that will enhance this process are: Why are we in this situation? Is this acceptable? What can I do to change the situation? How can we as a community remove the physical and psychological effects of a debilitating colonialism? A collective critical awareness about living conditions is the beginning of social change; free will and determination can assist in collective action. Positive action for the improvement of living conditions for First Nations peoples must begin with the people and must be ably supported by all levels of government. The legacy of government action is not an impressive one; it is time for accelerated change and the distribution of power in the hands of the First Nations. Adult education can engender a radical revision of perception about who has power and who should have it. The work of Paulo Freire, Mahatma Gandhi, Moses Coady and Jimmy Tompkins will be instructive here. These icons of social change apprehended the oppressive realities and proceeded to act on them; indeed, this is the essence of adult education.

In preparing for self-government, the areas of cultural and civic renaissance are critical in creating the ballast that will steady the movement towards self-reliance. The cultural and/or spiritual development of the people will provide the social glue that will keep them together as a community. Civic renaissance will provide the world-view that is necessary for enhancing discipline, responsibility, direction and vision in a civil society. This philosophical base will allow people to create and maintain sustainable self-government. Adult education, in its many forms, can play a major role in developing this necessary base for community survival and prosperity.

Certain principles can assist in program planning for adult education in First Nations communities. These are: (a) inclusion of the values, culture and spirituality of the local people; (b) consideration of the context for which the program is being designed; (c) recognition of First Nations peoples as central decision-takers (d) consideration for the needs and priorities of First Nations peoples, not those of the bureaucrats; and (e) inclusion of indigenous knowledge and new communication methods (computers, television, film) that will utilize the growing knowledge of the digital society. This is not an exhaustive list, but it forms the basis upon which planners can develop adult education programs for training and education.

Conclusion

The First Nations leadership and people have initiated many programs to improve living conditions and procure self-government. They have used several adult education strategies that are part of their cultural legacy such as mentoring, apprenticeship, experiential learning and discussion groups (circle talks). Training programs were directly related to the problem at hand as adults knew what they needed. As the world unfolds in increasingly complex patterns, more sophisticated forms of problem-solving are required. This means that First Nations peoples have to train themselves to cope with the demands of an increasingly globalized society.

The implementation of adult education programs in First Nations communities (broadly defined) will require the full support of all levels of government, especially federal, in tangible practical forms. Rhetoric aside, the visions and missions of First Nations peoples must be respected and fully supported financially and technically. Local people must be trained to fill the positions available and to create new positions through sustainable economic development activities in First Nations communities. As First Nations peoples migrate to urban centres the idea of community becomes more complicated because reserves are not the only place of domicile, and cities (for example, Winnipeg and Saskatoon) are seeing a rise in population from this group; hence, the need to accommodate both rural and urban adults and youth in all programs is crucial if we are to progress towards the goal of social and economic equality.

Trainers must consider the multicultural nature of our society when planning adult education programs. In order for First Nations peoples to survive in this economy, bicultural education and training must be part of all programs (Martin 1993), not only for First Nations peoples, but also for members of the majority society.

What adult education did for building Canada in the first fifty years of the last century (see G. Selman in this volume), it can also do for First Nations peoples. It is clear that conditions have changed since then, but the spirit of adult education to improve the human condition is alive and well. The social movement approach in adult education has served this society for decades, but now the reality of entrepreneurship coupled with the advent of new technologies and corporate globalization must be added. First Nations peoples can adapt the adult education practices and approaches that have proven valuable by incorporating their values, culture and methods for their own empowerment.

References

Adams, H. 1975. *Prison of grass: Canada from the Native point of view.* Toronto: General Publishing.

Burke, J. 1976. *Paper tomahawks.* Winnipeg: Queenston House Publishing.

Burns, G.E. 1998. *Toward a redefinition of formal and informal learning: Education and the aboriginal people.* Proceedings of the 17th annual conference of the Canadian Association for the Study of Adult Education (pp.34-41).

Cardinal, H. 1969. *The unjust society.* Edmonton: Hurtig Publishers.

Carney, R.J. 1982. The road to Heart Lake. Native people: Adult learners and the future. *Canadian Journal of Native Education* 9 (3): 1-13.

Cevero, R.M., and A.L. Wilson. 1999. Beyond learner-centred practice; Adult education, power, and society. *The Canadian Journal for the Study of Adult Education* 13 (2): 27 -38.

Freire, P. 1971. *Pedagogy of the oppressed.* New York: Herder and Herder.

Hamilton, A.C., and C.M. Sinclair. 1991. *Report of the aboriginal justice inquiry of Manitoba.* Vol. 1. Winnipeg: Province of Manitoba.

Hawthorn, H.B., ed. 1967. *A survey of the contemporary Indians of Canada. Economic, political, educational needs and policies. Parts 1 and 2.* Ottawa: Minister of Supply and Services, Government of Canada.

Hookimaw-Witt, J. 1998. Any changes since residential school? *Canadian Journal of Native Education* 22 (2): 159-170.

Indian and Northern Affairs Canada (INAC).1999. *Basic departmental data, 1998.* Ottawa: Department of Indian Affairs and Northern Development, Government of Canada.

Indian Tribes of Manitoba. 1971. *Wahbung. Our tomorrows.* Winnipeg: Manitoba Indian Brotherhood.

Jordan, D. 1992. Australian aborigines: Education and identity. In *Education and cultural differences: New perspectives,* edited by D. Ray and D.H. Poonwassie. New York: Garland Publishing.

Livingstone, D.W. 1999. Exploring the icebergs of adult learning: Findings of the first Canadian survey of informal learning practices. *The Canadian Journal for the Study of Adult Education* 13 (2): 49-72.

Martin, P. 1993. Considerations for aboriginal adult education program planning. *Canadian Journal of Native Education* 20 (1): 168-175.

McFarlane, P. 1993. *Brotherhood to nationhood. George Manual and the making of the modern Indian movement.* Toronto: Between the Lines.

National Indian Brotherhood. 1972. *Indian control of Indian education.* Ottawa: National Indian Brotherhood.

Peters, R.S. 1972. *Ethics and society.* London: George Allen and Unwin.

Ponting, J.R., and R. Gibbins. 1980. *Out of irrelevance: A socio-political introduction to Indian affairs in Canada.* Toronto: Butterworths.

Poonwassie, A. 1993. Participatory programming in aboriginal adult education: A Manitoba model. Vancouver: *Native Issue Monthly* (May): 18-20.

Poonwassie, D.H. 1987. *The third world in Canada: Education of aboriginal peoples.* Paper presented at the Comparative and International Society of Canada Annual Conference. McMaster University, Hamilton, Ontario, Canada.

——. 1991. Issues in teacher education for aboriginal peoples: A Canadian perspective. *Florida Journal of Teacher Education* VII: 3-15.

——, and N. Kanhai. 2000. Struggle and resistance: Crafting First Nations in the new millennium. In *21st century Canadian diversity*, edited by S.E. Nancoo (pp.68-86). Mississauga, Ont.: Canadian Educators' Press.

Report of the Royal Commission on Aboriginal Peoples. 1996. *Gathering strength*. Vol. 3. Ottawa: Minister of Supply and Services.

Selman, G. 1998. The imaginative training for citizenship. In *Learning for life: Canadian readings in adult education*, edited by S.M. Scott, B. Spencer, and A.M. Thomas (pp.24-34). Toronto: Thompson Educational Publishing.

Wien, F. 1986. *Rebuilding the economic base of Indian communities: The Micmac in Nova Scotia*. Montreal: The Institute for Research on Public Policy.

Winnipeg Free Press. 2000. Suicides plague Northern Ont. reserves (September 16, A19).

Wuttunee, W.I.C. 1971. *Ruffled feathers. Indians in Canadian society*. Calgary, Alta.: Bell Books.

19

Distance Education for Adults

Walter Archer

In a recent publication from Statistics Canada entitled *Distance Learning: An Idea Whose Time Has Come,* Bernier (1995) presents considerable evidence to support her contention that distance education is emerging from the marginal position it has occupied in our education systems for the past century. Using data culled from the 1994 Adult Education and Training Survey (AETS; Statistics Canada 1995), the author concludes that distance education comprises a significant and growing proportion of all adult education in Canada. She states that 420,000 adults participated in some form of distance education in 1993 (the year on which the 1994 AETS is based), an increase of 35,000 over 1991 (Bernier 1995, 35). This is an increase of 8.3 percent over two years, while adult education in general increased only about 1 percent over the same period (Statistics Canada 1995, 1). Distance education accounted for about 7 percent of Canadian adult learners in 1993, and 10 percent of those in rural areas (Bernier 1995, 40).

Distance education is also a large and steadily increasing part of the adult education picture in the United States. *The Chronicle of Higher Education* (1997) reports that, in a survey of 1,200 higher education institutions done by the National Centre for Educational Statistics, of 14.3 million students enrolled in colleges in 1995-96, 750,000 were enrolled in distance education courses. Given this number, it is clear that distance education is now an important part of the practice of adult education, and it is well worth the attention of the discipline of adult education. Such attention has not been forthcoming. Bruce Spencer (1998) speculates that this may be because distance education has a mainly individualized focus, while adult education scholars have been concerned with adult education as a dialogical and social activity. If this is the case, then the situation should be rectified in the near future, as a large part of current scholarship in distance education has to do with variants of distance education that do permit group learning. These variants will be referred to in this chapter as *Generation 2* and *Generation 3* distance education.

An alternative explanation is that the neglect of distance education by the discipline of adult education is a symptom of a general skewing of the discipline as compared to the field of practice. Distance education occurs overwhelmingly within the 70 percent of all adult education that is work-related (Statistics Canada 1994). A quick inspection of the leading journals in adult education would indicate that the main interests of scholars in adult education appear to lie very largely within the 30 percent of adult education activity that is not work related.

Despite the relative neglect of distance education within the mainstream adult education literature, a substantial body of literature specific to distance education has emerged, including a number of national and international journals. Among these, the *Journal of Distance Education/Revue de l'éducation à distance*, published by the Canadian Association for Distance Education/Association canadienne de l'éducation à distance since 1986, is a particularly good source for developments in distance education in Canada and elsewhere. There are many descriptions of the distance education programs and courses in which adults enrol and of the specialized distance education institutions that provide a large proportion of them in literature such as Haughey and Anderson (1998), Mugridge and Kaufman (1986) and Sweet (1989).

Most of the literature mentioned above discusses relatively current developments in distance education. However, what is probably the most famous distance education program ever mounted in Canada took place in the 1940s, 1950s and early 1960s. This was the National Farm Radio Forum, a complex co-operative effort by the Canadian Association for Adult Education, the Canadian Broadcasting Corporation and the Canadian Federation of Agriculture. It involved weekly radio broadcasts, local listening and discussion groups and feedback from these groups to the organizers of the program. This program is described by Selman, Cooke, Selman, and Dampier (1998) as one of the most internationally recognized of all Canadian adult education programs, and one which was widely imitated in Third World countries looking for affordable and practical ways to deliver adult education to their largely rural populations. This is an example of how distance education has been able to play an important role in distributing knowledge throughout the entire world, helping to bring about a truly global society.

This chapter will not attempt to describe all the different distance education programs or types of programs that have contributed to this goal of adult education. Instead, it will provide a conceptual framework for understanding the nature of distance education. The scope of this chapter does not permit discussion of the many issues with which the field of distance education is currently contending; however, many of these issues are common to all forms of adult education and are addressed elsewhere in this volume.

Definitions and Divisions within the Field of Distance Education

A common factor in both distance education and adult education is that there are approximately as many definitions of each field as there are scholars active within it. Distance education is such a diverse field that no definition is ever quite satisfactory. The definition that will be used throughout this chapter was formulated by Garrison and Shale (1987, 11). They provide the following three defining criteria:

1. Distance education implies that the majority of educational communication between (among) teacher and student(s) occurs non-contiguously.

2. Distance education must involve two-way communication between (among) teacher and student(s) for the purpose of facilitating and supporting the educational process.

3. Distance education uses technology to mediate the necessary two-way communication.

At least one scholar (P. Juler, cited in Nunan 1993, 190) has argued that the third criterion is superfluous, being implied by the first two. I would disagree. The third criterion has the effect of eliminating the "circuit rider" or "silver bird" method of reaching out to a group or groups of learners by sending an instructor to conduct periodic face-to-face sessions at a site remote from the campus. The third criterion in Garrison and Shale's definition makes this mode of operation not a type of distance education but rather a practical alternative to it. (Some scholars do include the "circuit rider" as distance education; for example, Spencer 1998.)

The definition cited above is succinct, but broad enough to include just about everything that we commonly refer to as distance education. However, it is not the most commonly cited definition of distance education. That position is probably held by the definition presented in *The Foundations of Distance Education* (1986, 49-50) and in earlier publications by Desmond Keegan. From the definitions previously published by various scholars and agencies, Keegan assembled a set of six and then (by 1986) seven defining characteristics of distance education, as a sort of consensus of the field.

However, Keegan's (1986) definition has been criticized by some scholars, including Garrison and Shale (1987) and Garrison (1989), as being too narrow and too closely aligned with the mode of operation of what are usually referred to as *single mode* distance education. Such institutions provide only distance education and no face-to-face programs. *Dual mode* institutions, on the other hand, provide primarily face-to-face programs and some distance courses or programs.

Keegan's (1986) definition reads as follows:

> Distance education is a form of education characterised by
>
> - the quasi-permanent separation of teacher and learner throughout the length of the learning process; this distinguishes it from conventional face-to-face education.
> - the influence of an educational organisation both in the planning and preparation of learning materials and in the provision of student support services; this distinguishes it from private study and teach-yourself programmes.
> - the use of technical media; print, audio, video or computer, to unite teacher and learner and carry the content of the course.
> - the provision of two-way communication so that the student may benefit from or even initiate dialogue; this distinguishes it from other uses of technology in education.
> - the quasi-permanent absence of the learning group throughout the length of the learning process so that people are usually taught as individuals and not in groups, with the possibility of occasional meetings for both didactic and socialisation purposes.
>
> Distance education is to be regarded as being constituted of these five interdependent elements, which remain constant essential components even if their content is different in separate institutional situations. In addition there are two socio-cultural determinants which are both necessary pre-conditions and necessary consequences of distance education. These are:

- the presence of more industrialised features than in conventional oral education.
- the privatisation of institutional learning (pp.49-50).

Two of the descriptions in Keegan's (1986) definition exclude the types of distance education that are often carried on by dual mode providers. For example, one of his "essential" criteria for distance education is "the quasi-permanent absence of the learning group throughout the length of the learning process so that people are usually taught as individuals and not in groups, with the possibility of occasional meetings for both didactic and socialisation purposes" (p.49). This clearly excludes all classes conducted by audio- or video-teleconferencing, group-based methods that are used by many dual mode institutions.

Another one of Keegan's (1986) criteria is "the presence of more industrialised features than in conventional oral education" (p.47). Here he is referring to the pioneering work of the German scholar Otto Peters, who has described the characteristics of distance education that are similar to the industrial production of commodities, as compared to the craft-like approach taken in most face-to-face instruction. These characteristics include (a) division of labour in the course production process (large teams comprised of content experts, editors, graphic designers and so on); (b) use of technical equipment to convey this material to large numbers of students, thereby gaining economies of scale; (c) pre-testing of these materials; and (d) use of scientific methods to monitor and improve the quality of the course materials (Keegan 1994, 111-112; first published, in German, by Peters in 1967).

This "industrialized" nature is characteristic of much of distance education, particularly that carried on by single mode institutions. However, it is definitely not characteristic of the methods used by many dual mode institutions that are almost as craft-like as face-to-face instruction. Furthermore, industrialization is not confined to distance education. The large introductory lecture courses offered face-to-face in many educational institutions, particularly universities, are also very industrialized. Here the large team of specialists is employed by the publisher of the textbook which, in such lecture classes performs much the same function as the course package does in an "industrialized" correspondence course. Since the professor lecturing to a group of four hundred students is not really in two-way communication with the students, the face-to-face lectures in such courses fulfil much the same ancillary function as the televised lectures that are often used as supplementary materials in correspondence courses. The teaching assistants–who actually do engage in two-way communication with students in some lecture courses–are not the actual content experts for the lecture course; their role is similar to the role of tutors who interact directly with students in correspondence courses.

In short, the Keegan definition is unsatisfactory because it contains two criteria that apply to some distance education but not all of it. The remaining criteria from Keegan's definition are expressed more succinctly in the three criteria listed by Garrison and Shale (1987).

The Three Generations of Distance Education

The reader, even one previously unfamiliar with distance education, will have realized by this point that distance education is not one method of education but rather a complex mixture of many different methods, bound together by only a few very general characteristics. Fortunately, there is a conceptual framework that has been found to be very useful for imposing some clarity on this apparent confusion. This framework is in fact a metaphor that was arrived at independently by two different scholars–D.R. Garrison (1985, 1989) and S. Nipper (1989)–and has been referred to frequently in recent distance education literature. That metaphor consists of the comparison of changes in distance education to three "generations," marked by significant changes in the way distance education has been carried out.

The first publication to use the metaphor of three generations of distance education was Garrison (1985), modified slightly in 1989. This version of the metaphor is the more useful, although it is now in need of modification in the light of developments in the field since 1985. A different version of the three generations metaphor was presented in Nipper (1989). It is this version that has more frequently been cited, with or without modifications, by other scholars. This may be due to the fact that it was published in a very widely distributed book. However, it is considerably less satisfactory than Garrison's, as it does not rest on any clear conceptual base and excludes some forms of distance education.

Nipper refers to the "first generation" of distance education as correspondence education, which he notes has been practiced for many centuries in Western civilization, but which was expanded in scale and efficiency with the introduction of railways (for postal delivery) and new printing techniques. He describes "second generation" distance education as follows:

> "Second generation" distance education is also called multi-media distance teaching, and has been developed since the late 1960s, integrating the use of print with broadcast media, cassettes, and – to some degree–computers. Feedback processes are very similar to those of "first generation" systems, but include telephone counseling and some face-to-face tutorials.
>
> The main objectives of the first and second generation systems have been the production and distribution of teaching/learning material to the learners. Communication with the learners has been marginal, and communication amongst the learners has been more or less non-existent (p.63).

As stated so well by Nipper in the last paragraph cited above, what he calls second generation distance education differs from his first generation only in being somewhat more elaborate. The student is supplied with information in more different forms, but the basic individualized tenor of the educational experience–no communication with other students, usually only slow and infrequent communication with a tutor–is the same. In other words, what he calls second generation distance education has introduced only new "sustaining" technologies that make the same processes perform somewhat better, rather than a new "disruptive" technology that changes the basic nature of the process.[1]

This is not to denigrate the magnitude of the changes that Nipper describes as a new generation of distance education. Led by the British Open

University, founded in 1969, distance education in the 1970s became much more visible to the public. Its high-quality television broadcasts, in particular, were viewed by many members of the public who were not enrolled in the courses that the broadcasts were supporting. This was very effective in advancing distance education from its former status as an obscure and rather disparaged specialization on the fringes of education towards what Jevons (1987) refers to as "parity of esteem" with conventional face-to-face instruction. It also led to a world-wide flurry of foundings of single mode distance education institutions modelled on the British Open University, in both developed and developing countries. These included, within Canada, Athabasca University, Télé-université du Québec, the Open Learning Institute (later merged into the current Open Learning Agency) in British Columbia, and North Island College on Vancouver Island.[2]

These institutions, generally well funded by governments eager to avoid the truly massive cost of a major expansion in conventional adult and higher education, soon became very good at producing high-quality instructional materials in various media. These materials were created according to the relatively new discipline of instructional design and produced by the industrialized processes described by Otto Peters. This material was clearly more attractive and perhaps somewhat more effective than the materials used by the shoestring operations that had previously characterized distance education.

But despite Nipper's reference to this upgrading in quality of materials and distribution methods as a new generation of distance education, there is no new conception of distance education represented here, and hence no reason to characterize this as a new generation. Students were still basically isolated from each other, with only slow and occasional contact with a tutor. It was when this isolation began to be broken down that the nature of distance education underwent a true qualitative change.

The framework provided by Garrison marks this major qualitative change, from individual study to the formation of distance learning groups, as the change from Generation 1 to Generation 2. It is to this conceptually clearer and generally preferable framework that we will now turn.

According to Garrison (1985; 1989), each generation of distance education has been based on the use of a different primary technology to carry the all-important two-way communication between teacher and student. That this student-teacher communication is crucial has been noted by many scholars. A perceptive recent book about education in general, including distance education, has an entire chapter entitled "Education Is Communication" (Tiffin and Rajasingham 1995). It is not surprising, therefore, that Garrison should consider that changes in the carrier of this two-way communication between teacher and distant learner should mark the boundaries between generations of distance education.

The two-way communication technologies that have defined generations of distance education, according to Garrison (1985, 1989), have been correspondence via the postal system for Generation 1, teleconferencing in its various forms for Generation 2 and communication via microprocessor (computer) for Generation 3. He presents the following conceptual scheme (from Garrison 1989, 50):

Distance Education Technologies: (Two-Way Communication)

1. Correspondence (First Generation)

Message: Print

Delivery Mode: Mail

2. Teleconferencing (Second Generation)

Message: Audio/Video

Delivery Mode: Telecommunications

3. Microprocessor Based (Third Generation)

Message: Audio/Video/Alphanumeric

Delivery Mode: Microprocessor

Other media, used for one-way communication only, frequently play a secondary role in enhancing distance education built around one of the primary, two-way media. Garrison refers to these as "ancillary media" (1985, 239-240):

Ancillary Media: (One-Way Communication)

1. Print Material

2. Audio/Video Cassettes

3. Audiographics (may support two-way communication)
   - facsimile
   - slow-scan television
   - compressed video
   - telewriting
   - videotex

4. Laser Videodisc

5. Broadcast
   - radio
   - television

Garrison's conceptual scheme is very insightful; it highlights those changes in distance education that have made a significant difference in the experience of the learner. However, with a decade and a half of hindsight, one can see a need for at least two minor improvements. First, there are now forms of teleconferencing that are microprocessor based and forms of correspondence that are carried on primarily through non-print messages; consequently, Garrison's names for the first and third generations of distance education now seem inappropriate. Second, the large cluster of "ancillary media" placed outside the general conceptual framework seems rather awkward; the framework could be broadened so that they fit within it. The next section outlines the changes to Garrison's framework designed to address these two issues.

The Three Generations Metaphor Revisited: Focus on Communication

Education is communication, and almost all of the communication that takes place in education can be categorized as messages of four types: (a) spoken language, (b) written language, (c) still images, and (d) moving images. The first three types of communication have long been available in support of face-to-face education; however, their use in distance education depended on the invention of ways to transport each type of message. This occurred at different times for the different types of messages. Written language and still images (first hand drawn, then photographic) became transportable long before spoken language could be moved beyond shouting range. The first of the trompe-l'oeil techniques for creating the illusion of moving images, that of film, was inherently unsuited to two-way communication; techniques for convenient and inexpensive two-way transmission of moving images used for most educational purposes have been available only during the past two or three decades. This meant that early distance education was dependent on two-way transmission of written language supplemented by still images, since those were the only types of messages that could be transported.

Although Generation 1 distance education was originally confined to messages in written language or still images, one-way voice communication was eventually added (records, broadcast radio), followed by one-way communication in moving images (16mm films, then broadcast television). However, the introduction of audiotapes and videotapes in some distance education programs marked the beginning of two-way communication in spoken language and moving images–with open reel tapes and later cassettes–transported back and forth via the postal system. For example, Leslie (1986) provides an interesting description of a Generation 1 program operated by the University of Waterloo that makes extensive use of audiocassettes sent through the postal system.

The next generation-marking technological advance, after the advent of efficient postal service, was the development of speed-of-light transmission of messages. In theory at least, this meant that people distant from each other could now communicate in "real time," i.e., in the same rhythm that is possible in face-to-face communication. This is known as "synchronous" (same time) communication, as opposed to "asynchronous" (different time, or delayed) communication. This new medium, the telegraph, could transmit only written language, and the machinery was too expensive and cumbersome to be used for education on a large scale. However, it was soon modified to carry voice messages as well. It spawned a variant called the telephone. The telephone became the first practical, affordable means of transmitting the two-way exchange of messages necessary for carrying on distance education in real time. This was done on either an individual basis (telephone tutoring) or in groups (audio-teleconferencing). This mode of distance education was originally confined to spoken language. More recently, still images (audiographics), moving images (videoconferencing) and written language (audiographics; computer "chat" mode) have been added to the mix of messages that can be transmitted in synchronous distance education. It is the new attribute of *synchronicity* of communication—enabling the formation of learning groups—that justifies calling this Generation 2, a new kind of distance education qualitatively different from asynchronous techniques based on the postal system.

One beneficial effect of the introduction of synchronous communication into distance education was a very significant increase in the rate at which participants completed their courses. In "pure" correspondence courses the completion rate has often been very low—in some cases below 10 percent. The addition of telephone tutoring to correspondence courses (i.e., an individualized form of Generation 2 distance education) raised completion rates substantially. The addition of audio-teleconferences (i.e., a group-based form of Generation 2 distance education) further raised completion rates to the 90-95 percent range, essentially the same as for face-to-face courses (Garrison 1987).

Yet the synchronicity introduced by the new Generation 2 distance education, which re-created the atmosphere of immediacy and group interaction, had its costs. The major drawback was that participants were no longer free to take part at their own convenience. This had been one of the attractions of the original mode of distance education based on slow motion asynchronous communication through the postal system. The freedom from having to participate at a fixed time was restored by the development of computer-mediated communication. In this new medium, in contrast to teleconferencing, messages are not ephemeral but rather are stored on a central computer. The light speed of computer conferencing (and facsimile, a less commonly used method of Generation 3 distance education), plus the organizing capacity of the programs developed specifically for computer conferencing, improves on Generation 1 distance education by offering the practical possibility of group interaction. The fact that the messages are stored centrally improves on Generation 2 distance education by allowing asynchronicity, i.e., allowing participants to access the stored messages at their own convenience, rather than participating in the group experience at regularly scheduled times. This combination of the chief advantages of Generation 1 and Generation 2 distance education justifies calling this light-speed, asynchronous distance education a new generation, Generation 3.

This third generation was originally confined to transmission of written language when early experiments in communication via networked computers were first carried on in the 1960s. However, transmission of still images quickly followed. Currently, transmission of spoken language (audio files) and moving images (video files) is also possible and rapidly becoming commonplace. These developments, concurrent with explosive expansion of computer ownership and Internet connections, have made Generation 3 the growing edge of distance education.

In summary, the three generations of distance education may logically be renamed as follows:

1. Slow Asynchronous (Generation 1)

Learning Mode: Individualized Instruction

Delivery Mechanism: Postal System

Message Types (two-way communication):

- originally written language and still images
- spoken language added by mailing of audiocassettes
- moving images added by mailing of videocassettes

2. Synchronous (Generation 2)

Learning Mode: Individualized or Group

Delivery Mechanism: Telecommunications Systems (wired and wireless)

Message Types (two-way communication):

- originally spoken language only
- still images added by audiographics
- written language added by audiographics and computer chat
- moving images added by videoconferencing (various modes, some involving use of computer desktop systems and some not)

3. Fast Asynchronous (Generation 3)

Learning Mode: Individualized (e-mail) or Group (computer conferencing)

Delivery Mechanism: Telecommunications Systems Combined with Networked Computers (usually) or Fax Machines

Message Types (two-way communication):

- originally written language (first networked computers)
- still images added by graphics files and facsimile
- spoken language added as audio files
- moving images added as video files

This modification of Garrison's (1989) outline of the three generations is intended to make clear that all three generations are now capable of two-way transmission of all four kinds of messages that are most commonly communicated during educational processes. The altered names of the generations are intended to indicate whether communication is immediate (synchronous) or time shifted (asynchronous). Both of these communication modes have their function in the learning process, but they are qualitatively different experiences. Finally, a quantitative difference in the speed at which messages are transmitted translates into a qualitative difference in the nature of the learning experiences that are possible; participants in a computer conference can function as a group and learn from each other, while enrolees in a correspondence course cannot.

Some Further Remarks on the Three Generations of Distance Education

When Garrison (1985) originated the metaphor of the three generations of distance education, he stated very clearly that he did not mean to imply that the appearance of a new generation of distance education meant the disappearance or even the decline of the generation(s) that existed previously.

The three generations metaphor was intended to create greater conceptual clarity in discussing the welter of different technologies used in distance education. It did so by focusing on the way in which the vital two-way communication function is carried on between learner and instructor and, in some forms of distance education, among groups of learners. In actual practice, providers of distance education frequently combine technologies from different generations within a single course. For example, a course in which I recently served as instructor made use of a print package mailed out to the learners (Generation 1 distance education), several audioconferences (Generation 2), web pages and a computer conference (Generation 3), and one face-to-face meeting. The three generations of distance education are not unlike a multi-generation household of people in which some members of the family are older than others, but they all live under the same roof and frequently co-ordinate their activities.

In distance education, as in a family, there is not always complete concord and understanding among the family members. There is evidence in distance education literature of two different subfields pursuing different interests and holding somewhat different conceptions of the field. The split appears to be between scholars working in single mode institutions specializing in distance education, and scholars employed in dual mode institutions, in which distance education has been added to a basically conventional institution. To some extent, single mode institutions, such as the world famous British Open University, Canada's Athabasca University, Open Learning Agency (British Columbia), and Télé-université (part of the Université du Québec system), have tended to offer mostly Generation 1 distance education programs, while dual mode institutions have been quicker to shift to Generation 2 delivery methods. The reasons for this are mostly related to cost structure.[3] Single mode institutions typically produce elaborate course packages of very high quality. They usually include very well designed print materials, plus a variety of other one-way communication instruments such as broadcast television lectures. These are the products of teams of specialists—the "industrialized" model of distance education described by Otto Peters. Such high-quality course packages are very expensive to produce; development costs can exceed $200,000. However, once developed, such packages can be delivered by Generation 1 technology—correspondence via the postal system—at relatively low cost per student. Such courses, then, have high fixed (one-time, start-up) costs but low variable (per student) costs. Obviously, they make economic sense when course enrolments are high.

Dual mode institutions often find it more economical and more convenient to offer their generally much smaller scale distance programs via Generation 2 technologies. Such courses tend to have low fixed (start-up) costs, particularly when the institution already offers the course on campus using face-to-face instruction and can have the same instructor offer the course in distance mode. The number of people involved in each pocket of distance education at a dual mode institution can be very small as compared to the large teams at the single mode institutions. In some cases, the "team" producing a distance delivered course or program sometimes consists of one person; this is sometimes referred to as the "Lone Ranger" model of distance education. Such small groups of non-specialists often find that teaching via Generation 2 technologies–particularly videoconferencing–is easier to adopt, since it is much more like classroom teaching as opposed to the very different experience of creating a correspondence course. The chief disadvantage of programs offered via Generation 2 technologies is that they do not have the same economies of scale as do the "industrial" processes of Generation 1 distance education. Variable (per student) costs can be very high, particularly when two-way video communication is used (Bates 1995).

The effect of this basic split in the field of practice has been a corresponding split in the distance education literature. The scholars in the field whose work is chiefly involved with single mode institutions have tended to discuss Generation 1 distance education as if it were the entire field. It is the rapid expansion of Generation 3 distance education that seems to be bringing the field of distance education back together. Both single mode and dual mode distance teaching institutions are intensely interested in it, both as an opportunity and as a threat. The opportunity is obvious: delivery via the Internet is not only very attractive to learners, but it also offers the freedom of Generation 1 coupled with the immediacy and group interaction of Generation 2, and it is a form of electronic distance delivery whose costs do not rise with increasing distance, as do most forms of teleconferencing. Generation 3 distance education creates a truly world-wide market for distance education courses (Turoff 1997; Graves 1997).

While this is an opportunity for all, it is also a threat to all. The threat to single mode institutions is obvious, since the competition faced by their programs is no longer regional; it comes from public and private providers the world over. The threat to dual mode institutions is less obvious. Certainly their relatively small (and, from the institutional viewpoint, usually not very important) distance programs are also vulnerable to increased competition and may succumb. However, Generation 3 distance education is proving attractive to many employed adult learners, mostly because it grants freedom from time constraints (Turoff 1997). It is proving so attractive, in fact, that dual mode institutions may soon begin to see some erosion of their on-campus programs.

The predictions of the total demise of conventional higher education in the face of the onrush of Generation 3 distance education seem somewhat exaggerated; however, they are at least plausible. As a result, most conventional institutions are beginning to incorporate into their face-to-face classes some features of Generation 3 distance education–particularly web pages and various types of computer conferencing. This hybrid of conventional classroom instruction and Generation 3 distance education is coming to be known as "distributed education" (Bates 1997; Hall 1996; Tait 1998). It is far too early to make an accurate prediction about the future of this new hybrid. It is possible, however, that it may eventually displace both conventional face-to-face instruction and distance education as we know it, and the lonely distance learner may finally become re-integrated into the mainstream of adult and higher education.

Notes

1. See Archer, Garrison, and Anderson (1999) for an extended discussion of disruptive technologies in higher education.
2. See chapters in Mugridge and Kaufman (1986) on each of these institutions by Ross Paul; Patrick Guillement, Roger Bédard, and Francine Landry; Ian Mugridge; and John Tayless, respectively.
3. Bates (1995) contains an excellent and comprehensive discussion of the factors involved in the selection of technologies for distance education, including cost. One important point that has been noted by Bates and many other scholars is that media, assuming they are intelligently employed, do not differ significantly in their effectiveness in supporting learning. That is, experiments comparing the effectiveness of different media and combinations of media have for the most part reported a finding of "no significant difference." It should be noted, also, that distant students who complete their courses consistently score as well on performance evaluations as do students completing the same courses in conventional classrooms. In sum, the educational effectiveness of distance education in general, and various delivery modes in particular, is a non-issue.

References

Archer, W., D.R. Garrison, and T. Anderson. 1999. Adopting disruptive technologies in traditional universities: Continuing education as an incubator for innovation. *Canadian Journal of University Continuing Education* 25 (1): 13-44.

Bates, A.W. 1995. *Technology, open learning and distance education.* London: Routledge.

——. 1997. Restructuring the university for technological change. Paper presented at a conference titled *What Kind of University?* sponsored by The Carnegie Foundation for the Advancement of Learning, London (June 18-20). Available online at: http://bates.cstudies.ubc.ca/.

Bernier, R. 1995. Distance learning: An idea whose time has come. *Education Quarterly Review (Statistics Canada)* 2 (3): 35-49.

Christensen, C.M. 1997. *The innovator's dilemma: When new technologies cause great firms to fail.* Boston: Harvard Business School Press.

The Chronicle of Higher Education. 1997 (October). Website: http://chronicle.com/chedata/news.dir/dailarch.dir/9710.dir/97100703.htm.

Garrison, D.R. 1985. Three generations of technological innovation in distance education. *Distance Education* 6: 235-241.

——. 1987. Researching dropout in distance education. *Distance Education* 8: 95-101.

——. 1989. *Understanding distance education: A framework for the future.* London: Routledge.

Garrison, D.R., and D.G. Shale. 1987. Mapping the boundaries of distance education: Problems in defining the field. *The American Journal of Distance Education* 1 (1): 7-13.

Graves, W.H. 1997. "Free trade" in higher education: The meta university. *Journal of Asynchronous Learning Networks* 1 (1). Website: http://www.aln.org/alnweb/journal/jaln_Vol1issue1.htm.

Hall, J. 1996. The revolution in electronic technology and the modern university: The convergence of means. In *Opening education: Policies and practices from open and distance education,* edited by T. Evans and D. Nation (pp.7-20). London: Routledge.

Haughey, M., and T. Anderson. 1998. *Networked learning: The pedagogy of the Internet.* Montreal: Chenelière/McGraw-Hill.

Jevons, F. 1987. Distance education and campus-based education: Parity of esteem. In *Distance education and the mainstream: Convergence in education,* edited by P. Smith and M. Kelly (pp.12-23). London: Croom Helm.

Keegan, D. 1986. *The foundations of distance education.* 2d ed. London: Croom Helm.

Keegan, D., ed. 1994. *Otto Peters on distance education: The industrialization of teaching and learning.* London: Routledge.

Leslie, J.D. 1986. Use of audiocassettes. In *Distance education in Canada,* edited by I. Mugridge and D. Kaufman (pp.234-246). London: Croom Helm.

Mugridge, I., and D. Kaufman. 1986. *Distance education in Canada.* London: Croom Helm.

Nipper, S. 1989. Third generation distance learning and computer conferencing. In *Mindweave: Communication, computers and distance education,* edited by R. Mason and A. Kaye (pp.63-73). Oxford: Pergamon.

Nunan, T. 1993. Distance education: What is it and can it have an educational future? In *Theoretical principles of distance education,* edited by D. Keegan (pp.189-210). London: Routledge.

Selman, G., M. Cooke, M. Selman, and P. Dampier. 1998. *The foundations of adult education in Canada.* 2d ed. Toronto: Thompson Educational Publishing.

Spencer, B. 1998. Distance education and the virtual classroom. In *Learning for life: Canadian readings in adult education,* edited by S.M. Scott, B. Spencer, and A.M. Thomas (pp.343-352). Toronto: Thompson Educational Publishing.

Statistics Canada. 1995. *Adult education and training in Canada: Report of the 1994 adult education and training survey.* Ottawa: Author.

Sweet, R., ed. 1989. *Post-secondary distance education in Canada: Policies, practices, and priorities.* Athabasca, Alta.: Athabasca University.

Tait, A. 1998. The convergence of distance and conventional education: Some implications for policy. Paper presented at the 1998 conference of the Canadian Association for Distance Education in Banff, Alberta (May).

Tiffin, J., and L. Rajasingham. 1995. *In search of the virtual class: Education in an information society.* London: Routledge.

Turoff, M. 1997. Alternative futures for distance learning: The force and the darkside. *Online Journal of Distance Learning Administration* 1 (1). Website: http://www.westga.edu/~distance/turoff11.html.

20

Lifelong Learning, Voluntary Action and Civil Society

Alan M. Thomas

From the perspective of only fifty years, the development of the education of adults in Canada and the rest of the world is little short of as-
tounding. It is not that some adults before that time, especially in the
case of members of various elites, were not engaged in learning or forms of
adult education, but that the latter has been extended to so many more "ordinary" adults. In 1997, Statistics Canada reported that 6 million Canadians, or 28 percent of adults, participated in adult education or training activities (Statistics Canada 1997, 13). Ten years earlier, UNESCO reported that
approximately 20 percent of the population of the world were classified as
students, of which an increasing proportion were adults (UNESCO 1998,
11).

The dominant concerns of the 1950s were to demonstrate, first, that
adults could learn and that what they learned was of social and economic
significance to any society, and second, that adults had a right of access to
all the publicly provided opportunities for formal education. Today, the education of adults has spread through every facet of Canadian society; industry, commerce, health, citizenship, and the arts and humanities. The
inclusion of adults in education is now understood not as a matter of privilege but as a matter of survival, collective and individual. This is not to say
that equity in opportunity for adults in education has been achieved any
more than it has for children and youth, but that the participation by those
adults who gain access is both normal and necessary.

One might conclude that, from the perspective of the 1950s, the principal battle has been won, and to a degree, it has, though much of the history
of that struggle remains unexplored. However, what was not anticipated,
nor much imagined, were the cultural implications of including so many of
the adult population in transforming themselves through learning and education. The purpose of this chapter is to explore three of these cultural implications as they manifest themselves in the form of *lifelong learning,*
voluntary action and the *civil society.* Indeed, it will be argued that these three
new postmodern concepts are the result of the spread of the education of
adults and can only truly be understood in that context.

Lifelong Learning

Lifelong learning presents an immediate difficulty to the "establishment"
of adult education. In Western history the education of adults evolved sepa-
rately, though not entirely separate, from the millennial growth of formal
education devoted, as it has been, primarily to children and youth. While

much initiative for the inclusion of adults into formal provisions came from individuals and groups within those growing formal agencies, there was an older, more powerful tradition of separate concern for adults imbedded principally in non-educational agencies in society, such as religious bodies, trade unions, and commercial and cultural agencies. This tradition has been largely indifferent, if not antagonistic, to the child-centred movement, which was correctly perceived to attract most of the public attention and financial resources. Adult educators by and large invested their energies in agencies and organizations distinct from formal schools, and developed not only distinct organizations and a specific vocabulary, but a unique theory of adult learning and instruction called *andragogy* (see chapter 1 in this volume), which is still in use. The Lifelong Learning Movement challenges that functional and intellectual separation. In fact, this separation has been steadily undermined in practice by the inclusion of more and more adults in formal education, the spread of the principles of adult education throughout the formal system and the reciprocal inclusion of practices associated with the formal education of the young in the education of adults, such as compulsory attendance.

At present lifelong learning is both a movement and a reality. The movement, principally European in origin, gathered steam in the early part of the last decade, supported by a different mixture of public and private interests than had been characteristic of adult education. To a degree it has captured the "movement" quality that was characteristic of adult education in the early part of the twentieth century, but was declining as the education of adults spread throughout diverse interests and practices of most modern societies. The roots of the new movement lie in two phenomena: the shift from the focus on *education*, so dominant in mid-century, to a focus on *learning* and the increasing role of technological change to which all current private interests are harnessed and which ensures a constantly changing environment. A consequence of the latter is the desire of entrepreneurs of all kinds to harness the learning capacity of their employees to their particular objectives; hence the public attempt to organize support for lifelong learning throughout all societies and to explore the precise nature of those supports.

The reality is, of course, related to those activities in the sense that learning, lifelong learning, is in large part a function of external changes in the environment of the learning organism, mainly we human beings. One need only point to the impact of the computer on all phases of public and private life as an example. Support for the achievement of computer "literacy" is spreading inexorably through Canada and the world. To a large degree, increasing numbers of adults are already engaged in learning throughout their whole lives. However, the uneven impact and accessibility of the computer throughout the world is a direct reflection of the uneven spread of that engagement not only throughout the world but throughout Canada. What we need to concentrate on now is the cultural meaning of such engagement in terms of family life, politics, health and the arts. We have already witnessed some of those "meanings" in economics and organizational behaviour.

Learning has never, in the history of the world, encompassed so many individuals and groups. The Lifelong Learning Movement is the beginning of an attempt to understand what that means.

We have only begun to broaden our understanding of the cultural function of learning itself. Learning is an activity in itself; learning is doing. It is above all an individual activity in terms of its basic centre, the physical self, though it invariably takes place in a social context; it takes time and effort; it is irreversible in effect and is fundamentally uncoercible. In general we are at our best when we are learning, a fact that underlies almost all of the representations of ourselves in art, science and religion (Thomas 1991). The latter fact underlies the intent of large organizations to not only harness but to capture human learning on an unprecedented scale.

The attempt to harness, indeed to capture, learning has always been the main preoccupation of formal education. Its primary tasks are to instil a sense of belonging and commitment in a particular group, society or nation and to identify and perfect talent in the service of that society. That is, we wish to develop willing and enthusiastic citizens and workers whose individual satisfactions are derived from both roles. That we do not always succeed is evidenced by the extent of poverty, misery and alienation in the world, including Canada, but the intent persists. The gradual extension of formal education to more and more people over longer and longer periods in their lives has been a major preoccupation of what can be reasonably named the "Educational" Millennium. In that manner we try to transform private learning—the learning traditionally concentrated in families, at work and in the fields and streets—to public learning, credentialled, marketable and commodified.

But formal education throughout that millennium has not always succeeded in capturing learning despite relentless attempts. There has been throughout the period a "discourse" between learning and education that, in terms of the history of the world, has been a constant and fundamental exchange over what the most important knowledge is, and who should, or does, have access to it (Thomas 1998). For example, the rise of the Academies in Europe in the sixteenth century signalled the rise of learning outside of the educational establishment and intense competition between the two. A new dominance of education over learning culminated in the middle of the twentieth century, but we are now living in a period in which its predominance in the control of knowledge is under intense challenge from independent sources of learning lodged in so-called "think-tanks," private laboratories and the like, which are contemporary versions of the Academies. What the emergence of these new sources suggests is that systematic, formal education, with its procedures for establishing and transmitting relevant knowledge is not capable, despite its wealth and power, of maintaining absolute control of significant learning.

A response to this current challenge by learning is manifest in the emergence of a new practice called prior learning assessment (PLA) (and recognition; PLAR). This is a procedure for establishing academic credit for learning outcomes acquired outside of formal instruction. It is a recognition of both the existence of legitimate knowledge available outside of education and of the continuing power of right to certify that knowledge possessed by accredited teaching agencies and some professional bodies. PLA(R) is now available Canada-wide from secondary schools, colleges and universities, though, characteristically in Canada, there are differences among provinces. Significant use of PLA(R) under various names has been developed in France, the United Kingdom, Australia, South Africa, and, the source of the PLA(R) movement, the United States. The characteristic mechanisms for assessment are the challenge examination, the demonstration and the portfolio. The latter has taken on a life of its own as a means of stimulating an awareness of learning accomplishments among individuals, independent of their formal educational recognition.

The use of PLA(R) can be seen as an important individual and social liberation of legitimate knowledge acquired in a great variety of ways, which it certainly can be. For example, hundreds of thousands of Canadians have been subject to "training" with no resulting academic credit. PLA(R) allows them to regain a position in the mainstream of formal education with all of its rewards. On the other hand, the act of submitting such knowledge to the evaluative authority of an educational agency resembles an act of selective seduction in which some knowledge is acknowledged and some is not. It may, in fact, be an attempt by formal education to recapture its pre-eminence in the control of learning, as it succeeded in doing so in the beginning of the nineteenth century. Whatever the future outcome of this struggle, the process represented by the use of PLA(R) seems as inherently useful as existing methods of identifying new and valuable knowledge, particularly on a global basis. It is essential that it becomes a permanent part of the society. (See chapter by Wong in this volume.)

Lifelong learning is both a growing reality throughout human society and a movement devoted to understanding its implications. One of the most prominent implications is to be found in the renewed rise of the voluntary organization throughout the world.

Voluntary Action

All human groups from families to states must cope with the learning capacity among its members. With learning, we encounter a unique phenomena in the sense that the capacity is inherent in each individual member and cannot be eliminated or even tightly controlled. It is a, if not *the*, fundamental essence of human existence. At best the state can direct or influence (that is, manage) the direction of learning and its outcomes. To pervert or try to eliminate outcomes of learning pursued by even a relatively small number of members seems to be impossible, despite recurring attempts to do so. The recent collapse of communist states in Eastern Europe is a cogent manifestation, and an example of defiance is the rise of the Solidarity Union in Poland. Each of those states wished to develop an efficient, competent, modern workforce, and in doing so, unleashed learning throughout all of the society. What evolved, quickly and remarkably peacefully, was, in each case, support for a democratic state that seems so far to be the best vehicle for the successful, relatively stable, management of learning.

The democratic state provides an environment for the pursuit of learning by its members. In fact the chief characteristic of a democratic state is its ability to manage the learning of its citizens. A central factor of that environment is the constitutional guarantee of the *freedom of association*. Since adults learn more from other adults than from any other source, that freedom is essential for successful communal management of fundamental learning in a society. It is certainly equal in importance to the more frequently cited *freedom of speech*. Among other things it secures the freedom of citizens to associate with one another for the pursuit of desirable aims of both a public and private character. These organizations are sometimes called not-for-profit, or non-governmental, organizations or interest groups, usually all included in the voluntary sector. It is also clear that more adults learn more as *members* than they ever do in the more familiar learning role of *student* (Thomas 1967), which means that the activities of all manner of voluntary organizations are substantial manifestations of the politics of learning–not the graded, detached learning associated with education, but often unselfconscious learning, always instrumental, always on the edge of action; "not the barren politics of abstractions and principles, but the warm cruel politics of the heart" (Durrell 1962, 72). They are the engines of learning by which private citizens meet their needs, other people's needs or the attributed needs of the state itself.

Though freedom of association has not always been guaranteed in Canada, we have a long history of voluntary association pre-dating the creation of the country. In the earliest days voluntary organizations provided resources that the state was unable or unwilling to provide. By the early part of the twentieth century, they were heavily involved in advocacy; that is, in attempts to persuade the state to introduce public policies embracing all citizens, for example, the establishment of public education. Since that time they have continued in that role and increasingly accepted responsibilities of performing services in the interest of the state with varying degrees of financial support, public and private. Canada, as have other democratic states, has evolved a policy of controlling these groups by granting them a privileged tax position that allows taxes that would have been collected by the federal government to be diverted through private donations to private organizations. To achieve that status they must fulfil certain criteria and obey certain rules.

Through such groups a large part of the public business of the country is carried on. Individuals who choose to participate in such groups gain substantial technical knowledge about the pursuit of myriad complicated causes in this society, as well as acquiring considerable skills in negotiating, organizing, conducting meetings, managing finances and engaging in the competition for public attention and support. This is where the skills and understanding of citizenship are learned and expressed. In recent years such groups have emerged internationally, often linked with groups in Canada, and have begun to exert considerable influence on official international organizations. The so-called "Battle of Seattle" where thousands of members of a variety of international organizations laid siege to the World Trade Organization in November of 1999 is a dramatic example. In fact, these global voluntary organizations are similar to commercial corporations in their freedom to act "globally," as distinct from "internationally." The latter context is precisely designed to limit the actions of states. It is here, abetted by new communication resources that these groups have rapidly learned to use, that the skills of genuine global citizenship are being defined and learned. Here we can witness skills and knowledge that in the present world cannot be taught, only learned; learned in an environment frequently characterized by conflict, argument and misunderstanding.

Consequent on the new prominence of voluntary organizations in both their roles of advocacy and service is the increase in systematic and scholarly exploration of their character and function. Attention has been directed to two primary areas in Canada in the past decade: the extent of participation by Canadians in giving either time or money or both to voluntary organizations (Statistics Canada 1998); and the matter of the financial and governmental integrity of such private organizations operating, self-appointed, in the public interest (Panel 1999).

Organized voluntary behaviour is not the only way to learn to be a citizen, since in the year the survey was conducted, more than seven of every ten Canadians engaged in "helping and supporting on their own without going through an organization" (Statistics Canada, 1998). However, in the larger sense of organizational support, "88% of the population, aged 15 and over made donations … [that] totaled $4.51 billion…. [A] small proportion of donors accounted for the majority of donations…. [S]ome 7.5 million Canadians, or 31.4% indicated that they volunteered…. [T]his represented an increase of 40% in the total number of volunteers since 1987…. The average volunteer contributed 149 hours over the year, down from 191 in 1987…. This … amounts to 1.11 billion hours … [an] increase of 9%" (p.10). "Close to one half of Canadians (49.5% totaling 12 million) reported that they were members of, or participants in community organizations" (p.11).

If adult educators are to take seriously, as we must, the politics of learning embodied in voluntary action, then we must pay attention to the political, administrative and financial contexts in which, and with which, these organizations carry on their affairs. A review of anyone's monthly total of requests for donations is sufficient to remind us of the scope and poignancy of the activities of voluntary organizations addressing public issues. Conventional questions are directed to financial integrity, efficiency in the utilization of private donations, cost of administration and the like. While they get considerable attention from the press when a scandal erupts, given the number of such organizations, incompetence and/or corruption is relatively rare in Canada and elsewhere in the world. As important as these questions are, there are newer ones arising from the increase in private advocacy throughout the world. When legions descend on international meetings, as in Seattle (1999), and other international conferences (World Bank in Washington, 2000), participated in by duly appointed or elected representatives of nation-states, we are entitled to ask who these legions represent and what authority they should be accorded. What weight should we, or our official representatives, give to the enthusiasm and passion resulting from the learning that they embody? It is these questions to which the *Building on Strength Report* addressed itself, in Canada. Its recommendations cover major aspects of our social and political life reflecting the basic principle of voluntary action in a democratic society; within the legal framework of this society any citizen, or group of citizens, is free to learn to organize and to advocate ideas or provide services privately and publicly. The provision of preference within the tax system, and the delegation by public bodies to voluntary organizations to provide public services, presents considerable complication, but the principles remain the same. Those principles lie at the heart of enlisting, as distinct from capturing, learning in the service of the society.

Citizens have two things to give to these organizations and causes: time and money. These essential reports indicate that, first, Canadians give substantial amounts of both, though giving to organized causes is not distributed evenly across Canadian society and, second, how they make these voluntary gifts to us all is both complicated, and to a large degree, obscure. The optimum amount of giving, or what is normal for a healthy society, is unclear. It is a matter of debate, though there is powerful evidence that there is a strong relationship between the maintenance of a healthy civil society and voluntary participation. There has been, so far, less attention paid to the relationship between voluntary participation, lifelong learning, and the civil society, though there can be no doubt that the three concepts and realities are intimately linked. We have distinguished between an attempt to "capture" learning, and an attempt to "enlist" learning in the service of varying collective goals. The emergence of the concept of the civil society offers a larger canvas on which to consider the two.

Civil Society

Some adult educators seem to have embraced the concept of the civil society (Gronholm and Katus 1999). Even though half-realized as a concept, they have recognized its close relationship with voluntary action and organizations (Putnam 1995) and its promise for a new understanding for the proper order of state, economy (corporate power) and individual citizens. What is essential to acknowledge is that this new conception of what is basically a new "social contract" has evolved, in part, because of the universal spread of the education of adults. An American educator early in the last century asked whether the schools ought to build a new social order. The question was rhetorical because the schools in that period were totally preoccupied with, and inhabited by, children and young people incapable of such a task. But when adults are added, the question assumes a new cogency.

The new conception of the civil society emerged in the last two decades as Eastern Europe struggled to overthrow the communist regimes it had lived under since the 1940s. Those regimes represented the fact that "the state, at least in Europe, would become an omnipresent Leviathan bent on shrinking the autonomy of individual areas of life and asserting its control over even the most intimate spheres of private existence" (Geremek n.d., 3). "The idea of a civil society–even one that avoids overtly political activities in favour of education, the exchange of information and opinion, or the protection of the basic interests of particular groups–has enormous antitotalitarian potential" (Geremek n.d., 2). The echoes of the Enlightenment preoccupation with the precedence of society over the state, and in the postmodern case, over corporate power, are clear.

There is however another factor in this formulation that influences Canada, and other Western, immigrant societies, more than experience with totalitarianism. The vast movement of peoples throughout the world since World War II has transformed these countries from "high-context" to "low-context" societies (Hall 1985). The influx of "strangers" means the transformation from societies based on shared languages and common heritage, where much of the context of daily life and civic behaviour can be taken for granted, to societies of diverse languages, even if one or two are "official," and disparate histories, in which daily life must be constantly explained and increasingly debated. A great deal of constant learning about, and from, "strangers" is necessitated if the society is to survive. Canada's adoption of official "multiculturalism" has imbedded the praxis, and made us a leader in the experience of postmodern societies. It has also provoked a new political philosophy in the attempt to reconcile "particularism" with new concepts of citizenship in a nation state (Angus 1997). In terms of the classical social contract discussion, it is not royalty that has been overthrown, it is one version of the liberal ideal of a civilized life.

There is a powerful thread of "communalism" in the emerging concept of the civil society. This suggests that one new problem of the politics of learning is to reconcile the capacity for learning (which resides exclusively with the individual citizen, despite the fact that it takes place almost as exclusively in a social context) with the possibility of the voluntary organization as mediator between the citizen and the state. Such possibilities have been implicit in so-called "identity" politics and some theories regarding ethnic groups. While the principal theorists of the classic concepts of the social contract, such as Hobbes, Locke and Rousseau, accompany their political arguments with theories of education, confronting learning itself is another matter of far greater significance. While the argument does imply a greater role for voluntary organizations (one that some, in fact, play unofficially), it also cuts to the heart of the individualism on which the democratic law is based and opens the door to the far less attractive aspects of "communalism" that we have witnessed in Eastern Europe since the decline of communist states.

Global society (the term seems increasingly appropriate) is by definition a "low-context" society. We have already commented on the growing presence and influence of voluntary organizations in that context as well as of commercial corporations. The latter are generally absent from the classical discussions of the social contract but must figure in ours. To the extent that both voluntary organizations and corporations are able to act globally, without the rules and safeguards of international action, we are seeing the early struggles in the development of a global civil society, not the least of which is seen in the competition between enlisting learning and capturing it.

At first glance the concept of the civil society suggests something close to the equally vague, but fashionable concept of the learning society. Certainly it embodies lifelong learning and freedom of association in terms of guaranteeing voluntary action and organizations. But it is in essence a dynamic society, which depends not only on the existence of apparent political constants such as the law, the legislature and a free press, but also on the proper balance between those factors and others. Primary among those balances is that between learning and education. As we have already argued, the discourse between the two is one of the constants of history never more evident and critical than in the recent century. In a changing environment, predominantly of human origin, learning constantly outstrips education. We observe that fact dramatically in the realms of science and technological change, and are slowly learning how to cope with its more drastic social consequences, but we have thought little about its implications for politics and, over all, our culture. With the explosion of "entertainment" in the past half century, led by film, television, the Internet and its accomplices, we have some glimmer of those implications, but relevant theory has been slow to appear.

Historically, new learning outcomes have been translated into education and transmitted to subsequent generations. When the rate of change eclipsed generations, we thought to compensate by extending education to adults. That now seems insufficient, and we must seek means of coping with learning independently of education, or at least in a new balance between the two. The recent national survey of informal learning in Canada indicates that it has increased from an average of ten to sixteen hours a week among adults (NALL n.d.). What is important is not only to know the extent of learning among adults, but to know, regularly and accurately, what it is they are learning. To know what they are learning tells us where their hearts and aspirations are, and what they wish Canada as a country to become. More important, it will also tell the degree of discrepancy between what we are teaching and what is being learned. That information is essential to address problems associated with the politics of learning, the dominant politics of the postmodern world. (See also Conley and Barot in this volume.)

Conclusion

We began by arguing that the new problems and opportunities in the education of adults are manifest in three emerging phenomena: lifelong learning, voluntary action and the civil society—the first, because it challenges the separation of the education of adults from the education of children and youth, particularly benefiting those caught in the vagaries of those definitions and allows us to see the educational enterprise as a whole, that is, to see it in the way in which it is experienced by its participants; the second, because voluntary action has always offered a larger learning enterprise for adults, and increasingly for children and youth, than has education, and that sector of the society, national and global, is assuming increasing importance; and the last, because the first two are its principal constituents and it is incomprehensible and unimaginable without understanding them. In the idea of the civil society we find, for the first time, the opportunity to consider the social and political implications of learning and education as first principles of a society rather than only as subsidiary means to other human goals. It compels us to question our own activities in terms of whether there is enough learning to sustain our society, or any society or group. Or, perhaps the unthinkable, that there is too much learning for the stability of our society or any other. In either case we are obliged to consider on what basis one could draw either conclusion.

As adult educators, as providers of education in an enormous variety of circumstances, locations and contexts, we have the opportunity to witness the distinction between learning and education and to ponder the different cultural implications of the two. Our argument is that those differences are critical to the maintenance, indeed the survival, of postmodern societies, including our own, and that in virtue of our experience, we have a special responsibility to understand and act on our experience. If we are only to grasp the vital distinction between enlisting and capturing learning, and ensure that, while both will exist, the former must predominate if any human collective is to survive peacefully and productively, then we will have fulfilled that responsibility in large measure.

References

Angus, I. 1997. *A border within: National identity, cultural plurality, and wilderness.* Montreal and Kingston: McGill-Queens University Press.

Durrell, L. 1962. *Prospero's cell: Reflections on a marine Venus.* New York: E.P. Dutton.

First National Survey of Informal Learning. 1998. New Approaches to Lifelong Learning. Toronto: OISE/UT.

Geremek, B. n.d. Civil society in the present age. In *The idea of a civil society.* Website: http://www.civsoc.com/links.html.

Gronholm, C., and J. Katus. 1999. *Issues of education and the civil society: Proceedings of the European symposium on voluntary associations.* Vol. 1. Helsinki: Fonda Publishing.

Hall, E. 1985. Unstated features of the cultural context of learning. In *Learning and Development: A Global Perspective,* edited by A. Thomas and E. Plowman (pp.157-176). Toronto: OISE Press.

NALL Website: http://nall.oise.utoronto.ca.

Panel on Accountability and Governance in the Voluntary Sector. 1999. *Building on strength: Improving the governance and accountability in Canada's voluntary sector.* Ottawa: Author.

Putnam, R. 1995 *The strange disappearance of civic America. American Prospect Journal* (volume 7, no 24).

Statistics Canada. 1998. *Caring Canadians, involved Canadians: Highlights from the 1997 national survey of giving, volunteering, and participating.* Ottawa: Government of Canada.

Statistics Canada. 1998. Adults upgrade with education and training. *Canadian Social Trends* 55 (winter). Ottawa: Government of Canada.

Thomas A.M. 1967. Studentship and membership: A study of roles in learning; *Journal of Educational Thought,* Vol.1 No. 2.

———. 1991. *Beyond education: A new perspective on society's management of learning.* San Francisco: Jossey-Bass.

———. 1998. Learning our way out. In *Learning for Life: Canadian Readings in Adult Education,* edited by Sue M. Scott, Bruce Spencer, and Alan M. Thomas. Toronto: Thompson Educational Publishing.

UNESCO. 1998. *Statistical Yearbook 1997.* Paris: UNESCO Publishing and Bernan Press.

Index